Markus Kress

Intelligent Business Process Optimization for the Service Industry

Intelligent Business Process Optimization for the Service Industry

by
Markus Kress

Dissertation, Universität Karlsruhe (TH)
Fakultät für Wirtschaftswissenschaften,
Tag der mündlichen Prüfung: 30.07.2009
Referent: Prof. Dr. Detlef Seese
Korreferent: Prof. Dr. Andreas Oberweis

Impressum

Karlsruher Institut für Technologie (KIT)
KIT Scientific Publishing
Straße am Forum 2
D-76131 Karlsruhe
www.uvka.de

KIT – Universität des Landes Baden-Württemberg und nationales
Forschungszentrum in der Helmholtz-Gemeinschaft

KIT Scientific Publishing 2010
Print on Demand

ISBN 978-3-86644-454-6

Intelligent Business Process Optimization for the Service Industry

Zur Erlangung des akademischen Grades eines

Doktors der Wirtschaftswissenschaften

(Dr. rer. pol.)

von der Fakultät für

Wirtschaftswissenschaften

der Universität Karlsruhe (TH)

genehmigte

DISSERTATION

von

Dipl.-Wi.-Ing.   Markus   Kress

Tag der mündlichen Prüfung: 30. Juli 2009

Referent: Prof. Dr. Detlef Seese

Korreferent: Prof. Dr. Andreas Oberweis

2009 Karlsruhe

Acknowledgment

> "People don't have to like or support you,
> so you always have to say thank you."
> Ruben Studdard

This research was conducted at the Institute for Applied Informatics and Formal Description Methods (AIFB) at the University of Karlsruhe (TH) during my time as external Ph.D. student. Besides my dissertation, I have worked part-time for Cirquent GmbH | NTT Data Group (former entory AG) as technical consultant and solution architect in the area of Business Process Management (BPM). At the time, I began my dissertation, entory switched its strategy and focused on BPM. I had one of the unique opportunities in this consultancy firm to participate in the BPM task force to support the implementation of this strategy.

It has to be said that it was a fruitful combination of scientific and practical work. My consultancy work provided insights into the challenges in the area of BPM in practice. In particular, my interest in business process design and optimization paved the way and led to the topic of this thesis. Nevertheless, it has to be mentioned that theory and practice have different requirements which can limit the synergy effects to a certain extent. It was also a double challenge to work in both areas as sometimes "hot" project phases coincided with deadlines of conferences.

There are several persons who made this combination possible and supported my scientific research. In particular, I would like to thank my supervisor Prof. Dr. Detlef Seese as well as Hagen Buchwald, former member of the board of directors.

I would like to thank my colleague Joachim Melcher (AIFB) with whom I initially collaborated and with whom I had several interesting and fruitful discussions. I would like to thank Dr.-Ing. Sanaz Mostaghim (AIFB) as well as Prof. Dr. Hartmut Schmeck (AIFB) for the collaboration in the area of Particle Swarm Optimization and Gap Search. Furthermore, I would like to thank Dr. Stephan K. Chalup (Newcastle Robotics Laboratory, School of Electrical Engineering & Computer Science, University of Newcastle) for the fruitful discussions and suggestions in the area of Machine Learning.

Also, I would like to thank Dirk Wölfing (Cirquent) for the common work on the article regarding business process performance. As a technical focused consultant, it was an interesting experience to work with a business expert. During this work, we personally experienced the gap between business and IT. Before we could start writing the article, we had several discussions in order to get a common understanding about BPM in general and the meaning of different terms such as business process integration. Another person I would like to thank is Peter Schönberg (Cirquent) who provided the details about the business process "new customer". His support made it possible to use the business process in my research.

I am also deeply grateful for Melanie Steurer's support and understanding in stressful times. Finally, I would like to thank my parents for the intensive support that allowed me to study and laid the foundation stone of my Ph.D. study. I dedicate this thesis to my parents.

Karlsruhe, 2009   *Markus Kress*

Contents

Acronyms

ABC	Activity Based Costing
ACL	Agent Communication Language
ACNP	Adapted FIPA Contract Net Interaction Protocol Specification
AI	Artificial Intelligence
ASAP	Asynchronous Service Access Protocol
ASM	Abstract State Machine
BDI	Belief-Desire-Intention
BO	Business Object
BOM	Bill of Material
BPEL	Business Process Execution Language
BPEL4People	Business Process Execution Language for People
BPEL4WS	Business Process Execution Language for Web Services
BPM	Business Process Management
BPMI	Business Process Management Initiative
BPMS	Business Process Management System
BPMM	Business Process Maturity Model
BPML	Business Process Modeling Language
BPMN	Business Process Modeling Notation
BPQL	Business Process Query Language
BPSS	Business Process Specification Schema
BPR	Business Process Reengineering
BS	Binary Search
CEO	Chief Executive Officer
CMMI	Capability Maturity Model Integration
COBIT	Control Objectives for Information and Related Technology
CPI	Continuous Process Improvement
CRM	Customer Relationship Management
ebXML	Electronic Business using eXtensible Markup Language
EAI	Enterprise Application Integration
EPC	Event-Driven Process Chain
EPM	Executable Product Model
EPML	Event-Driven Process Chain Markup Language

ERP	Enterprise Resource Planning
FIPA	Foundations of Intelligent Physical Agents
GA	Genetic Algorithm
GS	Gap Search
IBO	Intelligent Business Object
iEPM	intelligent Executable Product Model
IDE	Integrated Development Environment
IT	Information Technology
ITIL	Information Technology Infrastructure Library
KPI	Key Performance Indicator
KQML	Knowledge Query Manipulation Language
KRI	Key Risk Indicator
MAS	Multi-Agent System
MOF	Meta Object Facility
MOPSO	Multi-Objective Particle Swarm Optimization
MPS	Multi-Processor Scheduling
NDTM	Non-Deterministic Turing Machine
OASIS	Organization for the Advancement of Structured Information Standards
OMG	Object Management Group
PDM	Product Data Model
PNML	Petri Net Markup Language
PRNG	Pseudo-Random Number Generator
PSL	Process Specification Language
PSO	Particle Swarm Optimization
RA	Resource Agent
ROI	Return On Investment
RL	Reinforcement Learning
RRL	Relational Reinforcement Learning
RUP	Rational Unified Process
SDES	Sequential Discrete Event Simulation
SOA	Service Oriented Architecture
SOAP	Simple Object Access Protocol
SLA	Service Level Agreement
TQM	Total Quality Management
UBL	Universal Business Language
UML	Unified Modeling Language
WfMC	Workflow Management Coalition

WMS	Workflow Management System
WSCDL	Web Service Choreography Description Language
WSCI	W3C's Web Service Choreography Interface
WSCL	Web Services Conversation Language
WSDL	Web Service Description Language
WSFL	Web Services Flow Language
XMI	XML for Metadata Interchange
XSD	XML Schema
XPDL	XML Process Definition Language
YAWL	Yet Another Workflow Language

1. Introduction

1.1. Motivation

In the past, many companies operated in stable and large consumer markets. They were able to obtain competitive advantages by the mass production of standardized products. Economies of scale were not only a way to realize the cost leadership strategy as in Porter's view, but furthermore the main drivers of corporate success. Also, the company's strategy focused primarily on positioning in the right place on the value chain, the right business, the right products and market segments, the right value-adding activities. Information systems had the role to support business by the automation of certain business functions.

By contrast, companies today are challenged by a highly dynamic marketplace and increasing business complexity. The market is characterized by changing and varying customer preferences, new technologies and distribution channels, shorter time-to-market and product life cycles, stricter regulations, etc. Fig. 1.1 illustrates the influencing factors of a dynamic marketplace.

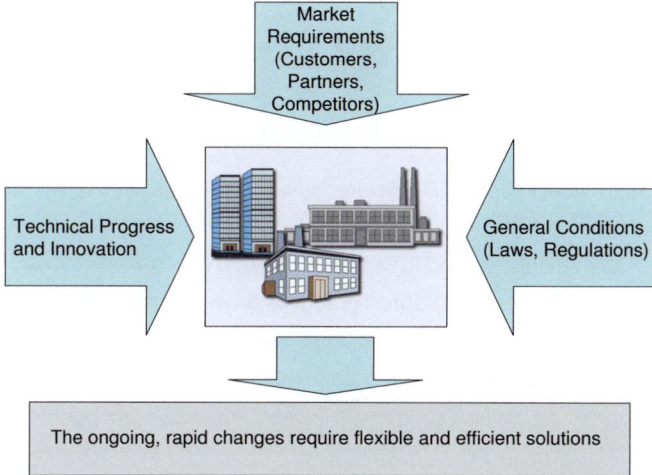

Figure 1.1.: Illustration of today's dynamic business environment.

1

Besides the high dynamic, the complexity arises also due to an increase of products and variants, among others. Another reason for the business complexity is the way value is created nowadays. Companies are organizing themselves in value networks in order to co-produce value by collaborating with different economic actors, like suppliers, business partners, allies and customers. This requires a close collaboration and coordination of business operations of the different actors. Fig. 1.2 exemplifies the relationship between product life-cycle, core processes and competencies and value networks. An increased complexity may lead for example to higher costs, error proneness or inadequate transparency. Thus, methods for coping with complexity have become increasingly important.

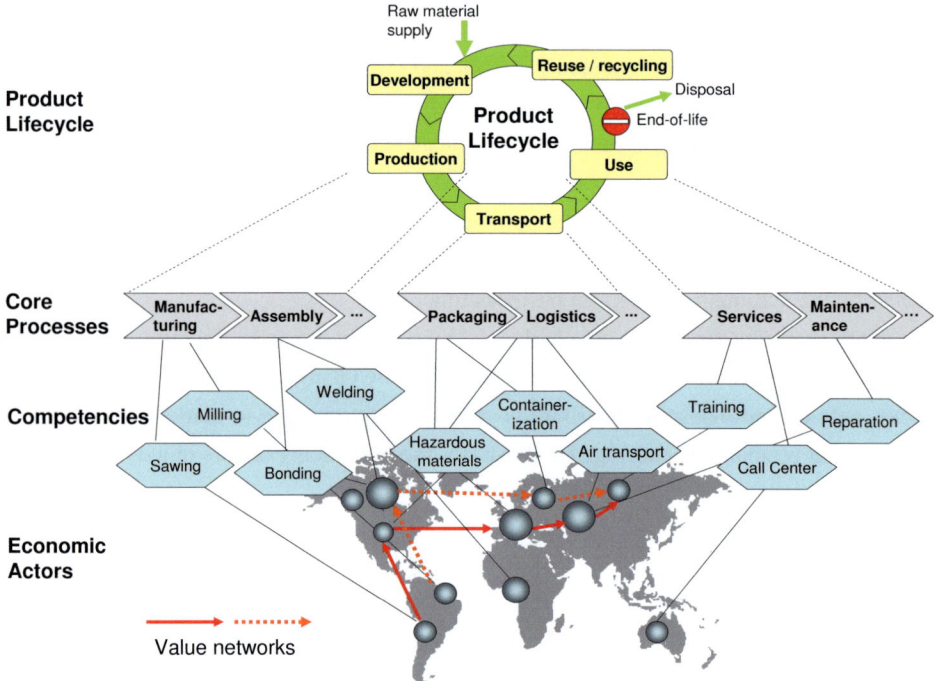

Figure 1.2.: Illustration of an world-spanning industrial value network (adapted from [255]).

The company's sustainable competitive advantage derives from its capacity to create value for customers and to adapt the operational practices to the changing situation. Business processes are the heart of each company. Therefore process excellence has become a key issue. A high-performing company must not only understand how to identify and correct its process weaknesses, but it must also be able to leverage process strengths and opportunities for strategic advantage.

The essential prerequisite for optimizing business processes is an integrated information system. The organization may be prepared to change business processes, but often the Information

Technology (IT) infrastructure cannot keep pace with change. The IT infrastructure is often characterized by a heterogeneous system landscape. Both, business and IT management, will benefit from a flexible software solution for managing business processes. Ultimately, IT must align with business goals. IT has to give employees, suppliers and customers access to all the information they need, at the exact time they need it. This provides the mean to guide them through the correct courses of action. The result is that speed and responsiveness are increased in all areas, defects in products and processes are eliminated and costs are dramatically reduced.

1.2. Objective and Contribution

The management paradigm Business Process Management (BPM) aims at the improvement of corporate performance by continuously monitoring, analyzing and optimizing the business processes in an end-to-end manner. Technology support makes the processing of business events and information simpler, faster and easier to follow.

The key element of BPM is the business process. A business process model is a model of one or more business processes describing the different ways in which activities are performed in order to accomplish the intended objectives of an enterprise. In practice, there is a variety of BPM approaches focusing on the automation of business processes. This automation comprises the creation of a process model for the business process to be automated and the execution of this model during runtime by a workflow or BPM engine [139, 211].

The process models do not necessarily provide the required flexibility for dealing with changing environments and competitors. Process models must be completely defined in the sense that every aspect and exception must be known and modeled in advance. If an exception occurs during runtime that has not been anticipated in the creation of the process model during design time, the implemented process may not be executable anymore. In this case, changes on the process model or process instance have to be performed in order to handle the exception accordingly.

In [245] a definition of flexibility pertaining to business processes is given: "business process flexibility is the capacity of the organization to respond to change by modifying only those parts of a process that require adaptation while keeping other parts stable." The importance of business process flexibility has been stressed by several authors [292, 109, 206, 147]. Consequentially, a variety of approaches regarding business process flexibility has been suggested. These approaches have provided deeper insights in the requirements of flexible BPM solutions on the basis of taxonomies [232, 292], change patterns [317] and process change strategies [147], among others.

In most cases, the control flow of process models is defined by a fixed number of business rules. Even if the control flow logic is separated by the use of a business rule engine, the flexibility is still restricted. A variety of approaches have been suggested for modeling business process variants, e.g. based on the process family engineering technique [252]. This technique allows to model and manage process variants in an efficient way, but as the actual variant is chosen on instantiation of the business process there is no possibility to change the variant during runtime as in the Executable Product Model (EPM) approach. Other techniques provide also more flexibility, e.g. constrained-based workflow uses a declarative style of modeling by defining a set of optional and mandatory constraints [221]. It provides the user with more execution options, but does not autonomously optimize the business process execution. How this autonomous optimization is achieved is discussed next.

The objective of the approach introduced in this thesis is to increase the process flexibility and to optimize autonomously the execution of business processes. It differs from regular BPM approaches as it is based on an EPM instead of an explicitly defined process model.

In [288] a Product Data Model (PDM) has been introduced, which is used in a business process design methodology called product driven workflow design. The PDM has been developed specifically for the service industry. It consists of data elements and the dependencies between them. In the PDM the order of activities is not as rigidly predefined as in common process models. In accordance to the design methodology, a process is derived from the PDM based on specific objectives during design time. The flexibility of the PDM is utilized only to create different processes. During runtime the PDM is not in use and therefore the flexibility is lost. In the approach presented in [288] there is also one problematic aspect. The algorithms for deriving process models rely on data like probabilities or durations that must be estimated. In practice the availability of this kind of information is often limited and also the data quality is not as accurate as required. This makes the realistic data estimation difficult and the resulting process model questionable. This pertains to regular BPM approaches as well, in which a process design is chosen that is optimal or most suitable in dependence on the considered operating conditions. But what may happen if these conditions change? In experiments it will be shown that a process design becomes suboptimal if certain changes occur such as an increasing volume of work or increasing processing durations due to quality problems.

In order to overcome these limitations, the PDM has been enhanced so it can be executed directly without deriving a process first. One of the enhancements was the development of an execution algorithm. Executing the product model directly provides the flexibility at runtime and bypasses the problem with the data estimation. The EPM contains a compact representation of the set of all possible execution paths of a business process. By defining information relationships instead of task sequences as in process models, the alternative possibilities or execution paths in the product model are defined independently from each other by default. This means that there are no precedence constraints between them. In a process model, such behavior has to be modeled explicitly. Modeling alternatives using one of the common process modeling languages may lead to a complicated and complex process model. Another advantage of the

EPM is, that the variant in execution can be changed anytime during runtime.

The flexibility provided by the EPM is utilized by using a Multi-Agent System (MAS). A MAS is an instance of distributed systems composed by agents [213]. The term agent denotes an encapsulated hardware or more commonly software based computer system that possesses the properties of autonomy, social ability, reactivity and pro-activity [329, 328]. As described earlier, companies are forced to cope with an increasing complexity. A MAS was chosen, as it is capable of solving complex tasks in distributed environments and has been applied successfully in practice, e.g. in the production industry [43]. In combination with self-adaption they are a powerful tool. Self-adaptation is the ability of a software system to adapt to dynamic and changing operating conditions autonomously [322]. Several MASs have been proposed for the execution of business processes. The approaches described in [75, 109, 45] make use of BDI agents. BDI agents act on the basis of plans in order to achieve the defined goals. In the BPM domain, a plan describes certain steps of a business process. By defining multiple plans, variants can be modeled. Thus, a business process is divided into separate plans. The EPM approach delivers the advantage of execution alternatives, that can be defined in one model using a compact representation for these alternatives. In order to provide the same degree of flexibility using BDI agents, each execution option results in one plan. Especially for complex business processes, this would not be an efficient approach.

The optimization of the execution of EPMs comprises two tasks: the determination of an execution path, as well as the assignment of the activities to resources[1] in such a way that leads to the optimization of the defined Key Performance Indicators (KPIs). As part of this thesis, it is shown, that a simplified variant of this multi-objective optimization problem has already a high complexity (i.e. the corresponding decision problem belongs to the class of NP-complete problems). This provides an argument as well as a motivation for applying approximation methods such as machine learning or heuristics to solve the optimization problem. As aforementioned, companies and their business processes are embedded in a highly dynamic environment. Consequently, business process optimization becomes a challenging task. One of the most frequently stated reasons for the application of machine learning techniques is their ability to automatically adapt to changing environments or expertise [61, 106, 192]. Regarding to business process optimization, machine learning provides a mechanism for automatically adapting to changing operating conditions. Therefore, machine learning was selected for solving the optimization problem.

The devised MAS manages and controls the execution of EPMs by making intelligent choices regarding the execution decisions. The intelligence stems from a hybrid learning mechanism which was developed based on two machine learning approaches, Relational Reinforcement Learning with a heuristic, such as Genetic Algorithm (GA) and Particle Swarm Optimization

---

[1]The term resource relates either to a human or technical resource that carries out an activity.

(PSO), termed RRL-GA and RRL-PSO, respectively. The learning mechanism in general is termed intelligent Executable Product Model (iEPM) approach. The behaviour of the agents is defined by a policy that comprises a number of manually pre-defined rules. A rule consists of a condition, an action and a probability. The action can be executed only if the condition is fulfilled. Whether the action is actually executed by the agent depends on the probability assigned to each rule. These probabilities are determined in an offline learning phase by a heuristic.

Combining EPMs with a MAS delivers two different practical application methods:

- during runtime as intelligent BPM engine and

- during design time as intelligent business process optimization methodology.

During runtime, the iEPM approach replaces a standard BPM engine and manages the control flow of business processes in an intelligent way by optimizing the objectives under consideration of the current operating conditions. The objectives are defined by a set of KPIs such as cycle times and costs. The current situation is influenced by the volume of work, availability and workload of resources, among others. The offline learning cannot only be used to adapt and optimize the behaviour of the agents, but also to perform what-if analyses, e.g. in order to make business forecasts. The advantage of this practical application method is that the execution of business processes is optimized autonomously. Thus, there is no manual work necessary in order to find alternative process designs. Of course, only the flexibility provided by the EPM can be utilized. If new requirements have to be implemented or if activities have become obsolete, the EPM must be adapted manually in accordance to the new situation.

During design time, the iEPM approach allows the examination of the system behavior. In regular BPM based simulation approaches, alternative process models must be explicitly defined. The iEPM approach delivers the advantage, that the EPM already contains the possible variants. The advantage of this methodology over regular approaches is that only one model needs to be created. The simulation logs the executed tasks of each EPM instance. This provides the possibility to make use of process mining tools in order to mine the optimal process model from the log files. Note that the availability and quality of the simulation data is a critical issue here as stated above.

As aforementioned, the probability vector is determined by using a heuristic. The use of heuristics requires the execution of simulation runs in order to evaluate the quality of the found probability vectors. Therefore, the learning mechanism belongs to the time intensive problems as for each evaluation one simulation has to be executed. In [159] a new search mechanism called Gap Search (GS) is introduced that aims at the acceleration of the PSO algorithm. The influence of using GS in combination with PSO in order to solve single, multi- and many-objective problems is studied using various standard test functions. For this reason, GS was integrated into the three possible parts of a PSO and Multi-Objective Particle Swarm Optimization (MOPSO) namely as initialization, diversity and feasibility preservation mechanisms. The major result from the conducted experiments reveals that GS improves the standard PSO and MOPSO methods even if it is deployed in solving many-objective problems.

In simulation-based experiments, the proof-of-concept of the developed approach is shown and the capabilities of the learning mechanism are analyzed based on simple EPM structures. The structures represent some of the standard situations found in business processes, such as the processing of tasks in a sequence and in parallel. The analysis of the simulations is based on various measures, such as throughput, cycle times, costs, among others. Moreover, the advantages of the two mentioned application methods are analyzed in detail on the basis of different business processes derived from examples found in the literature and in practice. The results of the conducted experiments show the advantages as well as the applicability of the iEPM approach. In particular, it is demonstrated how the iEPM approach can react on changing operating conditions by adapting the behavior of the agents. Thus, it is shown for different business processes that the iEPM approach outperforms the regular BPM approach based on a fixed process model in changing situations.

1.3. Outline of the Thesis

The outline of the thesis is as follows:

Chapter 1 describes the motivation as well as the objective of the thesis.

Chapter 2 introduces the theoretical background of this thesis as well as the applied scientific methods. The introduction comprises BPM, agents and machine learning techniques, among others. Moreover, the related work regarding BPM, product-driven approaches and business process flexibility is discussed.

In Chapter 3 the Executable Product Model (EPM) is introduced. It starts with the explanation of the original PDM, followed by the changes and enhancements that were performed in order to create the EPM. Several algorithms were developed for the execution which are explained and analyzed. Furthermore, a design methodology is introduced, which describes the necessary steps to design an EPM. This chapter also contains a discussion on the flexibility of EPMs.

In Chapter 4 the complexity of the optimization problem of the EPM approach is analyzed mathematically. It starts with a short introduction to computational complexity theory. Then, the multiprocessor scheduling problem is introduced, which was proven to be an NP-complete problem. Furthermore, the EPM is defined as optimization and decision problem for a special case. Finally, the NP-completeness is proved for this special case making use of the multi-processor scheduling problem. Since this simplified version of the EPM problem is already NP-complete, it motivates the usage of heuristic algorithms to solve the EPM problem.

In Chapter 5 the devised MAS is explained. The flexibility provided by the EPMs is utilized by intelligent agents, which constitute a MAS. The explanation of the MAS comprises the architecture, agent types, communication protocols, among others. Furthermore, details regarding the implementation of the MAS are given. This chapter also includes a discussion of the related work in the area of MASs.

In Chapter 6 the hybrid machine learning approach iEPM for managing the control flow of business processes on the basis of EPMs is presented. In particular, it is explained how the machine learning approaches are adapted, so they can be integrated and deployed in the MAS. Moreover, insights into the challenges and optimization efforts regarding the implementation of the machine learning mechanism are given. This chapter also discusses the related work in the area of machine learning.

In Chapter 7 the applicability of the iEPM approach in practice is studied. The chapter begins with the introduction of the two application methods of the iEPM approach in practice. It is explained how the iEPM approach can be applied as intelligent BPM engine and how it is used within an intelligent business process optimization methodology. Afterwards, it is explained how the learning mechanism can be integrated into commercial workflow or BPM tools. This integration has the advantage that it combines the complete functionality of a commercial tool with the capabilities of the learning mechanism. Furthermore, a scalability evaluation is performed. Based on the results, some areas of improvement are identified and suggested for future work.

Chapter 8 provides an excursion in an extension of the Particle Swarm Optimization (PSO) and Multi-Objective Particle Swarm Optimization (MOPSO) algorithms as suggested in [159]. The extension is a method termed Gap Search (GS) which is used to search the most unexplored regions of a search space similar. The use of Gap Search (GS) is proposed as an alternative to the existing population initialization, diversity preservation and feasibility preservation methods. The suggested methods are evaluated based on a variety of standard single-, multi- and many-objective test functions.

In Chapter 9 the conducted simulation based experiments for the iEPM approach are discussed. The proof-of-concept is shown and the different learning mechanisms are evaluated. The advantages of the iEPM approach are analyzed and discussed in detail on the basis of different business processes such as a mortgage application process and a credit application process.

Chapter 10 includes the conclusions and the directions for further research.

2. Theoretical Background

> "There is no sense of being precise about something
> when you do not even know what you are talking about."
>
> John von Neumann

This chapter introduces the theoretical background of the thesis as well as the applied scientific methods. As stated in the previous chapter, the domain of the thesis is Business Process Management (BPM). Therefore, this chapter starts with the foundation of BPM on the basis of a brief historical overview, the main definitions, and the BPM life-cycle, among others. As stated in the introduction, the intelligent Executable Product Model (iEPM) approach focuses on enhancing the flexibility of business process execution in the service industry[1]. Thus, the characteristics of services and in particular the service industry are investigated, followed by a discussion about the definitions of business process flexibility. The enhanced flexibility is utilized in order to optimize the business process execution. Therefore, an introduction to optimization is given. Afterwards, the theoretical background related to the applied solution techniques is explained. This comprises an introduction to agents, followed by the relevant machine learning techniques. The chapter concludes with a short summary.

2.1. Business Process Management

Sustainable competitiveness of companies can only be achieved if the products and services they provide are produced in an efficient and effective manner and fulfill the customer preferences at the same time. These products and services are the outcome of a certain number of activities performed. BPM organizes these activities with the help of business processes. Consequently, the business processes can be regarded as the foundation of commercial and economic collaboration between and within companies. Accordingly, business processes have a significant impact on the business success of an enterprise.

Another aspect that shows the importance of business processes is operational risk management. Regulations like Basel II or Sarbane-Oxley-Act have been enforced due to company scandals and bank defaults that were driven by poor operational risk management. A formal definition of operational risk is "the risk of direct or indirect loss resulting from inadequate or

---

[1]The enhanced flexibility of Executable Product Models (EPMs) will be shown on the basis of experiments. In particular, it is shown how the iEPM approach can utilize this flexibility to outperform BPM approaches based on regular process models.

failed internal processes, people and systems or from external events" [21]. The definition categorizes operational risk on the basis of its sources. The industry criticized this definition due to the lack of a clear definition of direct and indirect losses [55]. A refined definition of operational risk defines it as "the risk of loss resulting from inadequate or failed internal processes, people or systems, or from external events" [21]. Note that this definition omits the differentiation between direct and indirect losses.

Nowadays, companies are embedded in a highly dynamic environment, which is characterized by changing and varying customer preferences, new technologies and distribution channels, shorter time-to-market and product life cycles, stricter regulations, among others. These factors force companies to adapt their business strategies and operational tasks. Flexibility and agility have become key issues.

As aforementioned, business processes are one of the drivers for success and failure of companies. BPM enables companies to cope with the challenges arising due to the increased business dynamics and are the basis in order to achieve sustainable competitiveness. Before the relevant terms and concepts of BPM are explained in detail, a brief insight in its history is given.

2.1.1. A Brief Historical Overview

The history of BPM has been described as long and rich [261] or as a difficult one that has gained from success and failures of various other attempts [139].

The idea, that work can be viewed as a process, dates at least back to Frederick Taylor. His theories of management science comprise industrial engineering and process improvement regarding to labor work in production processes [274].

The next advance was the enhancement of Taylors process improvement by statistical process control. Shewart, Deming, Juran, Feigenbaum and others provided the basis for quality management. Their process improvement consisted of measuring and limiting process variants in a continuous effort. Their quality management approaches were enhanced in Japan leading to the development of Total Quality Management (TQM) in the 1980s.

In the early 1990s Business Process Reengineering (BPR) was introduced by Hammer and Champy. They promoted a radical redesign of business processes in order to achieve not only significant but dramatic improvements in critical performance measures like cost, quality, service and speed. A thorough analysis about the success of the BPR methodology and the undertaken projects and initiatives is given in [233]. Nowadays. some claim that BPR is outdated (see e.g. [211, Page 19]) or even that BPR has failed [7]. One of the reasons is that the "all-or-nothing" BPR projects are highly fraughted with risks that the companies are not willing to take.

In the mid- and late 1990s integrated standard business software was introduced, nowadays referred to as Enterprise Resource Planning (ERP) systems. They replaced the isolated business applications that existed in different departments but did not improve the efficiency or effectiveness of business processes. Often the processes were adapted to fit the system or the system was customized in order to comply with the existing processes.

The next kind of business software were Customer Relationship Management (CRM) systems, laying the focus on the customer view. Accordingly, CRM systems supported the front office but did not improve back office processes.

E-Business was becoming a hot topic with the new economy hype in 2000. At this time the focus laid on ideas and visions but not on the business processes. Many companies in the new economy did not have a sustainable business model and many were missing efficient or functional processes. After the crisis many companies reclaimed sustainable business models and rediscovered the business processes.

Recently, Six Sigma has started to become a widely accepted methodology for process excellence in the industry as well as in the service sector. Six Sigma is a business strategy that seeks to identify and eliminate causes of errors and defects or failures in business processes by focusing on outputs that are critical to customers [263]. In contrary to TQM, Six Sigma is based only on a relatively small number of methods that have been proved for decades [225]. It is a systematical quality management methodology for process improvement based on statistical methods.

2.1.2. Definitions

Despite the fact that BPM is still a hot topic in industry as well as in science, it has a long history as described in the previous section. In the following sections, the major concepts, terms and definitions that are relevant in the area of BPM are introduced.

Business Process

Back in 1990 Davenport and Short defined the concept of a business process as "a set of logically related tasks performed to achieve a defined business outcome" [70]. They also saw a tight relation between BPM and Information Technology (IT): "business process design and information technology are natural partners".

Michael Hammer and James Champy included the customer centric view to the definition of a business process in their seminal work "Reeinginerring the Coorporation" [114]. They defined a business process as "a collection of activities that takes one or more kinds of input and creates an output that is of value to the customer".

These definitions of business processes have been extended and adopted by other authors. Weske defines business processes as a "set of activities that are performed in coordination in an organizational and technical environment. These activities jointly realized a business goal..." [320].

Closely related to the term business process is the term workflow. The Workflow Management Coalition (WfMC) defines workflow simply as "the computerized facilitation or automation of a business process, in whole or part" [330]. Nevertheless, in practice, both terms are often mixed up. Sometimes they are used side-by-side [154] or they are explicitly used as synonyms [294].

In literature, three main types of business processes are distinguished:

Management Processes Typically, management processes can be found in the areas of "Strategic Management" and "Corporate Governance".

Operational Processes These are the core processes that generate the main value, e.g. procurement, production, marketing, and sales.

Support Processes To this category pertain processes that support the core processes, e.g. accounting and recruiting.

Another classification of business processes based on different dimensions was introduced in [320]. Based on this classification, the following dimensions are distinguished:

Organizational versus Operational The different levels in BPM range from high-level business strategies to implemented business processes. In Fig 2.1, each level is depicted with a corresponding description.

Intraorganizational versus Interorganizational Processes The differentiation is based on the aspect, whether there is an interaction with business processes of other organizations (interorganizational process) or not (intraorganizational). Interorganizational processes are more challenging due to the technical issues and legal matters that arise from the collaboration[2].

Degree of Automation The level of automation depends on the business process. There are processes that can be automated completely, so they are executed without any human interaction. An example are the technical processes found in the area of Enterprise Application Integration (EAI).

Degree of Repetition This dimension reflects the frequency a business process occurs. Frequently occurring processes are potential candidates for process automation.

---

[2]There exist several approaches for collaborative business processes (see e.g. [112, 316]).

Degree of Structuring A business process is structured, if the activities and their execution order can be prescribed completely[3]. Unstructured processes can be found in the area of knowledge workers[4].

Note that the above listed classification does not provide any formal definition for measuring the degrees. Especially the degree of structuring is difficult to measure whereas the degree of automation can be calculated e.g. as number of automated tasks divided by the total number of tasks of the business process.

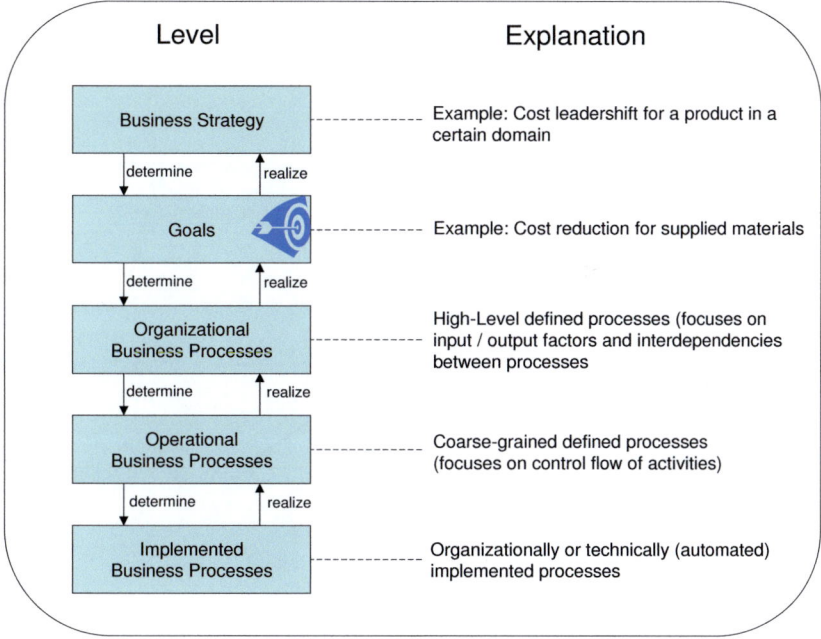

Figure 2.1.: From business strategy to implemented business processes [320].

Business process activities can be distinguished into two classes[5]: value adding and non value adding activities. A value adding activity meets all defining values as perceived by the customer without wasting any resources, whereas non value adding activities incur expenditure of time and/or money, but do not contribute to the customer satisfaction, service, or value. Non value adding activities are usually not profitable activities. However, they include essential functions such as accounting, inspection, storage, transportation, etc. Other non value adding activities

---

[3]The term production workflows has been introduced for well structured and highly repetitive workflows [171].

[4]Case handling has been introduced to support unstructured and knowledge-intensive processes [295]. Another approach for unstructured processes, also termed ad hoc processes, is based on the concept of ad hoc activities [133, 157].

[5]The definitions are taken from Six Sigma SPC's Quality Control Dictionary and Glossary w.sixsigmaspc.com/dictionary and the Business Dictionary w.businessdictionary.com.

such as recall, rework, and waste of effort have to be minimized or eliminated which is one major goal of any six sigma endeavor.

Business Process Modeling

In general, modeling aims at the retrieval of knowledge from a certain domain. The result of this effort can be a conceptual, graphical, or mathematical model. Accordingly, business process modeling is deployed to obtain knowledge from business processes, resulting in a business process model. The model is either a representation of a current or proposed business process. The former type is also termed as-is processes, the latter one to-be process. Business process modeling is deployed to facilitate a variety of purposes. In Fig. 2.2 various fields of application are depicted.

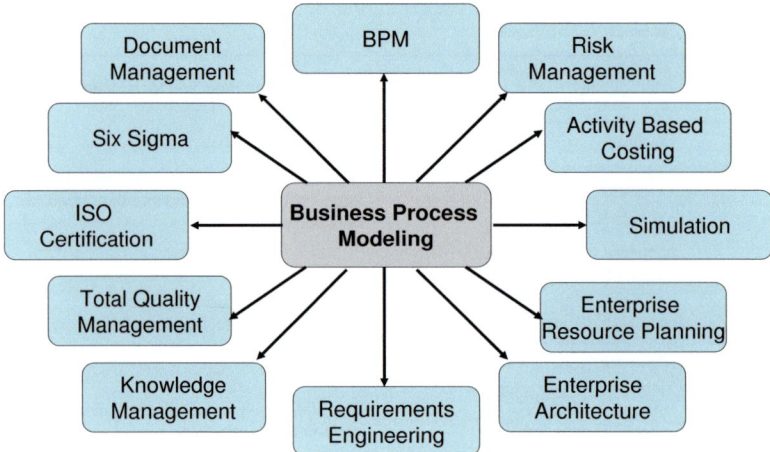

Figure 2.2.: The variety of application fields of business process modeling (adapted and extended based on [126]).

In the following, some of the depicted application fields are explained, to provide an insight into the variety. The major application field of business process modeling is obviously BPM as this kind of modeling is the core activity of BPM. But business process modeling is also deployed in Activity Based Costing (ABC), a cost management methodology introduced by Caplan and Atkinson [146]. In ABC the process model is the basis for calculating the direct costs of products and services. Six Sigma, TQM, and ISO certification focus on quality aspects. Six Sigma and TQM require a process model for the continuous improvement of the processes. A prerequisite of the ISO certification is, that processes are documented in procedures and work instructions. Business process simulation is carried out on the basis of process models using different simulation approaches such as discrete event simulation [313].

Accordingly to [208], a modeling language has to fulfill several requirements:

Expressive Power The expressive power of a modeling language determines what can be modeled at all and how concisely the model can be created. A modeling language must provide the means to model complex real world objects and the operations that are performed on them in an adequate way. Furthermore, aspects like the organizational structure, role concept, exception handling and business rules should be supported as well.

Formalism The modeling language should be based on a precise and formal notation in order to enable a computer aided analysis.

Visualization The modeling language should be visualized graphically in a clear and easy understandable way. Additionally, the language should provide multiple views on the model, e.g. for resources or activities.

Development support The modeling language should provide means for an incremental refinement of the model.

Means of analysis and validationability The modeling language should allow the application of analytical methods as well as simulation approaches.

There exists a huge variety of modeling languages that were either specifically developed or applied and extended for the modeling of workflows and business processes.

The two major modeling languages with a sound formal foundation that have been applied for process modeling are the Pi-calculus and Petri nets. The Pi-calculus was developed by Robert Milner in the 1980s [190]. It is a formal language for defining concurrent processes that interact with one another dynamically. Petri nets were introduced by Carl Adam Petri in 1962 [222]. Petri nets have a formal graphical notation based on elements like places, transitions, and tokens. Especially high-level Petri nets have been applied in the area of BPM [76]. High-level Petri nets are Petri nets that are enhanced by colour, time, and hierarchy allowing the modeling of more complex processes. Another type of high-level Petri nets are XML nets which combine Petri nets and XML [169, 170].

The Pi-calculus and Petri nets provided the foundation of major business process modeling standards. Fig. 2.3 shows the relationships between some of the existing modeling languages and theories. A relationship expresses what languages or theories are the basis of another language. The boxes represent modeling standards, circles theories and arrows dependencies, respectively. For example, BPEL is based on the languages XLANG and WSFL.

Also, the Unified Modeling Language (UML) was suggested for business process modeling, but it has not achieved the same reputation and success as in the area of software design. Most commonly, the UML activity diagram is applied for process modeling [212, 229, 239, 230]. In contrary to activity diagrams, state diagrams were suggested only rarely, e.g. the use of Harel's state charts [193, 326].

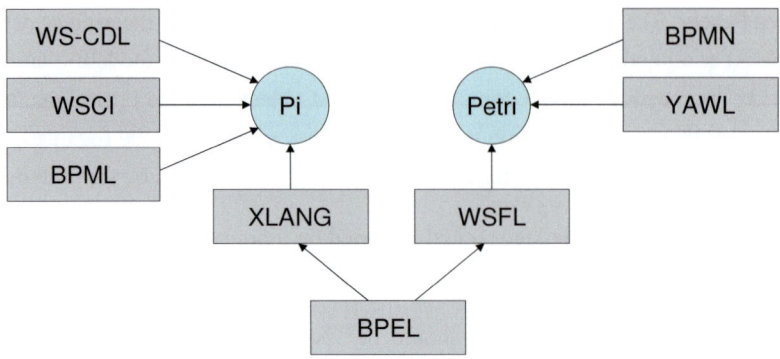

Figure 2.3.: The family tree of business process modeling languages (adapted from [117]).

Another control flow language is the Event-Driven Process Chain (EPC) based on events and functions developed by Wilhelm-August Scheer [148] in the early 1990s. It is a multiple view approach, in which the control view can link to other views like organizational, functional, and data views. In Germany, EPCs are widely used for modeling the business perspective of processes, especially in the banking sector. The strength of EPC lies on its easy-to-understand notation that is capable of portraying business information system, while at the same time incorporating other important features such as functions, data, organizational structure and information resources. EPCs use events, functions, and connectors. The extended EPC (eEPC) makes use of additional symbols for the data, organizational, and resource view. As Petri nets, EPCs have been further extended, e.g. based on an object-oriented process modeling approach oEPC [207].

In Appendix A an overview on BPM standards is given, particularly on process modeling languages. Due to the huge number of different standards, a lot of work has been done for the reuse of process models. These approaches are either based on model transformations[6] or exchange formats[7]. Model transformations have been developed not only for model exchange, but also for automatic analysis and verification purposes[8]

In Sec. 2.1.3, the use of modeling languages in the context of the BPM life cycle is explained. The expressive power and suitability of modeling languages have been evaluated on the basis of workflow patterns. As these patterns are distinguished by the different perspectives of process aware information systems, they are introduced after the process aware information systems.

---

[6]Many transformations have been introduced, e.g. from BPMN to BPEL [215] or from BPEL to Petri nets [123].

[7]Various standards exist that define exchange standards, like BPML, XPDL, PNML, and EPML (see Appendix A for a description of these standards). For a comparison of XML based exchange formats see e.g. [185].

[8]For example BPEL has been analyzed based on Abstract State Machine (ASM) [89] and Petri nets [308].

Process Aware Information Systems

Process aware information systems are software systems, whose execution occurs on the basis of business process models [80, 250]. They have a long history starting in the seventies, when so-called office information systems were introduced which were driven by explicit process models (see e.g. [85, 338]). A historical overview of office automation and workflow prototypes is given in [340].

Nowadays, accordingly to the differentiation between business process and workflow, the software systems are termed Business Process Management System (BPMS) (sometimes also called BPM suites) or Workflow Management System (WMS), respectively. The WfMC defines WMS as "a system that completely defines, manages and executes workflows through the execution of software whose order of execution is driven by a computer representation of the workflow logic" [330]. Today, vendors of BPM solutions offer BPMSs that cover the whole life-cycle of business processes. These systems can be defined as "specialist rapid application development software for the automation of rules based processes..." [224]. Despite the importance of BPM technology [189] many companies do not yet have a BPMS in use. If the process is implemented technically, most commonly an EAI, portal software or a self-developed solution is used instead.

In process aware information systems four perspectives can be distinguished in accordance to [250]:

Control-flow perspective This perspective describes tasks and their execution ordering.

Data perspective The data perspective deals with business and processing data. The data comprises business documents and other objects which flow between activities as well as local variables of the process.

Resource perspective The resource perspective provides an organizational structure in the form of human and device roles, responsible for executing activities.

Exception handling perspective Deviations from the normal execution (well-behaved cases) arising during a business process are often termed exceptions. The exception handling perspective deals with the various causes of exceptions and the corresponding actions that need to be taken for handling these exceptions.

For each of the perspectives so called workflow patterns have been provided, which are introduced in the next section.

Workflow Patterns

The objective of workflow patterns is the evaluation of modeling languages and tools in terms of suitability and expressive power. Here, the term expressive power is not used in the traditional or formal sense as if one abstracts from capacity constraints, any workflow language is Turing complete. Therefore a more intuitive notion of expressiveness is used which takes the modeling effort into account. This more intuitive notion is often referred to as suitability [151].

In general, a pattern "is the abstraction from a concrete form which keeps recurring in specific nonarbitrary contexts" [237]. The first patterns were systematically catalogued by Gamma et al. [100]. They identified 23 design patterns for describing the smallest recurring interactions in object-oriented systems. The advantage of design patterns is, that they provide independence from the implementation technology and from the essential requirements of the domain at the same time (see also [96, 287]).

In the past, workflow patterns were not precisely described, which led to ambiguous interpretations. Due to this deficiency, workflow patterns were described using formal languages such as ASM [34] or Pi-Calculus [223, 333]. The different perspectives of process aware information systems were analyzed on the basis of workflow patterns.

Initially 20 workflow patterns were defined [287], which were revised and extended resulting in 43 patterns for the control-flow perspective [314].

For the data perspective 40 workflow data patterns were identified, which describe the manner in which data is defined and utilized [290].

Furthermore, 43 workflow resource patterns were provided that describe the manner in which work items are distributed and executed by resources [289].

Finally, in [291] a pattern-based classification framework for exception handling in workflow systems is presented with 135 patterns.

Based on these different types of workflow patterns various modeling languages like UML activity diagrams [297] and Business Process Modeling Notation (BPMN) [296], as well as commercial and open source tools were analyzed. This analysis discovered to what extent workflow patterns are supported by modeling languages and tools. This led to the introduction of a new modeling language based on Petri nets: Yet Another Workflow Language (YAWL) was proposed with the objective to facilitate the modeling of complex workflows by supporting all control-flow patterns [293].

Even though a variety of workflow patterns was introduced, the completeness of the patterns cannot be assured. For example, the number of control-flow patterns was more than doubled in the past. But still, some relevant patterns could be identified in the future.

Constituents of BPM

After the introduction of the definition of business processes and the means of modeling and executing them, the question is clarified, what BPM constitutes. Analog to processes, BPM is defined in multiple ways. In the following, two management and objective oriented definitions are given:

In [115] BPM is defined "as a management discipline focused on improving corporate performance by managing a company's business processes."

Analogously, [139] defines BPM as "the achievement of an organization's objectives through improvement, management and control of essential business processes."

A definition that focuses on the business process life-cycle is given in [320]: "Business process management includes concepts, methods, and techniques to support the design, administration, configuration, enactment, and analysis of business processes."

In practice, BPM is considered as a management paradigm that defines an organization as a network of business processes. The quality of these processes is continuously monitored, analyzed and improved on the basis of facts. Fig. 2.4 depicts an organization as a network of business processes. This figure also illustrates the end-to-end view on business processes.

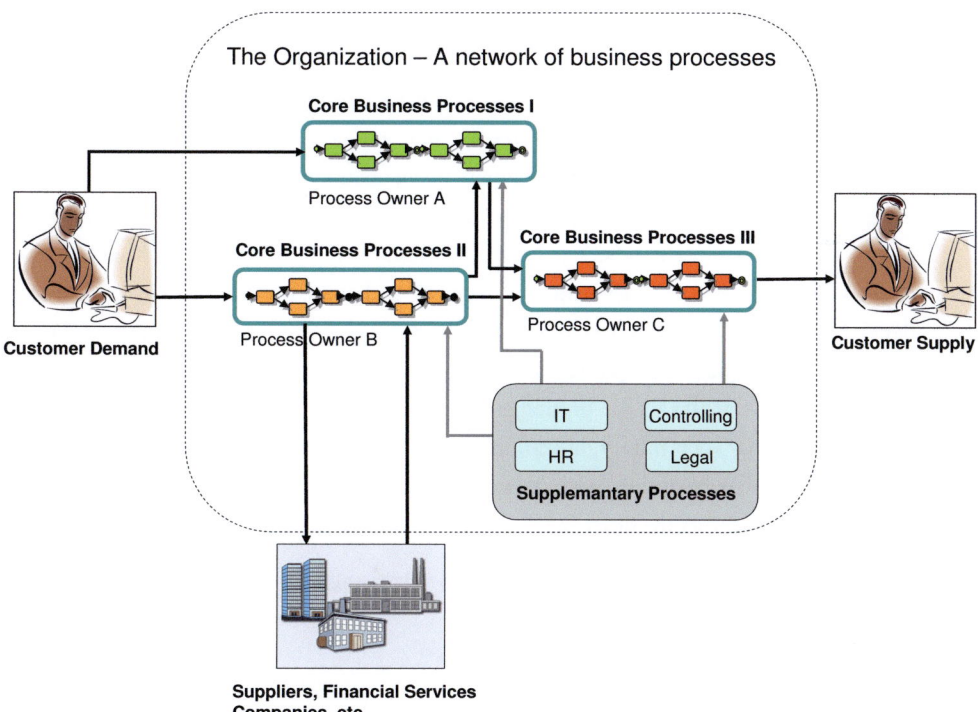

Figure 2.4.: The organization as a network of business processes.

Based on [211], the following main constituents of BPM can be identified:

Process Automation This is the automation of repeatable business processes based on a software solution, such as WMS or BPMS.

Enterprise Application Integration EAI can be defined as "unrestricted sharing of data and business processes among any connected application or data sources in the enterprise". To leverage the advantages of process automation, existing applications have to be integrated into the process solution. If the focus is more on the process than on the systems, EAI is sometimes called business process integration.

Business Rules A business rule defines or constrains one aspect of the business, that is intended to assert business structure or influence the behavior of the business [9]. The idea of the business rules approach is to extract the business logic from the systems and manage it separately [312]. The business rules approach has been proven to enhance the effectiveness, flexibility, and efficiency of business systems [248]. In the context of BPM, business rules play an important role as they describe the business logic of a business process. Business rules control the decision behavior and therefore determine how the process is actually executed [154]. Business rule engines are special software solutions for managing business rules.

End-to-end Management Business processes should be managed across their whole length. Focusing only on a specific part of a process, may not lead to the results expected [104]. Fig. 2.5 provides a department oriented view on an abstract business process. The department view is often termed silo due to department thinking and insufficient communication between different departments. The figure illustrates also the situation in which processes are considered only from a departmental view. Note that the borders of a business process depend on the considered system or environment in which the business process is embedded. The environment can pertain to the organization in which the business process is running or additionally to the participating organizations (see also the aforementioned differentiation between intraorganizational and interorganizational processes). Most often the environment pertains only to the organization due to the non existing or limited control over other organizations.

Continuous Improvement As described in Section 2.1.3, business processes are continuously improved.

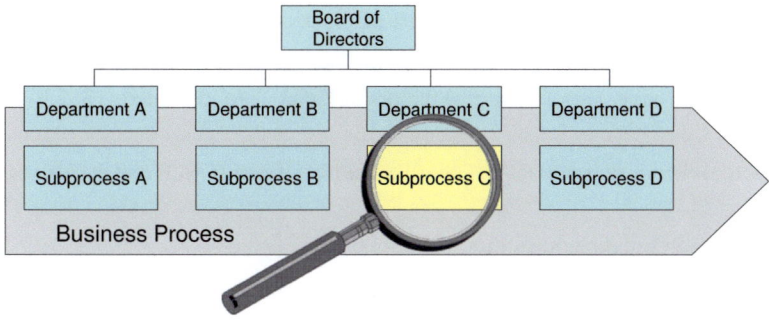

Figure 2.5.: Silo-oriented view on an abstract business process. The magnifying glass illustrates how a business process is considered only from a departmental view.

Real Time Monitoring This enables managers or process owners to retrieve information about the process performance in real-time. Note that the requirements regarding real time are dependent on the application. In general, the monitoring solution should be "able to produce the information in a timely enough fashion for it to be still meaningful and useful" [78].

Despite the technology centric view on BPM that sometimes prevails, processes are also executed by people. As people are the greatest asset of an organization and the key factor for project success, change management becomes an important issue when an organization introduces process automation [244]. Several approaches exist, that focus on human interactions [116, 125] or combine them with technical aspects [111]. Also, organizations have noticed the importance of the human role in BPM, leading to modeling languages like BPEL4People [2].

BPM potentially delivers a variety of advantages:

- Improved process transparency

- Improved processes in terms of cost efficiency and quality

- Increased customer satisfaction

- Advanced inter-divisional thinking

- Minimizing operational risks

Note that the above stated advantages are only potentially delivered by BPM, e.g. customer satisfaction can only be achieved if the customer needs are captured correctly. Furthermore, aspects such as business strategy, business model and business objectives play an important role in BPM. Therefore, these aspects must be mapped out in a promising and competitive way. Otherwise BPM initiatives or projects will not deliver any sustainable business success.

There exists a variety of pitfalls in the area of process modeling in general [242, 243] and when using specific languages such as BPMN [249]. As the advantages stated above are not automatically achievable, various success factors of BPM were identified [13, 139]:

- Support and commitment of the Chief Executive Officer (CEO) and senior management

- Embedding in organization strategy

- Availability of BPM know-how and experience

- Change management

- Governance and process architecture guidelines

- IT's ability to react quickly on changes

2.1.3. Business Process Life-cycle

Business processes have a continuous life-cylce which is divided into various phases. The different phases of the life-cycle group the activities which constitute BPM. The business process life-cycle is visually depicted as a circle in order to reflect the continuous repetition of the phases. The business process life-cycle generally focuses on the automation of business processes.

In the literature there is no uniform view on the number of these phases. Indeed, there exists a multitude of different divisions in practice[9] as well as in science [201, 219, 321].

The business process life-cycle is sometimes also defined on the basis of BPM and not on the business process. In this case, terms such as closed loop BPM, Business Continuous Management System or Continuous BPM cycle are in use.

The continuous cycle is based on the concept of Continuous Process Improvement (CPI) as in Kaizen [279] or Six Sigma [225]. CPI is a continuous effort for the discovering and elimination of the main causes of problems which is accomplished by using relatively small improvements, rather than one big bang improvement [240].

In the following, the main phases of the business process life-cycle are described under the assumption that the business process has already been introduced in the organization and is currently executed but not necessarily automated by means of an BPMS. Fig. 2.6 depicts the different phases with the most commonly used approaches.

---

[9]e.g. SAP does not depict an optimization phase with the argumentation that optimization takes place throughout all of the phases [251].

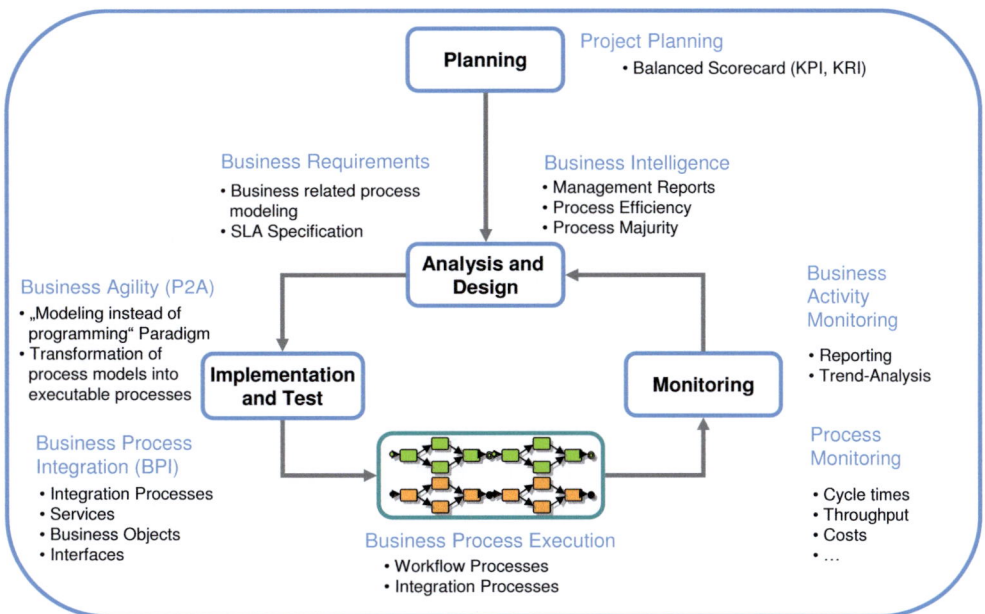

Figure 2.6.: The different phases of closed loop BPM.

Planning

This phase encompasses the creation of a business case that should contain a cohesive justification for getting the approval of the management for the project implementation. All feasible development approaches and realization strategies are evaluated using approaches like gap and scenario analysis. For each provisioned scenario, the benefits and costs must be estimated. Benefits and costs can be weighted based on the results of a risk analysis. During risk analysis, both the impact and probability of an event that may occur is estimated. Finally, the Return On Investment (ROI) is calculated for each development option as the ratio of net benefits over costs.

The different analyses demand a first requirements gathering and as-is analysis. Also, the affected business processes need to be identified. Balanced Scorecard is a performance and measurement tool that can be incorporated in the planning phase for specifying the performance targets [262]. These targets are specified based on different categories of indicators such as Key Performance Indicator (KPI) and Key Risk Indicator (KRI). While KPIs are used for the measurement of the process efficiency and process maturity[10], KRIs measure the operational risk.

---

[10]e.g. based on process improvement frameworks like OMG's Business Process Maturity Model (BPMM) [168] which is a derivation from Capability Maturity Model Integration (CMMI) [4, 59].

Analysis and Design

Once the project is approved, the initial as-is analysis needs to be extended and the requirements must be gathered completely by business analysts. Part of the requirements gathering is also the analysis of the current state of the running business process. The way this analysis is performed depends on whether the process has already been automated or not. If it is already implemented, the collected data and the calculated KPIs are the basis for the evaluation and for the comparison with the objectives planned. If the process has not been automated, the relevant data must be estimated.

If there is not yet a BPM tool in use, the BPM tool evaluation and selection becomes an important issue. Fig 2.7 shows a methodology for the BPM tool evaluation. In order to create a decision basis, technical as well as business requirements are considered. Commonly, the evaluation is done in multiple phases. First a long-list is created based on a market screening and a SWOT analysis[11]. Based on a criteria catalog, a short list is created from the long list which can be shortened again. The final tool evaluation is done for two or three options in a more thorough way by means of request for informations, proof-of-concepts, prototypes, among others.

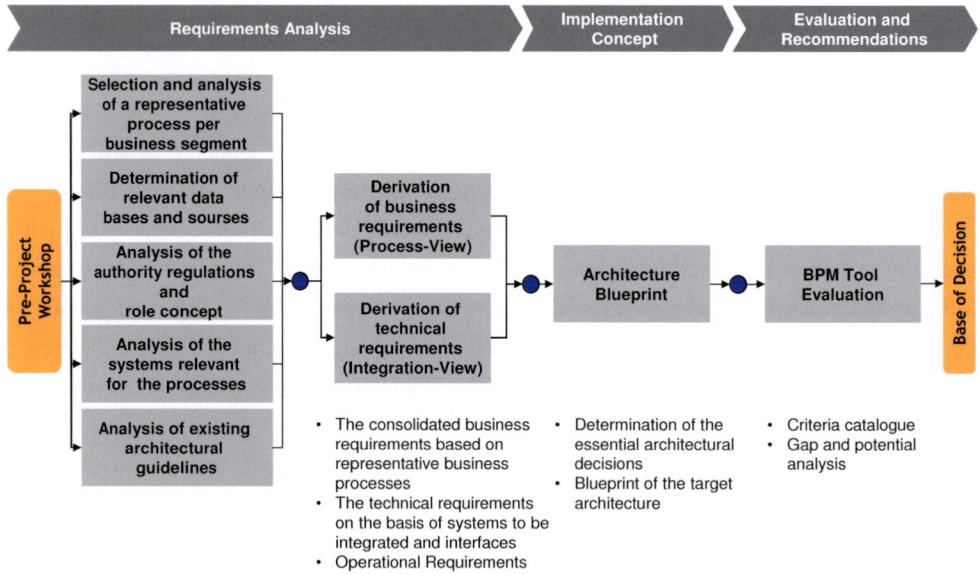

Figure 2.7.: Methodology for BPM tool evaluation and selection.

Process mining tools can be applied in order to analyze the executed processes. These tools generate graphical representations of process instances as well as process models based on

---

[11] A method for evaluating the Strengths, Weaknesses, Opportunities, and Threats of a project (see e.g. [138]).

logging data. Using these generated models, divergences and errors can be discovered, e.g. if activities have not been executed in the correct order. The flexibility and business agility of the processes and the implemented solution become an important issue at this point, if changes have to be performed.

Business analysts create a graphical process model based on the gathered business requirements. There is a multitude of proprietary and standardized modeling languages as described in Section 2.1.2. Business process modeling is in general a top-down approach with focus on the control flow of the activities of a process. But there are also alternative approaches for business process modeling. In contrary to the standard BPM approach, subject-oriented BPM is a bottom-up approach that focuses on the subjects of a process and not on its activities [92]. Another decentralized modeling approach in which models are created by process owners is introduced in [281].

Additionally, business analysts identify authority regulations, role concepts, data sources, and business rules that are relevant for the business process and its automation. Also the level of service is set, most commonly by defining a Service Level Agreement (SLA). The agreement comprises attributes like level of availability, serviceability, performance, operation, among others.

As the business analysts focus on the business requirements, the technical details for the actual execution of the processes are generally not considered in the process model.

Implementation and Test

Before the business process can be executed by a BPMS, the process must be implemented. This requires the transformation of the process models specified by the business analysts into executable process models. An executable process model is a process model that can be directly executed by a workflow or BPM engine. These are components that are part of a BPMS and are responsible for the execution of business processes. The aforementioned transformation is the responsibility of the process designers or technical consultants. As processes normally interact with different systems, the process integration is an important aspect. System architects interpret the business and technical (functional and non-functional) requirements and determine the architecture and software components needed for implementation. For this task, software or enterprise architecture modeling tools based on the UML are commonly used. IT developers then create these software components using programming tools (such as Integrated Development Environments (IDEs)) and integration software (such as EAI products). Nowadays, these components are normally implemented as reusable services as part of a Service Oriented Architecture (SOA). In this context, it is distinguished between choreography and orchestration of services. While orchestration refers to coordination at the level of a single participant's process, choreography refers to a more global view at the level of multiple participants [117, page 204]. In the latter case, the overall process behaviour stems from the interaction of the different components or participants following their own rules [246]. Process models based on service orchestration have committed to the Business Process Execution Language (BPEL) from Organization for the Advancement of Structured Information Standards (OASIS). Another language for executable processes is XML Process Definition Language (XPDL) developed by the WfMC.

The transformation of the process model into the executable software solution is often referred to as "business process to application" [11]. The created software solution must be thoroughly tested prior to the roll-out.

Execution

Once the acceptance tests of the implemented processes have been conducted successfully, the processes are deployed on the production system. The business processes are executed by humans, machines or both. Technically, for each execution, one instance is created from the process model template. Such an instance has a unique identifier termed process ID.

Monitoring

The monitoring of the business processes in execution is done with the help of Business Activity Monitoring or Business Process Performance Monitoring tools. They collect the data and calculate the KPIs of interest. Graphical dashboards provide a consolidated, target group oriented access, as well as an insight of the current state of the business processes and are the basis of the so called real time enterprise. Monitoring is also the basis for capacity management and business forecasts and can also be used for the evaluation of the success of the project previously executed.

2.1.4. IT Architecture

When it comes to process automation, the IT architecture is an important issue. This pertains not only to the software solution, but also to the enterprise architecture as business processes are executed company-wide. SOA has become the major architectural concept in the area of BPM with an increasing linkage between these two concepts [67].

The main advantages of a reference architecture and SOA in general are the clear separation of different functionalities and the loose coupling between components. The loose coupling of business process and the legacy systems is achieved by introducing a service layer which provides the abstraction required. This loose coupling together with the use of standardized technologies, leads an increased adaptability and flexibility. Due to its adaptable, flexible style of architecture, a SOA provides the foundation for shorter time-to-market, reduced costs, and risks in development and maintenance [216]. Furthermore the so called "service enabling" can leverage existing investments in legacy applications [46]. SOA should not be equated with web services, as these are only one way of implementing a SOA. Web services are widely-used, as they are based on platform-independent standards[12]. Therefore, they are the enabling technology and driver for the SOA trend.

2.1.5. Business and IT Alignment

Due to the business complexity and the highly dynamic marketplace, the role of the IT within organizations has changed. In the past, the IT had to support business and was more viewed and perceived as a cost factor. Nowadays, IT has to become a strategic enabler for business growth. This requires the alignment of business and IT which is a continuous process for optimizing the relationship between business and IT, especially by aligning the IT organization with the requirements of the business processes. Moreover, the IT strategy has to be embedded into the overall business strategy. Alignment has been defined also as the "capacity to demonstrate a positive relationship between information technologies and the accepted financial measures of performance" [267].

Although the business and IT alignment has been a topic for around two decades [120, 202], its importance has been increased dramatically in recent years. The so called gap between IT and business arises from the lack of understanding of the business needs by IT experts and of technical details by business experts (see Fig. 2.8).

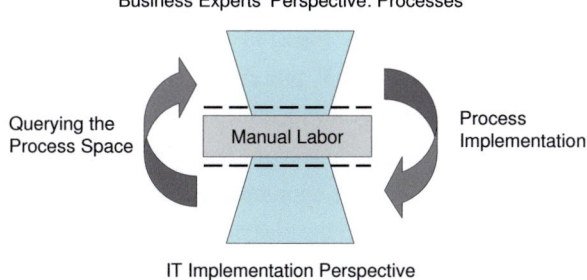

Figure 2.8.: The gap between business and IT [121].

Several approaches have been suggested to bridge the gap, e.g. by the integration of semantic web in BPM [321] or by combining the frameworks and methodologies Information Technology Infrastructure Library (ITIL), Control Objectives for Information and Related Technology (COBIT), and Rational Unified Process (RUP) [143].

---

[12]for an overview see e.g. [6, 280].

Furthermore, business processes have been identified for serving as a common language between IT and business. But as business analysts and process developers have different views on the processes and also normally a different educational background, the alignment is still a complicated and challenging task. The transformation from business models to IT implementations requires "an important and ephemeral human effort which is expensive and prone to errors" [321]. Furthermore, there exist fundamental differences between business modeling and process modeling, e.g. business modeling is centered around the notion of value, while process modeling focuses on how a process should be carried out in operational terms [105].

2.1.6. Business Process Complexity

In this section, the theoretical and empirical research on process complexity is briefly discussed[13]. In [48], process complexity is defined as "the degree to which a process is difficult to analyze, understand or explain. It may be characterized by the number and intricacy of activity interfaces, transitions, conditional and parallel branches, the existence of loops, roles, activity categories, the types of data structures, and other process characteristics."

Many approaches for measuring process complexity are based on metrics that are adapted from software metrics[14]. Examples of software metrics are lines of code and failure rate. Various requirements for software metrics were established such as consistency, computability, and validity [144, pages 70-72].

In the following, a short overview of different approaches is given: In one of the first publications about process complexity, several metrics are introduced for structural complexity based on graph-theory [164]. A control-flow complexity metric for business processes is suggested in [48] and tested by conducting a laboratory experiment [49]. In [184] the validation of process metrics is performed on the basis of 604 EPC processes of the SAP Reference Model by using the verification tool WofYAWL. In total, they identified 34 faulty processes.

Other approaches are developed in the context of a specific process modeling languages such as BPMN [3] or Petri nets [167]. Another approach that does not focus only on the process model perspective, but on the data-flow perspective is introduced in [47].

In [235], a heuristic for the proper size of individual activities in business processes is introduced. The heuristic is based on a Product Data Model (PDM). A PDM consists of data elements of the business process and dependencies between them. Such dependencies relate to basic operations. PDMs are introduced in more detail in the next chapter. The objective is to model a business process by grouping operations to activities in such a way that operations of one activity belong together (highly cohesive), whereas different activities are independent from each other (loosely coupled). For that purpose, a process cohesion and a process coupling

---

[13]A more detailed overview is given in [181].
[14]For an introduction to software metrics see e.g. [90].

metric are introduced.

Some critical remarks have to be mentioned regarding business process complexity. Despite the importance of the validation of metrics, the empirical research for the validation of process metrics is still rather limited [181]. Moreover, focusing only on the process model or control-flow perspective for measuring process complexity is not necessarily sufficient in order to make a statement about the complexity of the business process. In practice, business processes are often said to be complex, but the related process model does not reflect this complexity. In these cases, the complexity often arises due to the complicated work that must be carried out for some of the business process activities. Thus, the complexity is hidden "behind the activities" and complexity metrics that are only based on process models, are not capable of measuring this kind of complexity. Nevertheless, the understandability of process models may benefit from such analysis (see e.g. [187, 182]).

After the introduction to the different areas of BPM, the specifics of the service economy are discussed.

2.2. Service Economy

In this section the specifics of services are examined, as the iEPM approach has been developed specifically for the service industry. A good starting point for the examination of services is the three-sector hypothesis developed by Colin Clark and Jean Fourastié. This economic theory divides economies into the following three sectors of activity:

Primary To this sector pertains the extraction of raw materials like mining, agriculture and fishing.

Secondary The secondary sector of the economy manufactures (finished) physical goods. This means that all of manufacturing, processing, and construction lies within this sector.

Tertiary The tertiary sector of the economy is the service industry. It provides services to customers and businesses. This sector comprises services like retail, banking, insurance, and government.

Other suggestions have been made as to the need for further and more fine-grained subdivisions of the tertiary sector. This led to the addition of a fourth (quaternary) (see e.g. [107, 108]) and a fifth (quinary) (see e.g. [19, 20]) sector but with a variety of different definitions. The subdivisions focus on aspects like intellectual services, non-profit organizations, highest level of decision making in economies, quasi domestic services, among others (see also [103, 118]).

The transformation from manufacturing-based to predominantly service-based economies began in the mid-20th century and is happening on a global scale now. IT is the major enabler and the globalization one of the drivers for this structural change. Not only the scale of globally dispersed services is growing rapidly but also the complexity[15] [18]. Today, the service sector is highly important (see e.g. [276, 277]) as a large and increasing number of workers are employed in this sector in the industrialized nations. In Germany, the employment in the service sector is at 72.4%, the employment in the goods sector (manufacturing, agriculture, and fishing) is at 27.6% [16]. In the USA, the situation is similar, the employment in the service sector is at 82.1%, whereas the employment in the goods sector (manufacturing, construction, agriculture, and mining) is at 17.9% [17].

After showing the importance of the service sector, the question is clarified what this sector constitutes.

In [99], a historical view on the service sector is described: "the service sector was viewed as having little or no productivity growth and an inability to innovate... In contrast, the manufacturing sector, producing tangible outputs, was seen as the source of most innovation." A more modern characterization of the service sector is given in [259]: "service sector industries are characterized by a close interaction between production and consumption, high information content, the intangible nature of their output, and a heavy emphasis on labor capital in the delivery of their output." The definition of service sector in [204] is based on activities which contribute to productive values: the service sector "consists of services activities which are brought to bear on physical objects, human subjects, information or institutional entities in such a way that these are somehow influenced without being physically transformed; or where the focus is on the use and functioning of the objects which are subject to the activities rather than on the physical transformation".

Accordingly to [226], the service sector can be considered "to include all economic activities whose output is not a physical product or construction, is generally consumed at the time it is produced, and provides added value in forms (such as convenience, amusement, timeliness, comfort, or health) that are essentially intangible...". As common for most of the definitions of services, they are compared with physical products. In the following, the discussion about the differences is limited to the major aspects only. Services are intangible, heterogeneous, perishable, without transformation of material during the production, and required the joint participation of the consumer and producer with their skills and knowledge (see e.g. [39, 102]). In contrary to services, manufactured products are pre-produced, to a certain extent identical or substitutable in their production and use, physical tangible, storable (can be inventoried), recyclable, among others. This differentiation shows that the production and consumption of services and physical products have fundamental differences.

---

[15]For a detailed discussion about the complexity of services see e. g. [5]. Furthermore, a collection of recent developments in theory and empirical research regarding the complexity of economic systems is provided in [88].

[16]Source: Labour market statistics, Federal Statistical Office, Germany, 2007.

[17]Source: Bureau of Labor Statistics, USA, April 2006.

But this traditional understanding about the differentiation between goods and services has been challenged by alternative definitions and concepts. Examples are the definitions of physical products as "services waiting to happen" [113] or "frozen activities" [205]. Many authors also claim that virtually every product today contains a service component. This is referred to as "servitization of products", which generally includes the adding value to products through services [303]. But products can even be transfered to or offered as services. In this context, software-as-a-service is the most prominent example [27, 264]. In [305] the binary distinction between physical products and services is criticized due to their nested relationship. It is argued, that goods are appliances used in service provision. This work led to the development of the concept of Service-Dominant Logic (S-D logic) [304, 306], in which services are superordinant to goods. This hypothesis is based on the assumption that the aim of the customer's acquisition is the benefit available through the service of the provider and not products themselves. Furthermore, one of the nine foundational premises defined in the S-D logic denotes: goods are distribution mechanisms for service provision [176]. In the S-D logic, basically all economic exchange is considered as a service exchange.

As many products cannot be differentiated between the extremes pure physical products and pure services, the goods-services continuum was introduced. It reflects the spectrum of the different overlapping characteristics of services and physical products based on examples. An illustration of a goods-services continuum is depicted in Fig. 2.9.

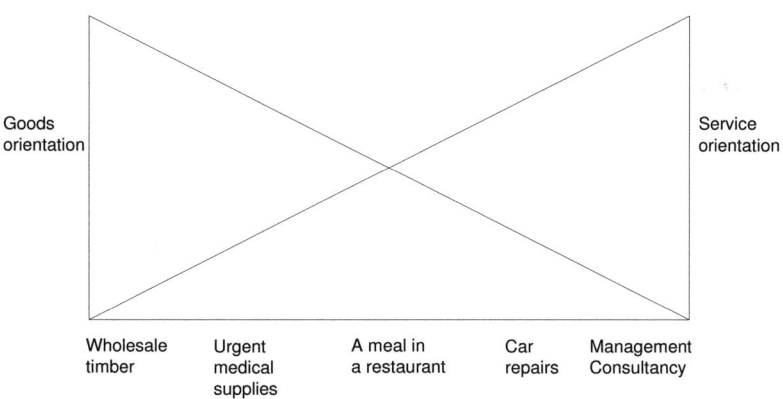

Figure 2.9.: An illustration of the goods-services continuum [17, page 592].

These insights concerning the relationship between goods and services have a high practical relevance, as they can reveal opportunities for innovation and furthermore lead to competitive advantages [113].

2.3. Flexibility

In this section a definition of flexibility, particularly for business processes, is provided. Furthermore, the requirements of flexibility in the area of BPM are discussed and different taxonomies introduced. Note that one of the objectives of the iEPM approach is the enhancement of the flexibility during the business process execution.

A general definition of flexibility is provided e.g. by the Meriam-Webster dictionary: flexibility is "characterized by a ready capability to adapt to new, different, or changing requirements."

In [245] a definition of flexibility pertaining to business process is given: "business process flexibility is the capacity of the organization to respond to change by modifying only those parts of a process that require adaptation while keeping other parts stable." Furthermore, they state that process flexibility consists of an extrinsic trigger for change and mechanisms for intrinsic process adaptation. They suggest context-aware process design that considers the extrinsic environment variables that denote drivers and requirements for process flexibility.

In [271] the term "Flexible Workflow" is introduced and five dimensions of workflow flexibility are identified:

Dynamic instance adaptation The adaption of a workflow instance is required due to unforeseen changes or situations during the execution. This means that a deviation from the standard way is created for one or more instances.

Process evolution Processes are not fixed over time, but they are subject to evolution. Process evolution may lead to an adaption of the process type.

Human learning curve This aspect is based on the assumption that any human who is new to a process experiences a learning curve. Workflow systems should provide support for users with differing experiences.

Optionality of control This reflects the degree of freedom, a user has regarding the processing of tasks, i.e. there are users that do not want to be ordained by a computer.

Autonomy of participants There are processes, in which autonomous organizational units are involved such as subcontractors or collaborators. Nevertheless, there may be the need to coordinate these participants, e.g. in order to achieve an improvement in customer service. On the contrary, there are organizational units without any autonomy.

Different taxonomies for process flexibility can be found in literature. For example, the taxonomy introduced in [292] distinguishes four types of process flexibility:

Flexibility by design This type pertains to the handling of anticipated changes in the operating environment, where supporting strategies can be defined at design-time.

Flexibility by deviation This type pertains to the handling of occasional unforeseen behaviour, where differences with the expected behaviour are minimal.

Flexibility by under-specification This type pertains to the handling of anticipated changes in the operating environment, where strategies cannot be defined at design-time, because the final strategy is not known in advance or is not generally applicable.

Flexibility by change This type is either for handling of occasional unforeseen behaviour, where differences require process adaptations, or for handling permanent unforeseen behaviour.

Another taxonomy for flexibility in business processes was suggested in [232]. In this paper, flexibility is classified with respect to the types of changes it enables. The taxonomy comprises three different dimensions:

Abstraction level of the change Changes can be considered on different level of abstractions. Here, changes in the business process type and process instances are differentiated.

Subject of change The different subjects of changes are differentiated by perspectives such as functional, organizational, and operational perceptive, among others.

Properties of the change Four different properties of change are distinguished: the extent (incremental or revolutionary), the duration (temporary or permanent), the swiftness (valid immediately or deferred), and the anticipation of change (planned or ad hoc).

Besides the enhancement of the flexibility, business process optimization is the second objective of the iEPM approach. Therefore, an introduction to optimization is given in the following.

2.4. Optimization

In this section, a brief introduction to global optimization as well as multi-objective optimization is given.

2.4.1. Global Optimization

In [128], a standard global optimization problem is defined as follows[18]:

Given a nonempty, closed set $D \subset \mathbb{R}^n$ and a continuous function $f : A \to \mathbb{R}$, where $A \subset \mathbb{R}^n$ is a suitable set containing D, find at least one point $x^* \in D$ satisfying $f(x^*) \leq f(x)$ for all $x \in D$ or show that such a point does not exist.

---

[18]Note that this definition is based on a closed set and on a continuous function. There exist optimization problems that are based on other classes of feasible sets and functions, such as a discrete feasible set (see [128] for more details).

A global optimization problem is denoted by

$$\text{minimize } f(x) \qquad\qquad [2.1]$$
$$\text{s.t. } x \in D$$

A point $x^* \in D$ satisfying $f(x^*) \leq f(x) \ \forall x \in D$ is called global minimizer of f over D. The corresponding value of f is called global minimum of f over D and is denoted by min $f(D)$. The set of all solutions of the global optimization problem (Equ. 2.1) is denoted by argmin $f(D)$.

Since max $f(D) = - $ min $(-f(D))$, global maximization problems are included in Equation 2.1.

2.4.2. Multi-Objective Optimization

In the previous section, global optimization has been briefly introduced which has the goal to optimize a single objective function. In a multi-objective optimization problem, multiple objective functions have to be optimized.

A multi-objective optimization problem is denoted by

$$\text{minimize } f = \{f_1(x), f_2(x), \cdots, f_m(x)\} \qquad\qquad [2.2]$$
$$\text{s.t. } x \in S$$

with $m \geq 2$ objective functions $f_i : \mathbb{R}^n \to \mathbb{R}, i = 1, \cdots, m$ that will be optimized. The vector $x = (x_1, x_2, \cdots, x_n)^T$ belongs to the feasible region $S \in \mathbb{R}^n$. The image of the feasible region is denoted by $Z \in \mathbb{R}^m$ and termed feasible objective region. The elements of Z are termed objective vectors and they consist of the objective values $f(x) = (f_1(x), f_2(x), \cdots, f_m(x))$.

In multi-objective optimization problems there does not necessarily exist a solution that is best with respect to all objectives due to conflicting objectives. One possibility to solve such problems is to combine the different objective functions to only one by using weights. This approach is termed scalarisation. It has been used for many years in the operations research and heuristic optimization community but suffers from several drawbacks, e.g. the use of weights implicitly assumes that the user preferences are known in advance [84]. Therefore, instead of searching for a single solution, methods for finding a diverse set of high quality solutions have been proposed. The concept of dominance provides such a method. In case of maximization, one solution is said to dominate another if their objective values are at least as high for all objectives, and is strictly better for at least one. Let A and B be two solutions, m the number of objectives and a, b m-dimensional vectors of the objective values of solution A and B, respectively. Then

$$A \text{ dominates } B \iff \forall i \in \{1, \cdots, m\} \ a_i \geq b_i, \text{ and } \exists i \in \{1, \cdots, m\} \ a_i > b_i$$

If conflicting objectives exist, there is no single solution that dominates all other solutions. A solution that is not dominated by any other solution is termed nondominated. The set of all nondominated solutions is termed Pareto set or Pareto front. Fig. 2.10 illustrates the concept of Pareto optimality.

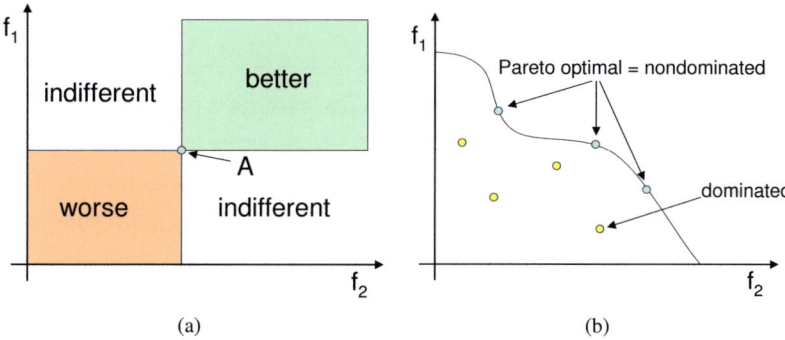

(a)   (b)

Figure 2.10.: Illustration of Pareto optimality for two conflicting objectives in case of maximization. (a) shows the different areas in which solutions are either worse, better or indifferent in relation to solution A. (b) illustrates a Pareto front and dominated solutions.

Based on the concept of Pareto optimality, a multi-objective optimization problem is solved by finding or approximating the Pareto optimal set. This means to find solutions as close as possible to the Pareto front, while maintaining a good diversity along the Pareto front. Accordingly to [339], the approximation of the Pareto optimal front should achieve the following three objectives:

- The distance of the resulting nondominated front to the Pareto optimal front should be minimized.

- A good (in most cases uniform) distribution of the solutions found is desirable.

- The spread of the obtained nondominated front should be maximized, i.e. for each objective a wide range of values should be covered by the nondominated solutions.

Various performance measures have been suggested for evaluating the quality of the solutions found. Note that good metrics should take the above stated objectives into account. Examples for such metrics are attainment surfaces and the hyper volume metric [339].

Several diversity preservation methods exist such as Kernel methods or nearest neighbor techniques [339]. The Pareto optimal solutions are typically stored in a data structure called archive. In certain problems, the number of Pareto optimal solutions can become extremely large. In this case, clustering has been successfully applied for reducing the nondominated set [339].

There are different techniques for the visualization of the results such as scatter plots, radar charts or heatmaps (see e.g. [183]).

The multi-objective optimization will be discussed again in conjunction with Particle Swarm Optimization (PSO) in Sec. 2.6.3. One solution technique for optimization problems is machine learning which is explained after the introduction to agents.

2.5. Introduction to Agents

Some researchers claim, that the requirements of today's software systems go beyond the capabilities of traditional computer science and software engineering abstractions, such as object-orientation [336]. In order to cope with an increasing complexity of distributed software systems, researchers have been developing and utilizing various tools of abstractions with the objective to improve the software engineering process. Accordingly to [336], four main characteristics distinguish future software systems from traditional ones which have led to the emergence of the agent paradigm:

Situatedness Software components are embedded in an environment, which they can influence and be influenced by. Thus, there is an explicit notion of the environment in which components are allocated and executed.

Openness It is common for software systems to interact with external software components that were designed independently. This interaction requires a certain openness of the software systems. Moreover, software systems are subject to decentralized management and can dynamically change their structure.

Locality in control Software systems components represent autonomous and proactive loci of control. As independent software systems have their own autonomous flows of control, there is no global execution control.

Locality in interactions Despite living in a fully connected world, software components interact according to local (geographical or logical) patterns.

These characteristics are typically used to characterize Multi-Agent Systems (MASs) in the research community of distributed artificial intelligence [136]. Agent-oriented techniques are based on the modularization of complex problems in terms of multiple autonomous components that can act and interact in flexible ways. Thus, they are well appropriate for complex, dynamic, and distributed software systems [137].

The term agent denotes an encapsulated hardware or more commonly software based computer system that possesses the properties of autonomy, social ability, reactivity, and proactivity [329, 328]. Other researchers emphasize different aspects of agency such as mobility or adaptability [323]. The characteristics depend mainly on the type of application in which certain attributes are more important than other ones. Nevertheless, in [135, page 5] it was stated that the power of the agent paradigm is provided only if the above mentioned four properties exist in one single entity which distinguishes the agent paradigm from related software paradigms such as object-oriented or distributed systems.

An agent is situated in an environment. It has certain sensing capabilities to retrieve knowledge or beliefs about this environment[19]. Moreover, it is able to perform certain actions to achieve the defined goals. Agents can communicate with each other by exchanging messages. Any communication language can be used within the constraints of the system's communication protocol. Examples of standardized languages are Knowledge Query Manipulation Language (KQML) or FIPA's[20] Agent Communication Language (ACL).

A MAS is an instance of distributed systems composed by agents [213]. In MASs, agents typically interact with each other in order to achieve the given objectives. The interaction comprises information exchange, coordination, cooperation, negotiation, among others. In the MAS developed for the iEPM approach, the assignment of the business process activities[21] to resources is done on the basis of negotiation. MASs have been applied in a variety of application fields such as sustainable resource management in ecosystems, enterprise modeling, manufacturing control, robotic soccer, among others [179].

Despite the variety of different areas in which agents have been applied, the agent paradigm may lead to a number of problems. In [135, page 10] three different problems are mentioned: First, there is no overall system controller which may cause problems in domains in which global constraints must be maintained. Second, there is no global perspective. Due to the distributed nature of agent based systems, a complete knowledge about the domain may be not achievable or at least not efficiently. As the agent's actions are based on its local state, its action may be suboptimal. Third, the delegation of tasks to agents requires trust as users have to gain confidence in the agents.

---

[19]A research field, focusing on the perception of the environment, is situation awareness. A general definition of situation awareness is "the perception of environmental elements within a volume of time and space, the comprehension of their meaning, and the projection of their status in the near future" [86].

[20]Foundations of Intelligent Physical Agents (FIPA) is an IEEE Computer Society standards organization that promotes agent-based technology and the interoperability of its standards with other technologies.

[21]These activities are termed production rules in the context of EPMs.

Agents are often referred to as intelligent agents, to emphasize the point that they achieve goals by learning or the use of knowledge. The agents developed for the iEPM approach[22] can be considered as intelligent agents as their behaviour is controlled and managed by machine learning techniques which are introduced in the next section.

2.6. Fundamental Machine Learning Concepts

In this section, the machine learning concepts relevant for the iEPM approach are introduced. Machine learning belongs to the field of Artificial Intelligence (AI). The term AI was originally coined in 19955 by John McCarthy. He defines AI as: "The science and engineering of making intelligent machines, especially intelligent computer programs. It is related to the similar task of using computers to understand human intelligence, but AI does not have to confine itself to methods that are biologically observable". Originally, research in the area of AI focused mainly on expert systems and problem solving algorithms. Nowadays, AI comprises a variety of subfields such as reasoning, knowledge, planning and learning. In [79] the importance of the subfield machine learning was stressed as "some people have posed that real intelligence is unattainable without the ability to learn". The research in the area of machine learning is concerned with computer programs that learn from experience and have the ability to adapt their behavior if necessary. A more scientific definition is provided by [191]: "A computer program is said to learn from experience E with respect to some class of tasks T and performance measure P, if its performance at tasks in T, as measured by P, improves with experience E." For example, in the domain computer chess, task T corresponds to the learning of chess, a performance measure P is the number of won games per number of played games. The number of played games corresponds to the experience E.

In [35] machine learning is categorized into four classes. In all classes, the agent[23] receives a sequence of inputs. As one of the classes is a generalization of reinforcement learning and is not sufficiently explained, only the other three classes are listed:

Supervised Learning Additionally to the input sequence, the agent is provided with the respective output. The input / output tuples are termed test data. The agent has the goal to learn based on the test data to produce the correct output for a new input. Examples are regression and classification.

Reinforcement Learning The agent interacts with its environment by performing actions which affect the state of the environment. Furthermore, the agent receives a reward that indicates how good it was to perform the respective action. The objective of the agent is to learn to act in a way that maximizes the future rewards.

---

[22]This pertains specifically to the agent type Intelligent Business Object (IBO) - see Sec. 5.1.1.
[23]A variety of different terms exists for the agent such as system, machine or learner.

Unsupervised Learning The agent obtains only input data but neither it receives supervised target outputs nor rewards from its environment. Unsupervised learning can be considered as finding patterns in the input data the agent receives. Examples are clustering and dimensionality reduction.

The following sections contain the introductions to the fundamental machine learning concepts that are relevant for the iEPM approach.

2.6.1. Introduction to Relational Reinforcement Learning

Despite the fact that Relational Reinforcement Learning (RRL) is quite a new topic, a variety of different approaches exists. For a thorough introduction see e. g. [83, 82]. RRL is a combination of reinforcement learning and relational learning which is also known as inductive logic programming. An important aspect in RRL is the knowledge representation as it is a key element in artificial intelligence. There are different kinds of knowledge representation such as propositional or relational formats (see e. g. [298]).

Reinforcement Learning

Reinforcement Learning (RL) is a try and error approach in which an agent takes actions in an environment in order to maximize a long-term reward [142, 269]. RL is based on the theory of Markov Decision Processes with the difference that RL relaxes some of the assumptions including determinism and complete knowledge of the domain model. The standard RL model consists of:

1. A set of environment states S,

2. A set of actions A,

3. A set of scalar rewards R in $\mathbb{R}$,

4. An unknown transition function $\delta : S \times A \rightarrow S$. For a given state s_t, the transition function determines the next state s_{t+1} following action a_t,

5. An unknown reward function $R(s_t, a_t) : S \times A \rightarrow R$.

At each time t, the agent perceives its current state $s_t \in S$ and the set of valid actions $A(s_t)$. The agent selects the action based on its current state and its policy. A policy determines which action should be performed in each state - thus a policy is a mapping from states to actions. The execution of action $a_t \in A(s_t)$ puts the agent into the new state s_{t+1}. Furthermore, the agent receives reinforcement (reward) r_{t+1} from the environment. The learning objective is to find an optimal policy. The interaction between an agent and its environment is illustrated in Fig. 2.11.

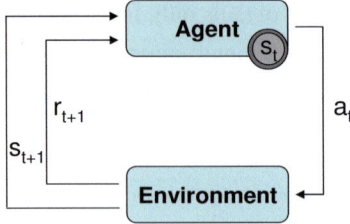

Figure 2.11.: Reinforcement Learning - Illustration of the interaction between an agent and its environment.

A commonly used objective is the maximization of the discounted sum of rewards (see. Equ. 2.3).

$$R = \sum_{t=0}^{\infty} \gamma^t r_t \text{ with } 0 \leq \gamma \leq 1 \qquad [2.3]$$

The constant γ is termed discount factor and is used to exponentially decrease the weight of reinforcements received in the future. Thus, it weights the near term reinforcement more heavily than the distant future reinforcement.

The goal of the agent consists of learning an optimal policy $\pi^* : S \rightarrow A$ that maximizes a given value function, here the discounted sum of the rewards $V(s)$:

$$V^\pi(s) = \sum_{t=0}^{\infty} \gamma^t r_t \text{ with } 0 \leq \gamma \leq 1 \qquad [2.4]$$

The optimal policy is denoted by π^* and the corresponding value-function by V^*.

In Reinforcement Learning, the representation of a state is mainly propositional, e. g. a state is decomposed in a set of state features. In accordance with [79], there exist two major directions to solve reinforcement learning problems: direct policy search and statistical value-function based approaches.

The first step in the direct policy search technique is the definition of the policy space. This definition includes the parametrization of the policy. Once the space is defined, this space is searched for determining an optimal policy. For example, Genetic Algorithms (GAs) are applied for determining such an optimal parameter vector.

Value function based approaches focus on the computation of the optimal utility of states (e.g. function V^*) to find the optimal policy. The optimal action in a state is the one leading to the state with the highest V^*-value. Various approaches have been suggested for computing the state or (state, action) values such as value iteration, Q-learning, or temporal difference learning. For details about these different techniques see e. g. [79].

In the following the idea of Q-learning is sketched. The optimal policy π^* selects the action that maximizes the sum of the immediate reward and the value of the immediate successor state, i.e. expressed by the equation

$$\pi^*(s) = \operatorname*{argmax}_{a} \left[r(s,a) + \gamma V^{\pi^*}(\delta(s,a)) \right] \qquad [2.5]$$

Based on this formula, the optimal policy π^* can be obtained by learning V^{π^*}, provided perfect knowledge of r and δ. But as these functions are unknown to the agent, π^* cannot be obtained even if V^{π^*} has been learned. Therefore a Q-function for policy π is introduced:

$$Q^{\pi}(s,a) = r(s,a) + \gamma V^{\pi}(\delta(s,a)) \qquad [2.6]$$

Let Q^* be the Q-function for the optimal policy. Then, the definition of π^* can be rewritten as:

$$\pi^*(s) = \operatorname*{argmax}_{a} Q^*(s,a) \qquad [2.7]$$

By learning Q^* instead of V^{π^*} the agent is still able to act optimally. An algorithm that learns an approximation to the Q-function in form of a lookup table is provided in [191].

After explaining RL and one of its solution techniques Q-learning, RRL is introduced next.

Relational Reinforcement Learning

RRL is a learning technique that combines reinforcement learning with relational learning. The need for relational representations is discussed in [82] by evaluating the RL Q-learning approach. The following limitations of RL Q-learning were identified:

- A lookup-table based approach is impractical for all but the smallest state-spaces.

- The method is unable to capture the structural aspects.

- The learned Q-function is dependent on the goal. Thus, if the goal is changed, the Q-function must be learned again.

- It is not clear how knowledge in form of a lookup table can be transfered from a small to a larger problem domain.

Accordingly to [82], the first problem can be solved by using an inductive learning algorithm (such as neural networks), whereas the three other problems can only be solved by using a relational learning algorithm that can abstract from the specific objects and goals using variables.

In RRL the state, actions, and the policy are described by using objects and relations. In many domains this kind of encoding is much more natural and has a higher expressiveness. Also the knowledge transfer may be easier using a relational representation. Knowledge transfer means to exploit the results of previous learning phases (experience) when solving more complex problems. This kind of knowledge transfer is also referred to as generalization.

The standard RRL model consists of the following input parameters:

1. A set of environment states S, represented in a relational format,

2. A set of actions A, represented in a relational format,

3. A set of scalar rewards R in $\mathbb{R}$,

4. An unknown transition function $\delta : S \times A \rightarrow S$. For a given state s_t, the transition function determines the next state s_{t+1} following action a_t (this function may be nondeterministic),

5. An unknown reward function $R(s_t, a_t) : S \times A \rightarrow R$,

6. Background knowledge about the environment.

The objective is to find a policy for selecting actions $\pi^* : S \times A$ that maximizes a value function $V^{\pi}(s_t)$ for all $s_t \in S$.

An environment state is represented as a set of basic facts that hold in the state. Background knowledge specifies knowledge that is generally valid across the whole domain, i.e. for all training examples. By providing background knowledge, the relational state description can be extended in the form of logical clauses. Based on these clauses, more complex knowledge can be derived about the (state, action) pairs.

An EPM is composed of information nodes and production rules. Thus, in the domain of EPMs, objects such as information-node and production-rule can be used. Relations are denoted by `name / n` where `name` corresponds to the name of the relation and `n` to its arity. Examples of relations are:

executable / 1: This relation describes a state and signifies that a specific production rule is executable, e. g. `executable(prodRule1)` means that the production rule with ID 1 is executable.

creates_info_node / 2: It signifies that a production rule creates an information node, e. g. `creates_info_node(prodRule2, infoNode3)` means that production rule with ID 2 has the information node with ID 3 as destination node.

execute / 1: This relation describes a specific action the agent can perform, e. g. if the action `execute(prodRule0)` is performed, the production rule with ID 0 is executed.

In the EPM domain, a variety of background knowledge can be defined, such as processing durations of production rules or detailed knowledge about the structure of an EPM.

As in RL, a variety of different approaches has been suggested for solving RRL problems based on policy search or value-function based techniques. For a survey or overview see e. g.: [270, 299, 300].

In relational domains policies have been used successfully as they can be defined in a compact way due to logical abstraction. Therefore, the iEPM approach is also based on a policy based solution technique.

One of the standard policy search techniques is the policy gradient search. Accordingly to [200] logical abstractions do not possess necessarily natural gradients. Therefore they applied a GA for searching the policy space. This critical remark was the reason for using heuristics in the iEPM approach instead of gradient search techniques.

In the next section the GA heuristic is introduced.

2.6.2. Genetic Algorithm and Evolution Strategy

A series of papers published by John Holland in 1962 on adaptive systems theory laid the conceptual foundation for the Genetic Algorithm's development [124]. Thereby, he became known as the father of Genetic Algorithms. J.D. Bagley finally coined the term Genetic Algorithm in his doctoral dissertation which was the first published application of genetic algorithms [15].

A GA is a search heuristic that belongs to the class of Evolutionary Algorithms (also known as Evolutionary Computation). These algorithms are derived from the process of evolution in biology[24]. The theory of natural evolution was developed by Charles Darwin. In his publication "On the Origin of Species" [69] he describes how biological organisms evolve over generations based on the principle of natural selection "survival of the fittest" in order to reach certain abilities [260]. Fig. 2.12 depicts the main steps of GA. Starting point is a set of individuals called population. Each individual represents a solution to the search problem. In analogy to the biological DNA alphabet[25], a GA operates on strings, usually bit strings of constant length. The string corresponds to the genotype of the individual. The phenotype of the individual is realized by a mapping onto the object parameters (genotype-phenotype mapping). Object parameters - also termed search space parameter - are genotype or phenotype variables which directly influence the fitness.

Each individual is evaluated by a fitness function based on the object parameters. Genetic operators are applied to evolve the population over time. For this evolution, individuals are selected from the population as parents for creating new individuals using operators such as crossover and mutation. Individuals are selected for the next generation based on their fitness

---

[24][268] provides a good insight into the theory of biological evolution.
[25]An introduction to genetics can be found in [258].

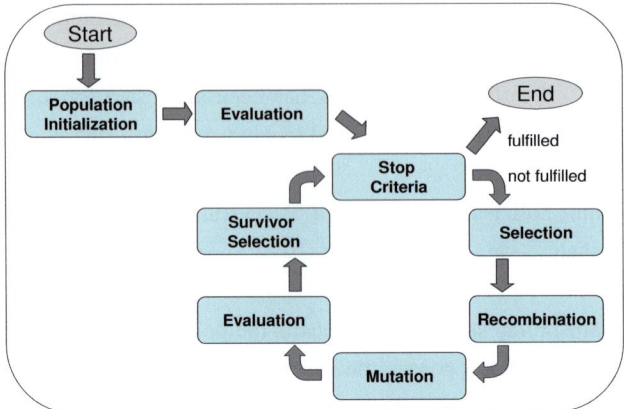

Figure 2.12.: Illustration of the Genetic Algorithm.

value. There exists a multitude of different genetic operators. For a detailed introduction see e. g. [324, 188]. Algorithm 1 is an example of a basic GA in pseudocode.

Algorithm 1 Genetic Algorithm.

1: **Initialization:**
   a) Generate initial population using an initialization method
   b) Evaluate initial population
2: **Repeat until termination:**
   a) **Selection:** Select individuals to reproduce using a selection mechanism
   b) **Reproduction:** Generate offspring from parents using genetic operators
   c) **Evaluation:** Evaluate the fitnesses of the offspring
   d) **Population Update:** Replace worst ranked part of population with offspring

---

Timetabling [41, 247, 25] and scheduling [334, 153, 273] problems appear to be particularly appropriate for applying GAs. Nevertheless, there are many other application fields, such as graphic layout [188], vehicle routing [16], investment strategy [52, 56], location decision [37], and data mining [97, 98], among others.

Accordingly to [188], a GA comprises the following five components:

- A genetic representation (encoding) for solutions to the problem,

- a method for creating the initial population,

- an evaluation function that rates the solutions in terms of their fitness,

- genetic operators for the breeding,

- values for the parameters such as population size and probabilities for applying genetic operators.

The different components are discussed in more detail in the following subsections.

Encoding

The encoding can be described as "a process of representing individual genes" [260]. This process links the original problem context with the problem-solving space in which the evolution takes place. Solutions of the original problem context are referred to as phenotypes, while their encoding is termed genotypes. The representation or encoding can be considered as a mapping from the phenotypes onto a set of genotypes. In the original problem context, a solution is called candidate solution, phenotype or individual, whereas in the GA context, terms like genotype, chromosome or individual are used instead. The elements of an individual are termed locus, position or gene. In other words, these genes form the chromosome of an individual. An object on such a gene is termed either value or allele.

The encoding can be based on bits, numbers, trees, among others. Which kind of encoding is used is problem specific. The mapping from genotypes to phenotypes is termed decoding.

Initial Population Method

The most common and easiest method for the creation of the initial population is the random generation of individuals. In case of a binary representation, each bit of the individual is initialized to a random zero or one. Further initialization methods have been proposed, such as using opposition-based learning [227], induced initialization method [145], uniform and unbiased initialization [58].

Evaluation Function

The fitness of an individual is "the value of an evaluation function[26] for its phenotype" [260]. Thus, the individual must be decoded and the fitness function has to be evaluated. The fitness indicates how good a solution is as well as the distance to the optimal solution. The evalution function can either be a single- or multi-objective function.

Genetic Operators

The breeding comprises the selection of parents, the creation of new individuals and replacement of old individuals with the newly created ones.

The genetic operator selection is responsible for choosing two parents from the population. An individual is termed parent if it has been selected in order to create new offspring. Accordingly to Darwin's theory of natural evolution, only the best individuals survive and create new offspring. The selection pressure is defined as "the degree to which better individuals are favored" [260]. This means that the higher the selection pressure, the more the better individuals

---

[26]The evaluation function is also termed fitness function or in case of an optimization problem objective function.

are selected for reproduction. The selection pressure is the driver of the GA for the improvement of the population over time. Furthermore, the convergence rate of GA is dependent on the selection pressure as a higher selection pressure results in a higher convergence rate [260]. Nevertheless, the selection must be balanced. A strong selection may lead to a reduced diversity[27] of the population whereas a weak selection may lead to a slow evolution and convergence. Diversity preservation is an important issue in GA as it helps to avoid premature convergence [260]. Investigations for diversity preservation based on the population size and niche radius have been made [60]. Such niching methods extend GA for the location and maintenance of multiple solutions.

A traditional selection operator is Roulette Wheel Selection. Here, an individual is selected from the population with a probability proportional to its fitness value. Each slot in the wheel corresponds to a specific individual. The size of the slot is proportional to the individual's fitness values. The Roulette Wheel Selection has the disadvantage that chromosomes with small fitness values have only very few chances to be selected if one chromosome has a very high fitness value.

Unlike the Roulette Wheel Selection, the Tournament Selection provides selective pressure by holding a tournament competition among a specific number of individuals k. In the first step, k individuals are selected at random from the population. The winner of the tournament is the individual with the best fitness value among the k individuals. The number of individuals k is termed tournament size. If the tournament size is large, weaker individuals have a smaller chance to be selected as they have to compete with more individuals. The Tournament Selection is more efficient than the Roulette Wheel Selection [260].

Once the parents have been selected, the offspring (also termed child) has to be created. This process is termed recombination or crossover. A variety of different crossover operators have been introduced (for a detailed overview see [260]). One of the traditional operators is Single Point Crossover. Here, a crossover point is randomly selected along the length of the encoding schema. At this point, both parents are cut and the sections after the point are exchanged. If the parents are cut at two or more points, the operator is termed Two Point or Multi-Point Crossover, respectively. In case of the Two Point Crossover, two crossover points are chosen at random and the contents between these two points are exchanged between the mated parents. The advantage of using more crossover points is that the search space may searched more thoroughly. The disadvantage is that the use of more points reduces the performance of the GA and the building blocks are more likely to be disrupted [260].

After the application of the crossover operator, the offspring is subject to mutation. As with the crossover, a variety of different mutation operators has been suggested. Mutation has the objective to explore the search space and to maintain the diversity of the population. Thus,

---

[27]A variety of diversity measures in GA have been proposed, see e. g. [42].

mutation helps to escape local minima and ensures ergodicity. A search space is ergodic "if there is a non-zero probability of generating any solution from any population state" [260]. How often parts of a chromosome are mutated depends on the mutation probability. If mutation appears too often, the operator changes in fact to a random search. A simple mutation operator is Interchanging. In case of a binary representation, the Interchanging Mutation chooses two random positions and interchanges the bits corresponding to the two positions. The Gaussian Mutation adds a random value from a Gaussian distribution to each gene of an individual to create the new offspring. The decision whether to add a value to a gene depends on the mutation probability.

The last step of the breeding cycle is the replacement also termed survivor selection or environmental selection. This process determines which of the current individuals of the population are replaced by the new created offspring. Two kinds of methods can be distinguished in accordance to [260]: generation updates and steady state updates. The basic generational update replaces the whole population of size N with N newly created individuals. Other examples of generational updates are (λ, μ)- and $(\lambda + \mu)$-update, where λ is the number of children and μ is the population size with $\lambda \leq \mu$. Firstly, λ individuals are created forming the offspring population. Secondly, the replacement takes place. In case of (λ, μ)-update, the best μ individuals from the offspring population form the next population. In case of $(\lambda + \mu)$-update, the best μ individuals from the population as well as from the offspring population form the next population. In the steady state update, the replacement takes place immediately after the creation of the individuals. The replacement requires the removal of an individual of the current population. This can be done for example by removing the worst or oldest individual. Also, Tournament Replacement can be applied for this replacement. Tournament Replacement is analogously to the Tournament Selection, except that less good individuals are selected more often than the better ones. In order to prevent the loss of the currently fittest individual, elitism may be used. This means that the fittest individual is always kept in the population if there is no better offspring.

Many refinements have been made on the different areas of breeding. In the following, a brief overview on the variety of approaches is given:

- Selection: Different selection operators have been investigated, e. g. a selection mechanism was proposed that incorporates user feedback [44, 272].

- Crossover: Various crossover operators have been introduced based on different approaches like fuzzy logic [10], virtual parents [214], and statistical methods [335].

- Mutation: The performance and quality of different mutation operators have been evaluated in [256, 166].

Parameter Settings

The performance of Evolutionary Algorithms depends largely on their parameters, such as population size, selection pressure, crossover and mutation rates [283]. The optimization of these control parameters is a time-consuming task. Different approaches making use of self-adaptation of control parameters have been suggested [110, 122, 94]. A good overview about the different approaches for the automation of parameter selection and control is given in [173].

The termination of the search is determined by one or more given stop criteria (also termed convergence criteria). Accordingly to [84], two types of termination conditions can be distinguished. If the optimal fitness value is known, then reaching this value or only with a given precision can be used as stop criteria. However, due to stochastic nature of the GA, the optima may never be reached. Therefore, other or additional stop criteria should be defined which form second type of termination conditions. In [260], a variety of such stop criteria are listed, among them:

- Maximum Generations: The GA stops after a specific number of generations evolved.

- Elapsed Time: The GA stops when a specific time has elapsed.

- No change in fitness: The GA stops if there is no improvement of the best fitness for a specific number of generations.

After explaining the the different parts of GA, the question is raised why GAs work. This can be explained by Holland's schema theorem and the building block hypothesis. The schema theorem is based on a binary string representation. "A schema is defined as templates for describing a subset of chromosomes with similar sections" [260]. A schema comprises the bits 0 and 1, and meta-character. The template describes patterns in similarities of different chromosomes. The building block hypothesis is stated as follows: "a genetic algorithm achieves high performance through the juxtaposition of short, low order, highly fit schemata, or building blocks". The knowledge of building blocks is important as the crossover operator must not be too disruptive of building blocks, but has to combine building blocks to create better solutions. A detailed discussion about how and why GAs work can be found in [188].

Another class of Evolutionary Algorithm is Evolution Strategy. It was created in the 1960s and 70s by Ingo Rechenberg and his colleagues [231]. In contrary to GAs, Evolution Strategy generally operates on the "natural" problem representation. This means that no genotype-phenotype mapping for object parameters is required. A further population based heuristic is PSO, which is explained in the next section.

2.6.3. Particle Swarm Optimization

As the GA, PSO is a population based heuristic. It belongs to the class of swarm intelligence methods. The term swarm intelligence was introduced by Gerardo Beni and Jing Wang in 1989 [26]. It is based on the collective behavior that emerges from groups of social insects, like ants and birds[28]. Typically local interactions of the individual agents are based on simple rules that lead to the emergence of global behavior. Ant Colony Optimization is another important technique inspired by swarm intelligence (see e.g. [31]).

PSO was originally introduced by Kennedy and Eberhart [149, 150]. PSO is motivated by the simulation of social behaviour in herds and schools of animals. A PSO contains a population of particles which explores the search space by moving with particular velocities towards the optimum. The velocity of each particle is influenced by a social impact coming from the population and the individual experience of the particle. PSO can be used to solve optimization problems. A solution x is a vector of n parameters which are bounded by a set of boundary conditions such as $i = 0, \cdots, n : x_i(L) \leq x_i \leq x_i(H)$. These bounds define the feasible search (parameter) space S.

In PSO, a set of N particles is considered as the population P_t at the generation t. Each particle i has a position x^i and a velocity v^i in the parameter space S. In generation $t + 1$, the velocity and the position of each particle i are updated as follows:

$$x^i_{t+1} = x^i_t + v^i_{t+1} \qquad [2.8]$$

$$v^i_{t+1} = wv^i_t + c_1 R_1 (P_{Best} - x^i_t) + c_2 R_2 (P - x^i_t) \qquad [2.9]$$

where w is called the inertia weight, c_1 and c_2 are two positive constants, and R_1 and R_2 are two random values selected in $[0, 1]$. In Equation 2.9, P is the position of the particle in the neighbourhood of particle i with the best function value. Some possible neighbourhood structures are discussed below. P_{Best} is the personal best position that particle i has visited so far which is like a memory for the particle i and is updated in each generation. The inertia weight w is employed to control the impact of the previous velocities on the current velocity.

There is a large range of possible neighbourhood structures. They do not necessarily refer to closeness in parameter space, but are defined by a graph having particles as nodes. Edges between nodes reflect social relationships. In [150], the following topologies are shown to be the most promising ones:

- Individual best (pbest): In this topology, particles are isolated, which means that there exists no connection between them. Each particle compares its current position only to its own best position found so far.

---

[28]More details about the biological foundations of swarm intelligence are provided in [23].

- Global best (gbest): This topology is defined by a fully connected graph, i.e. all members of the particle swarm are direct neighbours.

- Local best (lbest): Here, the topology is defined by a connected graph, but unlike the gbest topology the nodes are connected to only some defined neighbour nodes. With two neighbours, this topology is equivalent to a ring.

- Wheels: In this topology, one individual is connected to all others and they are connected to only that one. Individuals are isolated from one another, as all information has to be communicated through the focal individual.

The different topologies are depicted in Fig. 2.13.

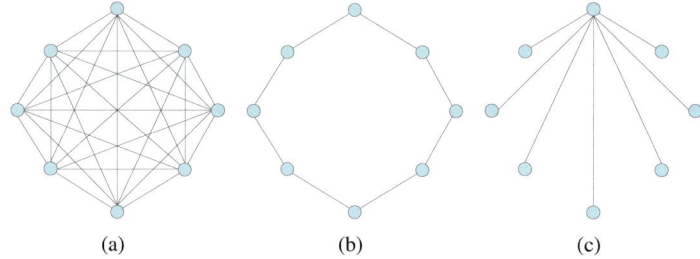

(a)   (b)   (c)

Figure 2.13.: Different neighbourhood topologies are depicted. (a), (b), and (c) illustrate the star topology known as global best, the ring topology known as local best, and the wheel topology, respectively.

The gbest populations tend to converge more rapidly than lbest populations, but are also more susceptible to suffer premature convergence, i.e. to converge to local optima [150]. It has to be denoted that the topology terms are used differently for network topologies. The depicted star topology corresponds to the fully connected network topology, whereas the wheel topology corresponds to the star network topology.

Initialization Methods

Different approaches for the generation of the initial population in PSO were suggested. The initialization comprises the position as well as the velocity of each particle of the swarm. Among the different approaches are:

- Uniform distribution method: This method is also termed "symmetric about the origin initialization method". This method uniformly distributes the initial population about the entire search space [12].

- Random initialization method: The initial population is randomly distributed about the entire search space.

- Asymmetric initialization method: Here, the initialization is limited to just a portion of the search space [12]. The use of non-uniform methods was motivated by Fogel and Beyer [93].

Diversity Preservation Methods

In PSO, diversity preservation methods are employed to avoid the convergence to a local optimum. There are several approaches to prevent the premature stagnation of the basic PSO most of which introduce randomness into the swarm:

- Quality-based: When particles do not improve their qualities over time, their positions are reinitialized [332, 307].

- Random method: After a fixed interval a particle is randomly reinitialized. This has been known as craziness [149] or turbulence factor [91, 197], where, after each iteration, some particles are randomly reinitialized.

- Self-organized criticality: In this method [175], a parameter called criticality is defined for each particle. If two particles get closer than a threshold to each other, their criticality values are increased. If the criticality value of a particle is larger than a certain value, that particle is a good candidate for reinitialization. The reinitialization means to locate the particle at a randomly selected position in the parameter space.

All of the above methods increase the diversity of the swarm. However, the randomness in the reinitialization leads to the following issues:

- It might happen that the particles revisit some parts of the search space by the reinitialization.

- Such randomness is meant to explore the unexplored regions in the parameter space. The above methods do not consider this aspect. In fact, it is desired to make sure that the swarm visits most of the search space and that there is no gap which has not been explored.

The proposed Gap Search (GS) method introduced in Chapter 8 considers these two issues by searching for the largest gaps instead of a purely randomized reinitialization.

Feasibility Preservation Methods

The boundary handling method or the so called feasibility preservation mechanism is an important issue in PSO [8, 195, 87, 220]. During the iterations, it can happen that particles leave the feasible region of the search space. These particles must be identified and sent back to the feasible space (usually the feasible space is defined by constraints; here the area surrounded by the boundaries of the search space is considered). Typically, if a particle leaves the feasible region, it is relocated either onto the boundary or on a random position. The velocity of the particle is either kept, set to zero or selected randomly. Setting on the boundaries has only an advantage if the global optimum is located on some boundary.

The PSO Algorithm

Algorithm 2 illustrates a PSO algorithm.

Algorithm 2 PSO Algorithm.

Input: S, N, T_{max}

Output: p^g

   1: **Initialization:** Initialize a set of N particles in S as the population P_t
      a) Set $t = 0$
      b) Set $p_t^i = x_t^i$
   2: **Evaluation:** Evaluate the population
      a) Find the global best particle: p_t^g
      b) Update the personal best particles
   3: **Update the population:** $P_{t+1} = Update(P_t, p_t^g)$
   4: **Termination:** Unless $t = T_{max}$
      a) t = t+1
      b) goto Step 2

The inputs to this algorithm are the feasible region S (the boundaries of the search space), N number of particles, and a maximum number of iterations T_{max}. The algorithm starts with the initialization of the particles at the generation $t = 0$. At the beginning the personal best memory of a particle is set to the position of the particle. In step 2 particles are evaluated. The global best and personal best particles are found. The function $Update(P_t, p_t^g)$ is used to update the population based on the global best particle. In this step, after updating the particles, it is examined if the particle is still in the feasible space. If not, a feasibility preserving method has to be applied to the infeasible particle (see Section 2.6.3). Also, the diversity of the particles in the population is preserved at this step using one of the methods as described in Section 2.6.3. The output of this algorithm is the global best particle after a stopping criterion is met. A typical stopping criterion is to select a fixed amount of iterations such as T_{max}.

Several studies regarding the convergence properties of PSO have been carried out. A summary about these studies can be found in [30], e.g. one of the discussed results is a condition for convergence of PSO: $w < 1$ and $w > 0.5(c_1 + c_2) - 1$.

A representative selection of PSO applications is provided in [30]. Among these applications are e.g. flowshop scheduling, bioinformatics, task assignment as well as multi-objective optimization. In the next section, multi-objective PSO is introduced.

Multi-Objective Particle Swarm Optimization

In order to solve multi-objective problems with PSO, the algorithm of a simple PSO has to be modified [8, 236]:

(a) After each generation, the set of non-dominated solutions has to be identified. Non-dominated solutions are the particles with at least one objective better than the others. These non-dominated solutions are usually stored in an external population called archive.

(b) For every particle, a global (local) best particle is selected from the archive. The way the global best particles are selected influences the quality of the solutions [236, 8]. The simplest strategy is to select them randomly from the archive, which have been proved to be successful in high dimensional objective spaces [196]. A variety of other strategies have been proposed such as Epsilon dominance, Pareto-dominance concept and the Sigma method [196].

(c) The personal best particle must be updated [36]. The simplest strategy is to replace it with the new position obtained by the particle, unless it dominates the new position.

The PSO algorithm for solving multi-objective problems is termed Multi-Objective Particle Swarm Optimization (MOPSO).

2.7. Summary

This chapter has investigated the fundamental concepts that are relevant for the iEPM approach such as BPM as well as the specifics of the service industry and business process flexibility. Additionally, the definitions of optimization problems, agents and several machine learning techniques have been discussed. The chapter provided a deeper insight in the motivation and need for flexible BPM solutions. In the next section, the EPM is introduced, which provides the fundamental concept of the iEPM approach for the flexibility enhancement in the service industry.

3. Executable Product Model

"There are many ways of going forward, but only one way of standing still."

Franklin D. Roosevelt

In this chapter, an alternative approach is presented to model service industry's business processes. Instead of using a pre-designed process model that is executed during runtime by a workflow or Business Process Management (BPM) engine, a special model called Executable Product Model (EPM) is used. It is based on the Product Data Model (PDM) introduced by van der Aalst, Reijers and Limam in [288]. This model is explained in Section 3.1. A product model[1] provides a compact representation of the set of possible execution paths of a business process by defining information dependencies instead of the order of activities. Due to the way of modeling, product models may provide more execution options, especially for complex business processes. In the original work, the PDM is used in a business process design methodology called product driven or product based workflow design. The execution options are utilized to derive business processes based on specific objectives during design time. The EPM approach differs in the way that the product model is "executed" directly which results in a higher flexibility during the execution. As the EPM approach differs from the original approach by its focus and objective, several changes and enhancements on the original model had to be performed which are described in Section 3.2. Also, an execution algorithm is required that determines the production rules to be executed. This algorithm is explained in detail in Section 3.3. In Section 3.4, a design methodology is introduced which describes the necessary steps to design an EPM. In the next sections, some specifics of the EPMs are explained, particularly how EPMs can provide more flexibility than regular process models. This chapter also contains the related work regarding BPM, process flexibility and product-driven approaches. The chapter ends with a brief summary.

---

[1]The term product model referrers to both, PDM and EPM.

3.1. Original Product Data Model

The original PDM is an adaptation of a Bill of Material (BOM) which can be found in manufacturing of physical products. A BOM has a tree structure with the final end product as its root and raw materials and purchased products as leafs. The nodes correspond to products (end-products, raw materials, subassemblies). The edges represent an *is-part-of* relation and have a cardinality to indicate the number of products needed. Think of a car composed of an engine and a subassembly. The subassembly is composed of four wheels and one chassis (see Fig. 3.1 left side).

The PDM is an equivalent for the information-intensive service industry. Fig. 3.1 illustrates the relationship between BOM and PDM. In a PDM, information nodes correspond to the material in a BOM. The dependencies between the information nodes reflect the production order and are modeled as arcs in the graph. There is exactly one root information node representing the final result of the process (e. g. the rejection or approval of an insurance claim or a credit application).

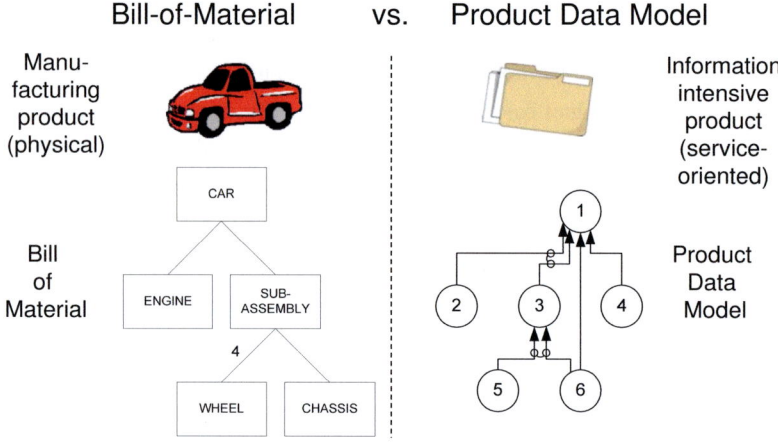

Figure 3.1.: Illustration of the relationship between Bill of Material and Product Data Model (adapted from [301]).

There are three main differences between a BOM and a PDM: (1) As making copies of (especially electronic) small pieces of information is trivial and takes hardly any time or resources, cardinalities on edges make no sense. (2) In contrary to a BOM, the PDM can use the same piece of information multiple times to create various kinds of new information. (3) Typically, there exist multiple ways to create a piece of information (variants). Using information nodes multiple times may lead to non-tree structures. As no cycles are allowed, the PDM is an acyclic graph.

In a PDM, AND and OR dependencies exist (see Fig. 3.2). In an AND dependency, all child

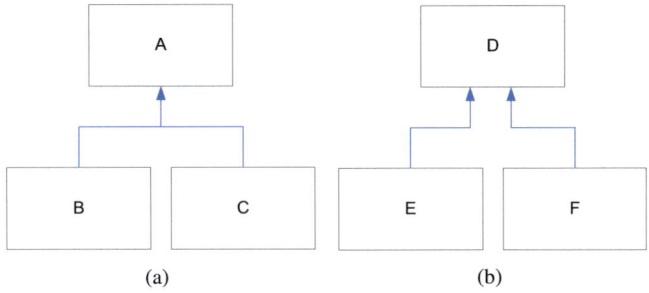

Figure 3.2.: (a) AND and (b) OR dependencies.

information nodes of the AND dependency *(B and C here)* must exist[2] in order to produce the parent information node *(A here)*. In contrary to the AND dependency, the OR dependency requires only one of the child information nodes. So it models a variant with different ways to compute the value of an information node. In Fig. 3.2(b), either E or F must exist to produce D.

An example of a PDM is depicted in Fig. 3.3. You can see an AND dependency e. g. from quality of reflexes and quality of eye-sight to physical fitness as well as an OR dependency from psychological fitness/physical fitness (nested AND dependency), quality of eye-sight or latest suitability result to suitability as helicopter pilot. The information about quality of eye-sight can be used twice. There are three variants to produce the final decision. If, for example, the quality of eye-sight is too bad, the final decision can immediately be made, leading to the result that the examinee is not suitable.

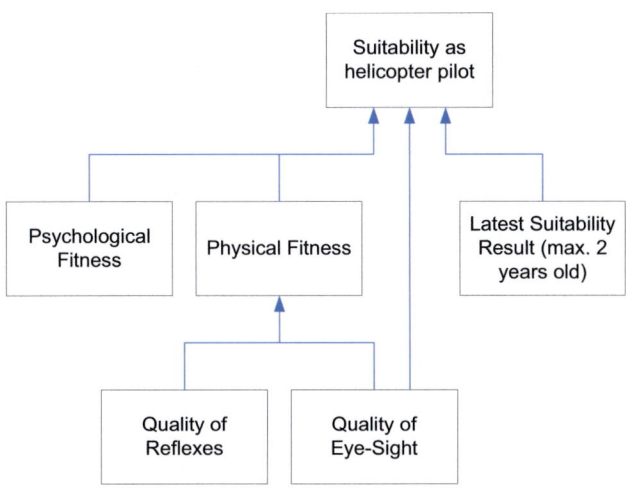

Figure 3.3.: Product data model example [288].

---

[2]To be more precisely, the values of the origin information nodes must have been generated.

3.2. Modifications to obtain the EPM

Van der Aalst *et al.* transform the PDM into a (Petri net) process model processable by a traditional workflow engine [288]. As the EPM approach is supposed to replace the process model, some extensions and changes were necessary to obtain an EPM. The modified elements are presented in this section.

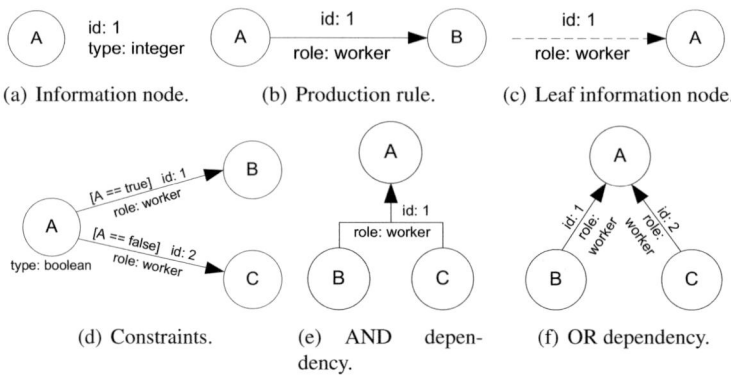

(a) Information node. (b) Production rule. (c) Leaf information node.

(d) Constraints. (e) AND dependency. (f) OR dependency.

Figure 3.4.: Visualizations of parts of an EPM.

Note that the formal definitions of the different elements of an EPM are provided in Chapter 4 in the context of the NP-completeness prove as well as in Appenidx E as part of the mathematical model for the execution semantics.

3.2.1. Information Nodes

Information nodes[3] are supposed to contain abstract information like documents, decisions, etc. For simplification purposes, the implemented prototype supports only certain data types. The type of an information node can be either a basic data type (integer, double, boolean, date, string) or a set (array) of elements with one of those data types. Additional to its type, an information node has a (descriptive) name and a unique ID of type integer.

The visualization of an information node is depicted in Fig. 3.4(a). Information nodes are visualized as circles instead of rectangles like the production parts in a BOM.

Root and leaf nodes are two special kinds of information nodes. (1) Each executable product model has exactly one root node that represents the final result of the corresponding process. This information node has no outgoing arcs. If a business process has multiple outcomes, a dummy node can be included in the EPM. (2) Leaf nodes do not depend on any other information node. So, they are the starting point of the execution. The values of leaf nodes are retrieved "externally", e.g. from a customer.

---

[3]Information nodes are also termed information elements.

3.2.2. Production Rules

Analog to the PDM, dependencies between information nodes are modeled as directed arcs. These arcs represent *production rules* that describe which task has to be performed to "create" a new value stored in the information node the corresponding arc is pointing at. Fig. 3.4(b) shows an example. Each production rule has a unique ID of type integer. The information node(s) that the production rule depends on is/are called *origin node(s)* or *input information element(s)*, the created node is the *destination node* or *output information element* of the production rule.

Each information node is the destination node of at least one production rule (or several in the case of variants). As leaf nodes do not depend on any other node, they have special production rules that can be executed at any time—visualized as dashed arcs (see Fig. 3.4(c)).

Fig. 3.4(e) shows an example for a production rule with an AND dependency. Here, both origin nodes B and C must have been created before the production rule becomes executable. A production rule with an OR dependency is depicted in Fig. 3.4(f). Here, A can be created using production rule 1 *or* 2. Both production rules depend on only one origin node (B and C respectively) and can be executed independently from each other. Thus, there are two different options for creating A.

As all tasks have to be processed by resources (machines or humans), a *role*[4] describing what skills a resource must have in order to execute this production rule is assigned to each production rule. Thus, the simplification was made that the execution of a production rule requires exactly one resource with a specific role.

Additionally, a *constraint* can be attached to a production rule. Constraints consist of variables (containing the generated value of information nodes) and logical operators that can be evaluated to true or false. They determine if a production rule can be executed. In general, constraints can be used to determine which path to follow at branches. All information nodes that appear in a constraint, have to be origin nodes of the production rule to which the constraint is attached. See Fig. 3.4(d) for an example.

3.2.3. Cycles

In the original work by van der Aalst *et al.*, cycles are not allowed[5]. But in real world processes, cycles often exist (e. g. in loops where tasks are repeated until a special goal is achieved). Therefore, cycles are allowed in the EPM. There are three restrictions that are necessary for the

---

[4]Accordingly to [285], a role is a special kind of resource class. "To facilitate the allocation of work items [tasks] to resources, resources are grouped into classes. A resource class is a group of resources with similar characteristics. There may be many resources in the same class and a resource may be a member of multiple resource classes. If a resource class is based on the capabilities (i.e. functional requirements) of its members, it is called a role. If the classification is based on the structure of the organization, such a resource class is called an organizational unit (e.g. team, branch or department)." [285].

[5]Cycles are not required in the original work as process models are derived from the PDM. The derived process models can contain cycles.

algorithms described in section 3.3 to work: (1) Leaf nodes are not part of a cycle. That would cause a deadlock. By including a dummy information node, this restriction can be bypassed. (2) An information node belongs to at most one cycle. (3) At places where a production rule leaves a cycle and another continues within the cycle, mutually exclusive constraints have to prevent that both paths are executed in parallel. Otherwise, further processing of the cycle could return to that place and overwrite the node with another value. But the leaving production rule is already executed with the old value. The parallel execution of one and the same production rule would cause inconsistencies. In the next section variants are introduced which will be used for the execution of EPMs.

3.2.4. Variants

In this section, the term variant is introduced. A variant is a minimal set of unordered production rules whose execution leads to the creation of the root node[6].

A variant is defined as a minimal set of production rules, as the execution of all production rules of this variant is necessary in order to create the root node. Based on the definition of variants, an EPM can be considered as a set of variants which describes the different possibilities to execute the product model. The variants are determined in a backwards directed approach starting at the root node and considering the OR and AND dependencies. At most one iteration through each cycle is considered when determining the variants. Therefore variants may contain production rules twice. Also, a production rule may appear in more than one variant.

Prerequisite of the usage of variants is their determination. Therefore, an algorithm has been developed that determines the variants existing in an EPM. A variant can be understood as a specific path to the root node. Therefore, one possibility to determine the set of variants is a backwards directed approach starting from the root node. Each of the incoming production rules of the root node belongs to a separate variant. In the next step, the origin nodes of these incoming production rules are evaluated again which means that their incoming production rules are added to the respective variant. This is done until the production rules creating leaf nodes are reached. Obviously, this procedure can be implemented as recursive algorithm.

The developed algorithm for the determination of variants has two stages. In the first stage, the variants without cycles are determined by using a recursive algorithm. The pseudo-code of this algorithm is listed in Algorithm 3. In the second stage, the already determined variants without cycles are checked, whether they generate an information node that belongs to a cycle. If yes, a new variant is generated that considers one iteration through the cycle. This is done by adding the production rules of the cycle to the set of production rules of the variant.

---

[6]An alternative definition of variants could be based on the set of ordered production rules as well. This would require also a possibility to define parallelism, e.g. like pr_0 | pr_1, pr_3 which would mean that production rule 0 and 1 are executed in parallel followed by production rule 3.

Algorithm 3 Determining variants without cycles.

Function DETERMINEVARIANTSNOCYCLES($currentNode$, $currentVariant$)

Input: start information node $currentNode$
current variant $currentVariant$

Output: set with variants without cycles

```
1:  variants ← ∅
2:  if currentVariant.getNumberOfVisits(currentNode) = 0 then
3:      currentVariant.incrementNumberOfVisits(currentNode)
4:      for all prodRule ∈ INCOMINGPRODRULES(node) do
5:          newVariant ← currentVariant.clone()
6:          newVariant.addProductionRule(prodRule)
7:          if prodRule.getNumberOfOriginNodes = 0 then
8:              variants ← {newVariant}
9:          else if prodRule.getNumberOfOriginNodes = 1 then
10:             originNode ← prodRule.getOriginNode()
11:             variants ← determineVariantsWithoutCycles(originNode, newVariant)
12:         else
13:             variantsAnd ← ∅
14:             for all originNode ∈ ORIGINNODES(prodRule) do
15:                 variantsAnd ← variantsAnd ∪
                                    determineVariantsWithoutCycles(originNode, newVariant)
16:                 newVariant ← currentVariant.clone()
17:                 newVariant.addProductionRule(prodRule)
18:             end for
19:             variants ← composeVariants(variantsAnd)
20:         end if
21:     end for
22: end if
23: return variants
```

Algorithm 3 makes use of a data structure for a variant that contains a set of production rules, and a counter for counting which information nodes have been visited by the algorithm. The variants are determined in a backwards directed search. Thus, starting point is the root node and a variant with an empty production rule set. First, it is checked whether the current node has already been visited. This check prevents that the algorithm traverses cycles. In the next step, the incoming production rules of the current node are processed. First, a copy of the current variant is made as each variant has to be stored in a separate object. Then, the current production rule is added to the set of production rules of the current variant. There may be multiple incoming production rules in case of an OR dependency. If an incoming production rule has no origin node, the current node corresponds to a leaf node. If there is one origin node, a recursive call is made with the origin node as current information node and the copied variant as current one. If there is more than one origin node (in case of an AND dependency), the different paths must be joined due to the AND dependency. First, for each origin node, a recursive call is made with the origin node as current information node. The determined variants are temporarily stored in set $variantsAnd$. To assure that for each variant a different object is used, a new variant is created as described above. The subsequent joining is done by helper method *composeVariants*. Finally, the set of determined variants (*variants*) is returned.

The algorithm's efficiency is analyzed by using the Big-O-notation[7]. The Big-O-Notation is used as an upper-bound on the growth of an algorithms effort to solve a problem [65]. Thus, by the way the Big-O-Notation is defined, it is a worst case measure for the algorithm's running time. As the algorithm is executed for a specific EPM, the structure of this EPM has to be considered when analyzing the algorithm's efficiency on the basis of the Big-O-notation.

In case of a strictly linear EPM (which means that the EPM contains a sequence of production rules), there is always only one incoming production rule and the number of origin nodes equals one. The command *currentVariant.clone()* creates a new object and copies the production rules that have been added to the variant so far. At the beginning there is no production rule to copy and one to add. At the last call of this command n-1 production rules must be copied and one added. Let n be the number of production rules. The number of operations equals $\sum_{i=1}^{n} i = n(n+1)/2$. This results in a quadratic runtime complexity $O(n^2)$ for linear EPMs.

The same result pertains to EPMs with a parallel structure, but no AND dependencies.

If there is an AND dependency whose origin nodes are created only by one variant, the runtime complexity is $O(n^2)$ as the method *composeVariants(variantsAnd)* has only to merge the different paths to the origin nodes to one variant. The situation is different if there is an AND dependency whose original nodes are created by multiple variants. Let us consider a AND dependency with three origin nodes whose origin nodes are created by two variants respectively. Then there will be $2*2*2 = 8$ different variants. In general let s be the number of origin nodes of the AND dependency and d_i the indegree of origin node $i, i = 1, \cdots, s$. Then the number of variants created by method *composeVariants(variantsAnd)* is $\prod_{i=1}^{s} d_i$.

The definition of a variant is explained using the EPM depicted in Fig. 3.5. This EPM contains two variants without cycles (variant 0 and 1) and two with cycles (variant 2 and 3):

- Variant 0: {0, 1, 2, 4, 5, 7}

- Variant 1: {1, 3, 4, 5, 7}

- Variant 2: {0, 1, 2, 4, 5, 5, 6, 7}

- Variant 3: {1, 3, 4, 5, 5, 6, 7}

As a variant is defined as a set of unordered production rules, different execution instances may be grouped, e.g. the production rules 0, 1, 2 of variant 0 can be executed in one of the following orders: in a sequential order 0, 1, 2 or 1, 0, 2 or by executing 0 and 1 in parallel followed by 2.

---

[7]The definition of Big-O-notation is provided in Chapter 4´as part of the complexity evaluation.

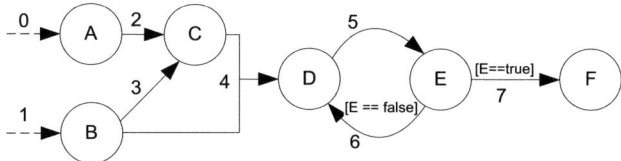

Figure 3.5.: An EPM containing two variants without cycles and initially two variants with cycles.

The following set is not a valid variant as it violates the minimal set requirement: {0, 1, 2, 3, 4, 5, 7}. Either production rule 2 or 3 could be omitted, but the root node could be created nevertheless. Another example of an invalid variant is the set {0, 2, 4, 5, 7}. As information node 1 cannot be created with these production rules, production rule 4 never gets executable and therefore the EPM cannot be executed completely.

In the next section the algorithms for the execution of an EPM are presented.

3.3. Execution of the EPM

The EPM is supposed to be executable without explicitly transforming it into a process model first. To do so, the set of executable production rules has to be determined at every processing step of the product model. The subsequent resource allocation is done by the Multi-Agent System (MAS) as described in Section 5. In the following, the execution is explained on the basis of algorithms and examples. In Appendx E, a mathematical model of the execution semantics of EPMs is provided.

3.3.1. Execution Algorithms

The developed algorithms for the execution of EPMs were published in [158]. A production rule is executable if all its origin information nodes have been created[8] and its possibly existing constraint evaluates to true. For that purpose, each production rule gets a counter storing the number of not yet created origin nodes. When this counter gets zero, the constraint of the corresponding production rule is evaluated. If it is fulfilled, the production rule becomes executable.

During execution, information nodes have one of the following states: (1) They start with `not_yet_created`. (2) After creation, they change to `created`. (3) During cycle processing, an already created node can get `invalidated` when the cycle is processed once again indicating that this node's value can be overwritten during further execution.

Each information node has a *history set* containing all information nodes used for creating its value (and including itself). Before an information node is created the first time, its history

---

[8]As production rules creating leaf nodes have no origin nodes, they are always executable.

set is empty. More details are explained during the description of the algorithms later in this subsection.

The execution of an EPM starts with an initialization (Algorithm 4): For each production rule, it computes the number of origin nodes and stores this value in the corresponding counter. Each information node is set to `not_yet_created` and gets an empty set as its history set. The function returns a set with all executable production rules (i. e. those that "create" the leaf nodes). For these production rules, appropriate resources have to be searched.

Algorithm 4 Initialization.

Function INITIALIZE()

Output: set with all executable production rules

1: *executableProdRules* ← ∅
2: **for all** production rules **do**
3:      *productionRule.counter* ← number of origin nodes
4:      **if** *productionRule.counter* = 0 **then**
5:          *executableProdRules* ← *executableProdRules* ∪ {*productionRule*}
6:      **end if**
7: **end for**
8: **for all** information nodes **do**
9:      *informationNode.state* ← `not_yet_created`
10:     *informationNode.history* ← ∅
11: **end for**
12: **return** *executableProdRules*

Again, the algorithm's efficiency is analyzed by using the Big-O-notation. Let k be the number of production rules, l be the number of information nodes and $n = max\{k,l\}$. Algorithm 4 has two loops, one iterates through the set of production rules, the other through the set of information nodes. As the loops are not nested, the running time of Algorithm 4 is linear with $O(n)$.

Each time a production rule execution has finished, Algorithm 5 is processed. Its main purpose is to decide whether the created value is stored in the destination node or not. This decision is made in line 9. If the destination node (created node) has already a value (status `created` or `invalidated`) but is not part of the origin nodes' history set, another variant (due to an OR dependency) has already created a value for that node. The node's value is not overwritten as the result of the first finished variant is used[9]. If the destination node has not yet a value, this production rule has created a value for that node for the first time (or the second, third, etc. in case of cycle). Then, the value is stored, the destination node's status is set to `created`, its history set is adjusted and the next executable production rules are determined using Algorithm 6.

---

[9]This means that the principle first-come, first-served is used.

Algorithm 5 Processing production rule result.

Function PROCESSRESULT(pr, v)

Input: finished production rule pr, created value v

Output: set with new executable production rules

```
 1: createdNode ← DESTINATIONNODE(pr)
 2: originHistory ← ∅
 3: for all originNode ∈ ORIGINNODES(pr) do
 4:     originHistory ← originHistory ∪ originNode.history
 5: end for
 6: if (createdNode.state = not_yet_created or created) and createdNode ∈ originHistory then
 7:     {ERROR}
 8: end if
 9: if (createdNode.state = created or invalidated) and createdNode ∉ originHistory then
10:     {do nothing, node already created by a variant}
11:     return ∅
12: else
13:     createdNode.value = v
14:     createdNode.state ← created
15:     createdNode.history ← originHistory ∪ {createdNode}
16:     return DETERMINENEXTEXECUTABLEPRODUCTIONRULES(createdNode)
17: end if
```

Algorithm 5 is analyzed by using the Big-O-notation. The method call DETERMINENEXT-EXECUTABLEPRODUCTIONRULES(*createdNode*) is not considered in the analysis, as the corresponding algorithm is analyzed separately (see Algorithm 6). The algorithm contains one loop that iterates through the origin nodes of the production rule that was finished. Let n be the number of information nodes of the EPM. In the worst case there are $n-1$ origin nodes. This would mean that the EPM contains one AND dependency with the root node as origin node and $n-1$ origin nodes. Therefore, the running time of Algorithm 5 is linear with $O(n)$.

Algorithm 6 decreases the counters of all outgoing production rules of the just created node by one. If a counter gets zero and its possibly existing constraint evaluates to true, the production rule is potentially executable. For all these production rules, it is checked (like in Algorithm 5) whether their destination nodes have already been created by a variant. In that case, the production rule is not executable. Otherwise, the production rule is executable and it is checked in line 21 whether the destination node has already been created and is part of the origin nodes' history sets. In that case, this production rule "closes" a cycle and will create a new value for the destination node. The status of all nodes within this cycle is set to invalidated indicating that their values can be overwritten. Also, all outgoing production rules of all cycle nodes are increased by one. Finally, the set of executable production rules is returned. Again, appropriate resources have to be determined. The execution ends after the creation of the EPM's root node.

Algorithm 6 Determining next executable production rules.

Function DETERMINENEXTEXECUTABLEPRODUCTIONRULES(*node*)

Input: start information node *node*

Output: set with new executable production rules

1: *executableProdRules* ← ∅
2: *potentiallyExecProdRules* ← ∅
3: **for all** *prodRule* ∈ OUTGOINGPRODRULES(*node*) **do**
4:     *prodRule.counter* ← *prodRule.counter* − 1
5:     **if** *prodRule.counter* = 0 **and** EVALCONST(*prodRule.constraint*) = true **then**
6:         *potentiallyExecProdRules* ← *potentiallyExecProdRules* ∪ {*prodRule*}
7:     **end if**
8: **end for**
9: **for all** *prodRule* ∈ *potentiallyExecProdRules* **do**
10:     *originHistory* ← ∅
11:     **for all** *originNode* ∈ ORIGINNODES(*prodRule*) **do**
12:         *originHistory* ← *originHistory* ∪ *originNode.history*
13:     **end for**
14:     *destNode* ← DESTINATIONNODE(*prodRule*)
15:     **if** *destNode.state* = not_yet_created **and** *destNode* ∈ *originHistory* **then**
16:         {ERROR}
17:     **end if**
18:     **if** (*destNode.state* = created **or** invalidated) **and** *destNode* ∉ *originHistory* **then**
19:         {do nothing, node already craeted by a variant}
20:     **else**
21:         **if** *destNode.state* = created **and** *destNode* ∈ *originHistory* **then**
22:             {cycle processing required}
23:             *cycleSet* ← DETERMINECYCLE(*destNode*)
24:             **for all** *cycleNode* ∈ *cycleSet* **do**
25:                 *cycleNode.state* = invalidated
26:                 **for all** *cycOutProdRule* ∈ OUTGOINGPRODRULES(*cycleNode*) **do**
27:                     *cycOutProdRule.coutner* ← *cycOutProdRule.counter* + 1
28:                 **end for**
29:             **end for**
30:         **end if**
31:         *executableProdRules* ← *executableProdRules* ∪ *prodRule*
32:     **end if**
33: **end for**
34: **return** *executableProdRules*

The efficiency of Algorithm 6 is analyzed by using the Big-O-notation. Let k be the number of production rules, l be the number of information nodes and $n = max\{k,l\}$. In case of a linear EPM, there is always at most one executable production rule with at most one origin node. Furthermore, no cycles exist. Thus, each loop of Algorithm 6 is traversed at most once which results in a constant running time for linear EPMs. For more complex structures, a simple worst case approximation is given. In that case, there exists a triple nested loop, the first iterating through the potentially executable production rules, the next inner loop through the cycle nodes, and the innermost loop through the outgoing production rules. This results in a polynomial running time of $O(n^3)$.

3.3.2. Production Rule Based Execution

An EPM execution example is given in Fig. 3.6. It contains AND and OR dependencies, a cycle (nodes D and E) and constraints for all outgoing production rules of node E (boolean type).

The execution of an EPM is explained based on the assumption that the execution of a production rule is immediately started as soon as it becomes executable. The execution starts with invoking INITIALIZE() (see Algorithm 4) (result in Fig. 3.6(b)). The production rule counters for the leaf nodes A and B are zero, so the production rules are started. First, node A is created. Consequently, the production rule from A to C becomes executable (Fig. 3.6(c)). Second, leaf node B is created. As node C has not yet been created by the already started production rule from A to C, the production rule from B to C is now started, too. The AND dependency from B and C to D is not yet executable because node C has not been created so far (Fig. 3.6(d)). Next, the production rule from A to C finishes. Now, all origin nodes of the production rule creating D are available, so the production rule gets executable (Fig. 3.6(e)). After that, the production rule from B to C finishes. As C has already been created, the resulting value is discarded. When the production rule from B and C to D finishes, also the production rule from D to E gets executable (Fig. 3.6(f)). After the creation of E (let E be `false`), the status of E is first set to `created` and the counters of the outgoing production rules are decreased to zero. As E is `false`, only the production rule from E to D is executable. But as D has already been created *and* is contained in E's history set, the algorithm's cycle processing is necessary. Now, D and E are set `invalidated` and their outgoing production rule counters are increased by one[10]. The resulting situation is depicted in Fig. 3.6(g). Subsequently, node D is created once again and the new value is stored (Fig. 3.6(h)). Then, node E is also created for the second time and its old value is overwritten (Fig. 3.6(i)). Let E be `true`, now. Consequently, the production rule from E to F is executed. After root node F is created (Fig. 3.6(j)), the execution is successfully finished.

---

[10]Nevertheless, the production rule from E to D stays executable.

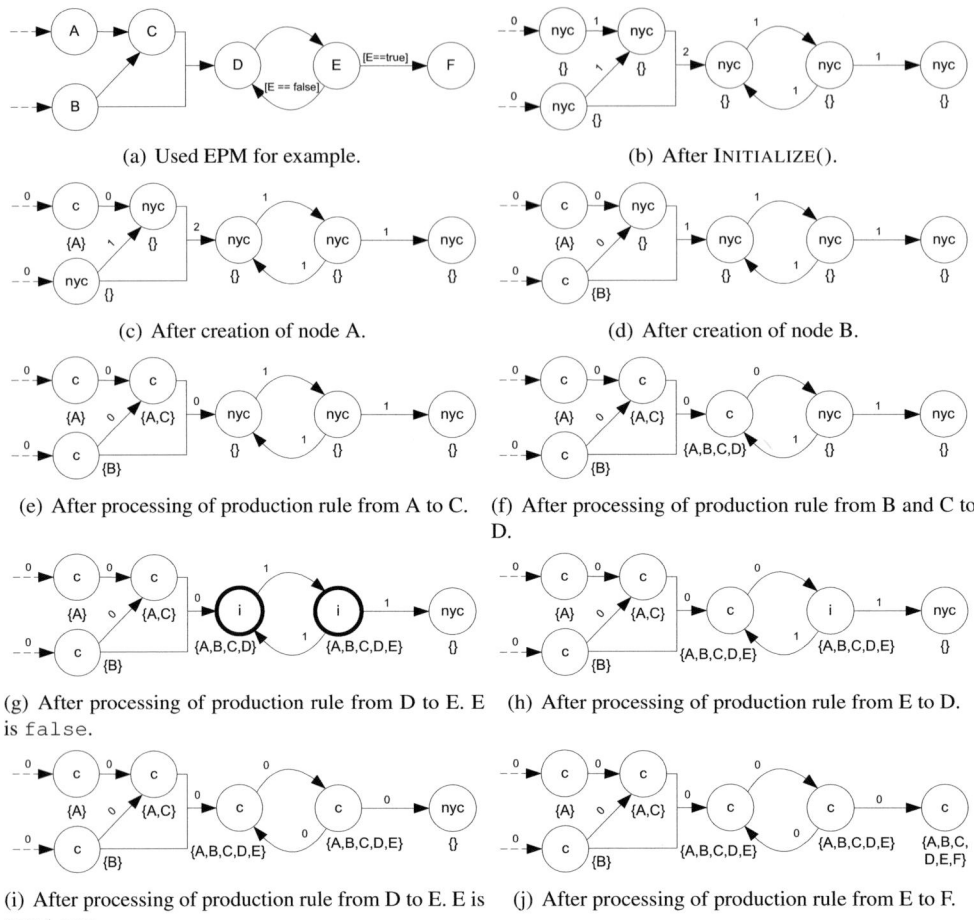

(a) Used EPM for example.

(b) After INITIALIZE().

(c) After creation of node A.

(d) After creation of node B.

(e) After processing of production rule from A to C.

(f) After processing of production rule from B and C to D.

(g) After processing of production rule from D to E. E is false.

(h) After processing of production rule from E to D.

(i) After processing of production rule from D to E. E is now true.

(j) After processing of production rule from E to F.

Figure 3.6.: Example of an EPM execution. In Fig. 3.6(b)-(j), the information nodes are labeled with their status instead of their names. "nyc" stands for not_yet_created, "c" for created and "i" for invalidated. Below each information node, you can find its history set. The arcs representing the production rules are labeled with the number of not yet created origin nodes.

3.3.3. Variant Based Execution

So far, it has been explained how executable production rules are identified and executed. Additionally, an EPM can be executed by making use of the variants it contains. In Sec. 3.2.4, variants were introduced and explained on the basis of the EPM depicted in Fig. 3.5. This EPM contains four variants at the beginning of the execution due to the cycle defined.

The determination of executable production rules follows the aforementioned procedure. Once the executable production rules are identified, the corresponding feasible and executable variants are determined. A variant is said to be feasible if it contains at least one executable production rule. Variants may get infeasible during the execution due to non-fulfilled constraints. At the beginning, all variants are feasible and production rule 0 and 1 are executable. As all four variants contain either production rule 0 or 1, all variants are executable. The explanation of the execution is based on the assumption that variant 1 {1, 3, 4, 5, 7} is activated as the only variant. By activating a variant, all executable production rules belonging to this variant are executed. Thus, by activating variant 1, production rule 1 is executed. As soon as the production rule is executed, the set of executable production rules is determined. Production rules 0 and 3 are executable. Still all four variants are executable. As variant 1 is considered only, production rule 3 is executed next, followed by production rule 4 and then production rule 5. The execution of production rule 5 or more precisely the value of the created information node, influences the further processing due to the constraint defined. If the value is true, the production rule 7 can be executed which leads to the creation of the root node. If the created value is false, variant 1 becomes infeasible and cannot be further executed. Only the variants with cycles are valid then. Lets assume that variant 3 is activated next. When production rule 5 has been executed again, the feasibility of the variants depends on the created value again. If the created value is false, the variants with only one iteration through the cycle become infeasible and two additional variants are generated considering two iterations through the cycle:

- Variant 4: {0, 1, 2, 4, 5, 5, 5, 6, 6, 7}

- Variant 5: {1, 3, 4, 5, 5, 5, 6, 6, 7}

The generation of variants takes place until the created value of production rule 5 is true. Then, the production rule 7 can be executed which creates the root node.

Different strategies exist, for deciding which variant has to be activated:

Random execution: This strategy selects pseudo randomly[11] one variant and executes it. Each variant is randomly selected with the same probability. If this variant becomes infeasible during the execution, another one is randomly activated.

Number of executions: This strategy selects the variant that was activated most frequently.

Estimated duration: The variant with the lowest estimated remaining processing duration is activated. Workload and resource failure rates may cause delays. If such information is available, it is included in the calculation of the estimated duration.

Estimated costs: The variant with the lowest estimated costs is activated.

---

[11] By using a Pseudo-Random Number Generator (PRNG).

Note that if there are multiple variants with the same highest (number of executions) or lowest value (costs), then one of them is selected pseudo randomly.

3.4. Modeling Methodology

In this section, the main steps in order to create an EPM are described. The modeling methodology comprises all tasks that are necessary for creating the EPM. In the original work, four phases were defined that are briefly summarized:

Scoping: The main tasks in this phase are the selection of the business process, the definition of performance targets and the feasibility check for applying the product model approach.

Analysis: In the analysis phase, the actual product model is created.

Design: In this phase, one or more business processes are derived from the created product model under consideration of the performance targets.

Evaluation: The evaluation comprises the verification, validation and performance estimation of the derived business processes. The best or most suitable process design is chosen in this phase.

As the EPM approach does not require the creation of a process design, the design phase as described in the original approach is obsolete. In the following sections, each phase of the EPM approach is explained in more detail.

3.4.1. Scoping Phase

In the scoping phase, the business processes to be designed or redesigned are identified. There are many criteria based on which business processes are chosen for automation. Furthermore several approaches exist for identifying business processes for automation (e.g. [22]) as well as best practices for design and re-design (e.g. [178], [152]). Once the business process is identified, the boundaries must be fixed. That means that the parts of the process must be defined that are subject to automation. It has to be defined whether the focus lies e.g. on the whole process (end-to-end view) or only on a specific part. Also the involvement of customers and suppliers must be identified. These open points must be clarified in order to fix the scope. Another important aspect in the scoping phase is the definition of performance targets and metrics often referred to as Key Performance Indicators (KPIs). These objectives are derived from the business targets (e.g. derived from balanced score card). The performance targets are required in order to evaluate the performance of the process. Also the feasibility and utility of applying the product model based approach needs to be checked. Once the scope is fixed, the analysis phase succeeds.

3.4.2. Analysis and Design Phase

In the analysis and design phase the EPM is created. A simplified business process of a credit application is used in order to explain how the model is created. The analysis phase comprises the following steps:

1. Analysis of the product specification

2. Determination of the production logic

3. Determination of the design characteristics

The first step comprises the determination of information elements and their dependencies. The identification and selection of the relevant information elements is not only crucial for the creation of the model but also for the applicability of the EPM approach. First, all information that accrues during the execution of the business process are potential candidates as information elements. But the information elements can be defined on different level of abstractions. On the lowest level of abstraction, data elements are considered like name, surname, street, etc. It would not be very efficient to execute one task for each single data element. On the other side, neither it would be very efficient if the abstraction level is chosen too high. For example if only two elements were selected like "Application Data" and "Processed Application". The approach requires that the EPM contains alternative execution paths. If there are no alternatives, there is no increased flexibility. Therefore the level of abstraction must be chosen carefully. Note that the approach for the proper size of workflow activities introduced in Sec. 2.1.6 can be adapted and applied for that purpose.

For the credit application example, information elements are selected on the level of business objects and their attributes. The class diagram containing the designed business objects is depicted in Fig. 3.7.

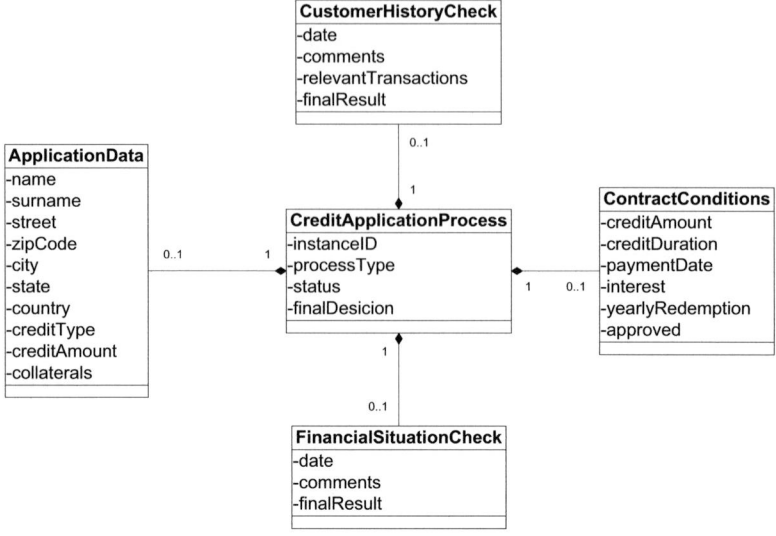

Figure 3.7.: Credit application - class diagram of the business objects

One has to keep in mind that the business object ApplicationData could be divided into further business objects like Customer, Address and CreditApplication. This means that the level of abstraction of the EPM is related to the design of the business objects as well. Business objects and their attributes can be used as information elements in the EPM. If attributes are selected as information elements, they should be referenced by the following notation: <Business Object Name>.<Attribute Name>. The explanation of these information elements is listed in Table 3.1.

Table 3.1.: Information elements of the credit application.

Information Element	Explanation
ApplicationData	Application data of the customer
FinancialSituationCheck	Result of the financial situation check of the customer
CustomerHistoryCheck	Result of the check of past financial transactions of the customer
ContractConditions	Calculated contract conditions based on the checks and on the application data
ContractConditions. ContractApproved	Indicates whether the contract for the credit was approved or not
CreditApplicationProcess. FinalDecision	Indicates whether the credit was granted or denied

For creating the EPM, these information nodes must be included in the model and the dependencies between them must be specified. The determination of the dependencies / production rules is done in a backwards directed approach. Starting point is the root information node. It must be determined what information must be available for creating the node under consideration. The required information nodes are added as origin nodes of the respective production rule(s). This is done until all information nodes and dependencies have been added to the model. The identified production rules are listed in Table 3.2.

Table 3.2.: Production rules of the credit application.

ID	Activity	Dependency
0	Take application from customer	First data entered, therefore no dependency to other data exists.
1	Perform financial situation check	Application data (name of applicant, etc.) must be available in order to perform the financial situation check.
2	Perform customer history check	Analog to production rule 1.
3	Calculate the contract conditions	This calculation requires the data from the application as well the outcomes of both checks.
4	Send refusal correspondence and set final status REJECTED	This activity requires data from the application such as name and address. Furthermore, due to the defined constraint, the outcome of the financial situation check is required.
5	Send refusal correspondence and set final status REJECTED	Analog to production rule 4.
6	Check contract conditions	This check requires the calculated contract conditions and the application data.
7	Recalculate the contract conditions	The recalculation of the contract conditions requires the same input data as production rule 3. Furthermore, the previously calculated contract conditions are required. Due to the constraint defined, the outcome of the approval check is required.
8	Send acceptance correspondence and set final status GRANTED	This activity requires application data such as name, address, and amount. Due to the constraint defined, the outcome of the approval check is required.

The table contains a short description of the activity that is performed. Furthermore, an explanation of the dependencies is given. It is explained which information is required as input data for each production rule.

The resulting EPM is depicted in Fig. 3.8.

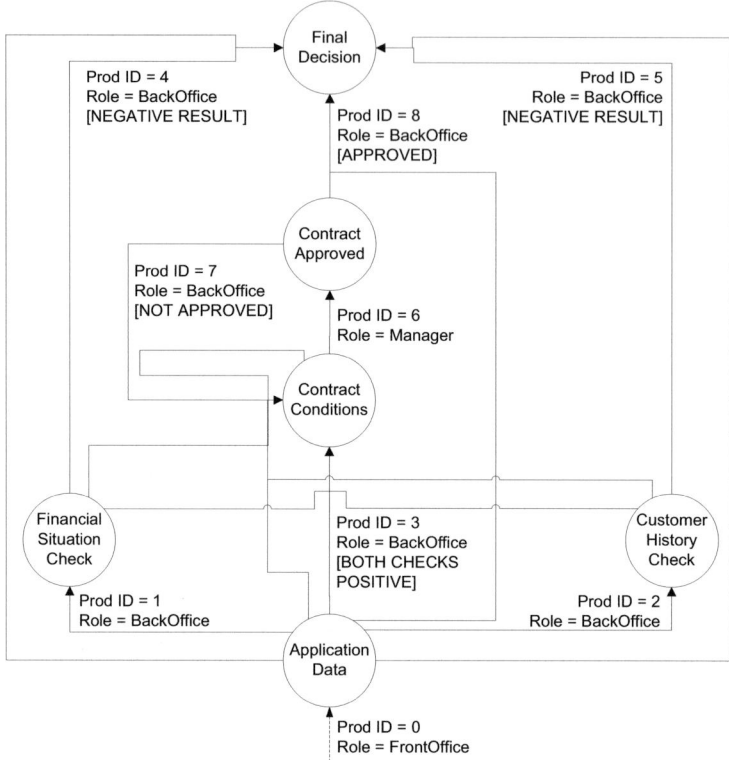

Figure 3.8.: Credit application as Executable Product Model.

The production rule with ID 3 is an AND dependency which means that the information nodes `ApplicationData`, `FinancialSituationCheck` and `CustomerHistoryCheck` must have been created before the production rule becomes executable. In the example, the final decision can be generated by three different production rules. This is another example of an OR dependency. For simplification, the suggested notation for attributes of business objects has been omitted in the figure.

For clearness, the following simplification regarding the dependencies is introduced: If it can be assured that an information node has been created, it can be omitted in a dependency as input data. In the credit application example, the information node `ApplicationData` is created at the beginning. Therefore, after the creation of this information element, it is available during the whole execution of the EPM. As described in Tab. 3.2, the production rule with ID 4 requires the application data as input data. But as the information node `ApplicationData` has been created at this point, it must not be modeled as origin node of the production rule. Fig. 3.9 depicts the resulting EPM with a much clearer design.

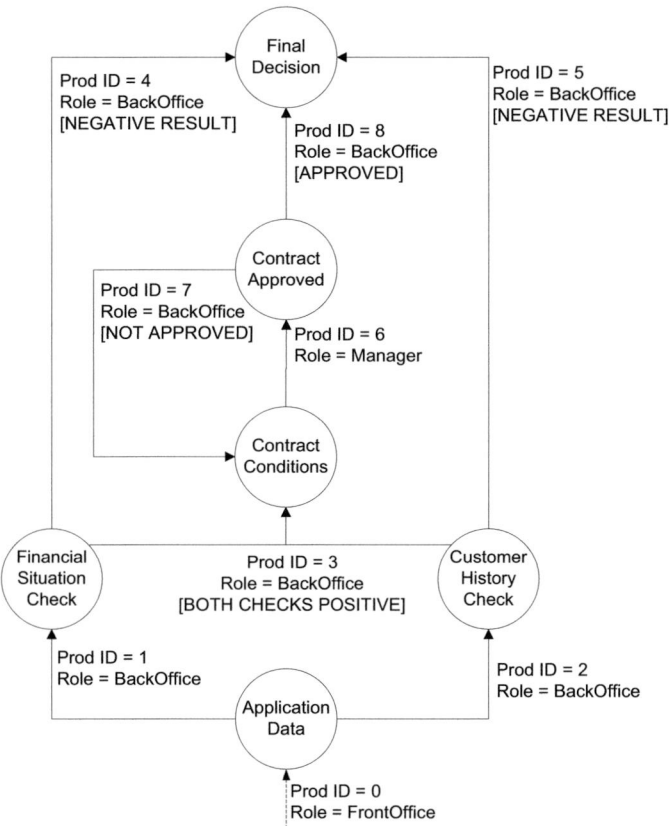

Figure 3.9.: Simplified credit application.

Using this simplification affects the robustness of the approach as the designer has the responsibility, that information that is required for the execution of a production rule is available when the production rule becomes available.

3.4.3. Evaluation Phase

The evaluation phase has the objective to identify the best design of the EPMs created in the analysis and design phase. Due to the different levels of abstractions and simplification possibilities, more than one EPM may be created for a business process. How EPMs are evaluated based on a simulation approach is explained in detail in the following chapters.

So far, it was examined how the original model (PDM) has been enhanced to become the EPM. In the next section, the flexibility of EPMs is discussed.

3.5. Enhanced Flexibility

In this section, the flexibility aspects of the EPM approach are discussed. It is argued, how the EPM approach enhances the flexibility in business process execution.

The enhanced flexibility of the approach stems from the way information is modeled. As mentioned earlier, in the product data model approach, business process models were derived from product models. Assume the process model was derived from a product model with the objective to minimize the costs. The resulting process model has a fixed order of activities. In such a cost minimizing scenario, activities which do not incur much costs but lead potentially fast to a final decision (e. g. NO GO decisions) are placed as early as possible in the process. If the workload is heavy, it can happen that the corresponding resources of these activities are not available in the required number while other resources are not fully occupied. If the execution is performed on the basis of an EPM, only the order based on the information dependencies has to be considered but not the order which was set based on an additional criteria as costs or cycle time. Therefore, other activities could be executed earlier.

The flexibility of EPMs is evaluated in more detail on the basis of various examples in Sec. 9.7. In the next section, the optimization problem is introduced.

3.6. Optimization Problem

The flexibility of the EPMs is utilized in order to optimize the KPIs of interest such as cycle time or costs. The optimization comprises two tasks for each EPM to be executed:

(1) A set of production rules has to be selected for execution.

(2) The selected production rule have to be assigned to resources.

Both tasks have to be performed in such a way that leads to the optimization of the KPIs of interest. Note that not all production rules have to be executed necessarily as the EPM may contain variants. Furthermore, the assignment of production rules to resource can be considered as a scheduling problem.

The optimization problem is formalized and evaluated in more detail in the next chapter as part of the complexity analysis. In the following, the related work is discussed.

3.7. Related Work

In this section, the related work regarding BPM and business process flexibility is discussed. Note that the objective of the intelligent Executable Product Model (iEPM) approach is the enhancement of the flexibility by using the EPMs introduced in this chapter. This flexibility is utilized in order to autonomously optimize the execution of business processes as described in the introduction. In addition to the related work, a differentiation from related models is provided.

3.7.1. Differentiation from Related Models

The goal of this section is to give a deeper insight in EPMs by differentiating them from related models and concepts.

AND/OR Graph

The PDM as well as the EPM resemble an AND/OR graph that is used in Artificial Intelligence research [203]. An AND/OR graph has a tree structure that describes the decomposition of a goal in terms of alternative subgoals (OR nodes) or combinations of subgoals that must all be satisfied (AND node) [233]. AND/OR graphs have been widely used, e.g. for parsing the human body in static images [337], for genetic linkage analysis [180], and for the representation of assembly plans in manufacturing [72]. The latter approach makes use of AND/OR graphs in a similar way as the product models with the difference that physical products are considered instead of business processes. Their conclusion shows the similarity of the usage: "The AND/OR graph representation of assembly plans described in this paper constitutes a compact representation of all feasible assembly sequences. It provides a useful tool for the selection of the best assembly plan for the selection of the best disassembly or repair plan, recovery from execution errors, and opportunistic scheduling. Unlike the directed graph of assembly states, the AND/OR graph can show explicitly the possibility of parallel execution of assembly operations and the time independence of operations that can be executed in parallel."

Entity-Relationship-Model

One type of model that contains data as well as dependencies are Entity-Relationship-Models (ER-Models) (see e.g. [54, 53]). They are used to create a semantical data model of a system by using entities and relationships between these entities. An entity can be defined as a uniquely identifiable thing which is relevant for the problem under consideration. Relationships capture how two or more entities relate to each other. This modeling technique is widely used for designing relational database models. The entities are tightly related to the information elements that are used for the EPMs. The main difference exists between relationships in ER-Models and dependencies in EPMs. The dependencies capture the production order by defining which information must be available to create new information, whereas relationships can define any relationship that exists between entities. As ER-Models are used to create database models they define more a static structure how information is stored in a database, whereas EPMs capture dynamic aspects by defining the production order of information. In an ER-Model the two entities "customer" and "address" could have the relationship "customer has address", whereas in EPMs they could have no dependencies[12].

Digital Information Product

A related concept are digital information products (see e.g. [209, 217]). In [217] a detailed introduction is given of an approach for creating variants of information product within a product line. In this work, an information product is defined as "a special type of digital product whose core benefit is the delivery of information or education". Examples are electronic newspapers, magazines, and weather reports. Various models are introduced that define what products can be built. Additionally, a workflow model is created that defines how the product is built.

The term digital product used in the aforementioned definition is defined in [217] as "a bundle of properties or features which are constituted by artifacts that are digitized or produced electronically...". Additionally, digital products are defined as distributable purely in digital form and that they serve a specific purpose. As this pertains to EPMs, they can be defined as digital products. But the approach differs by its understanding of variants. In the EPM approach, a variant is one possibility or execution path that leads to the creation of the final information node. In the digital information products approach, a variant is one valid configuration of an information product. In an EPM two different variants may contain exactly the same information elements which is not the case for variants of digital information products. Furthermore, the focus is different. The digital information product approach focuses on the efficient creation of variants of the products, whereas the EPM approach focuses on the efficient execution by using variants. Even if EPMs belong to the class of digital products, they have a significant difference. EPMs are more process focused and may contain information that is not delivered to the customer but required during the execution of an EPM. An example for this kind of information is rework required due to internal processing errors, e.g. if contract conditions were not calculated correctly. On the other hand, the digital information product contains all features that are subject for the customer delivery.

In the following section, general and product-driven BPM approaches are discussed.

3.7.2. Business Process Management

The widely used approach for business process execution is based on explicitly defined business models. There exist a multitude of vendor-specific (e. g. FileNet, Staffware) and standardized modeling languages (see Section 2.1.2). The suggested approach is not based on an explicitly defined process model, but on an EPM. Moreover, EPMs may be more flexible than regular process models as mentioned above.

---

[12]Alternatively there could be a dependency between "customer" and "address" in an EPM if the customer name has to be used in the address.

An approach related to business process variants is introduced in [156]. They developed an algorithm based on an ontology for determining linguistic similarities between business process model variants. The objective is the detection of process model variants in order to facilitate process redesign. Thus, it focuses on process design and not on the autonomous optimization of business processes.

The latest product-driven workflow approaches are based on life cycles of objects instead of product structures. In [163] these life cycles are used to check the compliance between the life cycles and the business processes whereas in [199] they are used to manage large process structures, especially the sub-processes related to a complex product are considered. Obviously, these approaches have another focus. Nevertheless, they were listed as they belong to the product-driven workflow approaches as the iEPM approach.

The most related product-driven workflow approach is introduced in [302], which directly executes Product Data Models, but does not integrate machine learning in order to autonomously optimize the process execution. The authors state that their presented execution strategies may not necessarily lead to the best overall execution path. Furthermore, it is not mentioned how iterations are handled which are fundamental in business processes.

There are a number of related research efforts in the area of BPM that examine flexibility issues which are discussed next.

3.7.3. Business Process Flexibility

Several approaches exist that focus on the flexibility of business processes. The approach described in [252] makes it possible to model and manage process variants on the basis of process family engineering techniques in an efficient way. But as the actual variant is chosen on instantiation of the business process there is no possibility to change the variant during runtime. As EPMs contain all feasible variants in one model, the variant in execution can be changed anytime during runtimne.

Another approach introduced in [275] uses fuzzy logic for decision making. This handles the problem when decisions have to be made based on uncertain data. The approach enables flexible decision making but does not provide more execution options as the EPM.

Further approaches improve the flexibility by allowing dynamic changes on workflow instance or schema level during runtime. The approaches mainly give an overview about the different kinds of changes and how they affect the instances and schema. For an overview of these adaptive and dynamic workflows approaches see e.g. [238]. The suggested approach differs from these approaches as a fixed model is created, whose flexibility is utilized by intelligent agents, controlling the process flow automatically. The adaptive workflow approaches could be used to extend the iEPM approach to further improve the flexibility of EPMs.

In [317] a set of change patterns is introduced which is the basis for an evaluation of industry and academic approaches. Regarding the iEPM approach the late binding of process fragments pattern is of interest. Process fragments can be selected during runtime. It differs from the iEPM approach as these process fragments are selected manually or based on fixed rules without any autonomous optimization.

In [221] a constrained-based workflow approach is introduced for providing flexibility by using a declarative style of modeling. The model comprises a set of optional and mandatory constraints. This approach is well suited for variants handling and exception handling by giving the user more choices regarding the actual execution order of activities. An automatic optimization as in the iEPM approach has not been integrated so far.

One of the core features of the case handling approach described in [295] is very similar to the iEPM approach. The decision about the activation of activities is also based on the information available instead of the activities already executed. But the approach focuses more on the user by providing all case information and a flexible way of data entry.

3.8. Summary

In this chapter, the EPM has been introduced. First, the PDM has been explained which is the basis of the EPM. The various extensions of the PDM has been explained that allow the direct execution of the product model. By these enhancements, the PDM became the EPM. Furthermore, a modeling methodology has been explicated by using an example of a simplified credit application process. Additionally, the two different ways of executing an EPM have been explained. Two assumptions were made for the explanation of the different executions. One assumption was that all executable production rules are executed immediately. The other one was that a specific variant is chosen. These assumptions were necessary in order to explain the execution without introducing the MAS and the learning mechanism. The MAS is introduced in Chapter 5 and the developed machine learning mechanism for the autonomous optimization is explained in Chapter 6. Moreover, it has been discussed, how the EPM provides more flexibility in comparison to regular business process models. Finally, the related work was discussed which included also a differentiation from related models in order to provide a deeper insight in EPMs. In the next chapter, the complexity of the optimization problem of the EPM approach is analyzed.

4. Complexity Evaluation

> "I think the next century will be the century of complexity."
>
> Stephen Hawking

In this chapter, the complexity of the optimization problem of the Executable Product Model (EPM) approach is analyzed mathematically. In the following, the optimization problem of the EPM approach is referred to as EPM problem. The objective of this chapter is to show that the EPM problem belongs to the class of NP-complete optimization problems. NP-complete problems are the most difficult problems of the complexity class NP. Until now, no deterministic algorithm could have been found that solves problems of this class in polynomial time. Thus, applying exact methods on large problem instances would not be very efficient. In such cases, approximation procedures are normally applied such as heuristics or machine learning algorithms.

The chapter is outlined as follows: In the first section, a short introduction to complexity is given. Then, the Multi-Processor Scheduling (MPS) problem is introduced as this kind of problem is used in the NP-completeness proof. In the next section, the EPM and the corresponding optimization and decision problem are formulated as mathematical models, followed by the mathematical prove that the EPM decision problem is NP-complete. The chapter ends with a brief summary.

4.1. Introduction to Complexity Theory

In this section, the formal details of the theory of NP-completeness are introduced. As the theory is based on mathematical models, several definitions have to be introduced. Further information about these concepts and definitions can be found e.g. in [65, 101, 127, 218]. Before the details are presented, complexity theory is briefly distinguished from the computability theory.

4.1.1. Computability vs. Complexity Theory

Computability theory originated with the seminal work of Gödel, Church, Turing, Kleene and Post in the 1930s. Computability theory studies which problems are computationally solvable [64]. It is based on the concept of *effective procedures* also termed *effective methods*. An effective procedures is a procedure that can be carried out by following specific rules. Thus, these rules can be considered as an exact instruction such as a program or algorithm. A function is *effectively calculable* if there is an effective procedure for calculating the function.

Complexity theory is "the theory of determining the necessary resources for the solution of algorithmic problems and, therefore, the limits of what is possible with the available resources" [318]. Complexity theory has a relationship to algorithm design as an understanding of these limits prevents the search for non-existing efficient algorithms. Accordingly to [318], the goal of complexity theory "is to prove for important problems that their solutions require certain minimum resources. The results of complexity theory have specific implications of algorithms for practical applications."

4.1.2. Basic Terms

First, several basic terms have to be introduced which are relevant for explaining the theory of NP-completeness. Accordingly to [101], a *problem* is "a general question to be answered, usually possessing several parameters, free variables, whose values are left unspecified." In [318, page 11], Wegener argues that the notion of problem is commonly used in such a general way, that it is impossible to formalize. Therefore, he restricts the definition to algorithmic problems: "a problem that is suitable for processing by computers and for which the set of correct results is unambiguous". The description of a problem comprises (a) a general description of the input parameters and (b) the properties the answer to the problem must satisfy. The answer to such a problem is also referred to as *solution*. An *instance* of a problem assigns particular values to each input parameter of the problem. An *algorithm* is a general step-by-step procedure for solving a problem. An algorithm solves a problem Π if that algorithm can be applied to any instance I of Π and produces always a solution for instance I. An *encoding scheme* allows to describe an instance of a problem by a single finite string of symbols. Thus, an encoding scheme maps problem instances to string representations. The formal measure of the size of an instance I of a problem Π is the *input length* which is defined by the number of symbols that describe instance I based on the encoding scheme of Π.

The *time complexity function* for an algorithm expresses the largest amount of time needed by the algorithm to solve a problem instance for each possible input length. This function characterizes how efficient an algorithm is able to solve a specific problem. A simple distinction of algorithms divides algorithms into two classes: "efficient enough" and "too inefficient" algorithms which corresponds to the distinction between polynomial and exponential time algorithms. It is only a simplified distinction due to the fact that there are problems whose polynomial algorithms are considered to be not efficient enough and problems that are efficiently solvable by exponential algorithms for small but in practice sufficiently large problem instances. Thus, in practice there may be the need for a more precise analysis than this theoretical distinction allows.

The two types of the simple distinction can be roughly differentiated on the basis of the Big-O-Notation[1].

Definition: Big-O-Notation

Let $f(n)$ and $g(n)$ be functions that map positive integers to positive real numbers. $f(n)$ is $O(g(n))$ (or $f(n) \in O(g(n))$) if there exists a real constant $c > 0$ and there exists an integer constant $n_0 \geq 1$ such that $f(n) \leq c * g(n)$ for every integer $n \geq n_0$.

The Big-O-Notation is used as an upper-bound on the growth of an algorithm's effort to solve a problem. Thus, by the way the Big-O-Notation is defined, it is a worst case measure. A polynomial time algorithm has a time complexity function which is $O(p(n))$ for some polynomial function p with n as input length. Exponential time algorithms have time complexity functions that cannot be bounded by any polynomial function. This kind of distinction has a significant impact on the growth rate of the execution time when solving large problem instances. The effect is illustrated in Table 4.1.

Table 4.1.: Comparison of several polynomial and exponential time complexity functions for different input lengths (taken from [101]).

	10	30	60
n	0.00001 seconds	0.00003 seconds	0.00006 seconds
n^2	0.0001 seconds	0.0009 seconds	0.0036 seconds
n^3	0.001 seconds	0.027 seconds	0.216 seconds
n^5	0.1 seconds	24.3 seconds	13.0 minutes
2^n	0.001 seconds	17.9 minutes	366 centuries
3^n	0.059 seconds	6.5 years	$1.3 * 10^{13}$ centuries

This table exemplifies why exponential time algorithms are considered as "too inefficient". Note that there are problems that are only exponentially solvable such as the board game Go [241]. Moreover, for problem instances with a small input length, an exponential algorithm can be faster than a polynomial algorithm. As one can see in Table 4.1, the 2^n algorithm is faster than the n^5 algorithm for input $n = 10$. A problem is referred to as *intractable* if there is no polynomial time algorithm that solves the problem.

The theory of NP-completeness provides a mathematically formalism in contrary to the infor-

---

[1] A real differentiation can only be made by a more precise estimation of the computational time.

mal notation of intractability. This theory is designed to be applied only to *decision problems*. A decision problem is a problem whose solution is either "yes" or "no". Thus, a decision problem Π consists of a set D_π of instances and a subset $Y_\Pi \subseteq D_\pi$ of "yes"-instances.

Decision problems have a natural, formal counterpart termed *language* which allows to study the problem in a mathematically formal way. That is the reason for the restriction to decision problems. For any finite set Σ of symbols, Σ^* denotes the set of all finite strings of symbols from Σ. If L is a subset of Σ^*, then L is a language over the alphabet Σ. For example, if $\Sigma = \{0,1\}$, then Σ^*, contains the empty string and all other finite strings of 0's and 1's. The set $\{01, 001, 111, 11011101\}$ is an example of a language over $\{0,1\}$.

An encoding scheme e for a problem Π describes each instance of Π by an appropriate string of symbols over some fixed alphabet Σ. The language which is associated with Π and e is defined by:

$$L[\Pi, e] = \{x \in \Sigma^* : \quad \Sigma \text{ is the alphabet used by } e, \text{ and } x \text{ is the encoding}$$
$$\text{under } e \text{ of an instance } I \in Y_\Pi \}$$

In the next section, the Turing Machine is introduced in order to formalize the notion of an algorithm.

4.1.3. Turing Machines and Time Complexity

Turing Machines were introduced by Alan Turing in 1936. A Turing Machine has a finite state control and an infinite input/output tape with a reading/writing head. Two types of Turing Machines can be distinguished, (a) the deterministic and (b) the non-deterministic Turing Machine.

A deterministic Turing Machine moves in each step in a unique way determined by its current state, and the symbol it is currently scanning. A move consists of a possible change of state and scanned symbol, and moving the head left or right. Fig. 4.1 illustrates a deterministic Turing Machine.

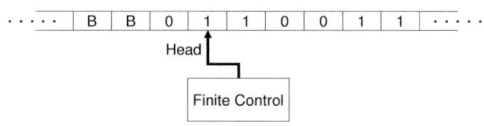

Figure 4.1.: Deterministic one tape Turing Machine.

A non-deterministic Turing Machine may have several legal moves, which are still determined by its current state and the scanned symbol. An input x is accepted by a deterministic Turing Machine if the computation starting with initial configuration ends in an accepting state. For a non-deterministic Turing Machine acceptance is defined by the existence of some sequence of legal moves that ends in an accepting state.

In the following subsections, the two types of Turing Machines are defined mathematically. Furthermore, the polynomial transformation is introduced.

Deterministic Turing Machine

A *program* for a deterministic Turing Machine has the following properties:

(1) A finite set Γ of tape symbols, including a subset $\Sigma \subset \Gamma$ of input symbols and a distinguished blank symbol $b \in \Gamma - \Sigma$,

(2) a finite set Q of states, including a distinguished start state q_0 and two distinguished halt states q_Y and q_N,

(3) a transition function $\delta : (Q - \{q_Y, q_N\}) \times \Gamma \to Q \times \Gamma \times \{-1, +1\}$.

The operation of such a program can be explained as follows: The input to the deterministic Turing Machine is a string $x \in \Sigma^*$ which is placed in the tape squares 1 through $|x|$. All other squares contain the blank symbol. The program starts in state q_0 with the read-write head reading tape square 1. The computation proceeds step-by-step until the current state q is either q_Y or q_N. If $q = q_Y$, then the answer to the decision problem is "yes", and "no" if $q = q_N$. Otherwise, the current state is $q \in Q - \{q_Y, q_N\}$, a symbol $s \in \Gamma$ is being scanned, and $\delta(q, s)$ is defined. Suppose that $\delta(q, s) = \delta(q', s', \Delta)$. Then, the read-write head erases s and writes s'. The head moves one square to the left if $\Delta = -1$ or one to the right if $\Delta = +1$. At the same time, the current state is changed from q to q' which completes one step of the computation.

In general, a deterministic Turing Machine program M with input alphabet Σ *accepts* $x \in \Sigma^*$ if and only if M halts in state q_Y when applied to input x. The language L_M *recognized* by the program M is given by:

$$L_M = \{x \in \Sigma^* : M \text{ accepts } x\}$$

A deterministic Turing Machine program M solves the decision problem Π under the encoding scheme e if M halts for all input strings over its input alphabet and $L_M = L[\Pi, e]$.

The Turing Machine allows the formal definition of "time complexity". For a deterministic Turing Machine program M that halts for all inputs $x \in \Sigma^*$, its time complexity function $T_M : \mathbb{Z}^+ \to \mathbb{Z}^+$ is given by:

$$T_M(n) = max \left\{ m : \begin{array}{l} \text{there is an } x \in \Sigma^*, \text{with} |x| = n, \text{ such that the} \\ \text{computation of } M \text{ on input } x \text{ takes time } m \end{array} \right\}$$

Such a program M is called a polynomial time deterministic Turing Machine program if there exists a polynomial p such that, for all $n \in \mathbb{Z}^+, T_M(n) \leq p(n)$.

Non-Deterministic Turing Machine

The class NP can be defined informally on the basis of a nondeterministic algorithm. Such algorithm is composed of two different stages, (a) a guessing stage, and (b) a checking stage. For a given problem instance I, the first stage guesses a structure S. In the next stage, I and S are used as input. The checking performs a computation in a deterministic manner, either halting with answer "yes", "no", or computing forever without halting. It can be said, that a nondeterministic algorithm "solves" a decision problem Π if the following properties hold for all instances $I \in D_\Pi$:

(1) If $I \in Y_\Pi$, the there exists some structure S that, when guessed for input I, will lead the checking stage to respond "yes" for I and S.

(2) If $I \notin Y_\Pi$, then there exists no structure S that, when guessed for input I, will lead the checking stage to respond "yes" for I and S.

The formal counterpart of a nondeterministic algorithm is a program for a nondeterministic one-tape Turing Machine. The Non-Deterministic Turing Machine (NDTM) has exactly the same structure as the deterministic Turing Machine, except that it has a guessing module with a write-only head. Fig.4.2 illustrates such a nondeterministic Turing Machine.

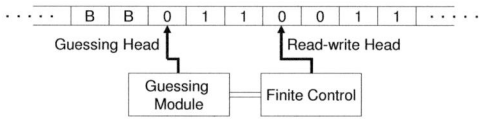

Figure 4.2.: Illustration of a nondeterministic one tape Turing Machine.

The NDTM program is specified as the deterministic Turing Machine, only that the computation proceeds in a different way. The computation takes place in two different stages.

The first stage is the so called "guessing" stage. Initially the input string x is written in the tape squares from 1 through $|x|$. The read-write head is reading square 1, the write-only head is reading square -1, and the finite state control is "inactive". The guessing module either writes a symbol from Γ into the square being read or moves the write-only head left to the next square. It can also stop which results in the inactivation of the guessing module and the activation of the finite state control in state q_0. The guessing module is able to write any string from Γ^* before it halts.

The second stage is called "checking" stage and begins with the activation of the finite state control in q_o. At this point, the computation proceeds in the same way as the deterministic Turing Machine. The computation stops if one of the halting states is entered, either q_Y or q_N. If it halts in state q_Y, it is said to be an *accepting computation*. All other computations (q_N or not halting at all), are *non-accepting computations*.

As explained in the previous section, a deterministic Turing Machine has a transition function that, for a given state and symbol, specifies the next state, the symbol to be written and the direction in which the head moves. The NDTM differs in that different actions may apply for the same combination of state and symbol. The aforementioned guessing module chooses one of the possible actions.

The NDTM program M accepts x if at least one of these is an accepting computation. The language recognized by M is defined by:

$$L_M = \{x \in \Sigma^* : M \text{ accepts } x\}.$$

The time complexity function $T_M : \mathbb{Z}^+ \rightarrow \mathbb{Z}^+$ for M is defined by:

$$T_M(n) = max\left(\{1\} \cup \left\{ m : \begin{array}{l} \text{there is an } x \in L_M, \text{with} |x| = n, \text{ such} \\ \text{that the time to accept } x \text{ by } M \text{ is } m \end{array} \right\}\right)$$

By convention, $T_M(n)$ is set to one if no inputs of length n are accepted by M. The time complexity function for M depends only on the number of steps occurring in accepting computations.

The NDTM program is a polynomial time NDTM program if there exists a polynomial p such that $T_M(n) \le p(n)$ for all $n \ge 1$.

Polynomial Time Transformation

In order to define the NP-complete class, the term polynomial transformation needs to be introduced first. A polynomial transformation from a language $L \subseteq \Sigma_1^*$ to a language $L \subseteq \Sigma_2^*$ is a function $f : \Sigma_1^* \rightarrow \Sigma_2^*$ that satisfies the following two conditions:

(1) There is a polynomial time deterministic Turing Machine program that computes f.

(2) For all $x \in \Sigma_1^*, x \in L_1$ if and only if $f(x) \in L_2$.

If there is such a polynomial transformation from L_1 to L_2, it is said that L_1 transforms to L_2, denoted by $L_1 \propto L_2$.

4.1.4. Complexity Classes

In general, a complexity class is a set of functions that can be computed within a given resource. The decision problems are classified on the basis of the definitions introduced in the previous sections. In the following subsections, some of the existing complexity classes are listed[2].

Class P

The class P consists of all decision problems that are solvable by a deterministic Turing Machines in polynomial time. Thus, the problems in P can be seen as efficiently solvable. P is formally defined by:

$$P = \{L : \text{there is a polynomial time deterministic Turing Machine program } M \text{ for which } L = L_M\}.$$

Class EXP

The class EXP comprises the class of languages (decision problems) accepted by an algorithm in exponential time.

Class NP

The class NP consists of all decision problems that are solvable in polynomial time by a non-deterministic Turing Machine. The abbreviation NP refers to "non-deterministic polynomial time".

The definition of a polynomial time NDTM program allows the formulation of class NP:

$$NP = \{L : \text{there is a polynomial time NDTM program } M \text{ for which } L_M = L\}.$$

Class NP-complete

Another important class is the class of NP-complete problems. It contains the "hardest" languages (decision problems) in NP.

A language is defined to be NP-complete if the two conditions are satisfied:

(1) $L \in NP$

(2) For all other languages $L' \in NP, L' \propto L$.

---

[2]For a more complete list of complexity classes see e. g. [318].

The first decision problem which was proved to be an NP-complete problem was the well-known satisfiability of Boolean formulas from proposition logic, denoted as SATISFIABILITY or shortly SAT problem.

If only the second condition of the NP-complete conditions is fulfilled, the problem belongs to class of NP-hard problems.

Relationships

For the complexity classes P, NP and EXP, the following proven relationships exist: P $\subseteq$ NP $\subseteq$ EXP. Fig.4.3 illustrates the relationship under the assumption that P $\neq$ NP [315]. Furthermore, it was proved that P $\neq$ EXP and P $\subset$ EXP.

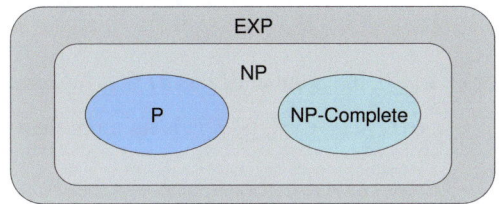

Figure 4.3.: The relationship between the complexity classes under the assumption that P $\neq$ NP.

The P-NP problem is considered to be the most important open problem in computer science[3]. The problem comprises the question whether P = NP holds. It is generally conjectured that P $\neq$ NP. If any NP-complete problem could be solved in polynomial time, then all problems in NP would also be solvable in polynomial time, which would lead to P = NP.

4.1.5. Proving NP-completeness

In accordance to [101], an NP-completeness proof for a decision problem Π consists of the following four steps:

(1) showing that Π is in NP,

(2) selecting a known NP-complete problem Π',

(3) constructing a transformation f from Π' to Π, and

(4) proving that f is a (polynomial) transformation

Step (2) requires the selection of a known NP-complete problem. Such a problem is introduced in the next section.

---

[3]This problem belongs to the Millennium Problems that were announced by the Clay Mathematics Institute which has offered a $1 million US prize for the first correct proof.

4.2. Multiprocessor Scheduling

The decision problem described in this section is used for proving the NP-completeness of the EPM decision problem. In accordance to Garey and Johnson [101], the multiprocessor decision problem is defined as follows:

Instance: Set T of tasks, number of $m \in \mathbb{Z}^+$ of processors, length $l(t) \in \mathbb{Z}^+$ for each $t \in T$, and a deadline $D \in \mathbb{Z}^+$.

Question: Is there an m-processor schedule for T that meets the overall deadline D, i.e., a function $\sigma : T \to \mathbb{Z}_0^+$ such that,

$$\text{for all } u \geq 0, \text{ the number of tasks } t \in T \text{ for which} \qquad [4.1]$$
$$\sigma(t) \leq u < \sigma(t) + l(t) \text{ is no more than } m$$

and such that,

$$\text{for all } t \in T, \sigma(t) + l(t) \leq D? \qquad [4.2]$$

It was proved, that the multiprocessor decision problem is NP-complete (see [101] - problem [SS8], page 238).

The m-processor schedule can be represented by a Gantt chart (see e.g. [29]). Without loss of generality, the m processors are integers from 1 until m. The Gantt chart is defined as function $\hat{\sigma} : T \to (\mathbb{N} \times \mathbb{Z}_0^+)$. Let $(r, s) \in (\mathbb{N} \times \mathbb{Z}_0^+)$, then r corresponds to the processor and s corresponds to the start time.

Thus far, the mathematical foundation of the NP-completeness was introduced and a known NP-complete problem described. The mathematical model for the EPM is explained next.

4.3. Mathematical Formulations

First of all, the relevant terms used in the mathematical model that were already introduced in Chapter 3 are shortly explained.

Information Element:
Information elements correspond to information or data that accrues during the execution of the business process.

Production Rule:
A production rule is an activity for determining a value of an information element. Each incoming arc of an information element reflects one possibility to determine a value for the corresponding information element. The activity can only be performed if all values of the input information elements of the production rule have been generated.

Resource:
A resource is either a human or technical resource. A resource can process at most one production rule at a time. As resources have only specific knowledge and capabilities, they are able to perform only specific production rules. For this reason, roles are introduced.

Role:
A role defines which resources are capable of performing a specific production rule. This means that a production rule can only be performed by a resource that has the same role assigned as the production rule. Each production rule and each resource has exactly one role assigned. Roles can correspond to skills, competences, positions, among others. In case of positions, examples of roles are manager and case worker.

4.3.1. Problem Reduction

The prototype of the iEPM approach allows a variety of different settings that are relevant for the practical application such as processing durations that are based on the gamma distribution or exponentially distributed arrival rates. As the EPM does not explicitly define the execution order of the production rules, it may be optimal (in terms of the defined Key Performance Indicators (KPIs)) to execute only a subset of the production rules in a specific order. Also, cycles are allowed in the EPM in contrast to the Product Data Model (PDM). Furthermore, multiple EPMs may have to be executed at the same time. For the NP-completeness prove, it is sufficient to prove the NP-completeness for a special case (subproblem) only. Therefore, the mathematical model of the EPM as well as the decision problem are defined for a special case. This method is referred to as problem reduction. The special case is characterized as follows:

- The EPM is an acyclic graph.

- Constraints are not considered in the EPM.

- Generated values of information elements are not considered.

- Processing times are constant values (integers).

- Only one execution of an EPM is considered.

- All production rules of the EPM are executed, which means that all production rules are assigned to resources.

4.3.2. The Executable Product Model

In this section, a mathematical formulation of the EPM is presented which is partly based on the definition of the PDM [233], e.g. the definition of function *pre*. Note that the definition pertains only to the EPM. Resources are not part of the EPM, but they belong to the corresponding optimization problem (see Sec. 4.3.4).

Definition: An Executable Product Model is a tuple (I, pre, P, f, R, g) with:

- I: A set of information elements with one special element, called top or root element:
  $$top \in I$$
  Additionally, without loss of generality, the elements are assumed to be integers from 1 to $|I|$.

- $pre : I \rightarrow \mathscr{P}(\mathscr{P}(I))$: This function defines for each information element the various possibilities of determining a value for it on the basis of different sets of other information elements, such that:

  - $D_{pre} = \{(d,o) \in I \times I | o \in \bigcup_{es \in pre(p)} es\}$ is connected and acyclic.
    Each information element is connected to at least another one. Furthermore, a value of an information element does not depend on itself.

  - $\forall (d,o) \in D_{pre} : o \neq top$
    The top element cannot be used for determining the value of any other information element.

  - $\forall e \in I : \emptyset \notin pre(e)$
    If there is a set of information elements that can be used for the value of another, this set is not empty.

- $P = \{(d,os) \in I \times (\mathscr{P}(I)) | os \in pre(d)\} \cup \{(d,\emptyset) | d \in I \wedge pre(d) = \emptyset)\}$
  A set of production rules which is based on the definition of function pre, extended with production rules for elements that do not require values of other information elements (leaf nodes).

- $f : P \rightarrow \mathbb{N}$: This function gives the time it takes to use a production rule (with the intended interpretation as processing duration of a production rule).

- R: A nonempty finite set. Let l be the number of elements of set R. An element of R is a role.

- $g : P \rightarrow R$: This function assigns a role to each production rule.

This mathematical model can be explained as follows: The EPM contains information elements, represented by the elements of I. The relationship between these information elements are expressed by function *pre*. This function defines for all information elements $d \in I$, one or more ways to create a value for d. The different ways are expressed by different subsets of I. For example let $a, b, c \in I$ and $\{a, b\} \in pre(c)$. This means that a value for information element c can be determined on the basis of the values of a and b. The corresponding production rule is denoted as $(c, \{a, b\})$. The information elements a and b can be considered as input and information element c as output of the production rule. A special case are production rules for an information element d with $pre(d) = \emptyset$. Information element d is a leaf node and its value does not depend on any other information element.

To illustrate the definition of an EPM, the helicopter example introduced in the Sec. 3.1 is used. The EPM consists of six information elements $1, 2, \cdots, 6$. Information element 1 of the EPM corresponds to information element (a) of the helicopter PDM, 2 to (b), $\cdots$, 6 to (f). Table 4.2 contains the production rules of the EPM and the assigned values of the different functions. For simplification, only one role is used for all production rules.

Table 4.2.: Example of an EPM.

pr ∈ F	f(pr)	g(pr)
$(2, \emptyset)$	60	caseWorker
$(4, \emptyset)$	30	caseWorker
$(5, \emptyset)$	60	caseWorker
$(6, \emptyset)$	30	caseWorker
$(3, \{5,6\})$	60	caseWorker
$(1, \{2,3\})$	45	caseWorker
$(1, \{6\})$	45	caseWorker
$(1, \{4\})$	45	caseWorker

Fig. 4.4 depicts this EPM. Information elements are depicted as circles. The circles are labeled by the information element. Production rules are depicted as arcs and the production rules leading to leaf nodes as dashed arcs. For simplification, the processing durations and roles are not depicted.

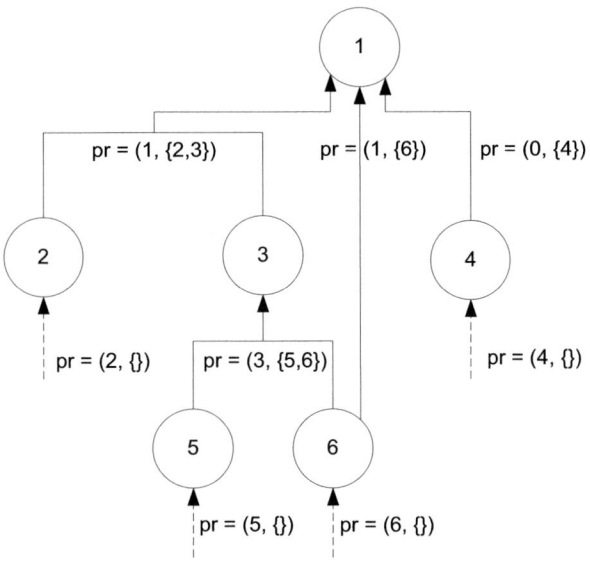

Figure 4.4.: Helicopter example as Executable Product Model.

4.3.3. The Execution of an EPM

Thus far, the structure of the EPM as well as the properties of the information elements and production rules have been defined. In this section, it is explained what the execution of an EPM comprises.

An EPM is executed completely if the value of the root information element was created. Note that this is always given for the special case as all production rules are assigned to resources. In general, an information element is created by assigning a production rule that has this information element as destination node to an adequate resource. Thus, in order to generate the root information element, the production rules must be assigned to resources. This results in a so called assignment.

Let RS be the finite set of resources. Without loss of generality, the resources are elements of $\mathbb{N}$, starting with one until $|RS|$.

Furthermore, let $h : RS \rightarrow R$ be the function that assigns to each resource $a \in RS$ one role $k \in R$. There must be at least one resource for each role: Let RS_k be the set of resources of role $k \in RS$ with:

$|RS_k| \geq 1$ for all k and $|RS| = \sum_{k=1}^{l} |RS_k|$.

Then, an assignment is defined as follows:

Definition Assignment: An assignment a is represented by function:

$$a : P \rightarrow RS \times \mathbb{Z}_0^+$$

Let $(r, s) \in RS \times \mathbb{Z}_0^+$, then r corresponds to the resource and s corresponds to the start time.

Let $p_i = (d_i, os_i), i = 1, \cdots, |P|$ be an enumeration of P and assume that $a(p_i) = (r_i, s_i)$, for certain elements r_i and $s_i, i = 1, \cdots, |P|$.

Definition Feasible Assignment: An assignment a is feasible if the constraints C1 until C4 are fulfilled:

C1 $\forall p_i \in P, i = 1, \cdots, |P| : \exists r_i \in RS \wedge \exists s_i \in \mathbb{Z}_0^+$ with $a(p_i) = (r_i, s_i)$
All production rules are assigned to resources.

C2 $\forall p_i \in P, i = 1, \cdots, |P| : g(p_i) = h(r_i)$
Production rules are assigned to resources that have the same role assigned as the production rules.

C3 $\forall p_i \in P, i = 1, \cdots, |P|$ with $\emptyset \notin os_i, \forall e \in os_i \exists p_j \in P$ with $d_i = d_j$:
$s_j + f(p_j) \leq s_i$
The precedence constraints of the assigned production rules as defined in the EPM must be fulfilled. It means that all input information elements of the assigned production rule must have been created before the production is assigned. Thus, there must be one production rule for each input element whose completion time is prior to the start time of the assigned production rule.

C4 $\forall p_i, p_j \in P, i, j = 1, \cdots, |P|, i \neq j : s_i + f(p_i) \leq s_j$ or $s_j + f(p_j) \leq s_i$
A resource processes at most one production rule at a time. Thus, the start and completion times of two different production rules assigned to the same resource must not overlap

A possible assignment for the helicopter example is depicted as Gantt chart in Fig.4.5. Note that in this example, only a subset of production rules is assigned to resources which is valid for the general case only. Thus, this assignment fulfills only the constraints C2 until C4.

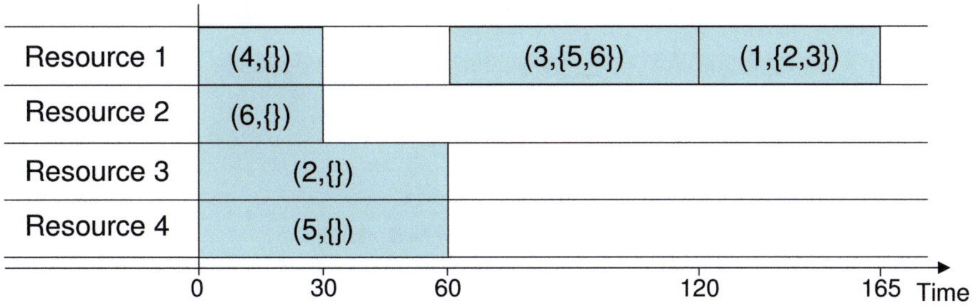

Figure 4.5.: Assignment for the Helicopter execution example. There are four resources with role case-Worker. Note that not all production rules are assigned to resources. Nevertheless, the EPM is executed completely with this subset of production rules.

4.3.4. EPM Optimization Problem

The optimization problem has the following input parameters:

- (I, pre, P, f, R, g): Executable Product Model.

- RS: The set of resources as defined in Sec. 4.3.3.

- h: The function assigning roles to resources as defined in Sec. 4.3.3.

The completion time C is considered as objective of the optimization problem which is defined as:

$$C = \max \{s + f(p) | p \in P \wedge \exists r \text{ with } a(p) = (r,s)\}.$$

Solution: A solution of the EPM optimization problem is a feasible assignment.

Remark: The term feasible assignment is defined in Sec. 4.3.3.

Optimal Solution: An optimal solution of the EPM optimization problem is a feasible assignment that minimizes C.

As the NP-completeness proof is based on decision problems, the EPM optimization problem is defined as decision problem in the next section.

4.3.5. EPM Decision Problem

The EPM optimization problem can be defined as decision problem as follows:

Input: The EPM (I, pre, P, f, R, g), a set of resources RS, RS_k is the set of resources of role k with $|RS_k| \geq 1$ for all k and $|RS| = \sum_{k=1}^{l} |RS_k|$. Finally, a given deadline $D' \in \mathbb{Z}^+$.

Question: Is there a feasible assignment with $C \leq D'$?

Remark: The term feasible assignment is defined in Sec. 4.3.3.

4.4. Proving NP-completeness of the EPM problem

This section contains the mathematical proof that the EPM decision problem as introduced in Sec. 4.3.5 is NP-complete. Remember that this problem is a special case of the general problem as explained in Sec. 4.3.1. The prove comprises the four steps as described in Sec. 4.1.5 and is based on decision problems.

Theorem III: The EPM decision problem is NP-complete.

Proof:

Step (1) The EPM decision problem is in NP as an algorithm has only to assign nondeterministically the production rules to the resources. Then, the algorithm only needs to check whether the solution fulfills the constraints which can be done deterministically in polynomial time.

Let $|P|$ be the number of production rules of the EPM. As we consider the special case that all production rules are assigned to resources, exactly $|P|$ production rules have to be assigned to resources. The check comprises the following steps:

- checking the feasibility of the assignment as described in Sec. 4.3.4.

- calculating the completion time and checking whether the overall deadline is met.

Step (2) The multiprocessor scheduling (MPS) decision problem as defined in Sec. 4.2 is selected as NP-complete decision problem.

Step (3) This step comprises two tasks. Firstly, the MPS decision problem must be transformed into the EPM decision problem by mapping the input parameters of the MPS decision problem to the parameters of the EPM decision problem. Secondly, the equivalence of both problems must be shown. Part of this equivalence proof is to show that a solution of the EPM problem is a solution of the MPS problem by using an adequate transformation.

As described in Sec. 4.2, there are four input parameters of the MPS decision problem that must be mapped to the EPM problem:

(a) T: Set of tasks. Let n be the number of tasks and $t_1, t_2, \cdots, t_n$ the elements of T.

(b) m: The number of processors.

(c) $l(t)$: The length of each task $t \in T$.

(d) D: The overall deadline.

The basic idea of the transformation is as follows: In the MPS problem n tasks are scheduled to m processors. Analogously, n production rules have to be assigned to m resources. Thus, one task relates exactly to one production rule. The m processors correspond to m resources that have the same role. The identifier "processor" was selected as role. The length $l(t)$ of a task $t \in T$ equals the processing duration of the corresponding production rule specified by function f. The EPM must be created in such a way that the production rules corresponding to set T are independently assignable which means there must not be any precedence constraint between them. This can be achieved by production rules that create different information nodes and do not have origin nodes. Furthermore, it must be assured that all of these production rules are assigned. This can be achieved by including an additional production rule corresponding to an AND-dependency that joins all other n production rules. As this is the last production rule in the EPM it creates the root node. This production rule is processed by another resource with a different role. The identifier "dummy" was selected as role. By using another role and resource, the assignment of the dummy production rule does not interfere with the assignment of the other n production rules.

In the following, the transformation from the MPS decision problem into the EPM decision problem is presented. The EPM is created as follows:

- I:

$$I = \{1, 2, \cdots, n+1\}$$

There are $n + 1$ information elements. The information element $n + 1$ is the top element (root node).

- *pre*:

$$pre(n+1) = \left\{ \ \{1\}, \cdots, \{n\} \right\}$$

$$D_{pre} = \{(n+1,1),(n+1,2),\cdots,(n+1,n)\}$$

Dependencies exist only between the top element and the other n information elements, i. e. the underlying graph is a tree and in particluar a star.

- *P*:

$$P = \ \{(n+1,\{1,\cdots,n\}),(1,\emptyset),(2,\emptyset),\cdots,(n,\emptyset)\}$$

with $(i,\emptyset)$ corresponding to task $t_i, i = 1,\cdots,n$. Additionally, one dummy production rule is added as explained above. Thus, there are $n+1$ production rules.

- *f*:

$$f(p) = \begin{cases} l(t_i) & \text{, if } p = (i,\emptyset), i = 1,\cdots,n \\ 1 & \text{, if } p = (n+1,\{1,\cdots,n\}) \end{cases}$$

The length of a task is transformed into the respective processing duration of the corresponding production rule. The processing duration of the dummy production rule is set to 1.

- *R*:

$$R = \ \{\text{processor}, \text{dummy}\}$$

There are two different roles.

- *g*:

$$g(p) = \begin{cases} \text{processor} & \text{, if } p = (i,\emptyset), i = 1,\cdots,n \\ \text{dummy} & \text{, if } p = (n+1,\{1,\cdots,n\}) \end{cases}$$

This EPM is depicted in Fig. 4.6.

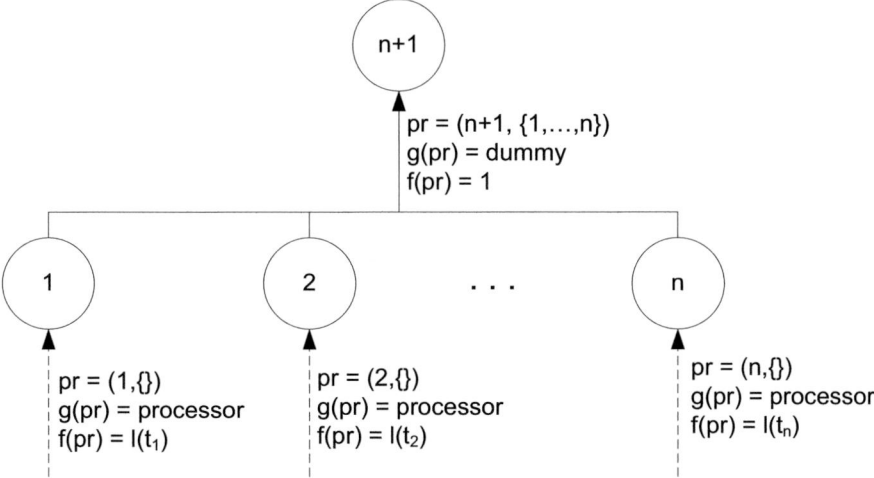

Figure 4.6.: The EPM for the multiprocessor scheduling problem. The production rule $(i, \emptyset)$ corresponds to the task $t_i, i = 1, \cdots, n$. As these production rules have no origin nodes, they are assignable at the beginning of the EPM execution. As production rule $(n+1, \{1, \cdots, n\})$ is an AND-dependency, all production rules must have been assigned in order to create the root element.

Additionally to the creation of the EPM, the processors and the deadline must be transformed:

- *RS*:

$$RS = \{1, \cdots, m, m+1\}$$

The processors are transformed into the resources $1, \cdots, m$ with role "processor". Additionally, there is one resource $m+1$ with role "dummy" for the assignment of the dummy production rule.

- D':

$$D' = D+1$$

As an additional production rule with a processing duration of 1 had to be included, the deadline is incremented by one.

After providing the transformation, the equivalence of the problems must be shown.

MPS $\Rightarrow$ EPM:

As stated in Sec. 4.2, a solution of the MPS decision problem is a schedule σ which is represented by a Gantt chart. The transformation of the solution is defined on the basis of the Gantt chart $\hat{\sigma}$:

$$a(p) = \begin{cases} (r,s) & \text{, if } p = (i,\emptyset) \text{ and } \hat{\sigma}(t_i) = (r,s), i = 1, \cdots, n \\ (m+1,s') & \text{, if } p = (n+1, \{1, \cdots, n\}) \end{cases}$$

with $s' = max\{s + l(t) | t \in T \land \exists r \text{ with } \hat{\sigma}(t) = (r,s)\}$.

As one can see, the processors are directly transformed to resources with role "processor" in such a way that processor i corresponds to resource $i, i = 1, \cdots, m$. Additionally, the dummy production rule is assigned to the resource with role "dummy". The start time of this production rule equals the completion time of the last task. It is obvious that the resulting assignment fulfills the deadline D'.

MPS $\Leftarrow$ EPM:

A solution of the EPM decision problem is an assignment. Two steps are necessary for transforming the assignment into a schedule σ. First, the assignment of the dummy production rule is omitted. Second, the first dimension RS of the range of the assignment $RS \times \mathbb{Z}_0^+$ is omitted. Thereby, the assignment becomes directly the schedule σ. This transformation is defined as follows:

$$\sigma(t_i) = \{s_i, \exists r_i \text{ with } a(p_i) = (r_i, s_i) \text{ and } p_i = (i, \emptyset), i = 1, \cdots, n.$$

As the production rules corresponding to the n tasks are distributed among m resources, the constraint Eq. 4.1 is fulfilled. As $D' = D + 1$, and the assignment of the dummy production rule was omitted, constraint Eq. 4.2 is fulfilled as well.

Step (4) It is obvious, that the transformation of the MPS decision problem into an EPM decision problem can be performed in polynomial time.

$\square$

Now, a detailed example is provided for explaining the transformation from an MPS decision problem into an EPM decision problem including the transformation of a solution.

The input parameters of the MPS problem are: three tasks t_1, t_2, t_3, 2 processors, $l(t_1) = 3, l(t_2) = 2, l(t_3) = 1$, and deadline $D = 3$.

Using the aforementioned transformation, the EPM decision problem has the following input parameters:
The created EPM is depicted in Fig. 4.7. There are two resources with role "processor" and one resource with role "dummy". The processing durations are set as depicted in Fig. 4.7. The deadline is $D' = D + 1 = 4$.

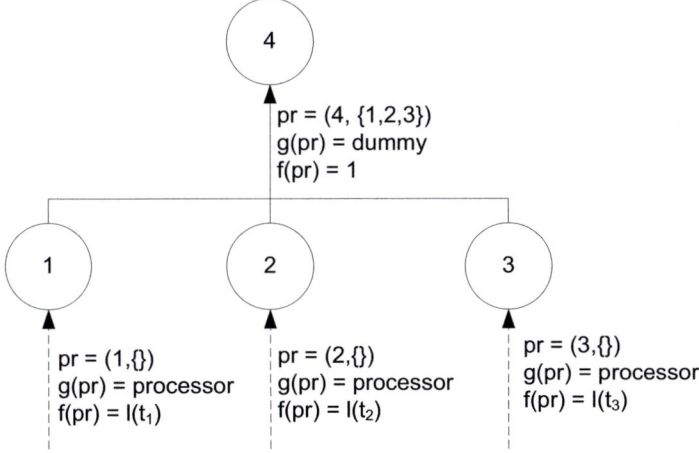

Figure 4.7.: The created EPM for the multiprocessor scheduling problem with 3 tasks and 2 processors.

A feasible assignment is depicted in Fig. 4.8.

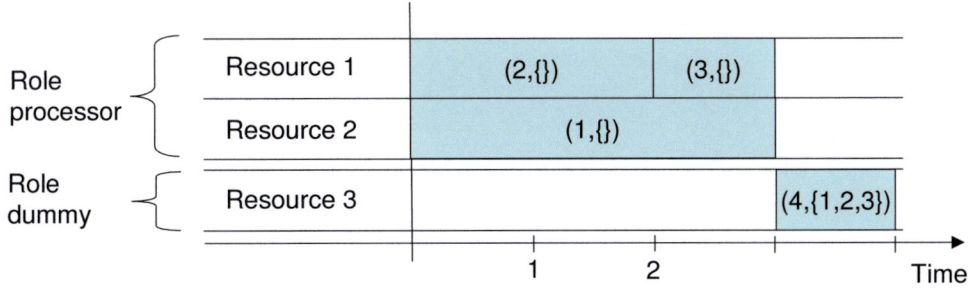

Figure 4.8.: A feasible assignment of the EPM decision problem.

Based on this assignment, the schedule σ can be created as follows: $\sigma(t_1) = 0, \sigma(t_2) = 0, \sigma(t_3) = 2,$. It is obvious, that this schedule fulfills the constraints of the MPS decision problem.

4.5. Summary

In this chapter, the motivation for using approximation procedures for solving the EPM problem was given. First, an introduction into complexity theory was provided and some of the essential complexity classes were introduced on the basis of Turing Machines. Then, the EPM and the corresponding decision problem were formulated as mathematical model for a special case. It was proved, that this EPM decision problem belongs to the class of NP-complete problems. This was done by using a standard method for proofing NP-completeness by transforming a known NP-complete problem into a special case of the EPM problem. As known NP-problem, the MPS problem was used. In the next chapter, the Multi-Agent System (MAS) is introduced.

5. Multi-Agent System

> "I not only use all the brains that I have, but all that I can borrow."
>
> Woodrow Wilson

The increased flexibility provided by the Executable Product Models (EPMs) is utilized by a Multi-Agent System (MAS). In the previous chapter it was shown that already a subproblem of the EPM decision problem is NP-complete. Thus, the EPM optimization problem can be considered as highly complex problem. As described in Section 1.2, a MAS is a promising paradigm for solving complex problems. Moreover, MASs have already been applied successfully in practice. Therefore, a MAS was chosen as software architecture.

The chapter is outlined as follows: First, the MAS architecture is explained with its different types of agents, their messaging capabilities and negotiation protocols. Then, the main steps that take place during a run of the MAS are denoted. In the next section, information about the simulation and analysis specific aspects is provided, followed by implementation details of the MAS. In the next section, the related work regarding MASs is discussed. Finally, the chapter ends with a short summary.

5.1. Architecture

In the following subsections, the MAS architecture is introduced by explaining the different agent types, the messaging mechanism, as well as the negotiation protocols.

5.1.1. Agent Types

The MAS comprises two different kinds of agents: *Intelligent Business Object (IBO)* and *Resource Agent (RA)*. Both agent types collaborate with each other in order to assure the successful execution of the EPMs. In order to achieve the collaboration, the agents have different capabilities and interact with each other. Both agent types are described in the following sections.

Intelligent Business Object

A new IBO is created for each execution of an EPM. This is similar to Business Process Management System (BPMS) in which a process instance is created for each process execution. The IBO replaces a standard workflow engine in the sense that it is responsible for the execution. Its behavior can be described by the following actions the IBO is able to perform:

Determination of executable production rules Once a product model execution is initiated or a task[1] has been completed, the IBO has to determine whether production rules are executable at this point of time (see algorithms in Section 3.3).

Scheduling of executable production rules For each production rule that has to be executed, a suitable RA needs to be found. This is done by means of a negotiation protocol (see Section 5.1.4).

Observation of production rules in execution Production rules that have been assigned to RAs must be observed in order to avoid delays due to error situations.

Resolving of error situations Once an error situation has been observed, it must be resolved by the appropriate action (e.g. if a resource is not available anymore, the tasks assigned to it are subject to rescheduling).

The main objective of the IBO is to assure the successful execution of the EPM. In the first version of the prototype implementation, *all* executable production rules are immediately executed which is termed *execute-all* approach. This means that presumably all variants of the EPM are executed which may lead to a high system load and potentially to unnecessary work. The enhancements include the determination of an optimal way through the product model by applying machine learning in accordance to special business objectives such as cycle times or costs and the current workload of resources (see Chapter 6).

As the IBO has to assure the successful execution, it must be able to handle error conditions and situations. The following types of error situations may occur:

Unavailability of a resource This means that an existing resource is not available anymore and the processing of the production rule is stopped. As the RA is decoupled from its resource, it is able to inform the IBO about this situation. In practice, such a situation may occur due to illness in case of a human resource or a system crash in case of a technical resource.

Delays in completion of production rules The completion of a production rule takes more time than estimated and communicated to the IBO. This can happen if the RA made a too optimistic estimation of the processing time. In practice, such a delay may occur due to unforeseen quality problems requiring rework.

---

[1] A task comprises exactly one production rule. Therefore, both terms are used as synonyms.

Deadlock in product model execution   No executable production rule can be determined but the product model is not executed completely (root information node is still not yet created). This can be caused by defining constraints leading to a deadlock.

Quality problems   In accordance to the assumption that bad quality leads to a longer processing time of the correspondent production rule (e.g. due to the required rework), quality problems can be simulated by causing additional delays in task completion.

Resource Agent

The second agent type within the MAS is the RA. A RA is modeled for each human resource (e.g. manager, caseworker) and technical resource (e.g. database, web service). A RA has a specific role assigned that describes for which production rules the agent is responsible for. Thus, there is a one-to-one relationship between RAs and roles which was sufficient for the conducted experiments. Note that this is a simplification as resources may have multiple roles in practice. Nevertheless, the relationship can easily be adapted if required by changing the implementation.

A RA is not processing tasks by itself. Instead, it negotiates with IBOs about tasks it is able to execute. The processing is done by the related resource, either a human or technical one like mentioned above. A RA can be considered as a mediator between one specific resource and IBOs. Its main objective is to achieve an optimum workload which corresponds to a minimum idle time. The IBOs and RAs communicate with each other by exchanging messages. The main part of the communication is consumed by negotiation. The behavior of the RA can be described by the following actions:

Responding to IBO requests   The RA participates in the negotiation with the objective to get tasks assigned from IBOs. RAs make estimations based on a special factor, their willingness to risk. The higher their willingness to risk, the more optimistic is the estimation of the duration. A more optimistic estimation results in a shorter duration and therefore in an offering with an earlier completion time. The configuration parameter *willingnessToRiskFactor* can be configured in the XML file (see Appendix C.1). Configuring RAs that have the same role with different factors, allows to model the situation in which estimations of varying quality are provided to the IBO.

Providing status information   If the processing of a production rule cannot be proceeded due to error situations, the RA must inform the IBO in order to ensure the successful execution of the EPM.

Providing the processing result   Once a production rule has been executed, the IBO has to be informed so it can proceed with the execution of the EPM. Therefore, the RA sends the corresponding result of the execution of the production rule to the IBO.

5.1.2. Schematic Representation

Fig 5.1 illustrates the architecture of the MAS and shows how it is embedded in a business environment.

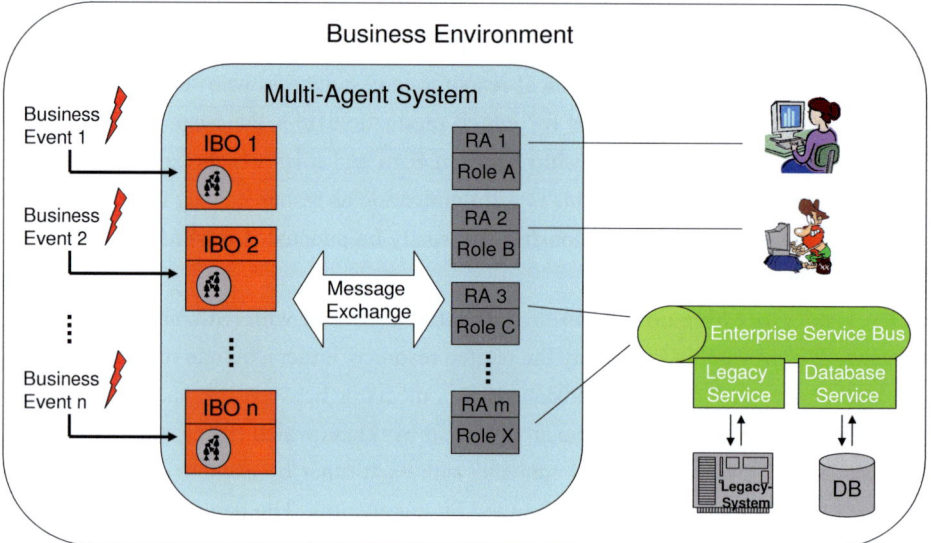

Figure 5.1.: Illustration of the MAS architecture.

For each business event that triggers the execution of a business process, a new IBO is created. This IBO is responsible for the execution of the business process. The IBOs make use of the machine learning mechanism in order to optimize the business process execution on the basis of the Key Performance Indicators (KPIs) of interest. Each RA is linked to one resource. Both agent types communicate with each other by exchanging messages.

As the RAs are either related to human or technical resources, a RA could also be related to a service, e.g. implemented as a web service. In this case, the destination node of a production rule corresponds to the outcome of a service invocation, whereas the origin nodes correspond to the data provided to the service. The orchestration of services could be done with the EPM, providing enhanced flexibility on the business process layer in a Service Oriented Architecture (SOA).

5.1.3. Messages

Agents communicate with each other by exchanging messages. A message is defined by the following elements:

- Message sender: Either the IBO, RA, or simulation control component[2].

- Message receiver: Either IBO, RA, or simulation control component. In case of a multi cast message, a role is set as receiver. All RAs with this role will get this message.

- Message type: Type of message, e.g. CALL_FOR_PROPOSAL, PROPOSAL, AWARD, among others.

- Message content: The content is dependent from the message type. Information such as the ID of the EPM to be executed or the estimated processing time can be part of the content. The message sender is not part of the content as it is already part of a message.

- Timestamp: Time when the event will be received by the message receiver. It corresponds to the earliest time the message processing can be started.

The complete list of the messages exchanged by the different agents can be found in Appendix B. A fixed priority is assigned to each type of message. This priority determines the order in which an agent processes the messages it has received, e.g. the PROPOSAL message has a higher priority than the CALL_FOR_PROPOSAL message. This allows the IBO, to consider PROPOSAL messages it has received at the same time as the CALL_FOR_PROPOSAL_DEADLINE_DUE message[3].

While running the MAS in simulation mode, a message can have the same agent as sender and receiver, for example when a timer must be realized. This kind of message is called self message. For example a self message is required when a call for proposal is made because the IBO waits until the corresponding deadline is due and evaluates then the received proposals. The same pertains to the observation of the task execution. The former corresponds to self message CALL_FOR_PROPOSAL_DEADLINE_DUE, the latter to self message ESTIMATED_TASK_COMPLETION.

5.1.4. Negotiation Protocols

Once the IBO has determined which tasks are executable, a resource needs to be determined for the processing. To find a suitable resource, negotiation is performed among the two agent

---

[2]The simulation control handles the simulation related operations within the MAS. It is explained in further detail in Sec. 5.3.

[3]First, the IBO evaluates the PROPOSAL messages received upon processing the CALL_FOR_PROPOSAL_DEADLINE_DUE message. Afterwards, PROPOSAL messages for this call for proposal are omitted. These message types are part of the negotiation protocol Adapted FIPA Contract Net Interaction Protocol Specification (ACNP) which is explained in Sec. 5.1.4.

types. An agent consists of two parts: (1) the agent core and (2) the negotiation protocol.

The agent core comprises the agent's main functionality like determining executable production rules (part of IBO) or providing the processing result (part of RA). The separation between agent core and negotiation protocol makes it possible to change the negotiation protocol without changing the respective agent core. There is the restriction that all agents within the MAS must have the same protocol.

Two very diverse negotiation protocols were implemented. One is based on an ACNP [95]. The second protocol is called picking protocol that was derived from standard workflow systems. The main difference between these two protocols is the time when tasks are assigned to RAs. If ACNP is used, tasks are assigned as soon as possible. Therefore, the RA must schedule the task it got assigned if it cannot process it immediately. If the picking protocol is used, a task is not assigned to a RA before the processing can be started by this RA. Therefore, the RAs do not use a schedule for storing tasks if the picking protocol is used. Instead of a schedule, the RAs store the announced tasks in a list.

In both protocols, a situation can occur in which a task cannot be assigned to a RA in a given time (deadline), e. g. because of the unavailability of resources. The deadline gives the IBO the possibility to react in case of deadline violations in the appropriate manner. The simplification is made, that if the deadline is exceeded, the task execution fails. If this task has been the only executable one and there is no other task currently in execution, the product model cannot be processed completely. This can be avoided by setting the deadline specific parameters appropriate. The assumption is made, that an IBO prefers the offer or request that comes with the earliest estimated completion time. In practice, there exist other Service Level Agreements (SLAs) (e. g. quality or costs), but for simplification only one criteria has been chosen.

In the following paragraphs, the ACNP is explained in detail. The picking protocol follows afterwards.

Adapted FIPA Contract Net Protocol

The messages exchanged during this negotiation protocol are shown in Fig. 5.2. This protocol comprises the following steps:

1. The IBO makes a call for proposal (CALL_FOR_PROPOSAL) for a specific production rule to all RAs with the required role. This message contains the corresponding communication ID. The communication ID is a unique ID identifying the call for proposal. At the same time, it sends a message to itself (CALL_FOR_PROPOSAL_DEADLINE_DUE) indicating when the deadline of the call for proposal made is due. By this, the IBO assures that it gets activated when the deadline is due.

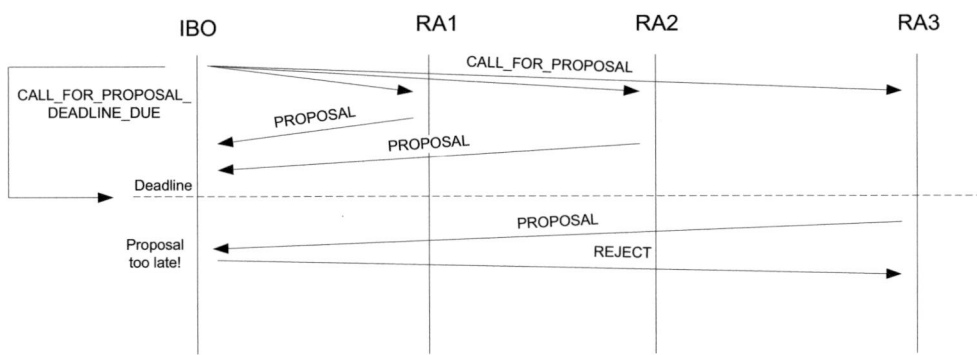

Figure 5.2.: ACNP messages.

2. RAs may respond with a proposal (PROPOSAL) to the call for proposals. The proposal contains the estimated completion time of the task. By making a proposal, the RA includes the task in its schedule marked as `pending`. A RA's schedule contains a list of timely ordered tasks, either with status `pending` or `fixed`.

3. By receiving the deadline due message previously sent, the IBO sends an award message (AWARD) to the RA with the best offer and sends a reject message (REJECT) to all other agents that submitted a proposal. If multiple best proposals exist, one is chosen randomly.

4. If no proposal has been received within the given deadline, the protocol is executed another time until a maximum number of retries is reached. If the maximum is reached, the task execution fails as mentioned above.

5. If a RA receives an award message, the status of the scheduled task is changed from `pending` to `fixed`. This means the task can be executed if the RA is not currently processing another one. If a RA receives a reject message, the pending task is removed from the schedule.

Picking protocol

To show that the generic approach makes it possible to use different negotiation protocols without the need of adapting the agent core, a very different protocol was chosen for second implementation. The so called picking protocol was derived from standard workflow systems where case workers have a work list containing tasks they are able to process. It depends on the case worker's role which task he is allowed to process. By starting work on a task, this task will be generally blocked for other case workers avoiding conflicts due to parallel work of the same task.

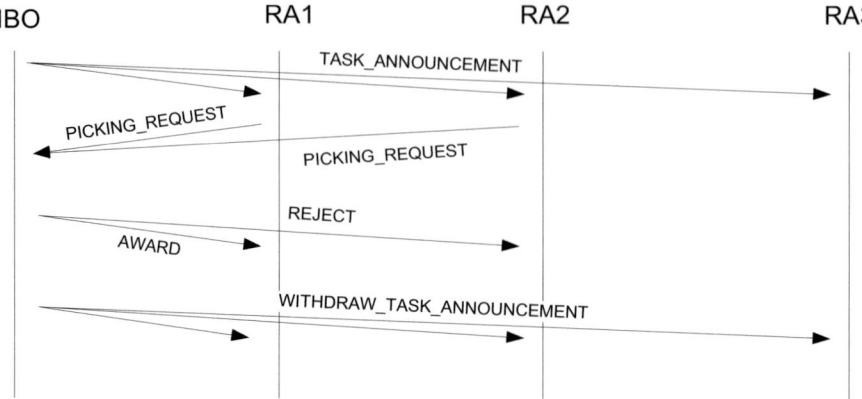

Figure 5.3.: Picking protocol messages.

This protocol is not similar to a FIFO protocol as RAs may not choose necessarily the first task in the work list / queue. For this task picking, a roulette wheel selection which is normally applied in Evolutionary Algorithms was implemented. The longer a task is waiting for execution, the higher is the probability that it is selected by a RA. This kind of selection was chosen due to performance reasons. If more than one RA can choose from several tasks at the same time, this protocol is supposed to prevent that all RAs select always the same task. Fig. 5.3 shows the message exchange during the picking protocol. The following steps are part of the picking protocol:

1. The IBO makes a task announcement (TASK_ANNOUNCEMENT) to all RAs with the required role. This announcement contains the ID of the task that needs to be executed. Moreover, the IBO sends a deadline due message to itself (TASK_ANNOUNCEMENT_DEADLINE_DUE).

2. The RAs store this task announcement and perform a request for processing (PICKING_REQUEST) if they are idle. As stated above, this picking is based on a roulette wheel selection. The picking request contains the estimated completion time allowing the IBO to select the best offer if more than one picking request is made at the same time.

3. The IBO sends an award message (AWARD) to the RA that submitted the first or best offer. Other RAs that have sent a picking request for the same task receive a reject message (REJECT). Furthermore, the IBO sends a withdraw announcement (WITHDRAW_TASK_ANNOUNCEMENT) informing RAs that a task is not longer available for processing. Then, RAs can remove the task announcement previously stored. If multiple best offers exist, one is chosen randomly.

4. If no picking request is made within the deadline, the task execution fails as mentioned above.

5.2. Main Steps of the Execution

In this section, the general steps of the MAS for the execution of EPMs are described without considering the simulation specific messages or the learning aspects. The start of an execution will be triggered by a user or automatically by a system. The trigger causes the MAS to create a new IBO. This IBO gets the information which product model it has to execute (START_PROCESSING). The first task of the IBO will be the determination of the executable production rules. This requires the analysis of the product model to retrieve all leaf information nodes and the production rules creating them. These are the executable production rules at the beginning of the execution. For each of these production rules, the IBO has to find a suitable resource for the execution. The role attribute of a production rule indicates which resources are capable of the execution. The negotiation between the IBO and the capable resources is done on the basis of the configured negotiation protocol (see Sections 5.1.4 and 5.1.4). The result of the protocol is the assignment of a production rule to a resource. When a resource is done with the execution of a production rule it provides the result to the IBO (by sending a TASK_COMPLETED message). On the basis of this result, the IBO determines the next executable production rules. If the processing is delayed, the IBO sends a RE-SOURCE_AGENT_STATE_REQUEST message to the resource that is processing the delayed production rule. Additionally, it sends a RESOURCE_AGENT_STATE_REQUEST_DEAD-LINE_DUE to itself to assure that it gets activated even if the RA does not send an answer. The RA answers by sending a RESOURCE_AGENT_STATE_INFO message that contains the state of the RA. If the RA is in state error, the IBO reschedules the production rule. The execution of one EPM finally stops when the value of the root information node has been generated.

5.3. Simulation Component

To simulate the execution of EPMs with the help of the MAS, a component is required for the control of the simulation. For this kind of control, messages are exchanged with the different agents. For example to inform a RA that the current task has been finished. This is implemented in the simulation control component.

The following aspects must be defined for the simulation:

- the simulation method

- distribution and calculation of inter-arrival times and durations

- simulation data for different scenarios (cases)

In the following sections, each aspect will be reviewed and its realization discussed.

5.3.1. Sequential Discrete Event Simulation

The simulation of the MAS is implemented as a Sequential Discrete Event Simulation (SDES) [165, pp. 6-11]. SDES belongs to the class of event scheduling approaches which have one advantage and one disadvantage as stated in [253]: "The advantage was that it required no specialized language or operating system support. Event-based simulations could be implemented in procedural languages of even modest capabilities". While the disadvantage "of the event-based approach was that describing a system as a collection of events obscured any sense of process flow". As such, "in complex systems, the number of events grew to a point that following the behavior of an element flowing through the system became very difficult" [253].

The time is defined abstractly on the basis of discrete time slots. All messages exchanged by the agents will be stored first in a special list called future event list. This is a 2-dimensional list: The first dimension is the message timestamp, the second one is the receiving agent. By processing events one after the other, the causal order between these events will be maintained.

During the processing of an event, the future event list can be modified by inserting new events into the list. The events will be processed in the order stored in the future event list. Therefore there will be time jumps from one event to the next one.

When a new event is created, the creator of this message has to compute the timestamp of this message. This timestamp indicates when the receiver retrieves the message. Therefore the timestamp corresponds to the earliest time the receiver can start the processing of the message.

In SDES the simulation time does not advance when an event is processed. In the simulation, message transportation is assumed to need no extra time.

As agents only react on messages, timers must be realized by sending self messages. In a "real world" implementation an IBO would have an internal timer in order to determine when a deadline is due, for example when the IBO waits for responses to a call for proposal.

It can be configured, that an agent has only limited resources. This is done on the basis of the maximum number of messages, an agent can process in one time slot (see Appendix C.1). If there are more pending messages than the agent can process at once (per time slot), the agent can process only the messages with the highest priority until the limit is reached. The remaining messages stay in its in-queue. The agent sends itself a SELF_ACTIVATION message in order to complete the message processing during the next time slot. Older messages have always a higher priority than newer ones in order to maintain the causal order.

5.3.2. **Probability-based Calculations**

The simulation requires the calculation of various values such as durations and costs. In simulation approaches such calculations are generally based on probability distributions or defined by constant values. If the calculations are based on probability distributions, pseudo-random samples are taken from the respective probability distribution using a Pseudo-Random Number Generator (PRNG).

Accordingly to [134], a PRNG generates random numbers by deterministic recursive rules, formulated in terms of simple arithmetic operations. Thus, the generated numbers can at best be pseudo random and it has to be ensured that the PRNG generates numbers that are sufficiently "random" for the intended use. This means that the quality of the results is dependent on the quality of the PRNG. For example, in the area of cryptography there exists a variety of attacks that can be launched against random number infrastructures [310]. "The standard random number generator provided within Java is fine for most purposes, however it does not adequately meet the needs of large-scale scientific applications, ..." [62]. Due to this reason, RngPack[4] was selected as PRNG. RngPack is a PRNG package for Java which was developed for large-scale scientific applications.

In the iEPM simulation, either constant or distributed values can be specified. In the following, an overview on the available probability distributions and their usage is given:

- The gamma distribution: $p_{\alpha,\beta}(x) = \frac{1}{\beta^{\alpha}\Gamma(\alpha)}x^{\alpha-1}e^{-\frac{x}{\beta}}$, $\alpha, \beta > 0$

    - estimated processing duration of a production rule

    - actual processing duration of a production rule

    - duration of a resource break down (non-availability)

- The (negative) exponential distribution: $p_{\beta}(x) = \frac{1}{\beta}e^{-\frac{x}{\beta}}$, $\beta > 0$

    - inter-arrival time between EPMs to be executed

    - inter-arrival time between break downs of a resource

The gamma distribution is often applied for processing times as it has the advantage that the values are greater than zero (e.g. in contrast to the normal distribution). The (negative) exponential distribution and the Poisson distribution are often used to model arrival processes. The Poisson distribution is strongly related to the negative exponential distribution. An introduction to the usage of probability distributions in the context of business process simulation is given in [286]. Further probability distributions can be easily added to the prototype by altering the configuration and the pseudo-random generator specific classes.

---

[4]RngPack web site: http://www.honeylocust.com/RngPack.

As described in Section 5.1.1 various error situations may occur. The delays in completion of production rules can be provoked by defining different α and β parameters for the estimated and real processing duration, e.g. α is set to 100 and β is set to 1 for the estimated processing duration, and α is set to 200 and β is set to 1 for the real processing duration. This leads to an estimated mean processing time of 100 and to a real mean processing time of 200. Thus, the mean delay is 100 time units.

As the EPM approach depends on the generated values of information nodes, a set of so called *execution data instances* must be specified that assign pre-defined and consistent values to the destination nodes of all production rules. Based on this data, different scenarios can be specified, e.g. in a credit application process, two different execution data instances could be specified, one instance leading to an approval, and another one leading to a reject of the application. During the simulation, each product model instance is either uniformly assigned to one of these execution data instances or based on the probability provided (depending on the configuration).

5.3.3. Analysis of Experiments

Process performance data obtained on the basis of metrics permits studying causalities and potential performance improvements. Therefore, for each experiment a variety of performance measures (KPIs) is calculated. The following performance measures are computed:

Workload (average and variance) The workload of a resource is calculated by summing up the time the resource is working on production rules and dividing this sum by the simulation duration. The average workload is calculated per resource and for all resources (total workload). This measure can be used for analyzing whether the work is evenly distributed among the available resources.

Average number of IBOs per interval The number of IBOs corresponds to number of EPMs in execution as for each EPM instance one IBO is created that is responsible for the execution. Thus, this measure indicates the volume of work. This measure is calculated for a fixed interval (1,000 time units). A continuous increase during the simulation may indicate that the number of available resources is not sufficient for processing the arriving EPMs.

Average costs per EPM This measure is calculated by summing up the costs incurred due to the execution of EPMs divided by the number of EPMs. This measure is important if a cost reduction strategy is pursued.

Average throughput per interval This measure is calculated by summing up the finished EPMs divided by the interval length (1,000 time units).

Average number of messages exchanged per EPM This value is calculated by summing up all messages exchanged between IBOs and resource agents (without considering simulation related messages) and dividing this sum by the number of EPMs.

Average waiting time per task The waiting time per task for one EPM is calculated by summing up all times tasks are waiting for a resource and dividing this sum by the number of tasks. High waiting times are an indicator that the number of available resources is not sufficient.

Average cycle time The cycle time of an EPM is the total elapsed time from the beginning to the end of the processing of one EPM.

Note that cycle time, costs and throughput are the most common KPIs used in businss process optimization. The simulation data is collected in fixed time intervals (each 1,000 time units). Additionally, an interval for the warm-up period can be specified. If such an interval is specified, simulation data is not collected within this interval. This allows the removal of the initialization bias[5]. Note that these performance measures are of quantitative nature. Qualitative metrics such as customer retention data and process flexibility could be integrated as well. For a detailed discussion on business process performance measures see [162].

5.3.4. Activities during a Time Slot

As mentioned above, the simulation proceeds in time slots[6]. During each time slot, a sequence of activities is processed in a special order:

1. The simulation control creates and sends messages to other agents if required. This is required for example in case of creation of new IBOs or status changes of RAs.

2. For each agent that has messages stored for the current time slot in the future event list (this could also be the simulation control itself), the simulation control proceeds as follows:

   a. All pending messages for one agent are sent to its message in-queue.

   b. Afterwards the agent is activated to process these messages (each agent is activated sequentially). As there are no dependencies between agents during one time slot, parallel processing is simulated in this way[7].

---

[5]An initialization bias may exist due to unrealistic initial conditions, e.g. the "system is empty". This can be handled by dividing the simulation into an initialization phase and a data-collection phase. For information on warm-up or transient periods see e.g. [50].

[6]Remember that time jumps are possible due to the SDES approach.

[7]The simulation control is activated as last agent in order to have all necessary information about events of the next time slot.

3. All events for the current time slot stored in the future event list are deleted by the simulation control.

4. Finally, the simulation control determines the next time slot for which events are stored in the future event list. This will be the following time slot.

5.3.5. Message Exchange During Simulation

Due to the simulation approach, additional messages as described in Section 5.2 are required. The messages exchanged by the agents and the simulation control are depicted in Fig. 5.4.

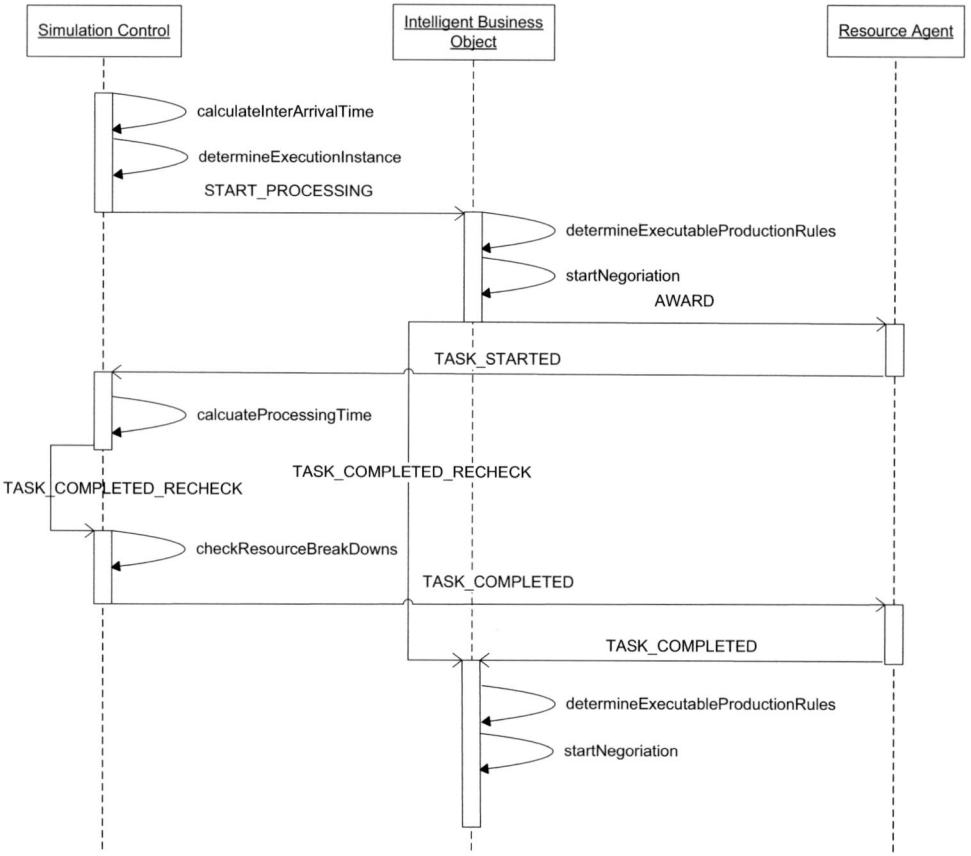

Figure 5.4.: Messages exchanged during simulation.

The simulation control calculates the inter-arrival time of the EPMs based on the exponential distribution. For each EPM to be executed, the execution data instance is selected. A new IBO is generated and a START_PROCESSING message is sent to it. By the START_PROCESSING message, this IBO gets the information which EPM it has to execute.

The first task of the IBO will be the determination of the executable production rules. Which of the executable production rules is actually executed is decided by the IBO on the basis of a machine learning approach that is explained in the next chapter.

The negotiation between the IBO and the capable resources will be done on the basis of the configured negotiation protocol. The result of the negotiation is the assignment of a production rule to a resource (by sending an AWARD or PICKING_GRANTED message). Furthermore, the IBO sends itself an ESTIMATED_TASK_COMPLETION message. This message allows the IBO to observe the processing.

The RA informs the simulation control about the processing start. The simulation control calculates the actual processing time. But it does not send directly a TASK_COMPLETED message to the RA. First, it send a TASK_COMPLETED_ RECHECK message to itself. The simulation control checks whether the processing of the production rule was interrupted due to the non-availability of the resource (break down). If yes, the new (delayed) processing time is calculated and another TASK_ COMPLETED_ RECHECK message is sent. This happens until the processing has not been interrupted. Finally, the TASK_COMPLETED message is sent to the RA. Part of this message is also the processing result, that the simulation control determines with the help of the execution data instance.

Then, the RA sends a TASK_COMPLETED message to the IBO. The IBO checks whether the root node has been generated. If not, it has to determine the next executable production rules. If the root node has been generated, it stops the processing by canceling the tasks that are still in execution (CANCEL_TASK) and the tasks in negotiation. Furthermore, it sends a PROCESSING_COMPLETED message to the simulation control.

The simulation control may also send a SET_RESOURCE_AGENT_STATE message to a RA. This is done when the non-availability of a resource should be simulated. Another message is sent to the RA to reactivate the RA. Both messages depend on the configured inter arrival times and durations. If a resource is not available anymore and is currently processing a production rule, the IBO that has scheduled this production rule is informed about the interruption of the processing by the RA.

5.4. Implementation Details

The development of MASs requires strong programming skills [228]. The usage of an agent framework or tool facilitates the development only to a certain extent. The extend of the support is depending on the maturity of the framework. Some frameworks are accompanied by an IDE with varying functionalities. But independent from the framework chosen, programming skills are still essential. Therefore, Java was chosen due to the personal experience and skills with this programming language.

There exist several agent-oriented programming languages and MAS platforms for Java that are freely available (for a survey see e.g. [33]). These platforms provide general techniques for the relevant aspects such as agent communication and coordination. Particularly, there are agent-based simulation models [228].

Despite the fact that tool support facilitates the development, it was decided to implement the MAS from scratch. As it was not intended to implement threading or parallelization, the implementation effort was manageable. Furthermore, the implementation from scratch provides the highest degree of flexibility.

In Fig. 5.5 the main classes of the MAS are depicted. In order to preserve the clearness of the class diagram, some of the associations between classes were omitted. Furthermore, helper classes as well as enumerations were not included in this class diagram. As the learning mechanism is introduced in the next section, the class diagram does not contain any learning specific classes. See Section 6.2 for implementation details regarding the intelligent behavior.

In the following a brief insight in the functionality and dependencies of the different classes is given:

The class `AnalysisControl` in package `analysis` contains the `main` method for starting the different kinds of experiments (either for a single configuration or a comparison of two configurations). Furthermore, it is responsible for the calculation and output regarding the statistical analysis.

The package `control` contains the classes for storing the configuration parameters specified in the XML configuration (`ConfigurationParameter`) file and the hard-coded constants (`ExperimentalSetup`). Class `ModelControl` encapsulates three main classes: `SimulationSystem` which implements the discrete event simulation, `EnterpriseModel` which comprises the enterprise model, and `MultiAgentSystem` which consists of the agent specific classes existing in the MAS.

The `FutureEventList` implements the functionality of the future event list which is part of the discrete event simulation approach. The `SimulationControl` controls the simulation by sending simulation related messages to the agents, like START_PROCESSING or TASK_COMPLETED messages. Part of the TASK_ COMPLETED message is the processing result which is determined based on the execution data instance (`ExecutionInstance`) assigned to the EPM.

The `EnterpriseModel` consists of the organization model (`OrganizationModel`) in which the relationship between roles and RAs is stored and the defined EPMs (`Executable-ProductModel`).

The package `messaging` contains the message handling specific classes. Classes derived from `CommunicationObject` retrieve messaging capabilities. Furthermore, the class `Agent` is capable of storing messages which is necessary if an agent cannot process all messages in one time slot due to its limited resources. Two kinds of message types exist: `MultiCastMessage`

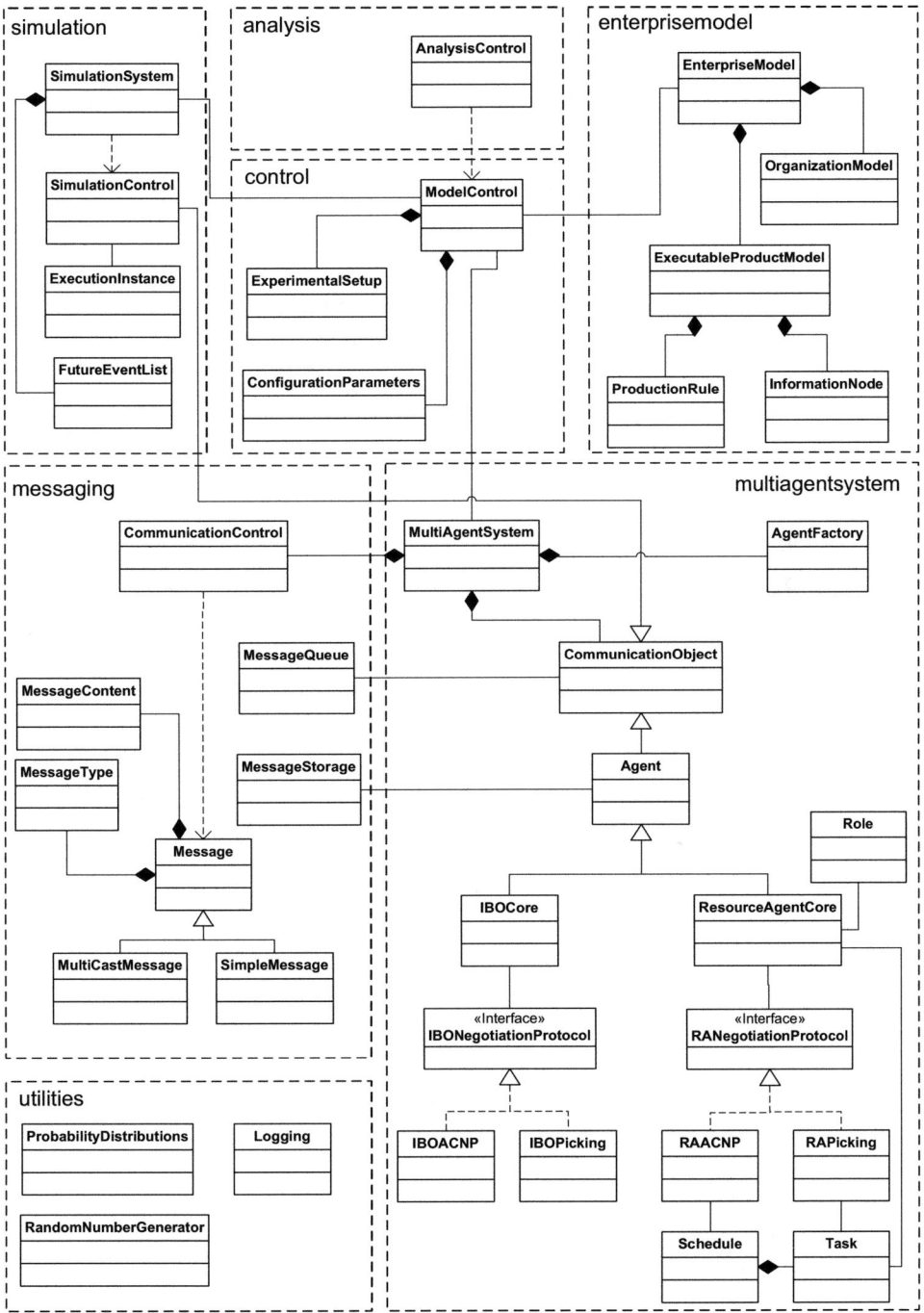

Figure 5.5.: Class diagram of the MAS showing the main classes.

for sending messages to all RAs with a specific role, and `SimpleMessages` for sending a message to a specific receiver. The message transportation is done by class `Communication-Control`.

RAs and IBOs are derived from class `Agent` as they may have limited messaging capabilities. In contrary to RAs and IBOs, the `SimulationControl` is derived from the class `CommunicationObject` as it must have unlimited messaging capabilities. RAs and IBOs have a core which implements the main behavior without the negotiation aspects. The negotiation specific aspects are part of the classes that implement the interface `Negotiation-Protocol`. These classes require different classes, e.g. class `RAACNP` implements the negotiation protocol ACNP on the RA side. It requires a schedule for scheduling the pending[8] and fixed[9] tasks. RAs and IBOs are created by the `AgentFactory`.

The dynamic behavior of the agents was modeled by using statecharts. Fig.5.6 shows an excerpt of the IBO statechart[10].

---

[8]The RA temporarily stores a task in its schedule marked as pending if it has sent a proposal to the IBO but has not received an answer yet.

[9]Tasks marked as fixed can be processed by the RA as it has received an award from the IBO.

[10]The complete statechart contains all messages the IBO receives. Accordingly, a statechart for the RA was created containing all messages the RA receives.

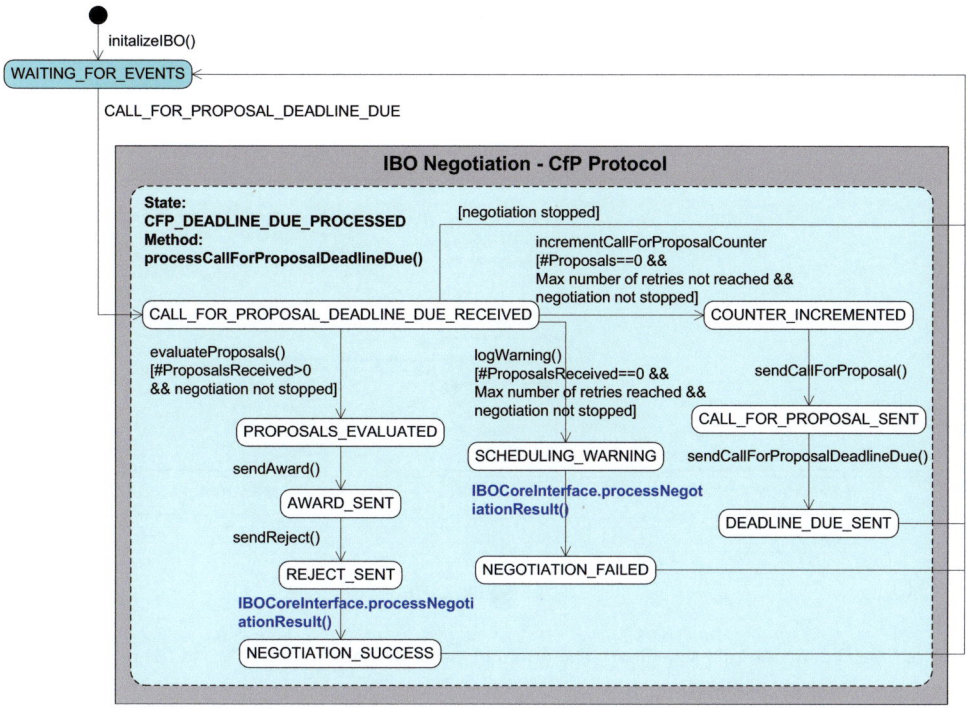

Figure 5.6.: Excerpt of the IBO statechart. It shows the different states and function calls for the message CALL_FOR_PROPOSAL_DEADLINE_DUE.

This excerpt shows the different states of an IBO if a message of type CALL_FOR_PRO-POSAL_DEADLINE_DUE is processed. After the initialization of an IBO it is in state WAIT-ING_FOR_EVENTS. If a message of type CALL_FOR_PROPOSAL_ DEADLINE_DUE has to be processed, method `processCallForProposalDeadlineDue` is called. If proposals have been received, the best one is determined and AWARD and REJECT messages are sent. If no proposal has been received, either another call for proposal is initiated or the negotiation has failed for this production rule. If the negotiation has been stopped, there is nothing to do.

Statecharts have also been used for modeling the more complicated dynamical aspects of the MAS as their usage facilitates the implementation. One such example is the statechart for production rules (see Fig.5.7).

Without considering the learning mechanism related classes, the MAS consists of *207* classes with around *31,500* total lines of codes. In order to achieve the correctness of the implementation, the software was thoroughly tested.

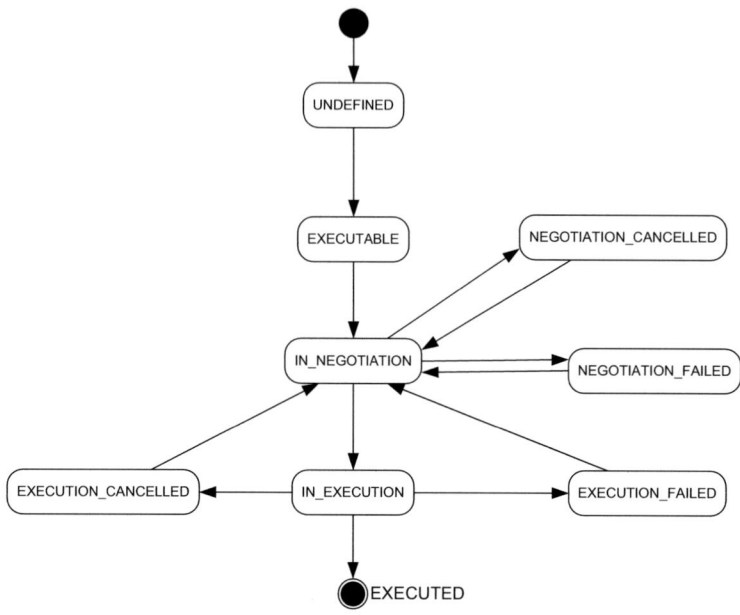

Figure 5.7.: Production rule statechart. The different states of a production rule and the possible transitions are depicted.

5.5. Testing the Implementation

In order to assure the correctness of the implementation, tests were implemented and executed by using the JUnit testing framework[11]. JUnit is a simple, open source framework to write and run repeatable software tests.

Moreover, the simulation results of the intelligent Executable Product Model (iEPM) approach were compared with other approaches such as business process simulation and queuing networks. If two approaches are compared, the respective experimental setups must be identical or at least similar in order to receive comparable results, i.e. the EPM must not provide more flexibility than the queuing network or process model.

In the following, an example is given based on an EPM in which two production rules are executed in a sequence (see Fig. 9.1(c)). Different roles (worker and manager) are assigned to the production rules. Two resource agents are available for each role. The experimental setup is defined as in Sec. 9.2.1.

The simulation results are compared with a queuing network using the Java Modeling Framework[12]. The corresponding queuing network is depicted in Fig. 5.8.

The labels in Fig. 5.8 have the following meaning: S1 and S2 correspond to the first and

---

[11]This framework is available on the website http://www.junit.org.
[12]This framework is available on website http://jmt.sourceforge.net/

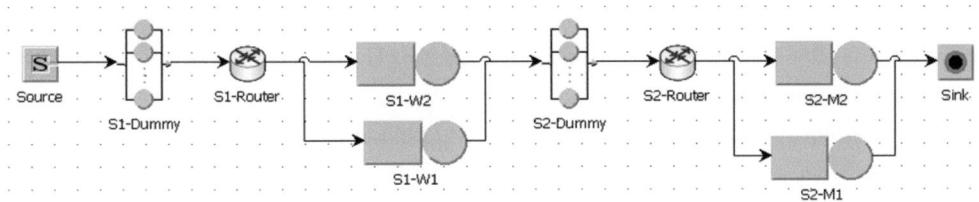

Figure 5.8.: EPM "linear" as queuing network.

second production rule, respectively. The MAS has a certain communication overhead, for example due to negotiation. This overhead is modeled by adding two stations with constant durations (four time units) corresponding to the overhead per production rule. These stations are denoted by dummy. A router needs to be modeled in order to assign jobs to the different stations. The minimum queue length is set as routing strategy. Each resource agent corresponds to one station, W1 and W2 correspond to the resource agents with role worker and M1, M2 to the resource agents with role manager.

Two scenarios are analyzed. In the first scenario, the workload is low (arrival rate: $\beta = 500$) and in the second one high (arrival rate: $\beta = 55$). The results for both scenarios are listed in Table 5.1. As one can see, both approaches lead to similar values regarding the cycle time and throughput which is the desirable result.

Table 5.1.: Comparing iEPM with queuing networks.

Scenario I		
Method	**Cycle Time**	**Throughput**
iEPM approach	209.0259 ± 0.218	$1.9966\text{E-}3 \pm 0.022\text{E-}3$
Queuing Network	209.8167 ± 4.2918	$2.020\text{E-}3 \pm 0.061\text{E-}3$
Scenario II		
iEPM approach	506.0928 ± 12.1772	0.01817 ± 0.00006
Queuing Network	502.6524 ± 20.0483	0.0180 ± 0.0006

The Java Modeling Framework doe not provide complex routing mechanisms, i.e. it is not possible to route a job based on process data as in the EPM. Therefore, further comparisons were conduced with the commercial business process simulation tool iGrafx using other EPM structures and scenarios. All of these comparisons were conducted successfully. An example of such an experiment is given in Sec. 9.6 by means of the "new customer" business process.

5.6. Related Work

In this section, the related work regarding MASs is discussed. The execution of business processes is performed with the help of a workflow or Business Process Management (BPM) engine which is either composed by regular software components, software agents (agent-based workflow [51, 266]) or both (agent enhanced workflow [141, 265]). There are two different approaches in agent-based workflow:

(1) Either, business processes are explicitly defined in a model or (2) the business process knowledge is distributed among the different agents participating in the process.

Also, MASs based on the Belief-Desire-Intention (BDI) model have been suggested. BDI agents act on the principles of beliefs, desires, and intentions. Agents basically identify the system state on the basis of their beliefs and perform their actions then by executing plans for achieving the objectives defined. These plans may have pre-conditions, based on which the plans become feasible.

The approach described in [109, 45] makes use of BDI agents. The execution order of the activities belonging to a business process is specified on the basis of plans. As in the iEPM approach, alternative execution paths can be specified. But then, each execution path must be specified within a separate plan, so the model for a business process is divided into separate plans. The iEPM approach has the advantage that execution alternatives can be defined in one model. Furthermore, the iEPM provides a compact representation for these alternatives. In order to provide the same degree of flexibility as the iEPM approach, each execution path results in one plan. Especially for complex business processes, this would not be an efficient approach. Also, there are no learning capabilities integrated. The pre-defined execution path is chosen under consideration of the objectives in a fixed manner.

Another approach, also employing BDI agents is described in [75]. As execution paths are defined on the basis of plans, the same limitations concerning complex business processes exist as stated above.

5.7. Summary

In this chapter, the MAS for the execution of EPMs was introduced in detail. The different agent types with their objectives and responsibilities were explained, particularly how the IBO manages the execution of EPMs using a simple strategy in the basic version of the MAS without learning capabilities. This strategy was termed *execute-all* approach. This strategy is characterized by the immediate execution of all executable production rules.

Furthermore, the simulation approach based on a SDES was explained extensively. The output analysis capabilities of the simulation were clarified, specifically the available performance measures (KPIs) were discussed. Moreover, an insight into the implementation of the MAS was given. Finally, the related work regarding MASs was discussed. In the next chapter, the question is answered, how the IBO can learn to execute the EPMs more efficiently than the basic execute-all approach. This efficiency gain will be achieved by applying a hybrid machine learning approach termed iEPM approach.

6. The Hybrid Machine Learning Approach

> "Experience is simply the name we give our mistakes."
>
> Oscar Wilde

In this chapter, the hybrid machine learning approach *intelligent Executable Product Model (iEPM)* for managing the control flow of business processes is introduced. In particular, the learning mechanism is capable of autonomously optimizing the execution of Executable Product Models (EPMs) in terms of the defined Key Performance Indicators (KPIs).

The motivation for applying approximation techniques was given in Chapter 4, by discussing the complexity of the EPM optimization problem. It was shown that the corresponding decision problem of a special case is already NP-complete. As stated in Chapter 1, machine learning provides a mechanism for automatically adapting to changing operating conditions which is an important issue for coping with the today's highly dynamic business environments. Therefore, machine learning is applied to the optimization problem.

The business processes are modeled as EPM as explained in Chapter 3. The flexibility provided by the EPMs is utilized by intelligent agents, which constitute a Multi-Agent System (MAS). The MAS was described without the learning capabilities in Chapter 5. The learning mechanism is integrated in the Intelligent Business Object (IBO) as this agent type is responsible for the execution of an EPM and has to decide which execution path should be taken. The learning mechanism aims at the efficient execution of EPMs by optimizing the objectives defined, under consideration of the current system state.

This chapter is outlined as follows: First, the iEPM approach is explained in detail. It is explained, how the machine learning approaches are adapted so they can be integrated and deployed in the MAS. Furthermore, different heuristics are applied as part of the performance optimization. In the next section, insights into the implementation challenges and details are given, followed by the related work regarding machine learning. The chapter concludes with a short summary.

6.1. Intelligent Executable Product Model

The fundamental machine learning concepts were introduced in Sec. 2.6. These concepts are the basis of the hybrid machine learning approach iEPM which is explained in the following.

As described in the introduction of this chapter, the IBO is equipped with learning capabilities. Thus, the IBO shall learn the efficient execution of EPMs. The learning capability of an

IBO is based on a hybrid machine learning approach termed iEPM. The IBO's behaviour is optimized by using Relational Reinforcement Learning (RRL) in combination with a heuristic. Before the iEPM approach is explained in detail, considerations regarding the integration of RRL in a MAS scenario are discussed.

6.1.1. Adaptations on Relational Reinforcement Learning

There are several aspects that need to be considered when using RRL in a MAS scenario, especially how actions of different agents interfere with each other. In a single agent scenario an agent chooses an action based on the current state. The next state is dependent only on this state and the action chosen. In a MAS, actions of other agents can interfere and influence the following state. Also depending on the design, an agent cannot be sure about the current state in a parallel scenario. This could be the case if the state changes between the observation of the state and the execution of the chosen action. In the MAS for executing EPMs, actions of other IBOs only affect the workload of resources, or more precisely the time a task waits for execution.

The MAS for executing the EPMs is designed as decentralized control system. This paradigm is not supposed to be changed for the learning mechanism. For deciding about the execution path(s) the IBO has a certain knowledge which can be distinguished between static and dynamic knowledge. Static knowledge is constant, whereas dynamic knowledge changes over time. An example of static knowledge is information about the product model structure. Examples of dynamic knowledge are information regarding the workload and error proneness of resources or the status of information nodes and production rules. Other aspects could be considered as well, such as priority and Service Level Agreements (SLAs), but are neglected for simplification and are subject for future work.

The learning approach is based on two main principles: individual learning and emergence. In the past it was shown in experiments that individual learning can produce group behavior that influences the performance positively [68]. The iEPM learning mechanism is designed to achieve this as well. In the iEPM approach each IBO learns by itself with the common goal to optimize the defined KPIs such as the average cycle time or costs. If this can be proved by experiments based on simulation, individual agent learning was sufficient.

6.1.2. RRL-GA

An intelligent control flow mechanism for learning optimal execution decisions is to employ RRL using probabilistic policies as in [132]. But instead of using a policy gradient method, a GA is applied for reasons described in Sec. 2.6.1. The hybrid machine learning approach *RRL-GA* that was developed is depicted in Fig. 6.1.

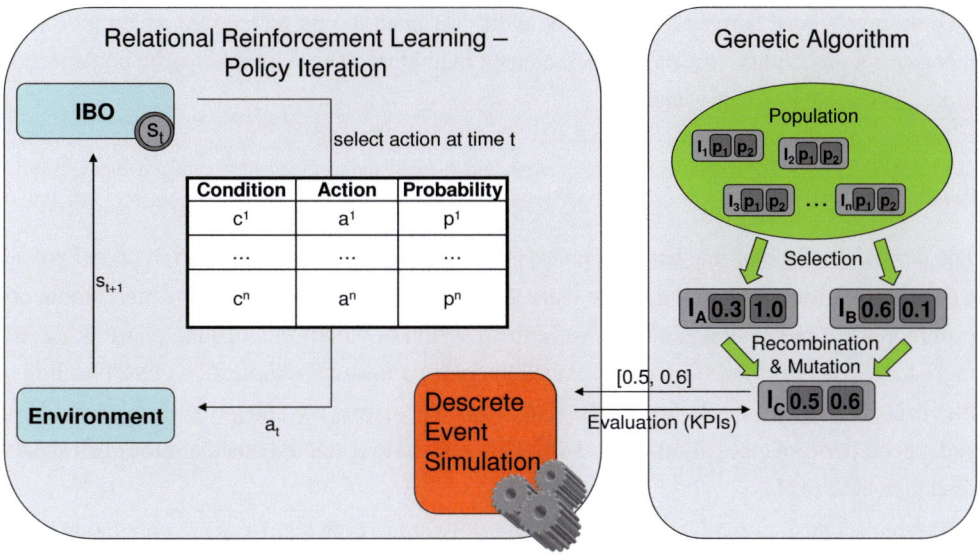

Figure 6.1.: The hybrid machine learning approach RRL-GA based on Relational Reinforcement Learning and Genetic Algorithm. The GA is depicted based on a policy containing two rules. In general, the number of genes of an individual corresponds to the number of policy rules.

The probabilistic policy contains a finite set of n predefined rules. Each rule has a condition c^i, an action part a^i, and a probability p^i $(i = 1, .., n)$. In order to select an action based on this policy, the condition part of each rule is consecutively evaluated until one evaluates to true. If the condition is fulfilled, the corresponding action is executed based on the assigned probability. If the action is not executed, the next rule in the policy is tested. This approach is termed *Policy Iteration*.

The probabilities of the policy must be determined for each scenario using an appropriate heuristic in an offline learning phase. A scenario pertains to a specific experimental setting which comprises the EPM, arrival rate, available resources, among others. The use of a heuristic requires the calculation of the fitness value for each probability vector. This means that for each evaluation, a simulation run is carried out. In general all agents use the same policy and probabilities in the simulation. Reinforcement learning requires a feedback mechanism, so the agents are capable of learning optimal actions. In standard reinforcement learning, agents receive a reward from the environment. In RRL-GA, the agents do not get a reward directly. Instead, the simulation runs are evaluated based on a fitness function which is composed of KPI of interest such as cycle times, throughput, or costs. The fitness function together with the policy rules must be carefully defined in order to achieve the desired behaviour of the agents.

As heuristic, a real-vector Genetic Algorithm is applied in order to find the probabilities for the pre-defined policy. An individual of the population contains one chromosome. The chromosome's gene is related to one probability assigned to one policy rule, so an individual represents a probability vector. For each created individual a simulation has to be performed in order to evaluate its fitness value.

6.1.3. RRL-PSO

The drawback of the offline learning phase is that for each fitness calculation of an individual, a time consuming simulation must be carried out. As GAs generally require a high number of evolution iterations to find good solutions, the duration of the offline learning phase is accordingly long. Therefore, the GA was replaced by Particle Swarm Optimization (PSO) leading to the machine learning mechanism *RRL-PSO*. PSO has several advantages such as ease of use and a good performance. In some cases PSO has proved to result in better solutions in a shorter time than GAs [32].

The replacement of the GA by PSO is straightforward as both heuristics are population based and require the evaluation of each individual or particle. As the individuals in GA, the particles in PSO represent a probability vector. Thus, the solution vector x is bounded by $i = 1, \cdots, n$: $0 \leq x_i \leq 1$. The number of parameters n equals the number of rules defined in the policy.

Fig. 6.2 depicts the learning mechanism RRL-PSO. In comparison to Fig. 6.1, only the right side of the figure is changed by replacing GA with PSO.

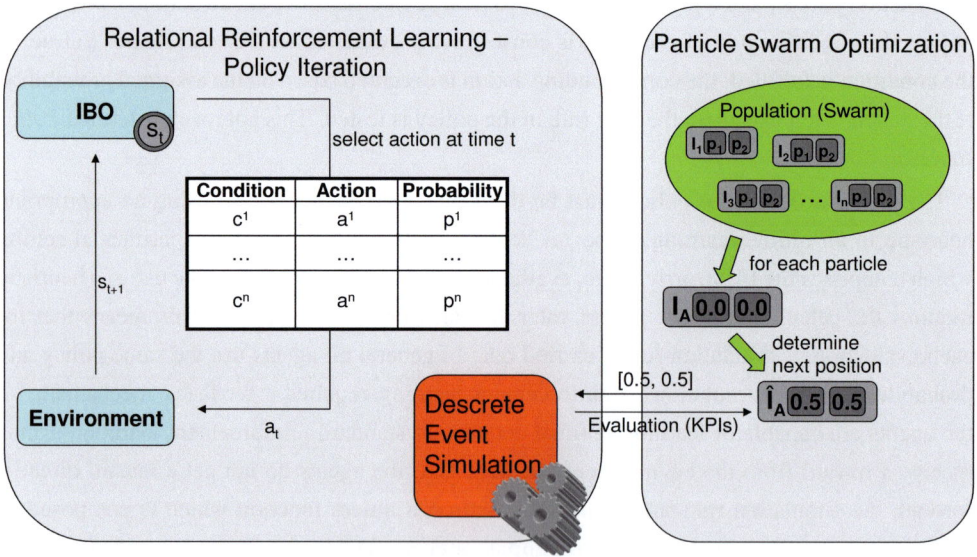

Figure 6.2.: The hybrid machine learning approach RRL-PSO based on Relational Reinforcement Learning and PSO. The PSO is depicted based on a policy containing two rules. In general, the dimension of the positions of the particles corresponds to the number of policy rules.

As aforementioned, the learning approaches RRL-GA and RRL-PSO require a policy and a fitness function that define the behaviour of the IBOs. In the following, both aspects are discussed in more detail.

6.1.4. Fitness Functions and Policies

The learning mechanism has the objective that IBOs learn the efficient execution of EPMs which means the optimization of KPIs. First, the KPIs of interest must be selected. These KPIs are used within the fitness function which is composed of the weighted KPIs. Once the fitness function is defined, a policy must be developed that leads to the adequate behaviour of the IBOs, and therefore to the optimization of the selected KPIs.

As the learning in RRL takes place by receiving a reward from the environment, the decisions of the IBOs are evaluated by the fitness function. Therefore the policy and the reward calculated on the basis of a fitness function determine the behaviour.

There is also the possibility that the IBO decides not to finish the execution of an EPM. As the cycle time is calculated for finished EPMs only, the mean cycle time is not negatively affected if some of the EPMs are not finished. This must be considered when creating the fitness function. If the IBO decides not to execute EPMs, the number of IBOs in execution is increased. Thus, the mean number of IBOs in execution can be used as penalty in the fitness function.

In Sec. 2.6.1 it was mentioned that RRL provides the possibility to reuse a learned policy on different problems. This kind of knowledge transfer is known as generalization. Generalization is successful if a previously learned policy delivers good results when it is applied on different product model structures. If such knowledge transfer should be achieved, the predefined policy must not be too product model specific. In general, two aspects must be considered when creating a policy:

1. Determining the level of abstraction

2. Defining the policy rules (condition / action pairs)

The policies are defined on the basis of PROLOG predicates. PROLOG was selected as it provides the functionality required for the Policy Iteration approach. The system state can be represented by a set of PROLOG predicates. Moreover, PROLOG queries are executed in order to evaluate whether the conditions of the defined policy are fulfilled. An introduction of PRO-LOG and the explanation of its application in the learning mechanism is given in Appendix D. Furthermore, the appendix contains the list of available PROLOG predicates.

In the following, two policies defined on different levels of abstractions are described which are used in the conducted experiments. The first one considers the product model structure and the current execution status. Here, production rules and information nodes are mainly used as predicates. The other one is defined on the level of variants. In the next section, an example of a fitness function is given. Afterwards, the two policies are listed and explained.

Fitness Function

As described above, the fitness function is composed of the weighted KPIs of interest. In Sec. 5.3.3 all measures (KPIs) are listed which are calculated for each simulation. All of these measures can be used in the fitness function. In the following example, the average cycle time is selected as KPI:

$$f(\vec{x}) = maxD - meanCT - 10 * meanN \qquad [6.1]$$

where *maxD* is the duration of the simulation[1], *meanCT* is the average cycle time, *meanN* the average number of IBOs in execution, which is used as a penalty. By this the IBO is forced to execute the EPM. Without this penalty, the IBO could decide not to complete the execution.

In the following, the different policies are explained.

Production Rules and Information Nodes

The first policy makes use of relations and objects reflecting the product model structure and the execution status using relations on information node and production rule level, for example:

- `in_execution(prodRule0)` means production rule with ID 0 is in execution.

- `creates_info_node(prodRule1, infoNode2)` means that by executing production rule with ID 1, the information node with ID 2 is created.

The following manually created policy was used in the experiments (see Table 6.1):

The seven policy rules are defined on the basis of PROLOG predicates[2]. The rules can be explained as follows: Rule (1) executes a production rule that creates the root node. Rule (2) does not execute an executable production rule if there is another active one. With the `do_nothing` predicate the IBO has the possibility not to perform any action. By applying rule (3), an executable production is not executed if another production rule is in execution that creates the same information node. Rule (4) executes an executable production rule if there is not another one in execution. Rule (5) assures that rescheduling is performed. In this case, a failed production rule is executed again. Rule (6) cancels a production rule if an alternative has already created the destination rule. This avoids unnecessary processing. Rule (7) executes a production rule that is executable.

---

[1]This technical constant ensures that the fitness values are nonnegative which is a requirement of the Java Genetic Algorithm Package (JGAP).

[2]Appendix D contains the list of defined PROLOG predicates.

Table 6.1.: The predefined policy utilizing the structure of an EPM by considering production rules and information nodes.

No	Condition	Action	P
1	executable(X), creates_info_node(X,Y), root_info_node(Y)	execute(X)	p_1
2	executable(X), active_production_rules(Y),Y>=1	do_nothing()	p_2
3	executable(X), in_execution(Y), creates_info_node(X,Z), creates_info_node(Y,Z), not created(Z)	do_nothing()	p_3
4	executable(X), not in_execution(Y)	execute(X)	p_4
5	execution_failed(X)	execute(X)	p_5
6	in_execution(X), creates_info_node(X,Y), created(Y)	cancel(X)	p_6
7	executable(X)	execute(X)	p_7

Variants

The introduction of variants allows the modeling on a higher level of abstraction. Additionally, background knowledge about the failure rates and workload of resources can be used by the IBOs. The policy described in Table 6.2 makes use of variants as well as background knowledge.

The rules can be explained as follows: Rule (1) requests work load information if it is not available and has not been requested yet. Rule (2) assures that work load information is kept up-to-date. Rules (3) and (4) pertain to error proneness information. The behavior is analog to rule (1) and (2). Rule (5) activates the variant with the shortest estimated execution duration[3]. If work load information and resource failure rates are available, they are used in the calculation of the estimated duration. Rule (6) assures that if the activated variant is still the one with the smallest estimated duration, its processing is continued. Rule (7) switches the variants if there is a shorter one than the activated.

For acquiring information about resource failure rates and workload of resources, a message exchange between IBO and the resources is required. An additional penalty can be configured that results in a fixed delay of each request regarding failure rates and workload.

6.2. Implementation Challenges and Details

This section describes the implementation challenges and details of the learning mechanism. The development of the learning approach and its implementation has passed through multiple phases and optimization efforts.

The definition of different policies does not only include the combination of predicates and objects, but may also lead to changes on the Java implementation as well. This is the case, when

---

[3]An activated variant results in the execution of one or more production rules (see Sec. 3.3.3).

Table 6.2.: The predefined policy making use of variants.

No	Condition	Action	P
1	not workloads_available, not workloads_requested	request_workload	p_1
2	workloads_available, workloads_outdated, not workloads_requested	request_workload	p_2
3	not failure_rates_available, not failure_rates_requested	request_failure_rate	p_3
4	failure_rates_available, failure_rates_outdated, not failure_rates_requested	request_failure_rate	p_4
5	number_of_activated_variants(No), No=0, minimum_weighted_duration(Variant, Duration)	activate(Variant)	p_5
6	activated_variant(VariantA), weighted_variant_duration(VariantA,DurationA), minimum_weighted_duration(VariantB,DurationB), DurationA=<DurationB	proceed(VariantA)	p_6
7	activated_variant(VariantA), weighted_variant_duration(VariantA,DurationA), minimum_weighted_duration(VariantB,DurationB), not VariantA=VariantB, DurationA>DurationB	switch(VariantA,VariantB)	p_7

new objects or relations are introduced such as variants or additional background knowledge. Therefore the creation of a policy may imply a high implementation and refactoring effort. On the other hand, the available predicates and objects can easily be combined to a new policy.

6.2.1. Optimization Efforts

Various efforts in performance optimization for applying the GA in the offline learning phase have been realized, among these are:

Abort criteria for stopping a simulation run:

For some probability vectors, the MAS is not able to execute EPMs at all or only a small amount. That leads to an explosion in the number of product models in execution, resulting in a high memory usage and very long simulation times. If the increase is too high in a fixed interval, the simulation is stopped and a constant fitness value is assigned to the corresponding individual indicating a bad solution.

Database for storing already evaluated individuals:

The number of different solutions is dependent on the precision of the probability values and the number of policy rules. There can be an efficiency gain if the simulation duration is long, and the number of different solutions limited.

Despite the optimizations performed, the duration of the offline learning phase was still not satisfying. As aforementioned, the drawback of the offline learning phase is that for each fitness calculation of an individual, a time consuming simulation must be carried out. Therefore, further optimization efforts followed up:

Runtime optimization:

After profiling the application and removing some minor performance bottlenecks, the operations of the PROLOG engine for updating the system state and the queries for evaluating the conditions were identified as main bottleneck. More than 50 percent of the duration was consumed by these operations.

As solution, a PROLOG cache that stores the results of evaluated operations was identified. If a system state occurs more than once, the result of the first conducted evaluation can be taken from the cache and the time consuming PROLOG engine operations can be omitted. The more often a state occurs, the higher is the efficiency gain of using a PROLOG cache.

Therefore, the system states that occur during a simulation were analyzed. Some of the relations defined caused a state explosion as they were based on timestamps. In order to achieve an improvement by using a PROLOG cache, these relations had to be changed. For determining whether the workload information should be updated or not, relations were used containing timestamps (e. g. `current_time(timestamp)` and `last_workload_request(timestamp)`). These relations were replaced with a simple relation (`workloads_outdated`) that has the same reasoning capabilities. Also, instead of defining relations with specific durations, ordinal scales were used. The changes of these relations resulted in a significant reduction of the number of different system states and solved the state explosion problem.

State abstraction:

Another way to decrease the number of different states is state abstraction. In the first version of the learning approach, relations and objects on information node and production rule level were used as described in Sec. 6.1.4. By introducing variants, the state and the actions could be modeled on a higher level of abstraction.

Using a PROLOG cache in combination with a significantly reduced number of states due to appropriate relations and state abstraction resulted in a reduced simulation duration of RRL-GA by approximately factor 10.

As stated in the Sec. 6.1.3, in some cases PSO is supposed to achieve better results in a shorter time in comparison to GA. As the further reduction of the simulation duration would increase the practicability of the learning approach, the GA was replaced by PSO. This actually led to a significant performance gain. In Chapter 9, the experiments comparing the performance of the learning approaches RRL-GA and RRL-PSO are discussed.

6.2.2. Implementation of the Learning Mechanism

The logic part is implemented making use of a PROLOG engine. Each IBO has to use the PRO-LOG engine to represent its state. Additionally, PROLOG queries are executed for determining whether a policy condition is fulfilled. Two Java PROLOG engines were evaluated thoroughly: TU-Prolog[4] and SWI-Prolog[5]. TU-Prolog has the advantage that multiple instances of this engine can be created. Thus, using TU-Prolog allows each IBO to have its own PROLOG engine in which the current state perceived by the IBO is stored. In SWI-Prolog only one instance can be created. Therefore, if there are multiple IBOs, the PROLOG engine must be reseted and the state of the current IBO must be created by storing the corresponding predicates. Despite the fact, that the state of the SWI-PROLOG must be reseted and created from scratch, it has a better performance than TU-Prolog. Therefore, SWI-Prolog has been chosen.

The GA was realized with the Java Genetic Algorithm Package (JGAP)[6]. The PSO algorithm was realized with the JSwarm-PSO package[7].

The main classes of the MAS were already described and depicted as UML class diagram in Sec. 5.4. Due to space limitation, only the main classes of the learning mechanism are depicted in Fig. 6.3.

In the following, the classes are briefly described. As the IBO shall learn the efficient execution of EPMs, it has to be provided with the corresponding functionality. Class `IBOCore` comprises the core functionality of the IBO. Several classes are derived from that core. Class `IBO_Basic` implements the basic execute-all approach without any learning capabilities. Here, the IBO executes immediately all executable production rules.

The classes `IBO_RRL` and `IBO_RRL_V` implement the use of the machine learning mechanism for deciding which production rule to execute. The IBO of type `IBO_RRL` makes use of the learning mechanism based on the level of production rules and information nodes, whereas the IBO of type `IBO_RRL_V` makes use of variants. These IBO types are equipped with a brain. The brain perceives the system state by using class `StatePerception` and stores the state in class `PersistentState`. The brain utilizes the PROLOG engine to represent the system state as well as for evaluating the conditions of the policy. PROLOG queries are executed only

---

[4]TU-Prolog web site: www.alice.unibo.it:8080/tuprolog.
[5]SWI-Prolog web site: http://www.swi-prolog.org.
[6]JGAP web site: http://jgap.sourceforge.net.
[7]JSwarm-PSO web site: http://jswarm-pso.sourceforge.net.

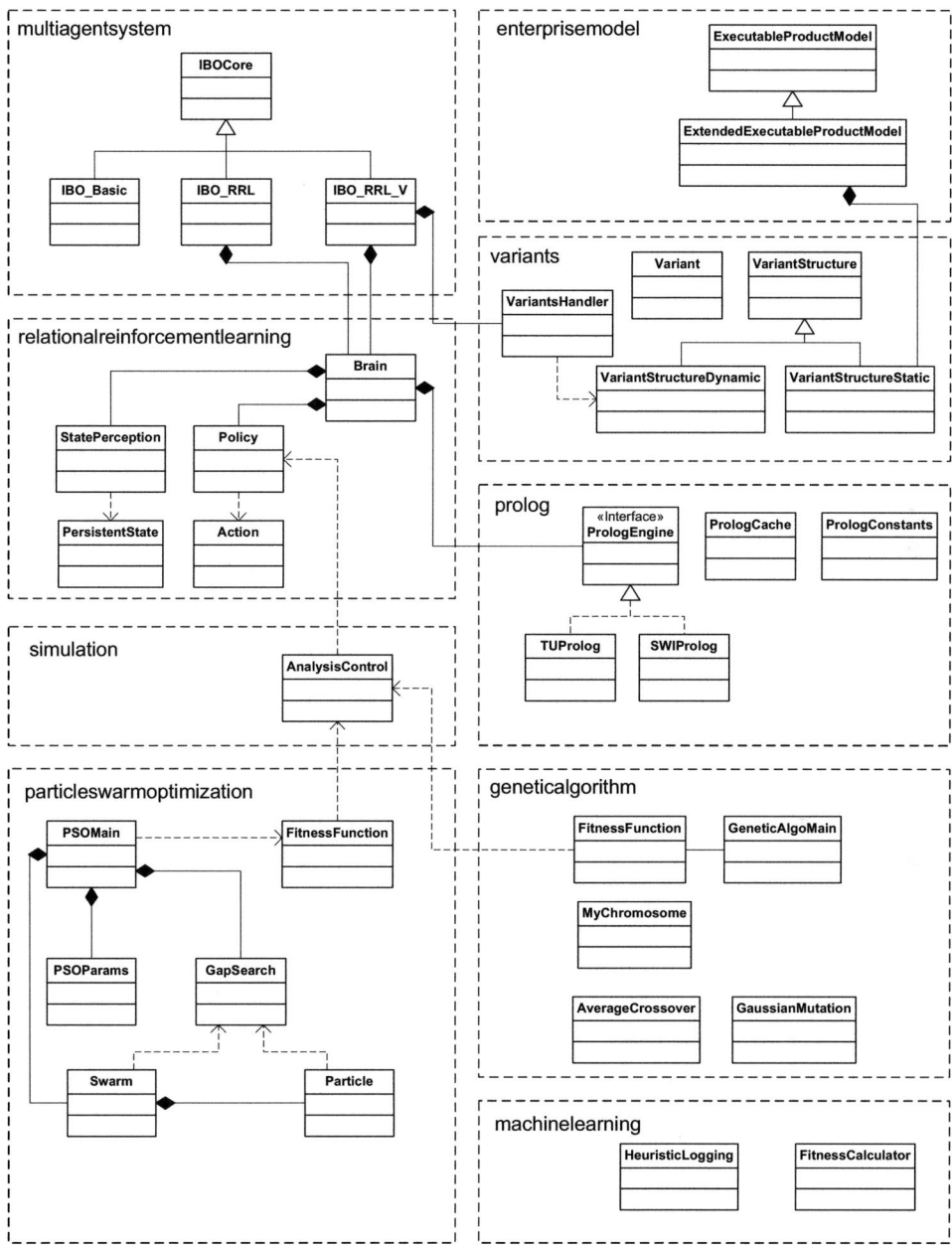

Figure 6.3.: Class diagram - the main classes of the learning mechanism.

if the system state is not already stored in the PROLOG cache. The interface `PrologEngine` was implemented in order to facilitate the integration of different kinds of PROLOG engines. The TU-Prolog and SWI-Prolog engines are integrated. The policy is stored in class `Policy`. The brain determines which actions the IBO has to perform. Thus, the brain passes an object of type `Action` to the IBO which finally performs this action. The use of variants led to the development of various classes. Class `ExtendedExecutableProductModel` is derived from `ExecutableProductModel` and contains the algorithm for determining the variants of the product model. The determined variants are stored in class `VariantStructureStatic`. As further variants may be generated during the execution of an EPM[8], class `Variant-StructureDynamic` was implemented in which the dynamically generated variants are stored.

Class `VariantHandler` manages the current state of the variants. This comprises the feasibility check as well as calculations such as for the estimated remaining processing duration or costs. The packages `particleswarmoptimization` and `geneticalgorithm` contain the PSO and GA related classes, respectively.

The number of learning mechanism related classes is *46* with around *8,250* total lines of codes. Together with the classes of the MAS, the total number of classes sums up to *253* with around *39,750* total lines of codes. The implementation was tested thoroughly as described in Sec. 5.5.

6.3. Related Work

One of the most frequently used machine learning approaches in Business Process Management (BPM) is the Genetic Algorithm (GA). It have been used in different areas of BPM:

- Process Mining: A technique for discovering models from event logs. These models may describe processes, organizations, and products [284]. GAs are used to discover models with non-trivial constructs or when dealing with the presence of noise [71] Obviously process mining has a different objective as the iEPM approach. The same pertains to the data mining approach introduced in [98]. Nevertheless, process mining can be used within the iEPM approach applied as intelligent business process optimization methodology (this application method is introduced in Sec. 7.2).

- Business process design: The approach in [311] uses a GA for determining the optimal order of activities in terms of the defined objectives. But as the process models are determined during design time, there is no possibility to change the model during runtime leading to the same restrictions as the regular BPM approach.

---

[8]The static structure contains variants which consider at most one iteration through existing cycles. If a cycle is traversed more than once during the execution, a new variant is dynamically created.

- Resource Allocation: There exists one approach in this area in which Swarm Intelligence is applied [234]. But this approach has another focus as Swarm Intelligence is applied for dynamic task assignment in ad-hoc processes.

Only two papers ([66], [282]) could be identified, addressing the combination of MAS and RRL. Both papers are based on the same approach and introduce a classification using properties of the learning problem and agent abilities, e.g. full observability or communication capabilities. They carried out preliminary experiments for the blocks world problem, as well as experiments for a planning task with full observability. Providing full observability would not be efficient for the iEPM approach as it would increase drastically the communication within the MAS.

6.4. Summary

In this chapter, the iEPM approach has been introduced that allows the IBO to make informed decisions regarding the execution of an EPM. The hybrid learning mechanisms RRL-GA and RRL-PSO utilize a hand coded policy that describes the behaviour of the agents. The IBO performs its actions on the basis of RRL using a Policy Iteration approach. The fitness function is used in the offline learning phase (as part of the heuristic) in order to evaluate the behavior of the agents. The application of the heuristic allows the optimization of the agent's behaviour. In order to evaluate the behaviour, a simulation run has to be executed. The fitness function is composed by the weighted KPIs of interest that are calculated during the simulation run. Furthermore, the details about the implementation and optimization efforts were explained. How the iEPM approach can be applied in practice is part of the next chapter.

7. Practical Application Methods

"Good ideas are not adopted automatically. They must
be driven into practice with courageous patience."
Hyman Rickover (1900 - 1986)

In this chapter, the applicability of the intelligent Executable Product Model (iEPM) approach in practice is studied. The chapter begins with the introduction of the two application methods of the iEPM approach in practice. First, it is explained how the iEPM approach can be applied as intelligent Business Process Management (BPM) engine. The next section shows another application scenario, in which the iEPM approach is used within an intelligent business process optimization methodology.

Afterwards, it is explained how the learning mechanism can be integrated into commercial workflow or BPM tools. This integration has the advantage that it combines the complete functionality of a commercial tool with the capabilities of the learning mechanism.

Another important aspect regarding the applicability in practice is the scalability of the implementation. Therefore, a scalability evaluation is performed. The identified limitations of the scalability are discussed and adequate suggestions for improvement are made.

The chapter ends with a brief summary.

7.1. Intelligent BPM Engine

The intelligent agents of the Multi-Agent System (MAS) can act as a BPM engine and control autonomously the execution of business processes on the basis of Executable Product Models (EPMs). Fig 7.1 depicts how the MAS can be embedded in a business environment as intelligent BPM engine using the GA as heuristic. In this application method, there exist in fact two MASs, one that is responsible for the real execution of the EPMs, and a second one that is used in the offline learning phase for simulating the execution of EPMs.

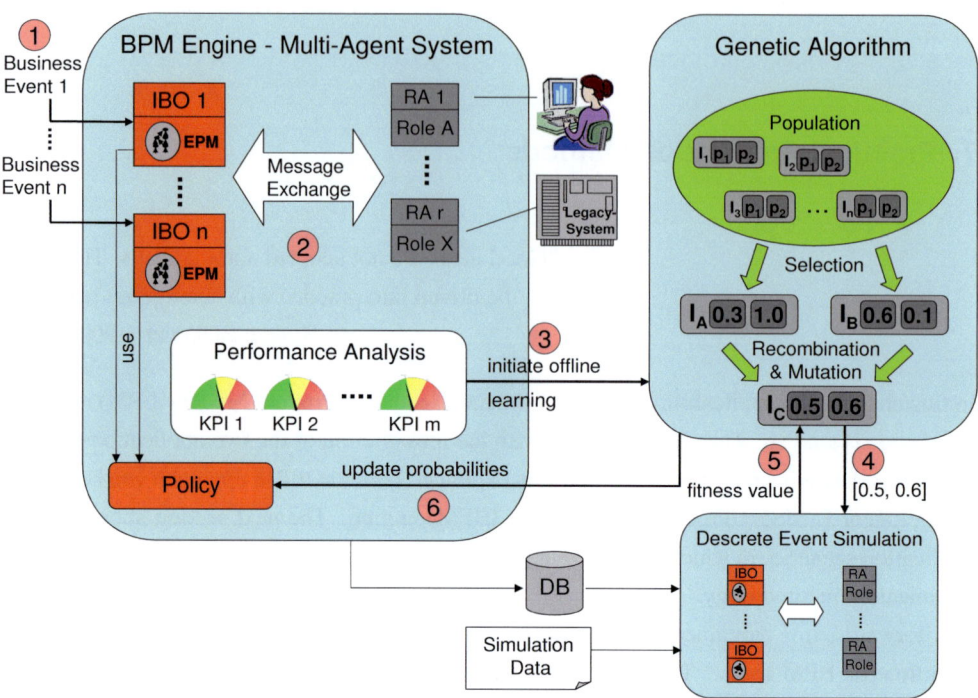

Figure 7.1.: The iEPM approach applied as intelligent BPM engine. (1) Business events trigger the
creation of IBOs and the execution of the corresponding EPM. (2) IBOs and RAs collaborate
in order to execute the EPMs. During the execution, operational data is stored in a database
and the defined KPIs are calculated. (3) If necessary, the offline learning phase is triggered.
The GA is illustrated on the basis of a two dimensional vector. (4) For each created individual
a discrete event simulation is carried out. The probability vector as well as operational and
simulation data are provided as input. (5) Result of this simulation is the fitness value. (6)
The policy is updated with the optimal probability vector found by the GA.

For each business event that triggers the execution of a business process, a new Intelligent
Business Object (IBO) is created. This IBO is responsible for the execution of the corresponding
EPM. The IBOs use the Policy Iteration technique in order to optimize the business process
execution regarding the Key Performance Indicators (KPIs) of interest. During the execution,
the performance is analyzed by calculating the KPIs of interest. The IBOs can adapt their
behaviour autonomously by initiating the offline learning phase. This means that a discrete
event simulation is carried out that runs in parallel to the real execution. Once the offline
learning phase has determined a new probability vector, the policy is updated. Thus, the IBOs of
the intelligent BPM engine act on the basis of this updated policy. The offline learning phase can
either be triggered periodically or if one of the KPIs is above or below a defined threshold. The
simulation utilizes either data that is manually provided or data that is automatically retrieved
from the operational database. The latter one, requires the analysis of the operational data in

order to retrieve and calculate simulation related settings, such as processing durations or arrival rates.

The offline learning phase can not only be used for the autonomous adaptation, but also for performing what-if analyzes in terms of a business forecast. The operational data could be enriched with prognosticated data. For example, a prospective increase of the business volume due to Christmas trade can be simulated by setting an corresponding arrival rate. By carrying out a simulation, the resulting KPIs can be analyzed and corrective actions can be identified and performed if necessary.

The iEPM approach may also be used in a hybrid approach with agents and users. The intelligent agents could make explained suggestions about the execution order of tasks, then the end users could have the final decision. Another hybrid approach is based on a process model and an EPM. The intelligent agents can find alternative execution paths using the EPM if the execution of the business process fails.

The advantage of this practical application method is that the execution of business processes is optimized autonomously. Thus, there is no manual work necessary in order to find alternative process designs. Of course, only the flexibility provided by the EPM can be utilized. If new requirements have to be implemented or if activities have become obsolete, the EPM must be adapted manually in accordance to the new situation.

In Sec. 9.7, the advantage of this application method is discussed in more detail by conducting several experiments on the basis of two business processes, a mortgage and a credit application business process.

7.2. Intelligent Business Process Optimization

The second practical application method is the use of the iEPM learning mechanism in an intelligent business process optimization methodology.

Despite the fact the business process simulation is not widely used in practice, it is well-known for its ability to assist in long-term planning and strategic decision making [331]. Simulation software allows the evaluation of different process designs and facilitates a what-if analysis. One major scenario comprises the evaluation of a specific number of process designs, e.g. an as-is process is compared with suggested to-be processes. The analysis based on standard process models requires the creation of one process model for each design. The iEPM approach has the advantage that it already contains the alternative execution paths. Thus, there is no need for modeling process models with different structures.

In the next section, the main steps of the intelligent business process optimization methodology are explained.

7.2.1. Main Steps of the Methodology

The main steps of the intelligent business process optimization methodology are depicted in Fig. 7.2.

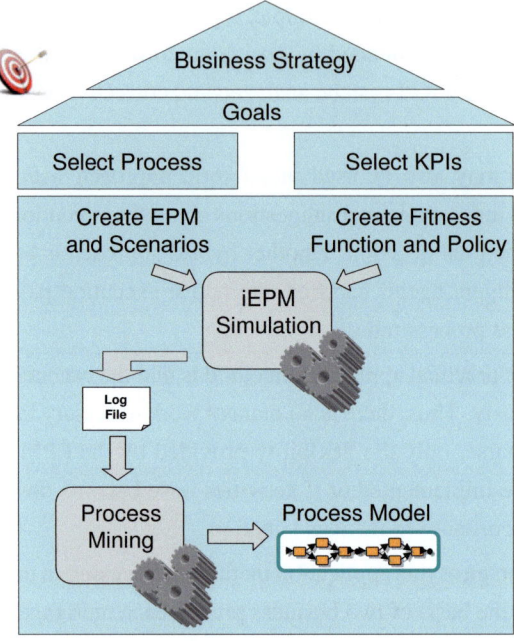

Figure 7.2.: The second practical application method of the iEPM approach: using iEPM as intelligent business process optimization.

The methodology is a top-down approach. First, the business strategy is defined from which the goals are derived in the successive step. Based on the goals derived, the business process to be automated or optimized is selected (see also the different levels of business processes in Sec. 2.1.2). Furthermore, the KPIs of interest are chosen together with their target values. The target values are required in order to assess the optimization effort and project success.

Once the business process is selected, the corresponding EPM has to be created and the scenarios of interest must be determined. A scenario setting defines the available resources, arrival rates, durations, among others. The fitness function is created on the basis of the previously chosen KPIs. Additionally, a policy must be provided based on which the intelligent agents make their decisions.

In the next step the iEPM approach is used to simulate the execution of the EPMs. The EPM with the scenarios of interest and the fitness function together with the policy are the input data for the iEPM simulation. In the first step, the heuristic is used determine an optimal probability vector. In the next step, the policy is configured with this probability vector and another simulation is executed During this simulation, the execution of each EPM is logged. Listing 7.1 shows an example of logging data.

Listing 7.1: Example of log file content.

```
processing started: instance id: 0, product model id: 0, time slot: 1
production rule executed: instance id: 0, product model id: 0, production
    rule id: 0, createdValue: '2', resource agent id: 2, start time slot: 3,
    end time slot: 103, number of failed executions: 0, delay: 0
processing completed successfully: instance id: 0, product model id: 0,
    time slot: 104
```

The logging data in Listing 7.1 comprises the three different kind of events which are logged:

- The start of the execution of an EPM.

- The end of the processing of the production rules.

- The end of the execution of an EPM.

This logging data is the basis for the analysis with process mining tools. Using a process mining tool facilitates the analysis of the different kinds of process instances. Each kind of instance is graphically depicted. Furthermore, process models can be created from the logging data. The open source process mining toolkit ProM[1] was used for this analysis. This toolkit requires a specific format of the log file which is termed MXML. MXML is an XML-based format for storing process event logs. The ProM toolkit provides an import framework which allows the implementation of custom import filters. For importing the EPM log files, such a filter was implemented. Once the log file is transformed into MXML, it can be loaded into ProM and analyzed.

Based on this methodology, one can study the influences of different KPIs or scenarios on the resulting business process structure. The advantage of this methodology over regular approaches is that only one model needs to be created. In Sec. 9.7, the advantage of this methodology is discussed again in more detail on the basis of a mortgage business process. Moreover, several diagrams generated with ProM are depicted and discussed.

After introducing the two practical application methods of the iEPM approach, the possibilities to integrate the learning mechanism in BPM tools are evaluated.

---

[1] ProM website http://is.tm.tue.nl/ cgunther/dev/prom/.

7.3. Integration in BPM Engines

In this section, the focus lies on the integration of the iEPM approach in commercial BPM tools. The advantage of this integration is that it allows to make use of the complete functionality of a commercial tool and to utilize the learning capabilities of the iEPM approach at the same time. The implementation of the iEPM approach is referred to as iEPM component. The component of a BPM tool which is responsible for the execution of a business process is called BPM engine.

The integration requires an information exchange between the BPM engine and the learning mechanism. The BPM engine must be informed by the iEPM component which activities it has to execute. If an activity has been executed, the iEPM component must be informed about it as the learning mechanism must know what information has been created in order to decide which activities are executed next. Furthermore, the iEPM component requires information about the workload of the available resources.

The modeling language Business Process Modeling Notation (BPMN) provides elements for modeling incoming and outgoing events. Furthermore, BPMN is widely used in practice. Therefore, the integration is explained on the basis of BPMN. Fig. 7.3 depicts the BPMN elements that are relevant for the transformation. Transitions between these elements are graphically depicted as directed arcs.

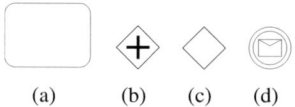

(a)   (b)   (c)   (d)

Figure 7.3.: BPMN elements. (a) represents an activity. (b) and (c) show special kinds of gateways. (b) is an AND split and join, whereas (c) corresponds to a decision. (d) depicts a message event which is used for incoming and outgoing events.

The transformation of an EPM into a BPMN model is achieved as follows: each production rule is related to one activity. The execution of an activity leads to the creation of one information node which is the destination node of the related production rule. The AND and OR dependencies must be transformed by using the available gateways of BPMN. The integration of the machine learning mechanism into a BPM tool requires an information exchange between the BPM engine and the iEPM component. This can be achieved by the event mechanism of BPMN which allows to model points for outgoing events and waiting points for incoming events. The two events that are explicitly modeled in the BPMN process model are:

infoNodeCreated By this event, the BPM engine informs the iEPM component about successful execution of an activity and the creation of the corresponding destination node. The event has three parameters: process ID, production rule ID and the value of the created information node.

executeProdRule By sending this event, the iEPM component informs the BPM engine to trigger the activation of an activity. This means that the activity appears in the inbox of the corresponding users if a human resource is responsible for carrying out the activity. This event has two parameters: the process ID and the production rule ID.

Further information exchange is necessary, which can be implemented as services as part of a Service Oriented Architecture (SOA). The following service methods are necessary for the information exchange:

startProcessing By this event, the BPM engine informs the iEPM component that a business process was started. It sends the product model ID and the process ID. The iEPM component creates an IBO which manages the execution of the corresponding EPM.

requestWorkloadInfo The iEPM component requests workload information from the BPM engine.

The usage of these events and service methods is explained by using a simple EPM having only one production rule and one information node. In Fig. 7.4 this EPM and its representation in BPMN is depicted.

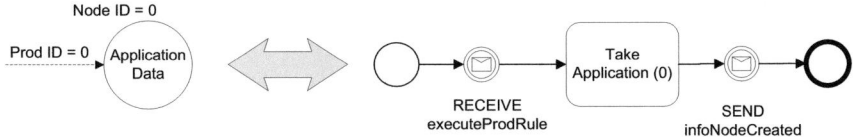

Figure 7.4.: Transformation of a simple EPM.

Fig. 7.5 illustrates the information exchange between the BPM engine and the iEPM component that takes place when the business process depicted in Fig. 7.4 is executed. In the following the numbered steps are explained: (1) A business event triggers the execution of a business process. (2) The BPM engine informs the iEPM component that a business process has been started by invoking service method `startProcessing`. Consequently, the iEPM component creates an IBO and assigns the corresponding product model to it. Furthermore, it stores the mapping between process ID and IBO ID. The IBO uses the machine learning techniques in order to decide which production rules have to be executed. For that, it may request workload information by invoking service method `requestWorkloadInfo`. (3) In the simple EPM, only one production rule is executable, thus the IBO sends the event `executeProdRule` with parameters `processID=XY`[2] and `prodRuleID=0`. This triggers the activation of activity "Take Application". (4) The activated activity is either executed by a user or technical resource. (5) Once this activity has finished, the event `infoNodeCreated` is sent to the iEPM component with parameters `processID=XY`, `prodRuleID=0`, and `value=123`. As the mapping between process ID and IBO ID was previously stored, the iEPM component forwards this event to the respective IBO. As the root node was created, the execution has been completed successfully.

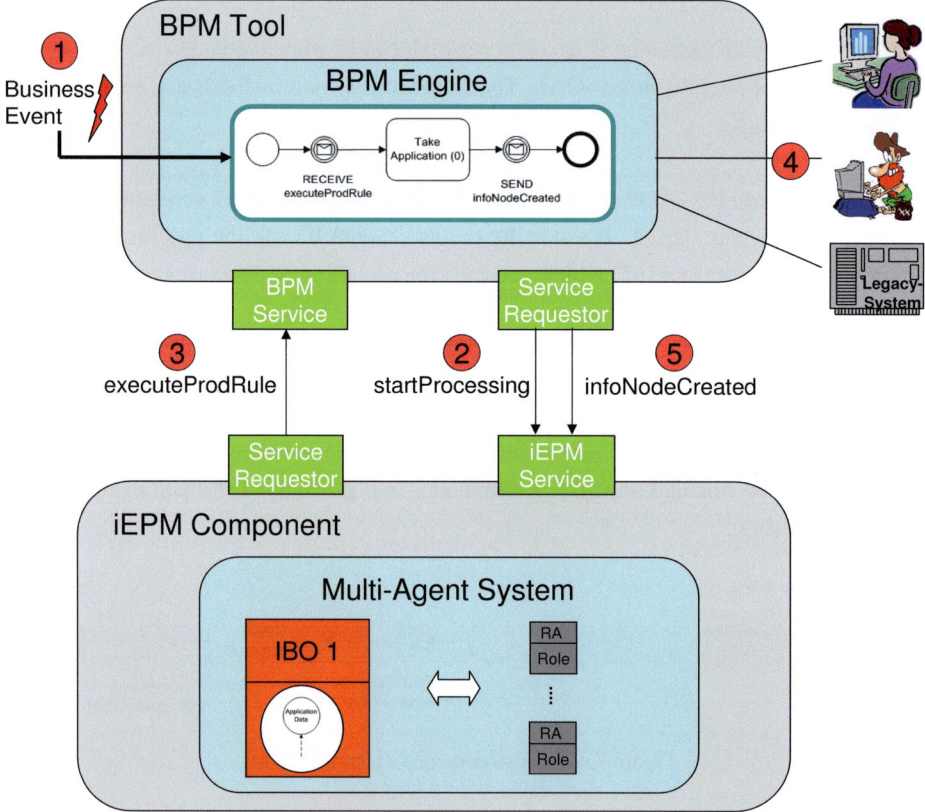

Figure 7.5.: Illustration of the information exchange between the BPM engine and the iEPM component.

---

[2]This value is arbitrarily chosen. The same pertains to parameter `value=123`.

One alternative to the suggested integration approach is the integration of the iEPM component as Java library (jar file) and the direct invocation of the respective Java classes. But this requires Java support by the BPM engine which is not necessary in the suggested approach due to the interoperability of SOA.

The complete list of transformation patterns is depicted in Fig. 7.6.

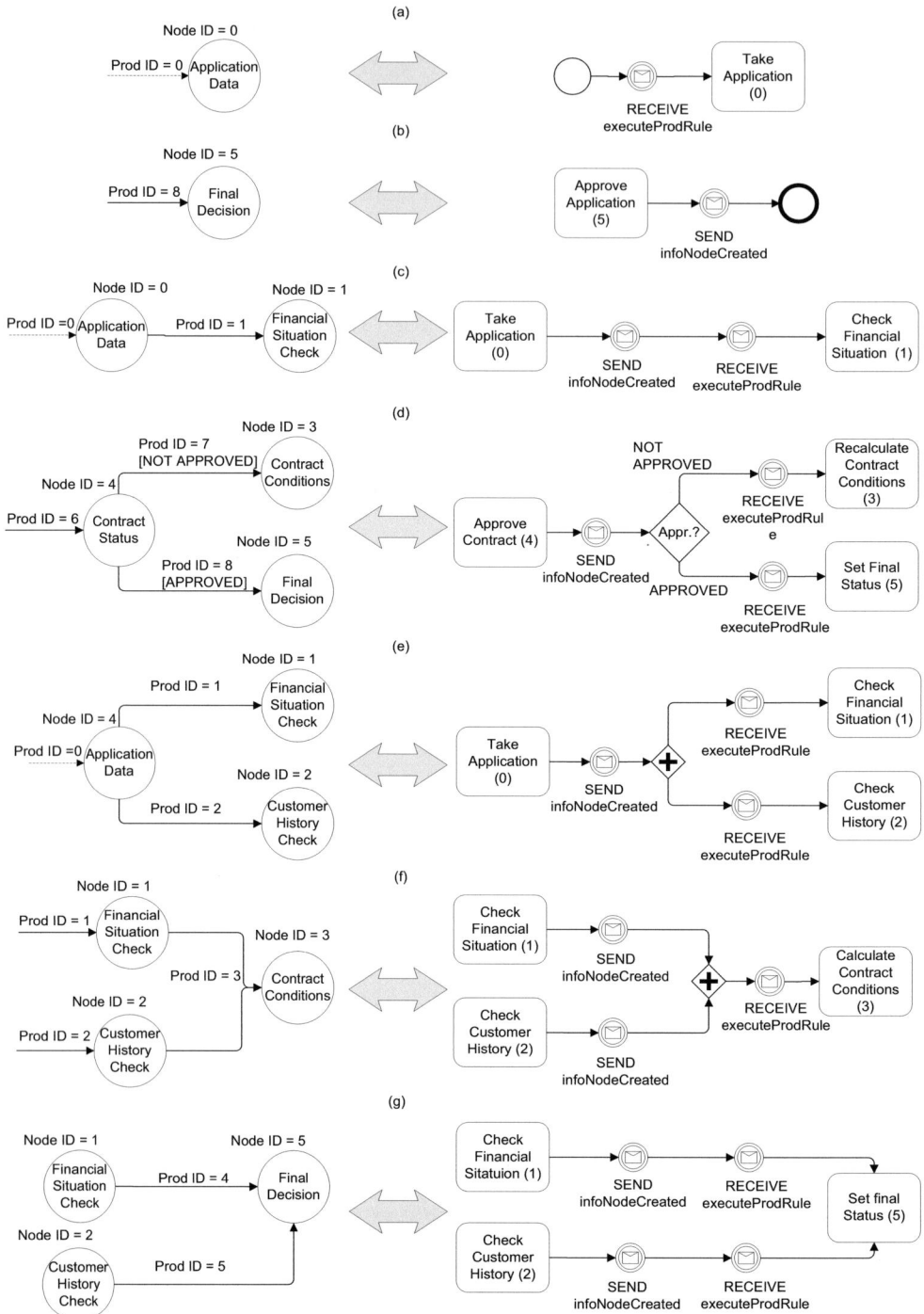

Figure 7.6.: The left side shows the different structural EPM elements and the right side the corresponding representation in BPMN.

Another example of a transformation from a more complex EPM into a BPMN process model is given in Sec. 9.6. This example is based on a "new customer" business process.

The transformation patterns depicted in Fig. 7.6 comprise the following EPM structures: (a) shows the transformation of a production rule creating a leaf node. (b) shows a production rule creating the root node. (c) shows a sequence of production rules. (d) shows how constraints are transformed into a decision. (e) shows how a parallel structure is transformed into BPMN using an AND split gateway. (f) shows how an AND dependency is transformed using a AND join gateway. (g) shows the transformation of an OR dependency.

7.4. Scalability

In [309] it was stated that the research in the area of business process optimization suffers from serious limitations in dealing with the scalability requirements and complexity of real-life processes. Therefore, evaluations of the simulation duration are conducted in order to identify bottlenecks and areas for improvement.

In the following, three influencing factors are analyzed: The number of IBOs, the number of Resource Agents (RAs), and the number of execution paths (variants). The number of IBOs equals the number of IBOs that are concurrently being processed. The number of RAs equals the number of RAs available per role. The number of execution paths equals the number of different execution paths in the EPM. Moreover, the effect of using workload and failure rate information is evaluated.

7.4.1. Experimental Setup

Each experiment is repeated 20 times. The average simulation duration in milliseconds is calculated for an increasing number of entities, such as EPMs, RAs and execution paths (variants). For each run, only one input parameter was increased, e.g. in run "EPMs" only the number of EPMs were increased while the other parameters were fixed. A simple EPM is used for the experiments. The EPM contains two production rules in a sequence. Moreover, a different role is assigned to each production rule. Thus, there are resources agents with two different roles.

A special generator was implemented in Java that allows to create EPMs with different structures. For the experiments, EPMs with two different structures were created. The first structure is an EPM, that has a varying number of execution paths. For example, the EPM with 1024 execution paths comprises 1024 different variants, each variant consisting of two production rules. Thus, this EPM comprises 2048 production rules and 1025 information nodes. The EPM with a varying number of execution paths is depicted in Fig. 7.7.

The second structure is an EPM, that has a varying number of intertwined variants. This

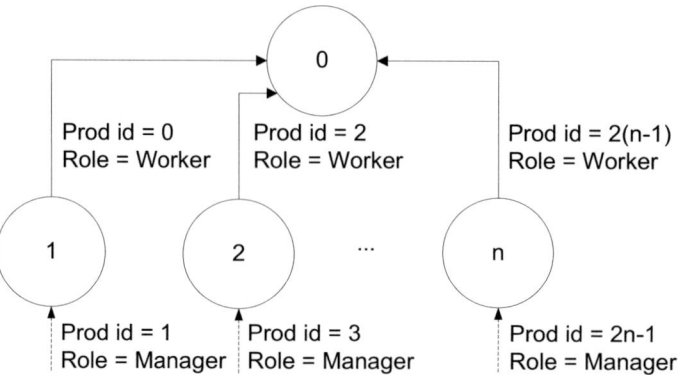

Figure 7.7.: EPM with a varying number of execution paths. For example, execution path 1 comprises the production rules 0 and 1, execution path 2 comprises the production rules 2 and 3, and in general, execution path n comprises the production rules $2(n-1)$ and $2n-1$.

means, that there are production rules belonging to more than one variant. If such a production rule was executed, the estimated remaining processing durations of all variants, that contain this production rule must be updated. The generator allows to create EPMs with a varying number of variants and production rules per variant. An example of such an EPM is depicted in Fig. 7.8.

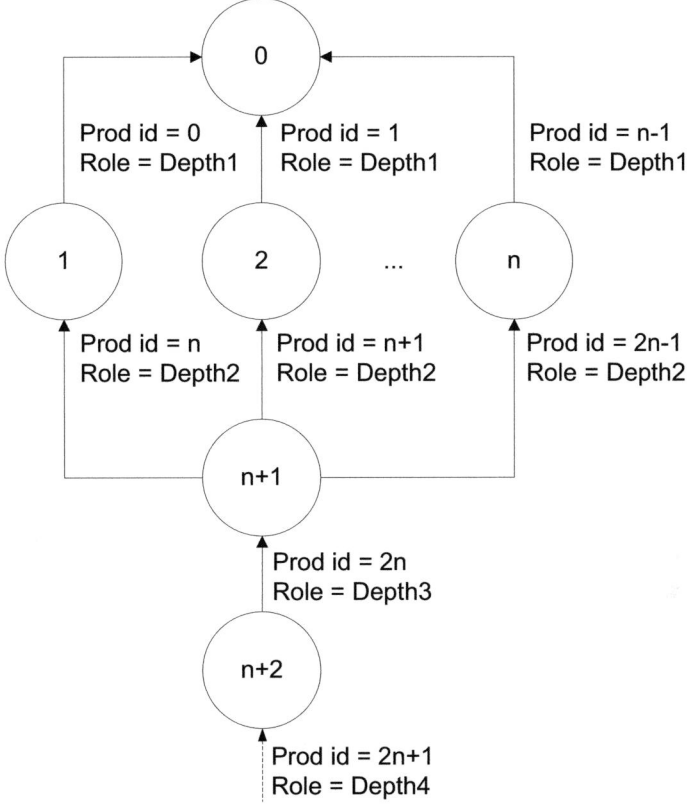

Figure 7.8.: EPM with a varying number of intertwined variants. The number of production rules per variant is four.

7.4.2. Results

Several evaluations are performed. In the first evaluation, a separate experiment is conducted for each influencing factor in which its input size is doubled. Fig. 7.9 shows the results of the first evaluation in which the input size is doubled.

All three figures show that the three influencing factors have a significant impact on the simulation duration. Note that the results cannot be compared with each other as the basic setting is different in each run. For example, for processing a large number of EPMs concurrently, a corresponding number of resource agents must be available. Therefore, a second experiment is conducted. In the second evaluation, the settings are exactly the same at the beginning: 10 concurrent EPMs, 10 execution paths, and 10 RAs per role. Then, one influencing factor is increased while the others are kept constant. This allows to compare the results of the different experiments with each other. Fig. 7.10 shows the results of this evaluation. As one can see, all three runs start (almost) from the same point.

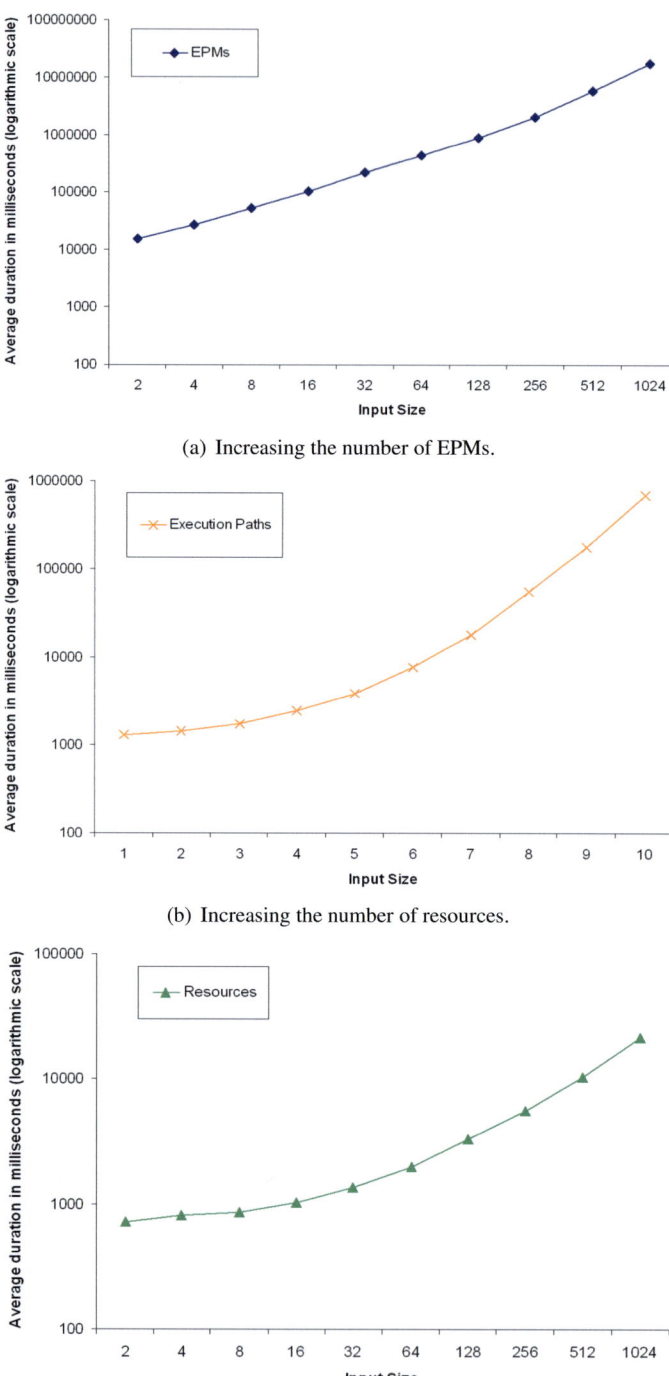

(a) Increasing the number of EPMs.

(b) Increasing the number of resources.

(c) Increasing the number of execution paths.

Figure 7.9.: Scalability evaluation of the iEPM approach. The figures show the average simulation duration in milliseconds for an increasing number of entities, such as EPMs, RAs, and execution paths.

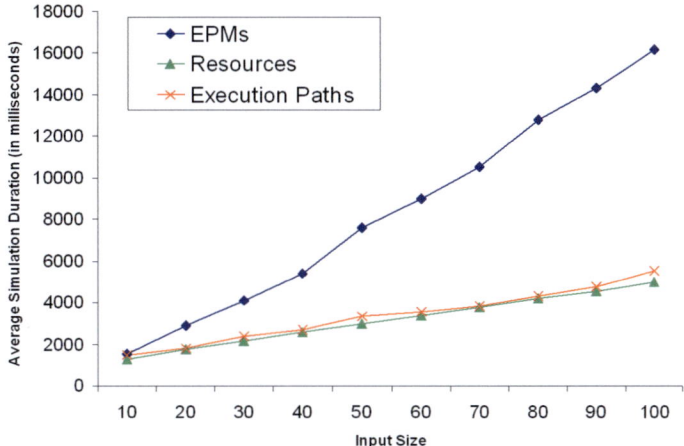

Figure 7.10.: Scalability evaluation of the iEPM approach. Each run starts with the same setting.

The highest impact on the duration has the number of EPMs. The reason for this impact can be explained as follows: The IBO sends a multicast message if it schedules a production rule[3] or if it requests workload information from the RAs. Thus, the more production rules are scheduled (due to the increase of EPMs), the more messages are sent and processed. The number of RAs and the number of execution paths show a similar effect. The effects can be explained as follows: Addressee of the multicast messages are RAs with a specific role. Therefore, a higher number of RAs per role leads as well to a higher number of exchanged messages. For each execution path, the estimated duration is calculated. Thus, the more execution paths exist, the longer is the simulation duration.

As the impact of the number of resources and execution path is very similar, another experiment is conducted with a different kind of EPM structure. Fig. 7.11 shows the result of this experiment in which the EPM with intertwined variants and different number of production rules per variant is used. Note that the impact of the number of resource agents is higher than the number of execution paths.

---

[3]e.g. a call for proposal message is sent to all RAs with a specific role if the Adapted FIPA Contract Net Interaction Protocol Specification (ACNP) is used.

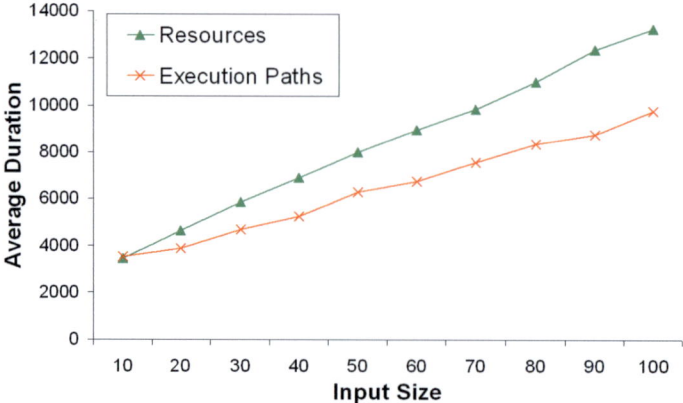

(a) Results using EPMs with intertwined variants and 5 production rules per variant.

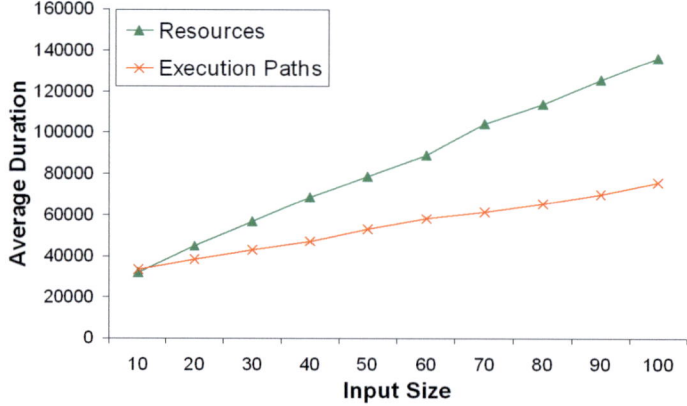

(b) Results using EPMs with intertwined variants and 50 production rules per variant.

Figure 7.11.: Scalability evaluation of the iEPM approach using EPMs with intertwined variants and different number of production rules per variant. The figures show the average simulation duration in milliseconds for an increasing number of entities, such as RAs and execution paths.

The conducted evaluation identified one important area for improvement. A more efficient communication topology (e. g. a central scheduling component which does not use multicast messages) or negotiation protocol (e.g. as in [77]) can be implemented.

In order to show, that changes on the communication topology would lead to a better performance, a simple scheduling strategy was implemented which is based on the Round-Robin method (see e.g. [172]). Using this method, the IBOs schedule the production rules directly to resource agents instead of sending multicast messages. In Fig. 7.12 one can see, that Run "EPMs - Round-Robing" has a better performance than run "EPMs". Run "EPMs and RAs" shows the result when the number EPMs and resource agents are increased simultaneously. Here, there is a significant negative impact on the performance. But again, the Round-Robin method has a much better performance if the number of EPMs and RAs are increased (Run "EPMs and RAs - Round-Robin").

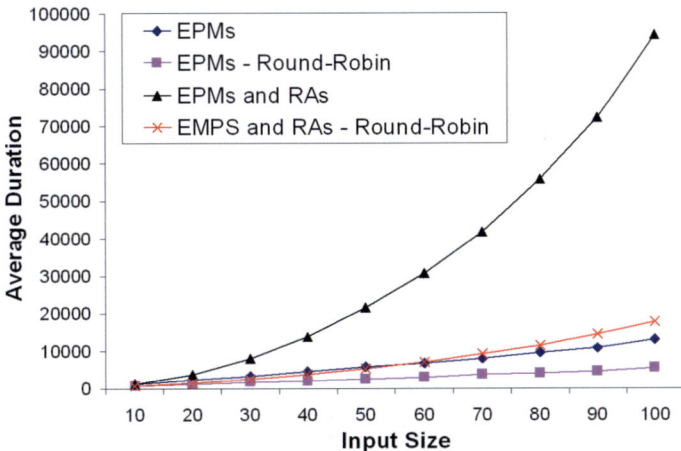

Figure 7.12.: Scalability evaluation of the iEPM approach. Evaluating a simple scheduling strategy based on the Round-Robin method.

Another aspect that influences the simulation duration is the usage of workload and failure rate information as the usage requires a message exchange between IBOs and RAs. Fig. 7.13 shows the results of this experiment. As one can see, the usage of this kind of information affects the simulation duration as expected.

Another improvement area pertains to the variants. Instead of considering all variants, only a subset of promising execution paths could be evaluated. Alternatively, the most promising variant (such as the cost or processing time minimal variant) could be chosen at the beginning. If this variant becomes infeasible, the next promising one could be selected for execution. There are several heuristics for determining minimal-cost solutions in AND/OR graphs. For acyclic AND/OR graphs different heuristics were developed, like the AO* algorithm [203] as well as more efficient heuristics, such as the CF and CS [177]. Furthermore, heuristics for cyclic AND/OR graphs were suggested [130]. As the EPM is a cyclic graph, the latter approach could be adapted and integrated in the iEPM approach. This is subject to future work (see Sec. 10.2).

The critical part of the iEPM approach is the offline learning phase, as each individual is evaluated by a simulation run. Thus, for providing real scalability capabilities, parallelism has to be implemented. Either the simulations for the evaluation of each individual are parallelized or within a simulation, the agents are distributed on different processors or machines. An additional performance enhancement would be the implementation of the identified areas for improvements as described above. The suggested improvements are subject to future work. Nevertheless, the scalability is once more evaluated on the basis of the new customer business process in Sec. 9.6. This evaluation considers the practical requirements regarding the quantity structure, such as the number of applications received per day.

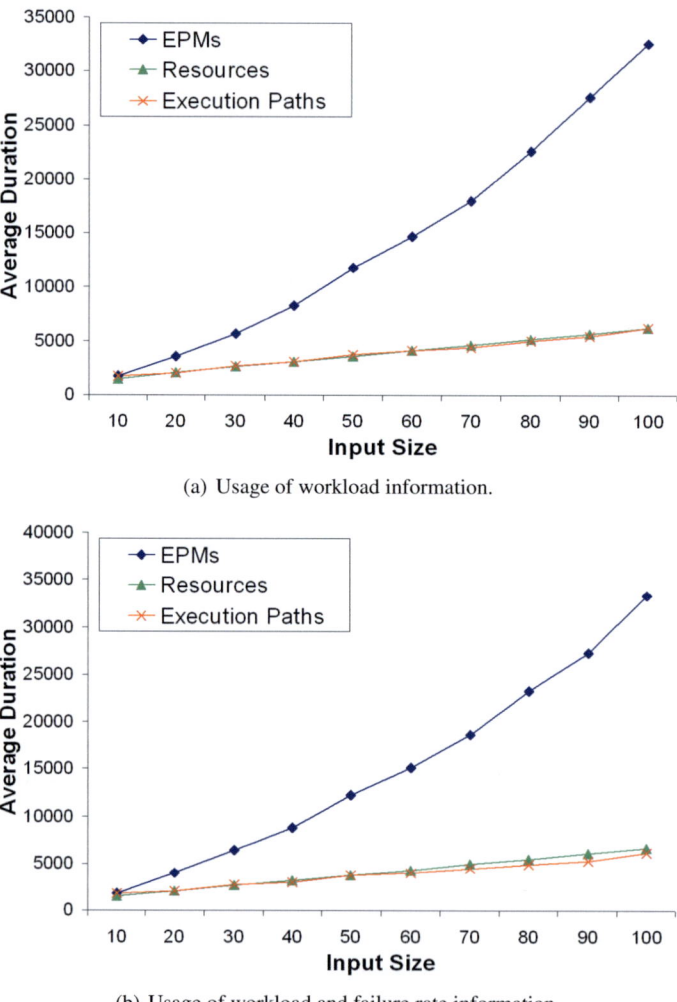

(a) Usage of workload information.

(b) Usage of workload and failure rate information.

Figure 7.13.: Scalability evaluation of the iEPM approach when workload and failure rate information is used. The figures show the average simulation duration in milliseconds for an increasing number of entities, such as EPMs, RAs, and execution paths.

7.5. Summary

This chapter highlighted the two practical application methods of the iEPM approach. It was discussed how this approach can be applied as intelligent business process engine, i.e. how agents autonomously optimize the execution of business processes in changing scenarios. Moreover, it was explained how the iEPM approach is used within an intelligent business process optimization methodology which does not require the modeling of multiple process designs. Both application methods will be evaluated with different business processes. The conducted experiments are discussed in Sec. 9.7.

Two further aspects relevant for the practical application of the iEPM approach were discussed. Firstly, the integration of the learning mechanism in commercial BPM tools was explained on the basis of the BPMN event mechanism and a SOA. Secondly, the scalability of the iEPM approach was evaluated on the basis of experiments.

As aforementioned, the offline learning phase is time critical as one simulation run is required for the evaluation of each solution. This led to the development of an extension of Particle Swarm Optimization (PSO) which is discussed in the next chapter.

8. Excursion - Accelerating Particle Swarm Optimization

> "It takes a long time to bring excellence to maturity."
>
> Publilius Syrus

This chapter provides an excursion in an extension of the Particle Swarm Optimization (PSO) and Multi-Objective Particle Swarm Optimization (MOPSO) algorithms as suggested in [159]. As described in Sec. 2.6.3, various methods for population initialization as well as diversity and feasibility preservation exist. In PSO, it is desired to ensure that the swarm visits most of the search space and that there is no gap which has not been explored. Considering this aspect, the use of Gap Search (GS) is proposed as an alternative to the existing population initialization, diversity preservation, and feasibility preservation methods.

In the first section of this chapter, the GS algorithm is introduced, particularly the different methods in which GS is applied. Then, the conducted experiments are discussed. The suggested methods are evaluated based on a variety of standard single-, multi-, and many-objective test functions. The chapter concludes with a brief summary.

8.1. Gap Search

The Gap Search (GS) algorithm is an extension of the Particle Swarm Optimization (PSO) Algorithm [159]. The GS is used to search the most unexplored regions of a search space similar to the Binary Search (BS) proposed by Hughes [129]. Binary Search is based on the iterative division of the search space into regions and exploring the large gaps. It has a similar but simpler mechanism than the Voronoi optimization. The proposed GS method starts with selecting a random point in the search space. Then the largest gap in the search space is found by computing the distances between the first point and the boundaries of the search space. The difference between GS and BS is that in BS the promising areas in the search space are successively refined through a binary search where in GS the largest gaps are sampled. Fig. 8.1 shows an example for a two dimensional space. In (a) one solution is randomly selected in the search space. The second solution is randomly selected in the largest gap (Fig. 8.1 (b)). This is an iterative method and can be performed to define any desirable number of solutions in the search space. These solutions are usually stored in a list termed GS-archive.

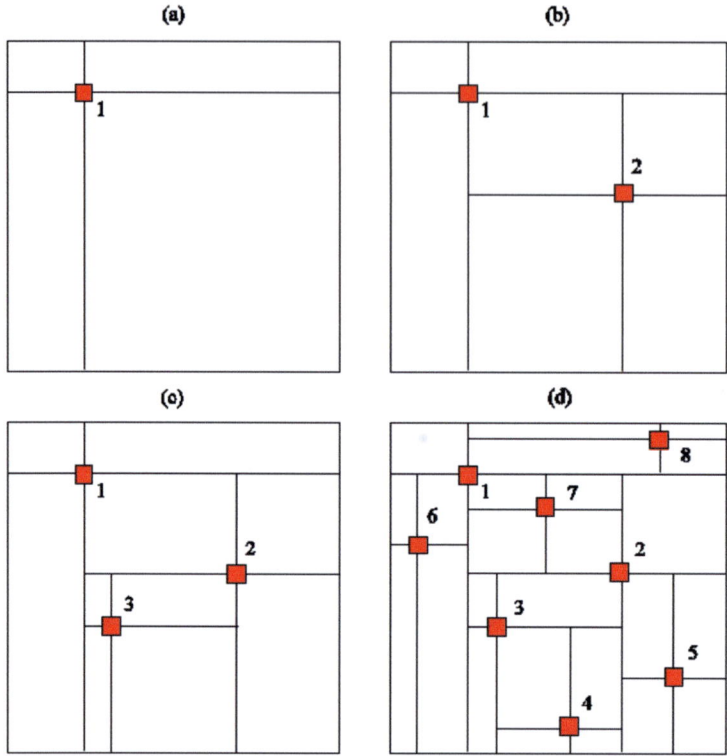

Figure 8.1.: An example of a Gap Search Method in a two dimensional search space. In (a) one point is randomly selected in the search space. The next point is selected in the largest gap defined in (b). (c) and (d) illustrate the selection of three and eight point.

There are two possibilities for storing the points the swarm has visited in the GS-archive. First, only the points generated by the GS method are stored in the archive. Alternatively one could also store all of the visited points of the search space. One disadvantage of GS could be that calculating a new position requires a relatively high computation time particularly for high dimensions (> 30) and large sizes of the GS-archive (> 8000). Indeed, the list size depends on the number of iterations and the GS rate. When using GS for feasibility preservation, the list size depends on the problem (where the local and global optima are located in relation to the border of the feasible space). If the fitness evaluations are very expensive and the lists are small enough, the computation time of the GS operations may have no significant negative influence on the total computational time. In the following, the GS mechanism is proposed for the initialization of particles, the diversity preservation, and feasibility preservation in a PSO.

8.1.1. Population Initialization Mechanism

The standard way of generating an initial population in PSO is to randomly find feasible positions of the particles. The goal is to ensure that the initial population is a uniform representation of the search space. In PSO, the initial population has a great impact on the exploration mechanism. The GS method is suggested for producing the initial solutions. Using the GS method instead of the random generator has a particular advantage as the GS tries to cover the entire search space. Of course, this depends on the number of initial particles and a very small initial population can never cover the entire search space. However, due to the storage of all of the found positions for the particles through the iterations, a good coverage of the search space can be preserved. Furthermore when using a random initial population, it has been shown that in high dimensional spaces, the probability that a particle is placed very close to the boundary is very high as shown in [119]. Therefore, it is very probable that particles leave the feasible search space. Here, it is intended to avoid this effect by intentionally initializing solutions in non-explored regions in the search space.

8.1.2. Diversity Preservation Mechanism

In order to prevent premature stagnation and convergence to a local optimum, some particles of the population are randomly re-initialized in the search space. The use of GS instead of a random initialization is suggested. A relatively small percentage of the particles are randomly selected and relocated by using GS. In this way, these particles are sent to the large gaps (most unexplored regions) in the space. Hence, it is ensured that the particles never visit the same part of the search space twice. GS is applied like the turbulence factor proposed in [91]; select one particle with a predefined probability at random and replace it in the search space by using GS. The other issue in re-initializing the particles is to set an appropriate value for the velocity. In the literature for example the papers from [175], and [307], the velocities of the reinitialized particles are set to zero, to a random value or are kept as before.

8.1.3. Feasibility Preservation Mechanism

Another issue in PSO is the boundary handling method or the so called feasibility preservation mechanism as also studied by Mostaghim et al. [195]. During the iterations, it is possible that particles leave the feasible region of the search space. Those particles must be identified and sent back to the feasible space (usually the feasible space is defined by the constraints; here, the area surrounded by the boundaries of the search space is considered). Typically if a particle leaves the feasible region, it is replaced either on the boundary or on a random position. The velocity of the particle is unchanged, set to zero or randomly selected. Indeed the most straight forward mechanism is to set the infeasible particles on the boundaries. This has an advantage when the global optimum is close to the boundary. In this chapter, also the performance of employing GS for replacing the infeasible particles in the search space is analyzed.

8.2. Conducted Experiments

In the following, the experimental setup and the results for the Gap Search (GS) experiments are described. A variety of experiments were conducted using single, multi-, and many-objective functions.

According to the no free lunch theorem, the performance of two different searching algorithms is exactly the same, when averaged over all possible test functions [327]. Therefore, the adequate choice of test functions is very important [325]. The selected functions allow it to draw conclusions on the performance of the different methods depending on the type of function.

In the GS experiments, the solutions generated by the GS method are stored in a GS-archive. The rate for applying GS to the diversity preservation part is set to 0.1 which means that 10 % of the particles are relocated per generation by the GS method.

8.2.1. Single-Objective Experiments

The selected single-objective functions used for the experiments are listed in Tab. 8.1.

Table 8.1.: Single-objective test functions.

Name	Function	Constraint
Rastrigin	$F(\vec{x}) = 10 \cdot n + \sum_{i=1}^{n} x_i^2 - 10 \cdot \cos(2 \cdot \pi \cdot x_i)$	$x_i \in [-5.12, 5.12]$
Ackley	$F(\vec{x}) = 20 \cdot exp(-0.2\sqrt{\frac{1}{n} \cdot \sum_{i=1}^{n} x_i^2}) - exp(\frac{1}{n} \cdot \sum_{i=1}^{n} \cos(2\pi x_i))$	$x_i \in [-32.768, 32.768]$
Griewank	$F(\vec{x}) = 1 + \sum_{i=1}^{n} \frac{x_i^2}{4000} - \prod_{i=1}^{n} cos(\frac{x_i}{\sqrt{i}})$	$x_i \in [-300, 300]$
Sphere	$F(\vec{x}) = \sum_{i=1}^{n} x_i^2$	$x_i \in [-100, 100]$
Rosenbrock	$F(\vec{x}) = \sum_{i=1}^{n-1} [100 \cdot (x_i^2 - x_{i+1})^2 + (x_i - 1)^2]$	$x_i \in [-10, 10]$
Schwefel	$F(\vec{x}) = 418.9829 \cdot n + \sum_{i=1}^{n} -x_i \cdot \sin(\sqrt{|(x_i)|})$	$x_i \in [-500, 500]$

The single-objective functions can be characterized as follows:

- Sphere: This convex, unimodal function has been used for a long time in optimization [140].

- Rastrigin: Originally this function was defined in a 2-dimensional form by Rastrigin [278] and has been generalized to N dimensions by Mühlenbein et al in [198]. This highly multimodal function is constructed from Sphere adding a modulator term $\alpha \cdot cos(2\pi x_i)$. Its surface is made up of a large number of local minima whose values increase with the distance to the global minimum. However, the locations of the minima are regularly distributed.

- Ackley: Originally this function was defined for two dimensions [1], but has been generalized to N dimensions [14]. It is a multimodal function obtained by modulating an exponential function with a cosine wave of moderate amplitude. The exponential term covers the surface with numerous regularly distributed local minima.

- Griewank: This multimodal function has a product term that introduces interdependence among the variables. As in the Ackley function, the optima are regularly distributed. The number of minima grows exponentially as the number of dimensions increases [174, 57].

- Rosenbrock: This function is also known as Banana function. It is a multimodal function for dimensions larger than three, otherwise it is unimodal [257]. The global minimum is inside a long, narrow, parabolic shaped flat valley. To find the valley is trivial, however to converge to the global minimum is difficult.

- Schwefel: This multimodal function was proposed by Schwefel [254]. Its global minimum is geometrically distant from the next best local minima. Therefore the search algorithms are potentially prone to convergence in the wrong direction.

For comparison purposes, the same degree of difficulty has been established in all the problems by defining a search space of dimensionality $n = 30$ for all single objective functions. The inertia weight w and the parameters c_1 and c_2 (see Equ. 2.9) are selected as follows: For the single objective functions, a parameter analysis has been performed for determining the best parameter combination based on the standard PSO (the standard has the following settings: random initialization of position and velocity, setting infeasible particles on the border and keeping the velocity unchanged, no diversity preservation mechanism, global topology). Each parameter is iterated from 0.2 to 1.0 in 0.1 steps. For each of the 729 combinations, a simulation with 1000 iterations, 50 particles, and 20 different initial seeds were executed. The best combinations (selected based on the best average value) are listed Table 8.2.

Table 8.2.: Computed parameter combinations.

Function	w	c_1	c_2
Sphere	0.9	1.0	0.9
Rastrigin	0.9	1.0	0.2
Ackley	ld[1]	1.0	0.2
Griewank	ld	1.0	0.2
Rosenbrock	0.9	1.0	0.5
Schwefel	0.9	1.0	0.9

The single-objective functions can easily be evaluated using the average and standard errors of the function value obtained for the best found solution.

The results of the experiments for the single-objective functions are shown in Fig. 8.3. It shows the progress over time of the different PSO methods. Additionally the means and standard errors are listed in Tab. 8.3. The abbreviations have the following meaning: Div., Feas., Init. are diversity preservation, feasibility preservation, and population initialization, respectively; -0, -R, and -K are the velocity values indicating zero, randomized, or kept unchanged. Standard was already explained above. Ring is defined analogously to Standard but with a ring topology. Border corresponds to the feasibility preservation method where the infeasible particles are placed on the border of the feasible space.

The results show that applying GS to a PSO can improve the behavior of the algorithm. Depending on the characteristics of the test function, different GS variants with PSO lead to a good result. More precisely, for the simplest function sphere, Div-GS-R, followed by Border-0, Div-GS-K, Div-GS-0 and Standard methods obtain the best solutions, respectively. This indicates that for a simple landscape the diversity preservation method using GS highly improves the solutions. One can observe a similar behavior of PSO when solving the Griewank and Ackley test problems: Div-GS-R obtains the best result followed by Border-0 method. The landscapes of Griewank and Ackley contain local optima, but still PSO can overcome the small local optima and has a similar behavior as when solving the sphere function. In Figure 8.3, one can observe that although Div-GS-R has a slower convergence than the other methods, it is able to constantly improve the solutions. It also obtains the lowest standard error.

For the Rastrigin function with several local optima, the GS has the best impact when it is used for the initialization of the particles. The best solutions are obtained from Init-GS-0, followed by Border-0, Init-GS-R, and Div-GS-K. This also indicates that the Init-GS variants lead to a good distribution of particles at the beginning which is helpful not to get stuck in (non global) local optima too early. A similar result can be observed for the Schwefel function. Div-GS-K followed by Init-GS-0 and Init-GS-R and Border-0 obtain the best results respectively. This illustrates the fact that when dealing with a number of local optima, a good initialization might lead to better results and in this case the GS method improves the PSO approach.

---

[1]The entry ld means a linear decreasing inertia over time starting from 1.0 to 0.4

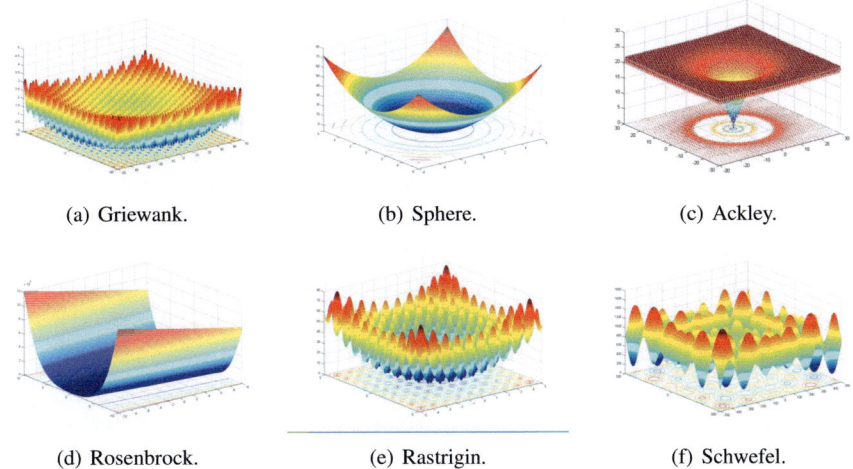

(a) Griewank.   (b) Sphere.   (c) Ackley.

(d) Rosenbrock.   (e) Rastrigin.   (f) Schwefel.

Figure 8.2.: Single-objective test functions.

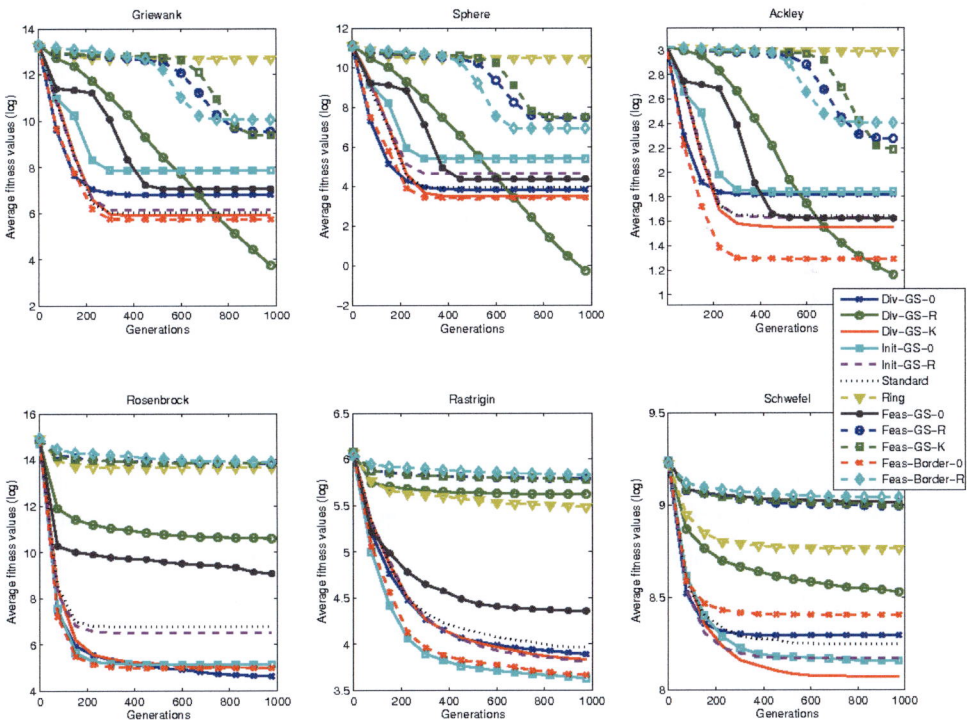

Figure 8.3.: The average function values of the best obtained solutions for the single objective function

Table 8.3.: The average and standard error of the best obtained solutions from different methods on the single objective test functions (ave.±Std.err).

Test	Griewank	Rastrigin	Rosenbrock
Div-GS-0	8.942e+2 ± 1.63e+2	4.86e+1 ± 3.17	**1.01e+2 ± 1.24e+1**
Div-GS-R	**3.35e+1 ± 2.55**	2.74e+2 ± 4.22	3.78e+4 ± 4.24e+3
Div-GS-K	3.67e+2 ± 5.91e+1	4.55e+1 ± 2.69	1.47e+2 ± 6.81e+1
Init-GS-0	2.59e+3 ± 5.67e+2	**3.73e+1 ± 2.18**	1.69e+2 ± 3.78e+1
Init-GS-R	4.66e+2 ± 4.56e+1	4.45e+1 ± 2.43	6.61e+2 ± 4.96e+2
Standard	4.10e+2 ± 8.73e+1	5.23e+1 ± 3.22	8.66e+2 ± 4.91e+2
Ring	3.17e+5 ± 1.38e+4	2.39e+2 ± 7.47	8.41e+5 ± 9.29e+4
Feas-GS-0	1.14e+3 ± 1.17e+2	7.79e+1 ± 8.76	8.58e+3 ± 1.59e+3
Feas-GS-R	1.37e+4 ± 1.04e+3	3.25e+2 ± 2.93	9.716e+5 ± 3.58e+4
Feas-GS-K	1.18e+4 ± 5.12e+2	3.23e+2 ± 3.71	1.02e+6 ± 4.80e+4
Border-0	3.08e+2 ± 5.11e+1	3.88e+1 ± 2.21	1.45e+2 ± 3.01e+1
Border-R	2.30e+4 ± 2.14e+3	3.39e+2 ± 2.8	1.065e+6 ± 5.25e+4

Test	Sphere	Ackley	Schwefel
Div-GS-0	4.57e+1 ± 1.03e+1	6.16 ± 2.87e-1	3.99e+3 ± 1.18e+2
Div-GS-R	**5.6e-1 ± 4.26e-2**	**3.12 ± 1.76e-1**	5.03e+3 ± 2.21e+2
Div-GS-K	3.34e+1 ± 1.61e+1	4.70 ± 2.77e-1	**3.21e+3 ± 1.89e+2**
Init-GS-0	2.2e+2 ± 4.65e+1	6.29 ± 3.87e-1	3.48e+3 ± 1.38e+2
Init-GS-R	1.04e+2 ± 3.2e+1	5.11 ± 2.52e-1	3.52e+3 ± 1.72e+2
Standard	5.04e+1 ± 1.07e+1	5.16 ± 2.65e-1	3.82e+3 ± 1.87e+2
Ring	3.47e+4 ± 1.55e+3	1.98e+1 ± 1.06e-1	6.39e+3 ± 1.37e+2
Feas-GS-0	7.81e+1 ± 8.37	5.06 ± 2.48e-1	8.18e+3 ± 3.43e+1
Feas-GS-R	1.75e+3 ± 1.22e+2	9.73 ± 2.62e-1	8.05e+3 ± 5.91e+1
Feas-GS-K	1.78e+3 ± 1.25e+2	8.88 ± 2.41e-1	8.06e+3 ± 5.98e+1
Border-0	3.03e+1 ± 6.48	3.63 ± 1.38e-1	4.47e+3 ± 1.64e+2
Border-R	1.01e+3 ± 8.81e+1	1.11e+1 ± 2.32e-1	8.43e+3 ± 6.09e+1

For the Rosenbrock function with a hidden global optimum, the diversity preservation methods are expected to be useful which is confirmed by the experiments conducted. Div-GS-0, followed by Border-0, Div-GS-K obtain the best results.

From the results above, one can conclude that the Border-0 method works as the second best for almost all of the functions independent from the different landscapes. This indicates that many particles leave the search space. It is also expected as the inertia values computed from the preliminary tests are in fact very high and this results in the effect that many particles leave the search space.

8.2.2. Multi- and Many-Objective Test Functions

The multi- and many-objective test function used for the GS experiments are listed in Tab. 8.4.

Table 8.4.: Multi- and many-objective test functions.

Name	Function	Constraint
FF	$f_1(\vec{x}) = 1 - exp(-\sum_i (x_i - \frac{1}{\sqrt{n}})2)$ $f_2(\vec{x}) = 1 - exp(-\sum_i (x_i + \frac{1}{\sqrt{n}})2)$	$x_i \in [-4, 4]$
DTLZ2	$f_1(\vec{x}) = (1 + g(X_M)) \cos(x_1 \pi/2) \cdots \cos(x_{M-1} \pi/2)$ $f_2(\vec{x}) = (1 + g(X_M)) \cos(x_1 \pi/2) \cdots \sin(x_{M-1} \pi/2)$ $\vdots$ $f_{m-1}(\vec{x}) = (1 + g(X_M)) \cos(x_1 \pi/2) \sin(x_2 \pi/2)$ $f_m(\vec{x}) = (1 + g(X_M)) \sin(x_1 \pi/2)$ $g(X_M) = \sum_{j=M}^{n} (x_j - 0.5)2$	 $x_i \in [0, 1]$ $M \equiv$ number of objectives

The test functions can be characterized as follows:

- FF: This function has two objectives and a concave shaped Pareto-optimal front [63].

- DTLZ(2): This scalable function was introduced to investigate the performance of algorithms for any desirable numbers of objectives and parameters. The Pareto-optimal solutions lie inside the first quadrant of the unit sphere [74].

As for the single-objective test functions, a dimensionality of $n = 30$ is used for the FF problem. The DTLZ2 function is evaluated for 20, 30, 50, and 100 parameters and 5, 10, and 15 objectives. For one type of experiment, 1000 iterations with 50 particles and 20 different initial seeds are run, except for the DTLZ2 function where 100 particles and 100 iterations are used. Furthermore, two different topologies are evaluated, gbest and lbest (ring). In MOPSO, the global best particles are selected at random from the archive of non-dominated solutions [196]. The maximum size of this archive is set to 100 using the k-means clustering technique [339]. The FF and DTLZ2 were run with 0.4, 1.0, and 1.0 (inertia weight w and parameters c_1 and c_2 - see Equ. 2.9).

The multi-objective function FF is evaluated using the hypervolume metric [339]. For this calculation, the reference point $x = (1.1, 1.1)$ was selected. All the Pareto-optimal solutions of the DTLZ2 function are located on the hyper-sphere and have the property $S = \sum_{j=1}^{m} f_j^2 = 1$ [74]. These S values are used to evaluate the solutions. The quality of different methods can be compared in terms of the number of solutions having S values close to one. This evaluation is done by computing the histograms of S for the solutions. Note, that due to the expensive computation of the hypervolume metric in the high dimensional objective spaces, this metric is not applied for the many-objective cases.

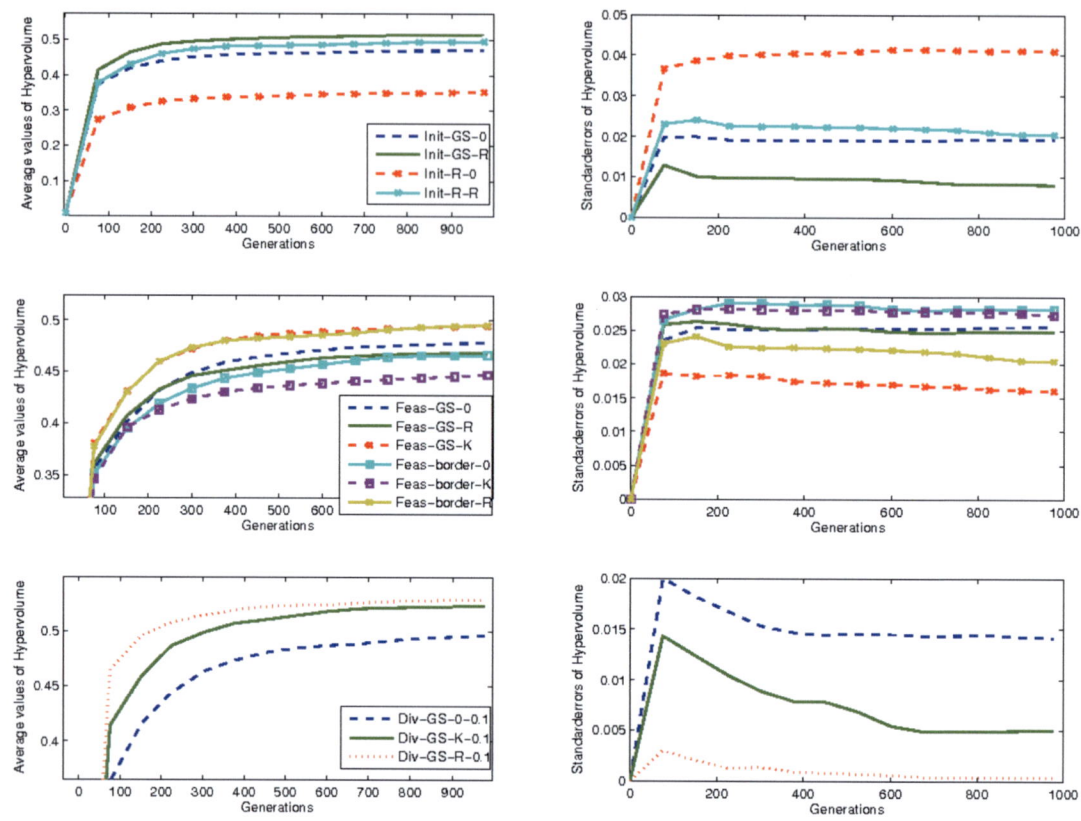

Figure 8.4.: Hypervolume values for the FF function.

The results of the experiments with the FF function are shown in Fig. 8.4.

The best results are obtained from Div-GS-R and Div-GS-K followed by Init-GS-R. This is also an expectable result, because in most of the MOPSO methods, the turbulence factor has a higher impact [91, 197]. Here, it can be observed that Init-GS improves the results in comparison to the application of a turbulence factor. In fact, this opens a new issue in bi-objective PSO methods.

In the following, the influence of the GS variants on MOPSO for the scalable test problem DTLZ2 is further studied. The results of the DTLZ2 function for different dimensions and objectives are shown in Fig. 8.5. Due to space restrictions, only the well performing methods are depicted. Additionally, two other methods are plotted as baselines, namely random search and NSGA-II [73].

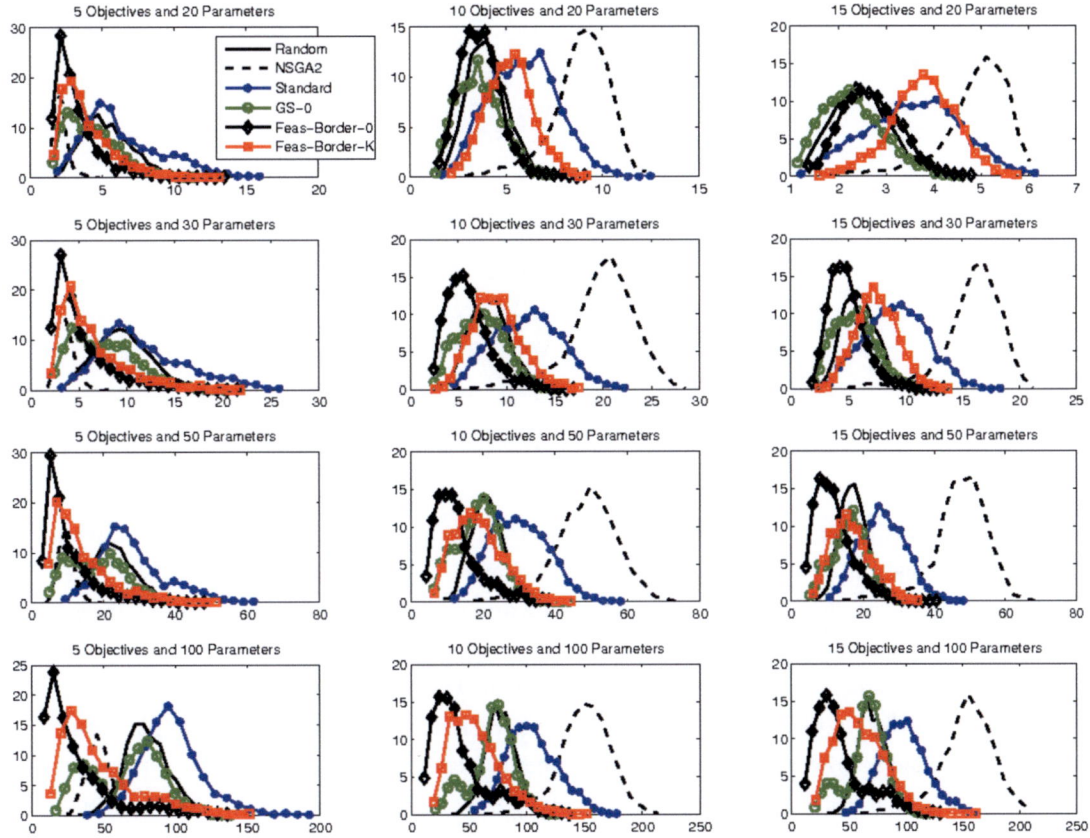

Figure 8.5.: Histograms of *S* values for the DTLZ2 function.

The experiments are conducted to analyze the impact of the number of parameters as well as the objectives. It is known that NSGA-II obtains very good results for a small number of objectives. This is also being observed in the experiments conducted and also in [196]. But as the number of objectives is increased, the MOPSO variants outperform NSGA-II. Among the MOPSO variants the Feas-Border-0 obtains the best. This is followed by Feas-Border-K and Feas-GS-0 variants. The Feas-Border-0 variant has a constant behavior independent from the number of objectives and parameters.

The diversity preservation methods do not perform well and are not shown. The above results indicate that the boundary handling methods play a very important role as for the single objective functions. Therefore, an analysis of the mean number of particles is performed, that leave the feasible space. Table 8.5 contains the mean number of infeasible particles for the DTLZ2 function with 5 objectives.

Table 8.5.: Mean number of infeasible particles for DTLZ2 with 5 objectives and 20, 30, 50, and 100 parameters.

Variant	20	30	50	100
Standard	9604.55	9924.75	9997.5	10000.0
Ring	9609.8	9930.2	9997.35	10000.0
pop-GS-R	9595.8	9930.25	9996.85	10000.0
pop-GS-0	9266.95	9682.1	9829.0	9882.6
pop-R-0	9270.7	9716.55	9841.9	9887.4
Div-GS-R	8659.15	8940.25	8997.0	9000.0
Div-GS-K	8634.0	8932.2	8997.4	9000.0
Div-GS-0	7319.8	7733.6	7967.95	8081.35
Feas-Border-0	2242.05	2548.5	2885.45	3494.75
Feas-Border-K	4461.85	5280.1	6531.6	8271.6
Feas-GS-R	9327.95	9870.4	9993.05	10000.0
Feas-GS-0	2718.05	3260.75	3976.1	4707.8
Feas-GS-K	4475.45	5981.75	7920.0	9603.3

Similar results for the other number of objectives were received. In an experiment with 100 iterations with 100 particles, the maximum number of infeasible particles is 10000. It is interesting to see, that the best performing variant Feas-Border-0 is the one with the lowest number of infeasible particles. A possibility to decrease the number of infeasible particles is clamping the particle velocity through the *vmax* method [150]. The critical remark concerning the *vmax* method in [38] is, that there is no single value for the maximum velocity parameter for all problems. However, this pertains to the inertia weight parameter as well.

All the results point out that boundary handling is an important issue in MOPSO and PSO and that the GS variants in PSO improve the performance for the different test problems.

8.3. Summary

In order to solve time intensive problems quite often methods such as Binary Search and Sub-division method are used to employ a reasonable search in the search space. In this chapter, a search mechanism called Gap Search (GS) has been introduced. The influence of using GS in combination with PSO in order to solve single, multi- and many-objective problems has been studied. For this reason, GS was integrated into the three possible parts of a PSO (MOPSO) namely as initialization, diversity, and feasibility preservation mechanisms.

The major result from the conducted experiments reveals that GS improves the standard PSO and MOPSO methods even if it is deployed in solving many-objective problems. However, applying a search mechanism like GS to solve a problem highly depends on the landscape of the problems. This fact was intentionally examined on some common test functions with known landscapes. For the problems including a large number of deep local optima the diversity preservation as well as the initialization using GS improved the results. For many-objective problems, the feasibility preservation methods using GS showed improvements.

After studying the application of GS in PSO, the conducted experiments for the intelligent Executable Product Model (iEPM) approach are discussed in the next chapter. One of these experiments studies also the usage of PSO in combination with GS when applied for the iEPM approach. The results show that a significant performance gain is achieved when using PSO in combination with GS in comparison to standard PSO or Genetic Algorithm (GA).

9. Simulation-based Experiments

> "In God we trust; all others must bring data."
>
> W. Edwards Deming

In this chapter, the conducted experiments for the intelligent Executable Product Model (iEPM) approach are discussed. For each experiment, the purpose and the experimental setup are explained. Furthermore, the results of the experiments are discussed in detail. The first section explains the general experimental setup. The objective of the first experiment is to show the proof-of-concept of the developed approach and its implementation. The next experiments evaluate the different hybrid machine learning approaches such as RRL-GA and RRL-PSO. These mechanisms combine Relational Reinforcement Learning (RRL) with Genetic Algorithm (GA) and Particle Swarm Optimization (PSO), respectively. Furthermore, policies defined on different levels of abstraction are evaluated. The next experiment compares the performance of GA and PSO in the offline learning phase. Finally, the advantage of the iEPM approach is discussed on the basis of different business processes such as a mortgage application process and a credit application process. The chapter ends with a short summary.

9.1. General Experimental Setup

A single system configuration (also termed scenario) relates to one instance of the EPM optimization problem. Such an instance comprises the set of Executable Product Models (EPMs), negotiation protocol, number of resources per role, among others. Furthermore, the simulation is repeated a specific number of times.

For the analysis of a single experiment (with n simulation runs), a point estimator and a $100(1 - \alpha)$ percent confidence interval ($0 < \alpha < 1$) for the expected average $E(X)$ of each interesting value X are computed (see [165, pp. 505-515] for details). The paired-t confidence interval approach (see [165, pp. 557-559] for details) is used to check whether there is a statistically relevant difference between two experiments with different configurations. If the confidence interval for $E(\Delta)$ contains zero, no statistically relevant difference is present. Otherwise, one also gets a quantifier for the difference.

In [233], simulation based experiments are conducted with the help of a so called workbench. It is a collection of Petri-nets with different characteristics which are grouped into three categories. The classification is not Petri net specific. Therefore, this classification is applied to the iEPM approach, i.e. all the EPMs used in the different experiments belong to one of these groups. The EPMs are grouped as follows:

1. Pathological EPMs: These are artificial, small EPMs incorporating a special feature. The small EPMs with different structures used in the following experiments pertain to this group. Examples are the linear EPM containing a sequence of production rules or the EPM containing a cycle.

2. Large EPMs: These are artificial EPMs as well, but with a simpler structure and a larger number of tasks. The EPMs with a varying number of execution paths used in the scalability evaluation (see Sec.7.4) pertain to this group.

3. Practical EPMs: These are EPMs derived from actual business processes used in practice. For example, the EPM of the new customer business process pertains to this group.

9.2. Proof-of-Concept

The proof-of-concept has the objective to evaluate the feasibility of the approach and the corresponding implementation. In particular, the successful execution of EPMs with the help of the Multi-Agent System (MAS) on the basis of a Sequential Discrete Event Simulation (SDES) has to be shown. As this experiment was conducted in an early stage of the development, the Intelligent Business Objects (IBOs) do not have learning capabilities. Instead of that, they use an *execute-all* strategy (see Sec. 5.1.1) for details). Additionally, the two implemented negotiation protocols are analyzed. This experiment and the corresponding results were published in [158].

9.2.1. Experimental Setup

Experiments are conducted for a comparison of the two negotiation protocols using the three structurally different product models depicted in Fig. 9.1.

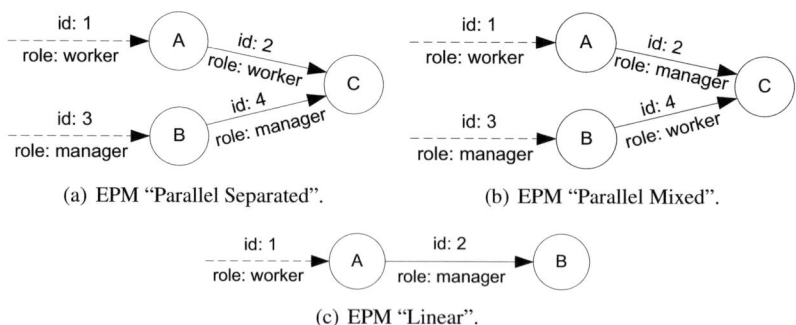

(a) EPM "Parallel Separated".   (b) EPM "Parallel Mixed".

(c) EPM "Linear".

Figure 9.1.: EPMs used for experiments.

These EPMs represent some of the standard situations found in business processes such as the processing of tasks in a sequence and in parallel. The models (a) and (b) consist of two different paths to the root node with two production rules each. The difference between (a) and (b) is the resource assignment. In Fig. 9.1(a) one resource type is sufficient if only one execution path is executed, while in Fig. 9.1(b) always both resource types are required. Model (c) is a linear model with two production rules that are executed by different resources. For each product model structure a separate experiment is carried out.

All production rule durations are gamma distributed with $\alpha = 100$ and $\beta = 1$. In all three cases, there are two resources with role "worker" (error inter-arrival time $\beta = 500000$, error duration $\alpha = 3$, $\beta = 2$) and two resources with role "manager" (error inter-arrival time $\beta = 500000$, error duration $\alpha = 2.5$, $\beta = 2.1$). The error settings result in relatively few resource breakdowns of short length. As the parallel execution of both paths in the models (a) and (b) needs twice the processing time of model (c), the product model instances inter-arrival times were accordingly adapted: $\beta = 100$ for models (a) and (b) and $\beta = 55$ for model (c). (The accurate values were determined through experiments.) This setting assures a comparable resource utilization.

In order to get relatively small confidence intervals, the simulation is repeated 50 times for each configuration and the duration is set to 10,000,000 time units. The following measures were analyzed: the average workload per resource, the average number of IBOs in the system (measured each 1,000 time units) and for each EPM instance

- the average number of sent messages (of its IBO and all resource agents having participated in negotiations with this IBO),

- the average waiting time (sum of all times tasks are waiting for a resource to perform an executable production rule) and

- the average cycle time.

For all measures, a confidence interval with error level $\alpha = 0.05$ is computed.

9.2.2. Results and Discussion

The results of the proof-of-concept experiments are shown in Table 9.1. The proof-of-concept was successful as the EPMs could be successfully executed with the developed approach.

As one can see, equal workloads for all configurations could have been reached. The behaviour of the two parallel models is quite similar—Adapted FIPA Contract Net Interaction Protocol Specification (ACNP) is significantly better (zero not within the confidence intervals) than the picking protocol. For the linear model, the results are different. Here, the picking protocol is significantly better. As one can see, different model structures may have a great impact on the results.

Table 9.1.: Results of the protocol comparison for the three EPMs ($\alpha = 0.05$, 50 simulation runs).

Parallel Separated			
	ACNP	Picking	Difference
# IBOs	5.80 ± 0.03	4.17 ± 0.01	1.63 ± 0.04
cycle time	579.9 ± 2.7	417.1 ± 1.0	162.8 ± 2.9
workload	0.90 ± 0.00	0.85 ± 0.00	0.04 ± 0.00
messages	27.27 ± 0.00	26.76 ± 0.01	0.51 ± 0.01
waiting	195.4 ± 1.4	118.8 ± 0.5	76.6 ± 1.5
Parallel Mixed			
	ACNP	Picking	Difference
# IBOs	5.72 ± 0.03	4.14 ± 0.01	1.57 ± 0.03
cycle time	572.3 ± 2.7	414.4 ± 1.0	157.9 ± 2.8
workload	0.89 ± 0.00	0.85 ± 0.00	0.05 ± 0.00
messages	27.29 ± 0.00	26.65 ± 0.01	0.64 ± 0.01
waiting	190.3 ± 1.3	115.3 ± 0.5	75.0 ± 1.4
Linear			
	ACNP	Picking	Difference
# IBOs	9.01 ± 0.07	10.39 ± 0.09	-1.39 ± 0.12
cycle time	495.4 ± 3.4	571.7 ± 4.5	-76.3 ± 6.1
workload	0.91 ± 0.00	0.91 ± 0.00	0.00 ± 0.00
messages	13.43 ± 0.00	13.51 ± 0.00	-0.08 ± 0.00
waiting	146.7 ± 1.7	184.8 ± 2.2	-38.1 ± 3.1

In another experiment, a similar analysis for a larger and more realistic product model for a credit application was conducted. Different from the findings above, no relevant performance differences between the protocols could be observed.

9.3. RRL-GA

This section contains the experiments for the RRL-GA learning mechanism which combines RRL with GA. These were the first experiments conducted with the learning mechanism. As stated in Sec. 6.1, the learning mechanism is based on the principles individual learning and emergence. An IBO learns by itself without interacting with other IBOs and pursue the common goal to optimize the defined Key Performance Indicators (KPIs) such as the average cycle time. Therefore, it has to be shown in the conducted experiments that such a common goal can be attained. The experiments and the corresponding results were published in [160, 161].

The first type of experiment has the objective to prove that RRL-GA increases the efficiency in comparison to the basic *execute-all* approach. Such an improvement implies also the attainment of the common goal.

The efficiency experiments are generally conducted in two stages. The conduction of a two-stage experiment can be motivated by considering the practical application method of the iEPM approach as intelligent Business Process Management (BPM) engine. As described in Sec. 7.1, the control flow of business processes is managed by using the iEPM approach. This means that the IBOs use the Policy Iteration method in order to decide about their actions. The offline learning phase is carried out either periodically or if a calculated KPI value has exceeded a defined threshold. Offline learning means here to use a heuristic and to perform simulation runs for the evaluation of the determined solutions. Once an optimal probability vector has been determined in the offline learning phase, the policy of the IBOs[1] is configured with this probability vector. Thus, the first stage corresponds to the offline learning phase and the second stage corresponds to the real execution of business processes.

The second type of experiment examines the generalization. Generalization is a special kind of knowledge transfer where previously learned knowledge is applied on a bigger or more complex problem. Objective of this experiment type is to show that learned policies (i.e. the probability vector) can be re-used and applied for other product models. If a re-use is possible, the duration of the offline learning phase can be reduced.

In all experiments, the objective is the minimization of KPI cycle time.

9.3.1. Experimental Setup

The same three product model structures and settings as in the proof-of-concept experiments are used.

The efficiency comparison is done using a two-stage experiment as mentioned above. The policy is given except the assigned probabilities. The policy on the level of production rules and information nodes is used (see Sec. 6.1.4). In the first stage, the RRL-GA algorithm is run to determine the optimal solution (probability vector) for each product model structure. The population size is set to 20 with 50 evolution iterations. Each individual is evaluated by a simulation run that is repeated two times with a duration of 100,000 time units. Once the probabilities are computed, the second stage begins. Here, the basic execute-all approach is compared with the RRL approach (again for each product model) using a paired-t confidence interval approach with a simulation duration of 1 million time units. The policy is configured using the optimal policy parameters (probability vector) taken from the previous RRL-GA experiment.

---

[1]These IBOs manage the real execution of business processes / EPMs.

Again, the second type of experiment examines the generalization. As aforementioned, generalization is a special kind of knowledge transfer where previously learned knowledge is applied on a bigger or more complex problem. To gather the first insights on this topic, the three learned policies are applied on a bigger product model with a higher number of elements and more complex structure. This product model is depicted in Fig. 9.2. For each configuration, 50 repetitions (1 million time units duration) were carried out.

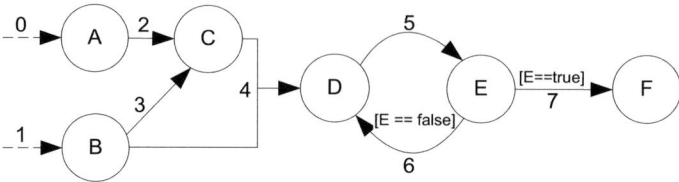

Figure 9.2.: EPM "Big" - used in the generalization experiments.

In both experiment types, ACNP is selected as negotiation protocol. The average number of IBOs and the average cycle time are compared. For these measures, a confidence interval with error level $\alpha = 0.05$ is computed.

9.3.2. Results and Discussion

Firstly, the results of the efficiency comparison are discussed. The following solutions were found by the RRL-GA approach for the different product model structures in the first stage of the experiment:

Parallel Separated: [1.0, 0.8, 1.0, 0.1, 0.7, 0.6, 1.0]
Parallel Mixed: [1.0, 0.9, 0.3, 0.1, 0.9, 0.7, 1.0]
Linear: [0.9, 0.4, 0.9, 0.3, 0.3, 0.3, 1.0]
Big: [0.0, 0.1, 0.9, 0.0, 0.2, 0.9, 1.0]

The results of the second stage of the experiment are listed in Table 9.2. It shows the difference between the execute-all (denoted as basic) and the RRL-GA approach for the four product model structures.

Table 9.2.: Results of the efficiency experiment comparing the execute-all and RRL-GA approach for the EPMs ($\alpha = 0.05$, 50 simulation runs).

Parallel Separated			
	Basic	RRL-GA	Difference
# IBOs	5.83 ± 0.11	3.50 ± 0.03	2.33 ± 0.11
cycle time	580.71 ± 9.51	350.0 ± 1.77	230.71 ± 9.79
workload	0.9 ± 0	0.71 ± 0	0.19 ± 0
messages	27.27 ± 0	21.97 ± 0.02	5.3 ± 0.02
waiting	195.91 ± 4.8	66.43 ± 0.76	129.48 ± 4.91

Parallel Mixed			
	Basic	RRL-GA	Difference
# IBOs	5.76 ± 0.11	2.60 ± 0.02	3.16 ± 0.11
cycle time	575.24 ± 9.1	260.47 ± 0.72	314.77 ± 9.33
workload	0.89 ± 0	0.61 ± 0	0.29 ± 0
messages	27.29 ± 0	17.96 ± 0.02	9.33 ± 0.02
waiting	191.82 ± 4.6	30.29 ± 0.36	161.53 ± 4.72

Linear			
	Basic	RRL-GA	Difference
# IBOs	8.87 ± 0.19	10.68 ± 0.33	-1.81 ± 0.35
cycle time	488.1 ± 9.36	491.4 ± 9.57	-3.3 ± 12.59
workload	0.91 ± 0	0.91 ± 0	$4.42e^{-4}$ ± 0.003
messages	13.43 ± 0	13.43 ± 0	0.003 ± 0.01
waiting	143.06 ± 4.68	144.73 ± 4.79	-1.67 ± 6.3

Big			
	Basic	RRL-GA	Difference
# IBOs	7.61 ± 0.16	7.60 ± 0.25	0.01 ± 0.31
cycle time	1517.8 ± 28.2	1276.8 ± 18.5	241.0 ± 36.2
workload	0.81 ± 0	0.73 ± 0	0.08 ± 0
messages	51.65 ± 0.03	51.69 ± 0.02	-0.04 ± 0.04
waiting	153.1 ± 4.56	103.41 ± 2.73	49.69 ± 5.64

For both parallel product models there is a significant improvement. For the linear product model, the execute-all approach is optimal as all production rules have to be executed. Therefore this result is not surprising. An experiment with the vector [0.0, 0.0, 0.0, 0.0, 0.0, 0.0, 1.0] showed no significant difference between the execute-all and RRL-GA approach. If the policy is configured with this vector, the behaviour of the IBOs is identical to the execute-all strategy. The results of the first experiment type show that the common goal of minimizing the average cycle time could be reached successfully by the individual agent learning approach.

Additionally, an experiment was conducted for evaluating the behaviour of the learning mechanism when inefficient policy rules are included in the policy. Here, the learning mechanism should be able to identify the inefficient policy rule and learn not to apply them. The rule that every production rule that is in execution is cancelled was included in the hand-coded policy: $in\_execution(X) \longrightarrow cancel(X)$. The policy rules' probability determined by the RRL-GA approach tended towards zero. Thus, the RRL-GA approach is able to learn not to apply inefficient policy rules.

The results of the generalization experiments are shown in Table 9.3.

Table 9.3.: Results of the generalization experiment ($\alpha = 0.05$, 50 simulation runs).

Policy	Objective	Basic	RRL-GA	Difference
Big Policy	# IBOs	7.61 ± 0.16	7.60 ± 0.25	0.01 ± 0.31
	cycle time	1517.8 ± 28.2	1276.8 ± 18.5	241.0 ± 36.2
Parallel Separated Policy	# IBOs	7.54 ± 0.15	7.38 ± 0.16	0.16 ± 0.18
	cycle time	1508.1 ± 25.2	1444.4 ± 21.9	63.7 ± 27.6
Parallel Mixed Policy	# IBOs	7.44 ± 0.16	7.74 ± 0.16	-0.31 ± 0.19
	cycle time	1490.6 ± 28.4	1547.8 ± 26.9	-57.2 ± 32.3
Linear Policy	# IBOs	7.64 ± 0.16	7.95 ± 0.24	-0.31 ± 0.31
	cycle time	1526.4 ± 28.4	1353.8 ± 18.6	172.6 ± 35.3

The EPM "Big" was used in all runs. The first row contains the results comparing the execute-all approach with the RRL-GA approach. These results are taken from Table 9.2 and are included for comparison purposes. The last three rows contain the results of the generalization runs. In column "Basic", the results of the execute-all approach are listed. Column "RRL-GA" shows the results when the RRL-GA approach is configured with different policies, e.g. the second row compares the execution of the "Big" EPM with the execute-all approach and the RRL-GA approach configured with the policy that was originally learned for the "Parallel Separated" EPM. As expected, the best result was retrieved by RRL-GA approach with the policy that was learned for the "Big" product model (row 1). When comparing the execute-all approach with the generalization runs, the RRL-GA approach with the policies learned for the "Parallel Separated" and "Linear" EPM were significantly better regarding the cycle time.

Due to the structure of the "Big" EPM, there is not that much room for improvement as in the parallel product model examples. In both parallel structures half of the production rules do not have to be executed. Therefore, in terms of the percentage better results were retrieved in the experiments with the parallel structures. The generalization was successful to some extent. At least the policies learned for the "Parallel Separated" and "Linear" EPM achieved an improvement compared to the execute-all approach when applied to the bigger product model. A desirable generalization result would be that the RRL-GA runs show no significant difference between a policy that was learned for the "Big" EPM and another policy that was learned for a smaller EPM.

To improve the generalization as well as the efficiency, the IBO requires more detailed background knowledge, so it is able to make an informed decision. This applies specifically to bigger product models. The more complex a product model gets, the more execution alternatives exist. If there are many execution alternatives, the IBO needs a possibility to evaluate each of them. Background knowledge like work load of resources and estimated duration times of alternatives could be used for this evaluation. Another possibility to improve the performance could be the number of evolution steps. The GA requires much more evolution steps than used in the experiment to find better solutions. Due to the long simulation times, more evolution steps can only be carried out when the performance of the application has been significantly increased. Specifically the PROLOG related actions are very time consuming. This led to the implementation of a PROLOG cache as described in Sec. 6.2.1. Moreover, the concept of variants was introduced that allows the definition of policy rules on a higher level of abstraction than with information elements and production rules. In the next section, the usage of variants and background knowledge is analyzed.

9.4. RRL-GA-Variants

This section contains the experiments for the RRL-GA learning mechanism that makes use of variants. The first type of experiment has the objective to prove that RRL-GA-V (V is the abbreviation for variant) with the usage of background knowledge increases the efficiency in comparison to the basic execute-all and the RRL-GA approach.

An IBO estimates the remaining processing duration of each variant. It can also request workload information which can be used in the estimation of the processing duration. This allows an IBO to make more informed decisions regarding the execution of production rules.

The second type of experiment examines the generalization on the basis of a larger model which is again the "Big" EPM.

In all experiments, the objective is the minimization of KPI cycle time.

9.4.1. Experimental Setup

The experimental setup is similar to the setup for the RRL-GA experiments described in the previous section. The only difference is the pre-defined policy. For these experiments, the policy defined on the level of variants is used as defined in Sec. 6.1.4.

9.4.2. Results and Discussion

The following solutions were found by the RRL-GA-V approach for the different product model structures:

Parallel Separated: [1.00, 0.00, 0.15, 0.15, 1.00, 1.00, 0.35]

Parallel Mixed: [0.70, 0.30, 0.15, 0.17, 1.00, 1.00, 0.00]

Linear: [0.61, 0.24, 0.15, 0.70, 1.00, 1.00, 0.50]

Big: [0.60, 1.00, 0.82, 0.68, 1.00, 1.00, 0.60]

As in the previous RRL-GA experiment, these probability vectors are used in the second stage of the experiment. Table 9.4 shows the difference between the execute-all and the RRL-GA-V approach. Table 9.5 shows the difference between the RRL-GA and RRL-GA-V approach. As one can see the usage of variants and background knowledge significantly improves the performance regarding the cycle time in comparison to the execute-all approach, except for the "Linear" EPM for which no significant difference exists. The RRL-GA-V approach improved significantly the cycle time in comparison to the RRL-GA approach for the parallel EPMs. For the other models there was no significant difference as they do not provide much more room for improvement.

Especially in the "Parallel Separated" EPM, the usage of workload information is important. If the same execution path is taken for all EPMs, half of the agents get all work assigned whereas the other half is idle. As the probability P_1 equals one, the IBOs always request workload. As the resource breakdowns occur only rarely, the IBOs also request failure rate information seldom, except for the "Big" EPM. The duration of the requests of workload information and failure rate information have only a small impact on the cycle time. If no extra penalty is configured for the requests, the delay is two time units if information is requested. Thus, it can happen due to the probability distributed durations, that vector [0.60, 1.00, 0.82, 0.68, 1.00, 1.00, 0.60] gets a better fitness value than vector [0.60, 1.00, 0, 0.68, 1.00, 1.00, 0.60]. Therefore, one cannot assume, that a high probability indicates the importance of applying the corresponding rule.

In another experiment, the situation was evaluated in which the request of workload information and failure rates is penalized. The experiment was conducted with the linear EPM in which these requests are not necessary for an optimal execution. The penalty was set to 50 time units per request. In the following, the probability vector which was determined in the previous experiment is compared with the probability vector determined in the experiment with penalties:

Linear: [0.61, 0.24, 0.15, 0.70, 1.0, 1.0, 0.50]

Linear with Penalty   [0.00, 0.33, 0.00, 0.00, 1.0, 1.0, 0.39]

Note that the agents do not request information regarding workload or failure rates if a penalty is enforced ($p_1 = 0$ and $p_3 = 0$). This result shows that the learning mechanism is capable of determining an optimal behaviour of the agents.

Table 9.4.: Results of the efficiency experiment comparing the execute-all and RRL-GA-V approach for the four EPMs ($\alpha = 0.05$, 50 simulation runs).

Parallel Separated			
	Basic	RRL-GA-V	Difference
# IBOs	5.80 ± 0.10	2.29 ± 0.01	3.50 ± 0.10
cycle time	578.51 ± 9.12	228.59 ± 0.27	349.92 ± 9.11
workload	0.90 ± 0.002	0.50 ± 0.001	0.40 ± 0.002
messages	27.27 ± 0.004	23.61 ± 0.01	3.65 ± 0.01
waiting	194.80 ± 4.60	12.03 ± 0.13	182.76 ± 4.60

Parallel Mixed			
	Basic	RRL-GA-V	Difference
# IBOs	5.76 ± 0.08	2.34 ± 0.02	3.42 ± 0.08
cycle time	575.02 ± 6.89	233.66 ± 0.31	341.35 ± 6.77
workload	0.89 ± 0.002	0.50 ± 0.001	0.39 ± 0.002
messages	27.29 ± 0.004	25.10 ± 0.02	2.18 ± 0.02
waiting	191.71 ± 3.48	14.36 ± 0.15	177.35 ± 3.41

Linear			
	Basic	RRL-GA-V	Difference
# IBOs	8.99 ± 0.18	9.03 ± 0.20	-0.04 ± 0.28
cycle time	493.71 ± 9.37	496.17 ± 10.0	-2.46 ± 14.38
workload	0.91 ± 0.002	0.91 ± 0.002	$-3.13E\text{-}4 \pm 0.003$
messages	13.43 ± 0.004	24.92 ± 0.015	-11.49 ± 0.016
waiting	145.87 ± 4.68	145.66 ± 5.0	0.21 ± 7.19

Big			
	Basic	RRL-GA-V	Difference
# IBOs	7.67 ± 0.15	6.63 ± 0.14	1.04 ± 0.20
cycle time	1528.84 ± 26.79	1317.28 ± 18.40	211.56 ± 32.11
workload	0.81 ± 0.003	0.62 ± 0.002	0.19 ± 0.004
messages	51.64 ± 0.04	137.61 ± 0.08	-85.97 ± 0.09
waiting	155.10 ± 4.30	112.76 ± 3.04	42.35 ± 5.22

Table 9.5.: Results of the efficiency experiment comparing the RRL-GA and RRL-GA-V approach for the four EPMs ($\alpha = 0.05$, 50 simulation runs).

Parallel Separated			
	RRL-GA	RRL-GA-V	Difference
# IBOs	3.51 ± 0.02	2.30 ± 0.02	1.21 ± 0.03
cycle time	351.54 ± 1.55	228.67 ± 0.03	122.87 ± 1.57
workload	0.71 ± 0.002	0.50 ± 0.001	0.21 ± 0.002
messages	21.99 ± 0.02	23.61 ± 0.01	-1.62 ± 0.02
waiting	66.96 ± 0.66	12.05 ± 0.14	54.91 ± 0.68

Parallel Mixed			
	RRL-GA	RRL-GA-V	Difference
# IBOs	2.60 ± 0.02	2.33 ± 0.01	0.27 ± 0.02
cycle time	260.62 ± 0.77	233.43 ± 0.31	27.19 ± 0.86
workload	0.60 ± 0.002	0.50 ± 0.001	0.10 ± 0.002
messages	17.95 ± 0.02	25.12 ± 0.02	-7.17 ± 0.03
waiting	30.39 ± 0.39	14.26 ± 0.15	16.14 ± 0.43

Linear			
	RRL-GA	RRL-GA-V	Difference
# IBOs	10.61 ± 0.31	9.21 ± 0.20	1.39 ± 0.37
cycle time	495.18 ± 7.88	506.52 ± 10.22	-11.34 ± 11.88
workload	0.91 ± 0.002	0.91 ± 0.002	-0.001 ± 0.002
messages	13.43 ± 0.003	24.93 ± 0.02	-11.50 ± 0.02
waiting	146.61 ± 3.94	150.82 ± 5.11	-4.23 ± 5.94

Big			
	RRL-GA	RRL-GA-V	Difference
# IBOs	7.73 ± 0.28	6.61 ± 0.13	1.12 ± 0.33
cycle time	1288.37 ± 24.86	1318.70 ± 21.71	-30.33 ± 32.28
workload	0.73 ± 0.003	0.61 ± 0.003	0.11 ± 0.004
messages	51.72 ± 0.02	137.56 ± 0.11	-85.84 ± 0.11
waiting	105.09 ± 3.73	113.08 ± 3.56	-8.0 ± 5.02

The results of the generalization experiments are analyzed next. In all generalization experiments, the EPM "Big" was executed either with a policy specifically learned for this EPM or for another EPM such as the "Linear" EPM. Table 9.6 shows the results of the generalization in comparison to the execute-all approach. In column "Basic", the result of the execute-all approach is listed. Column "RRL-GA-V" shows the results of the RRL-GA-V approach with different policies. As one can see, there is a significant improvement which means that the generalization with the RRL-GA-V approach leads to better results than the execute-all approach.

As stated in Sec. 9.3, a desirable generalization result is that there is no significant difference between the usage of a policy that was learned for the "Big" EPM and another policy that was

Table 9.6.: Results of the generalization experiment with the RRL-GA Variants approach in comparison to the execute-all approach ($\alpha = 0.05$, 50 simulation runs).

Policy	Objective	Basic	RRL-GA-V	Difference
P. Separated Policy	# IBOs	7.61 ± 0.14	6.78 ± 0.16	0.83 ± 0.21
	cycle time	1520.14 ± 24.90	1317.86 ± 23.34	202.28 ± 32.30
P. Mixed Policy	# IBOs	7.59 ± 0.15	6.69 ± 0.15	0.90 ± 0.19
	cycle time	1520.14 ± 25.51	1302.94 ± 20.96	217.19 ± 33.99
Linear Policy	# IBOs	7.52 ± 0.16	6.67 ± 0.17	0.84 ± 0.22
	cycle time	1508.27 ± 27.39	1299.73 ± 22.21	208.92 ± 32.46

learned for a smaller EPM. Therefore, in the next generalization experiment, the RRL-GA-V approach with the policy learned for the "Big" EPM is compared with the policy learned for the other EPMs. Table 9.7 shows the results of this experiment. Column "Big RRL-GA-V" contains the result of the run in which the policy learned for the "Big" EPM is used. Column "RRL-GA-V" shows the resuls for the different policies. The fourth row is included for control only. As both runs use the same setting, there must not be a significant difference between them. As one can see, there is no significant difference. Thus, the generalization with the RRL-GA-V approach has worked as desired.

Table 9.7.: Results of the generalization experiment with the RRL-GA Variants approach in comparison to the policy learned by RRL-GA-V for the big model ($\alpha = 0.05$, 50 simulation runs).

Policy	Objective	Big RRL-GA-V	RRL-GA-V	Difference
P. Separated Policy	# IBOs	6.64 ± 0.13	6.76 ± 0.17	-0.11 ± 0.23
	cycle time	1323.0 ± 21.01	1315.82 ± 24.09	7.18 ± 32.93
P. Mixed Policy	# IBOs	6.59 ± 0.11	6.63 ± 0.14	-0.04 ± 0.20
	cycle time	1317.04 ± 20.22	1300.12 ± 21.45	16.92 ± 29.68
Linear Policy	# IBOs	6.64 ± 0.11	6.67 ± 0.16	-0.02 ± 0.20
	cycle time	1326.32 ± 19.82	1316.04 ± 22.37	10.27 ± 28.52
Big Policy	# IBOs	6.63 ± 0.12	6.61 ± 0.14	0.02 ± 0.18
	cycle time	1321.84 ± 20.0	1318.64 ± 24.19	3.20 ± 30.48

Despite the fact, that the last experiment showed the generalization capability of the learning mechanism RRL-GA-V, there is one aspect that must be considered. The generalization can only work if the IBO has learned the knowledge that is required for the execution of the bigger EPM by executing the smaller EPM. If critical situations exist only in the bigger model, but not in the smaller one, the IBO may not act adequately. Of course, there is always the possibility to initiate the offline learning phase which allows the IBOs to learn. But in this case, the bigger model must be used in the offline learning phase.

In the next experiment it is shown what may happen, if an agent has not learned the required knowledge. The execution of the "Linear" EPM does not require workload information. On the contrary, the execution of the "Parallel separated" EPM is highly dependent on this information. If a smaller arrival rate is set, the usage of workload information becomes even more important when executing the "Parallel Separated" EPM. Thus, the arrival rate[2] is changed from 100 to 55.

Table 9.8 shows the results of this experiment. As one can see, the execution of the "Parallel Separated" EPM with the RRL-GA-V approach using the policy that was learned for the "Linear" EPM leads to a very bad result. The IBOs have not learned the importance of workload information when the "Linear" EPM was executed in the offline learning phase. As the "Parallel Separated" EPM was executed with a low arrival rate, the usage of workload information is important in order to distribute the work evenly among the resource agents.

Table 9.8.: Results of the generalization experiment with the RRL-GA-V approach using the policy learned for the "Linear" EPM on the parallel separated EPM ($\alpha = 0.05$, 50 simulation runs).

Parallel Separated		
Policy	# IBOs	cycle time
ParSep Policy	2.29 ± 0.01	220.67 ± 15.40
Linear Policy	228.79 ± 0.34	550.51 ± 10.88
Difference	-218.38 ± 15.4	-321.72 ± 10.84

9.5. Comparing RRL-GA and RRL-PSO

In this section, a variant of PSO is studied and compared with the GA. In Chapter 8 the Gap Search (GS) method in combination with PSO was introduced and analyzed on the basis of standard test functions. In the following, this PSO variant is evaluated for the iEPM approach.

Therefore, PSO instead of a GA is applied in the offline learning phase for determining the probability vector. Indeed, the GS method is applied in the different areas of PSO such as the random initialization of the solutions for the initial population as well as for the diversity and feasibility preservation methods.

As mentioned before, the offline learning phase is the critical part of the iEPM approach as for each solution determined by the heuristic, a simulation must be carried out in order to calculate the solution's fitness value. The objective of the experiment is to show that GS in combination with PSO leads to a better exploration in the search space and to a faster convergence to the optima. If this can be shown, the duration of the offline learning phase can be reduced by using PSO with GS instead of the GA.

The conducted experiments and the corresponding results were published in [159].

---

[2] A lower arrival rate results in the generation of more EPMs. Thus, the workload is increased by lowering the arrival rate.

9.5.1. Experimental Setup

In this experiment, the evaluation of the different heuristics is performed with the "Parallel Separated" EPM. The settings are defined as described in Sec. 9.2, except that the arrival rate is set to 55 instead of 100 which leads to a higher workload. A higher workload requires an even distribution of work among the resource agents. Therefore, the IBOs are under more pressure to learn an adequate behaviour than if the workload is very low.

The PSO method is run with 20 particles for 30 iterations and two different topologies (global best and ring).

The policy on the basis of variants is given as described in Sec. 6.1.4. As the policy consists of seven policy rules, the dimension of the positions is seven as well. The term "standard PSO" refers to use the global best topology without the GS method. The ring topology is indicated by the notation "ring". The inertia weight w and the parameters $c1$ and $c2$ are selected as 0.4, 1.0 and 1.0. The selection of these values is based on the best combination obtained through several tests on the application in preliminary experiments.

The GA is a real-vector GA using a Gaussian mutation. The mutation operator is applied to 15 percent of the genes of every individual selected through a binary tournament selection. This setting was determined in preliminary experiments. For comparison purposes, the population size of the GA is set to 20 as well.

Each run is repeated 20 times. In the following Random refers to the use of a pseudo-random generator for finding new positions.

9.5.2. Results and Discussion

In the following the different experiments for comparing PSO with GA are discussed. Each experiment analyzes a different aspect such as the influence of topologies on the convergence.

Influence of Topologies

The first experiment compares the PSO with different topologies with the GA. Fig. 9.3 shows the results over generations. It can be observed that the PSO with ring topology converges more slowly than the PSO with the global best topology (indicated as "standard" in the figure). The GA obtains the best results at the end, but has the slowest convergence. Note that the quick convergence is of great importance for the iEPM approach as the simulations and therefore the fitness evaluations are time-intensive.

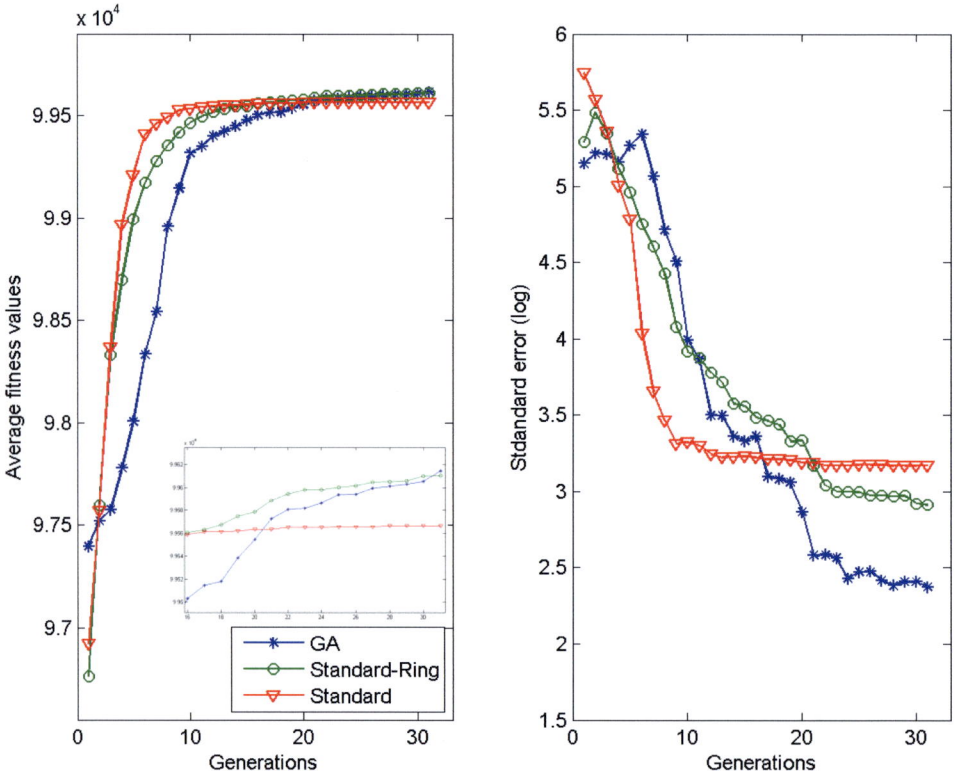

Figure 9.3.: The results of PSO with global best and ring topologies (denoted as Standard and Standard-Ring) and the results of GA. In the left figure, a zoom of the average fitness values is depicted.

Influence of Initial Population

These experiments are dedicated to examine the influence of the GS method in producing the initial population. In order to achieve this, 250 different initial particles are produced using GS and Random methods. Table 9.9 shows the minimum, average and maximum values of the fitness values of the produced initial populations. It can be observed that the GS method is able to find better fitness values in average and minimum cases and with lower standard deviation.

Table 9.9.: Fitness values of the initial population produced by GS and Random methods over 250 different runs.

Method	Minimum	Average	Maximum	Std. Deviation
GS	94200	97044	99253	1111.7
Random	93471	96936	99386	1136.1

The influence of the initial populations on the results of the standard PSO and other methods are analyzed next. By these experiments, the influence of the initial velocities are examined as well. Fig. 9.4 shows the results of a standard PSO with different initial populations.

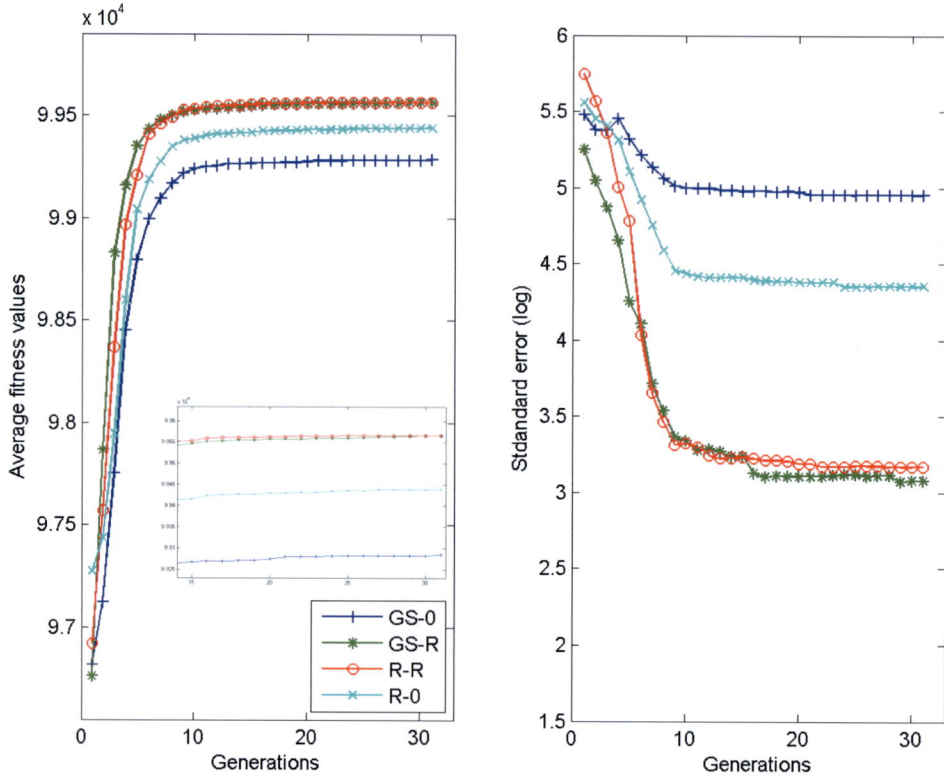

Figure 9.4.: PSO with different initial populations and initial velocities.

The initial population is selected at random (R) or using the GS method (GS) and the initial velocities are set to zero (denoted as -0) or a random value (denoted as -R). It can be observed that the PSO with the population produced by GS and initial random velocities can perform better compared to the other cases and this effect is consistent over the iterations. Also the standard error obtained by GS-R is the lowest among the others. These experiments illustrate that if a different initial population is selected, different results are obtained. This shows that the results depend on the initial population. For the further experiments, the best initialization method is selected from here, namely GS-R.

Influence of Diversity Preserving Methods

These experiments are carried out to observe the influence of employing GS to PSO in order to preserve the diversity in the population and avoid premature stagnation in local optima. Motivated from the promising results retrieved with the standard test functions (see Chapter. 8), the expectation is that the GS method improves the performance of the PSO compared to the standard PSO and the GA algorithm when applied in the iEPM approach.

In these experiments the positions and the velocities of 10 percent of the population are reinitialized after each iteration using the GS method. The velocities of those particles are either kept unchanged (denoted as -K), set to zero (denoted as -0) or selected randomly (denoted as -R). In Fig. 9.5, it can be observed that all the variations of PSO outperform the GA for the first 15 iterations. As expected, the GS method improves the performance of the standard PSO.

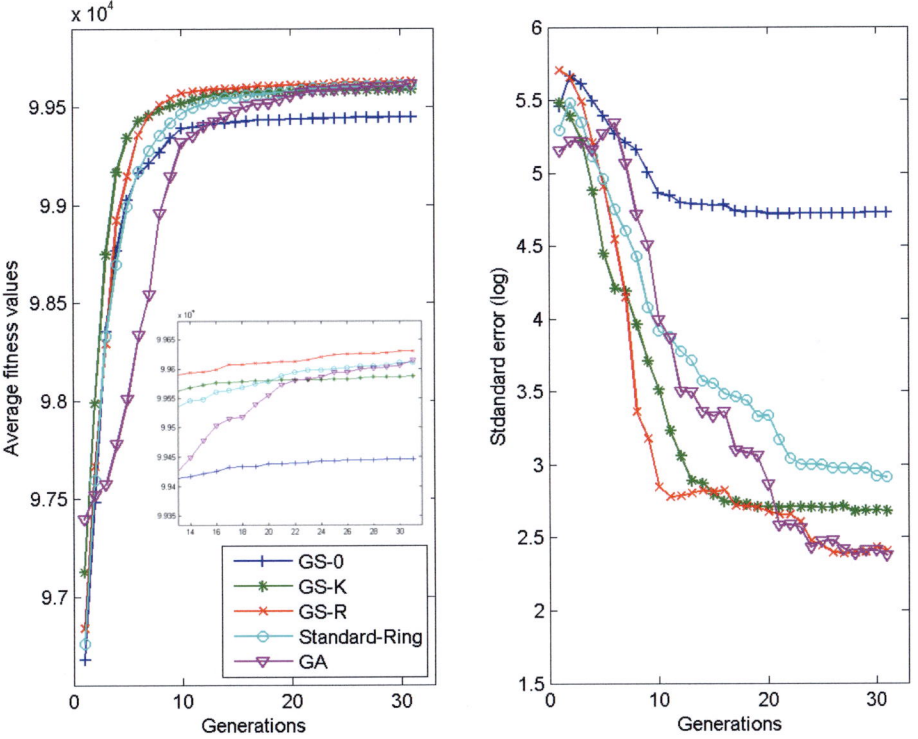

Figure 9.5.: A standard PSO and a PSO using the Gap Search method for diversity preserving. In the left figure, a zoom of the average fitness values is depicted.

Influence of Feasibility Preserving Methods

The following experiments examine a spectrum of different feasibility preserving methods for those particles leaving the feasible search space. Those particles are replaced on the boundary of the search space (denoted as border-) or reinitialized using the Gap Search method (denoted as GS-). Their velocities are either kept unchanged (denoted as -K), selected at random (-R) or set to zero (-0). The results shown in Fig. 9.6 indicate that setting the particles on the boundary and selecting a random velocity leads to better results than reinitializing the particles using the GS method. Also the standard error shown in Fig. 9.6 illustrates that the border-R method is the best choice in our experiments. In fact, this is a reasonable strategy to replace the solutions which tend to go out of the search space on the borders and just give them a new velocity vector. If their old velocity vector is assigned, the particles tend to go out of the search space again.

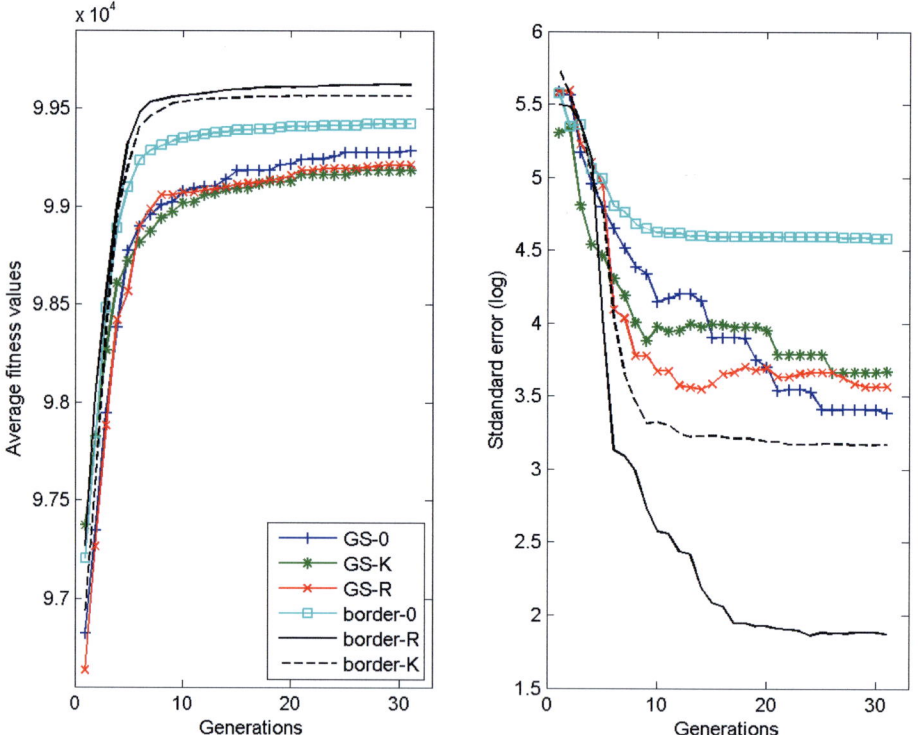

Figure 9.6.: Different PSO methods using different feasibility preserving methods (boundary handling methods).

Final Evaluation

Using all the above experiments, the best combination of the PSO and Gap Search methods is selected as follows:

(a) Initialize the population of PSO using the Gap Search method and set the initial velocities to random.

(b) Employ a Gap Search method to 10 percent of the particles for diversity preservation.

(c) Use a simple feasibility preservation method such as the one denoted as border-R (as described above).

This combination of GS and PSO is compared with the GA and the standard PSO. Fig. 9.7

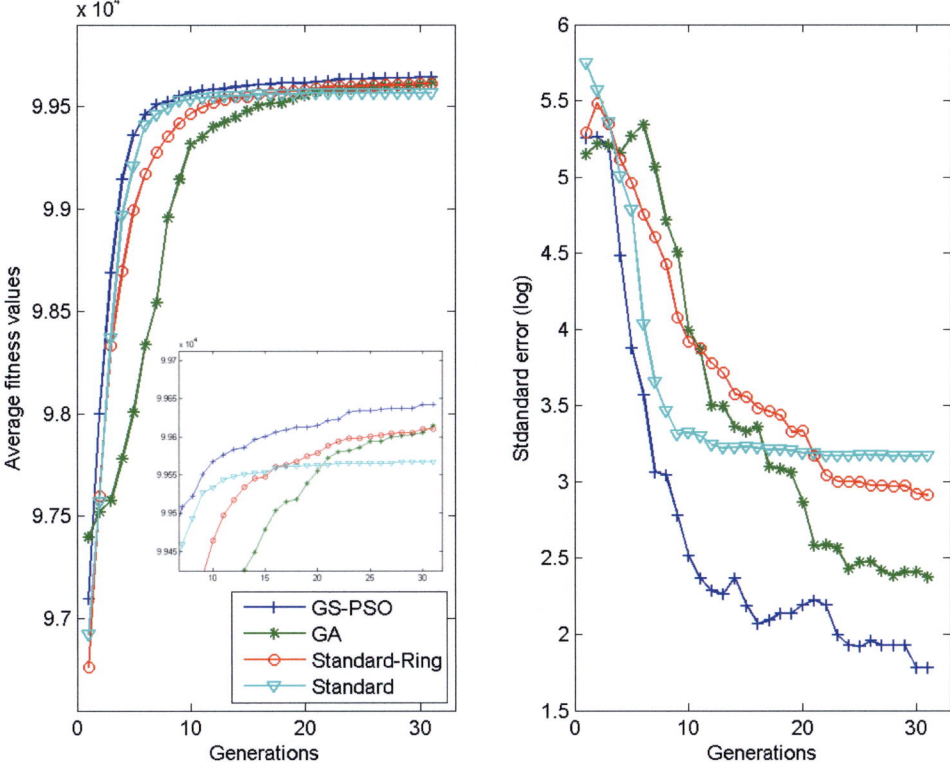

Figure 9.7.: Final evaluation of PSO variants and GA. In the left figure, a zoom of the average fitness values is depicted.

Fig. 9.7 left shows that the GS-PSO converges very fast to the optimal solution, whereas GA is relatively slow. Moreover, GS-PSO yields to a better final result in comparison to the other methods The standard PSOs with global best and ring topology perform much better in terms of a fast convergence than the GA but are outperformed by the GS-PSO. Also the standard PSO has a very large standard error compared to the others (see Fig. 9.7 right), whereas GS-PSO has the lowest standard error.

Around one third of the generations can be saved when using PSO with the GS method compared to the GA. Fig. 9.8 shows the zoom of the curve progression of the average fitness value as depicted in Fig. 9.7. The horizontal line illustrates the savings of generations. The GS-PSO yields the best fitness value obtained by the other methods at generation 20. Alternatively, if the same number of generations is carried out, the GS-PSO yields a better optimal solution than the other methods.

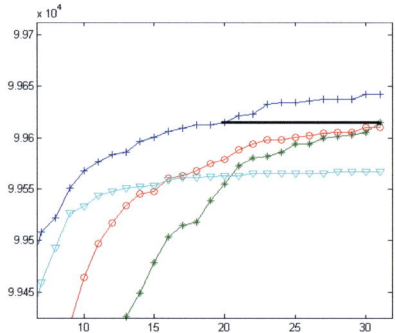

Figure 9.8.: Zoom of Fig. 9.7. As illustrated by the horizontal black line, around one third of the generations can be saved when using GS-PSO.

The standard PSO proposed by Bratton and Kennedy in [38] suggests a population size of 50. However, due to the timely intensive simulations, a smaller population size (20) was selected in the above experiments. For comparison purposes, the performance of the proposed GS-PSO containing 50 particles (denoted as GS-PSO50) is compared with the standard PSO (with the two topologies). Fig. 9.9 shows the results.

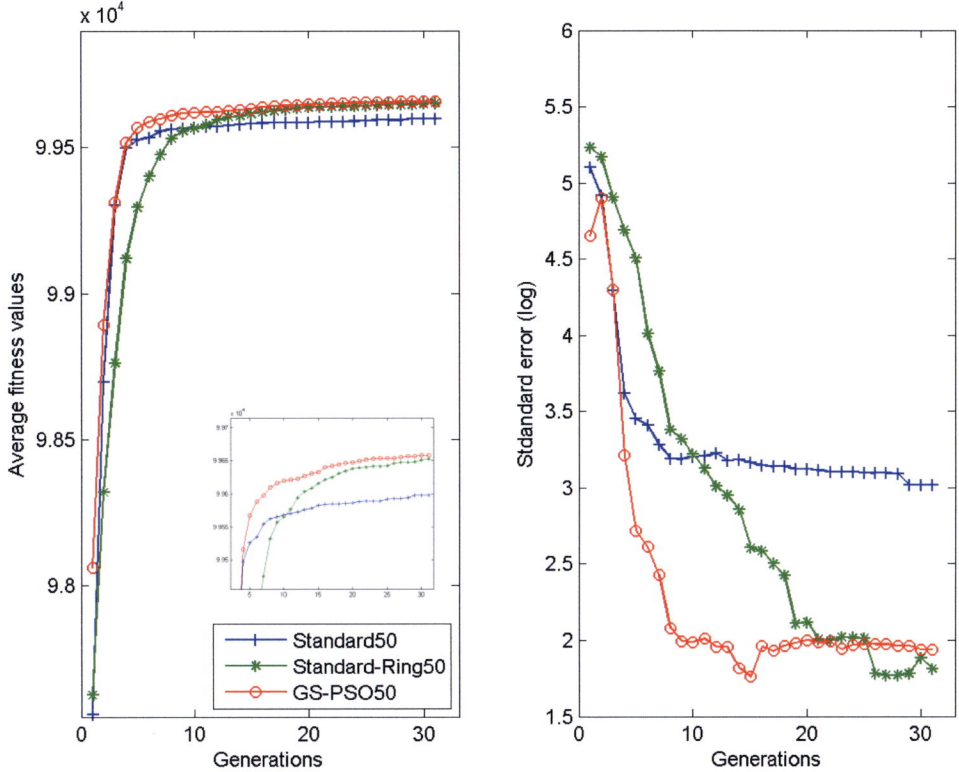

Figure 9.9.: Final evaluation of PSO variants and GA.

One can observe that during the early generations, the GS-PSO performs like the standard PSO (indicating the star topology) and both perform better than the standard PSO with ring topology. This result is expected as the ring topology has a slow convergence as studied by Kennedy and Eberhart in [150]. The GS-PSO outperforms both the standard variants at the end of the generations. Furthermore, the GS-PSO obtains much better average fitness value of the initial population than the other methods. This is due to the initialization of particles using the Gap Search method. Overall, GS-PSO is able to converge very fast to a good solution and this is a desirable behaviour for the iEPM approach with very time consuming fitness evaluations. In particular, a significant performance gain could be achieved by applying GS in PSO as initialization and preservation method. Either one third of the iterations can be saved or if the same number of iterations are carried out, a significant better solution is found in comparison to the other methods such as GA or regular PSO.

In this section, the performance of different heuristics were compared. In the next section, experiments are conducted using a more complex business process. The experiments include also a comparison between GA and PSO.

9.6. New Customer Business Process

The business process introduced in this section is a simplified version of a real "new customer" business process that was implemented in a large German bank. The simplification has been done in such a way that only the main information elements and activities are included. Moreover, the business process has been made anonymous. It is an example of a more complex business process with 14 information elements and 18 production rules.

Several objectives are attained with the conducted experiments. Firstly, the performance of the learning mechanisms RRL-GA and RRL-PSO is compared once more in order to show that PSO outperforms GA also for larger EPMs. Secondly, the execution of the "new customer" EPM is analyzed in different scenarios in order to show that the agents autonomously adapt their behaviour. The experiments shall provide first insights into the advantages of the iEPM approach. The advantages are further studied on the basis of a mortgage and credit application business process. Finally, it is shown that the iEPM approach works also in larger scenarios with a higher number of agents.

Business Requirements

The process is initiated when a new customer applies for one of the financial products the bank offers, e.g. a new customer intends to open a debit account. First, the application is filled out and checked for completeness as well as correctness in the next step. If the application is incomplete or incorrect, repair actions are performed which may also include requests for information or new documents. The process may be canceled if the requested information is not retrieved within a given time period. In this case, a letter is sent to the customer which informs him about the cancellation of the application and the final result is set to CANCELED. After the repair actions, the application is checked again. This iteration takes place until the application is complete and correct. Afterwards, the financial situation and the customer history are checked. If one of these checks has a negative outcome, the customer is informed about the refusal of his application and the status is set to REJECTED. In addition to the checks, the business object person is created. If the two checks have a positive outcome, the person is accepted as customer and the corresponding business object is created. After the creation of the customer business object, the signature is scanned and electronically stored. Additionally, the financial products are created. After this creation, the products are activated and the customer is informed about the successful processing and acceptance of his application. If these steps were carried out, the final status is set to APPROVED.

The EPM

All information that accrues during the execution of this process is listed in Table 9.10.

Table 9.10.: Information elements of the "new customer" EPM.

Information Element	Explanation
application	application data of the new customer
correctness check	result of the correctness check of the application data
Repair	missing documents and information requested
financial situation check	result of the customer's financial situation check
customer history check	result of the check of past customer's financial transactions
person, customer, product	the created business objects
product activation	activation of created product(s)
refusal, cancellation, acceptance correspondence	the generated correspondence for informing the customer about the outcome of his application
signature extracted	extracted and verified signature for future electronic processing
final status	indicates the final result of the new customer process

Once the information elements have been identified, these information elements must be included in the model and the dependencies between them must be specified. The resulting EPM is depicted in Fig. 9.10.

The explanations of the production rules and the dependencies are listed in Table 9.11.

Table 9.11.: Production rules of the "new customer" EPM.

ID	Origin Nodes	Description of the production rule	Explanation of the dependency
0	-	take application from customer	initial information, no dependency to other information
1	0	check correctness of the application	the application data must be available
2	0,1	repair of an incorrect or incomplete application (e.g. request of documents) available	the result of the correctness check (failure) and the application are
3	0,2	recheck of repaired application	repair was performed and the repaired application is available
4	0,1	check financial situation of the customer	the application data is complete and correct
5	0,1	check customer history	the application data is complete and correct
6	0,1	create Business Object (BO) person	the application data is complete and correct
7	0,3,4,5	create BO customer	BO person is extended based on
			Continued on next page

201

		Continued from previous page	
ID	**Origin Nodes**	**Description of the production rule**	**Explanation of the dependency**
			application data (only if checks had a positive outcome)
8	0,6	create BO product	BO product is created based on the application data and is linked with the customer
9	0,3	inform customer about refusal of the application	the outcome of the check and the application data are available
10	0,4	inform customer about refusal of the application	the outcome of the check and the application data are available
11	0,2	inform customer about the cancellation due to missing documents	the application data is available and the deadline exceeded
12	0,6	extract the signature and store it electronically for future checks	the application data is available and the customer is created (signature is linked with the customer)
13	6,9	inform customer about the successful processing of his application	customer and product related information is available
14	9	activate the product	bo product must be available
15	7	set final status REJECTED	negative outcome of the check and the application data is available
16	8	set final status CANCELED	negative outcome of the check and the application data is available
17	10,11,12	set final status APPROVED	customer and product specific data was created and the customer was informed about the acceptance

In order to increase the understandability and readability, the EPM is transformed into a BPMN model. In the BPMN model production rules become activities and the different kind of dependencies must be modeled using the available gateways of BPMN. As in the EPM, the information node is created after the successful execution of the related activity. The transformation is performed on the basis of transformation pattern as described in Sec. 7.3. The transformation has been developed for the integration of the iEPM approach in commercial BPM tools. Using these transformation patterns, the EPM is transfered into a BPMN model which is depicted in Fig. 9.11.

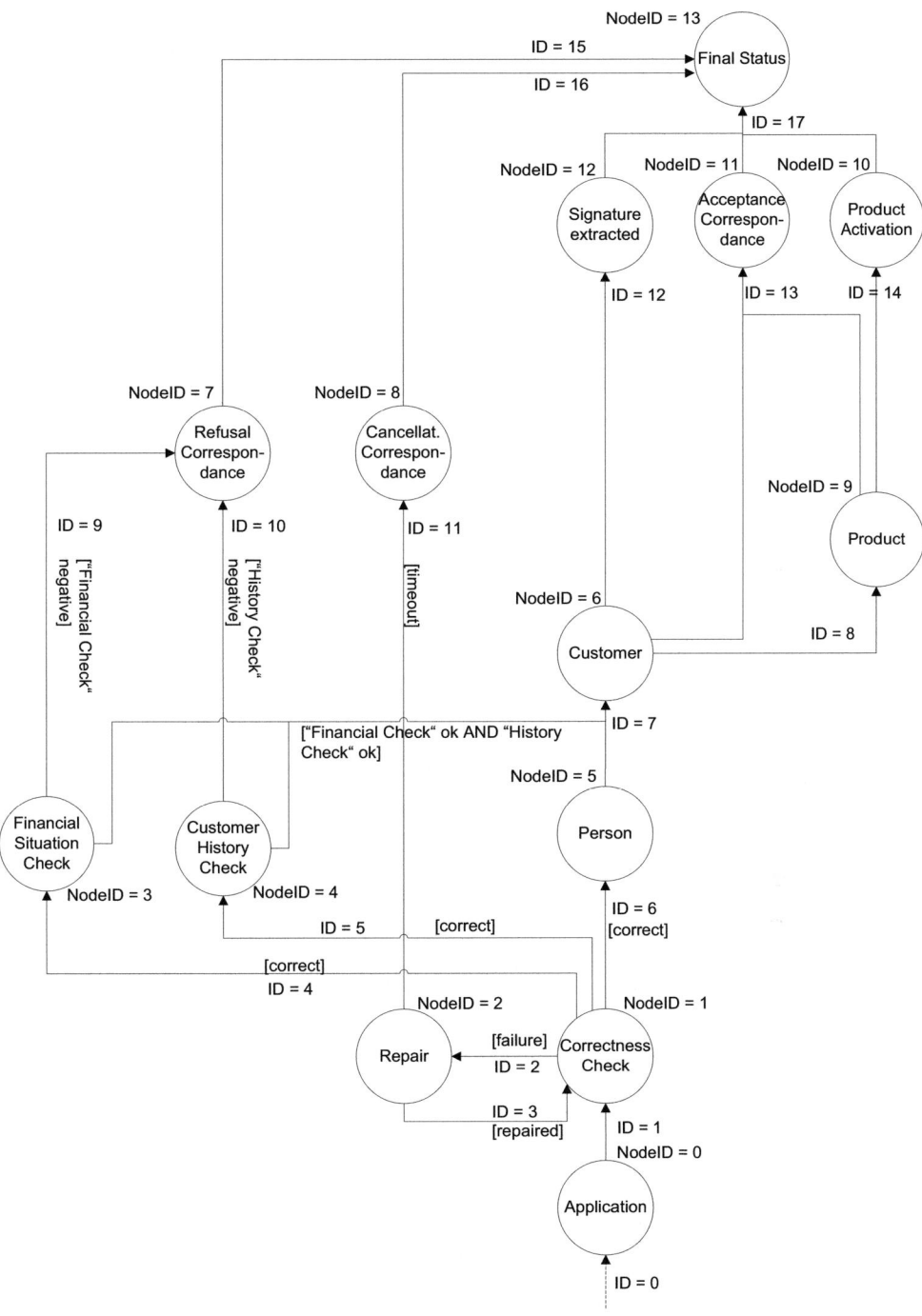

Figure 9.10.: EPM "new customer". In order to simplify the figure, not all connections are depicted in which node "Application" appears as a origin node. See Table 9.11 for the complete list of origin nodes.

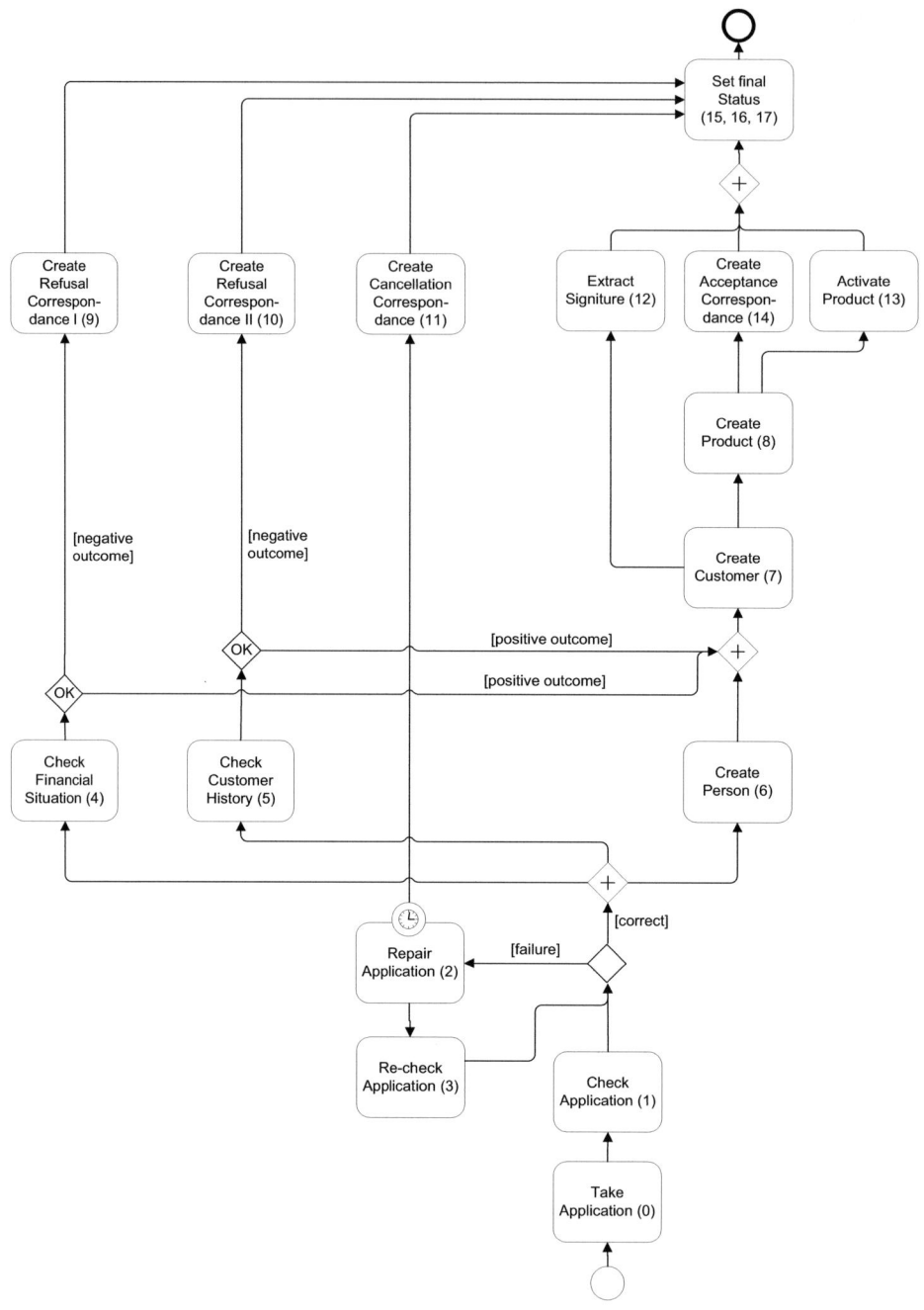

Figure 9.11.: Business process "new customer" as BPMN model. The numbers in brackets correspond to the production rule IDs. For simplifying the figure, the send and receive events are not depicted. If one information node is created by different production rules, one can model either multiple activities (e.g. production rules 9 and 10) or only one activity (e.g. production rules 15, 16 and 17). One has to keep in mind that this process model is still based on information dependencies as each activity creates one information element.

Experiments and Results

Before different scenarios are analyzed, once more the performance of GA is compared with PSO. In all experiments, the policy defined on the level of variants is used as defined in Sec. 6.1.4.

In the first step, preliminary experiments for determining the number of time slots (simulation duration of one run) and the number of repetitions of the simulation were determined. There is a trade off between the total simulation duration and the precision of the calculated fitness value. The more repetitions are carried out, the higher the precision but the longer is the simulation duration. Based on the first conducted experiments, the duration is set to 100,000 time slots and the number of repetitions is set to three.

In the next step, different parameter settings of the GA and the PSO were evaluated. The best parameter combination of the GA is: population size 30, no crossover, gaussian mutation with rate 0.15, tournament selection. The best parameter combination of PSO is as follows: inertia weight (w), c_1 and c_2 values are selected as 1.0, 0.8, 1.0 (see Equation 2.9). With these parameter combinations, experiments were performed with the "new customer" EPM in order to compare the offline learning phases of RRL-GA and RRL-PSO. The PSO method is run with 20 particles and the GA with 30 individuals for 30 generations and 20 different initial seeds.

In Fig. 9.12 one can observe that the application of PSO outperforms GA. PSO requires only 5 iterations instead of 20 in comparison to the GA.

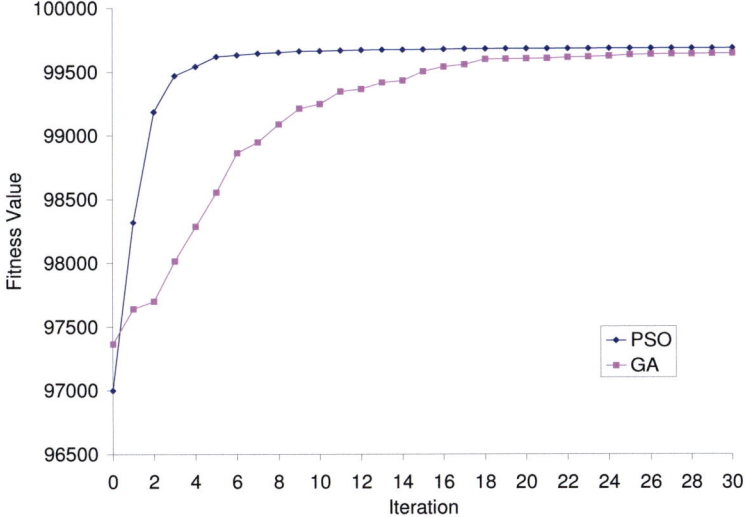

Figure 9.12.: Comparison of PSO and GA using the "new customer" EPM (average fitness value of the best solution per iteration). Observe, that the PSO has a faster convergence than the GA. At the end both find the optimal solution.

In the next experiments, different scenarios are analyzed in order to get first insights into the advantage of the iEPM approach. First, two different scenarios are considered. In scenario I the application of a new customer is accepted. In scenario II the application is rejected due to the customer's negative financial situation. In both scenarios no repair actions are necessary for the application. For each scenario, the optimal probability vector is determined in the offline learning phase. A low workload is chosen by setting a moderate arrival rate of new customers (process instances) and by providing enough resources. The resulting probability vectors of the GA runs are:

Scenario I: [0.0, 0.27, 1.0, 1.00, 1.0, 1.0, 0.27]
Scenario II: [0.0, 0.42, 1.0, 0.82, 1.0, 1.0, 0.46]

The behaviour of the IBOs in scenario I is as follows: The IBOs do not use work load information at all. The activation of variants is based on the execution number of the variants. The variant that has been most frequently successfully completed the EPM is chosen. Analyzing the log files shows that the IBO decides to execute all production rules of the variant immediately, e.g. production rules 4, 5 and 6 as well as 8 and 12 are executed in parallel[3]. As in scenario I, the behaviour in scenario II is mainly based on the execution number without considering work load information. As in scenario I, the IBOs start the execution of production rules 3, 4, and 5. In scenario II it would be sufficient to execute production rule 3 only as the negative outcome of the financial situation check finishes the process by the execution of production rule 9 and 15 (final status rejected).

By increasing the system load (providing less resources in combination with a higher arrival rate), the execution of unnecessary tasks has a negative effect on the mean cycle time. Scenario III is based on scenario II, except that it has a higher system load. The determined probability vector for scenario III is:

Scenario III: [0.0, 0.13, 0.2, 0.8, 1.0, 1.0, 0.53]

The behaviour of the IBOs in scenario III is different now. They activate the variants mainly based on the estimated duration of the variants. By this, the variants with the shortest processing time left are chosen. Now the IBOs only rarely execute unnecessary production rules. Another way to force the IBOs to a different behaviour is to use other KPIs in combination with an adequate policy. For example costs could be additionally considered, so the IBOs are punished if they execute unnecessary tasks. The conducted experiments show that the behaviour of the IBOs is highly dependent on the scenario, the fitness function (with its KPIs) and the policy. The

---

[3]The log file of the simulation is analyzed in order to evaluate the created EPM instances using the open source process mining toolkit ProM.

fitness function and policy must carefully be defined to achieve the results desired independent from specific scenarios. The capability of the agents to autonomously adapt their behaviour in changing scenarios will be discussed in more detail on the basis of two other business processes.

So far, experiments with a relatively small number of agents were conducted. In order to demonstrate that also a higher number of agents can be handled by the iEPM approach, an experiment considering a larger scenario is conduced. The actual requirement regarding the quantity structure of the new customer business process is as follows: The number of new applications per day is approximately 100. Based on this requirement, the simulation is configured as follows: If the time units correspond to minutes, the arrival rate has to be set to 4.8 (60*8/100) assuming that the arriving applications are equally distributed. Note that it is assumed that a day has 8 business hours and a month 20 business days. The simulation duration for the offline learning phase is set to one month which equals 9600 (60*8*20) time units. Sufficient resources are provided in order to avoid delays due to waiting times. The total number of resource agents equals 450. Thereby, the parallel processing of the production rules is the optimal strategy as this minimizes the considered KPI cycle time. In order to speed up the simulation duration, the Round-Robin scheduling method was used instead of a negotiation protocol (see Sec. 7.4). This scenario could be handled by the iEPM approach. The IBOs learned to execute the production rules in parallel as expected. Note that the larger the scenario, the longer is computational time (see also Sec. 7.4 concerning the scalability of the iEPM approach.). This pertains also to the configured simulation duration, e.g. if the simulation duration of the offline learning phase is set to one year.

In Sec. 5.5 it was explained, the correctness of the implementation and the statistical evaluation is verified by comparing it with the results of related approaches such as regular business process simulation. The experimental setup for both experiment types must be performed in such a way that there is no significant difference between the results. In particular, the EPM and the related process model must have the same degree of flexibility. This means that the EPM must not have more execution options than the process model. If there are more execution options, the EPM may yield better results. Furthermore, arrival rate, processing durations, number of resources, among others, must be equal in both experiment types. The average processing time is chosen as KPI. The comparison was successful as both experiments yielded the same average processing time (1499 time units).

9.7. The Advantages of iEPM

This section has the objective to show the advantages of the iEPM approach by means of different business processes derived from examples which can be found in literature and practice.

The enhanced flexibility of the EPM stems from the way information is modeled. In regular process models, the order of activities is fixed as the activities are modeled either in a sequence or in parallel. By modeling information dependencies, the EPM does not fix the actual execution order. In the following, two examples of business processes will be analyzed, a credit application and a mortgage application business process. Both examples show that the EPM comprises multiple process designs in one model. This enables the agents to choose the optimal path through the EPM for each instance. Furthermore, the execution path can be changed anytime. This is an advantage that other approaches do not provide as they choose a specific variant at instantiation without having the possibility to change it afterwards.

In Chapter 7 the two application methods of the iEPM approach in practice were introduced. The advantage of the iEPM approach as intelligent BPM engine is demonstrated on the basis of the credit and mortgage application examples. For these business processes, different design options are analyzed in varying scenarios, in particular it is examined how changing scenarios affect the KPIs. The changes that will be analyzed are the occurrence of quality problems, the increase of workload and the reduction of available resources. In simulation based experiments, it is shown that process models can become suboptimal in changing scenarios. Furthermore, it is shown how the iEPM approach is capable of handling such changes by adapting the behaviour of the intelligent agents in such a way that leads to the optimization of the KPIs under consideration. For two different business processes it is shown, that the iEPM approach outperforms the regular process model based BPM approach.

The advantage of the iEPM approach as intelligent business process optimization methodology is demonstrated on the basis of the mortgage business process. It is shown that the iEPM approach reduces the effort of modeling alternative process designs as it is required in regular business process optimization methodologies.

9.7.1. Experimental Setup

In this section, the general experimental setup is explained that pertains to both examples. The policy is given as defined in Table 9.12.

The policy is defined on the level of variants and comprises different execution strategies. The rules can be explained as follows: Rule (1) requests work load information if it is not available and has not been requested yet. Rule (2) assures that work load information is kept up-to-date. Rule (3) equals the execute-all strategy which means that all executable production rules are executed immediately. Rule (4) activates the variant that was activated most frequently (the one

Table 9.12.: The pre-defined policy with different execution strategies.

No	Condition	Action	P
1	not workloads_available, not workloads_requested	request_workload	p_1
2	workloads_available, workloads_outdated, not workloads_requested	request_workload	p_2
3	number_of_activated_variants(No),No=0	activate_exec_all	p_3
4	number_of_activated_variants(No),No=0, maximum_execution_number(Variant,NoExecutions)	activate_exec_no(Variant)	p_4
5	execution_mode(exec_no), activated_variant(Variant)	proceed(Variant)	p_5
6	number_of_activated_variants(No), No=0, minimum_weighted_duration(Variant, Duration)	activate(Variant)	p_6
7	activated_variant(VariantA), weighted_variant_duration(VariantA, DurationA), minimum_weighted_duration(VariantB, DurationB), DurationA=<DurationB	proceed(VariantA)	p_7
8	activated_variant(VariantA), weighted_variant_duration(VariantA, DurationA), minimum_weighted_duration(VariantB, DurationB), not VariantA=VariantB, DurationA>DurationB	switch(VariantA,VariantB)	p_8

with the highest execution number). Rule (5) proceeds with the execution of the variant that has been activated based on its execution number. Rule (6) activates the variant with the shortest estimated execution duration. Rule (7) assures that if the activated variant is still the one with the smallest estimated duration, its processing is continued. Rule (8) switches the variants if there is a shorter one than the activated.

9.7.2. Mortgage Application Business Process

This example is utilized in order to show the two practical application methods introduced in Chapter 7. The first conducted experiment shows the advantage of the iEPM approach in an intelligent business process optimization methodology. The second experiment has the objective to demonstrate the advantage if the iEPM approach applied as intelligent BPM engine.

In [131] different approaches for evaluating business process variants regarding the cycle time are discussed. They use approaches such as static path analysis, Monte-Carlo simulation, and ARIS simulation. Their analysis is based on a simplified business process of a mortgage application. In the following, this example is used as well in order to show the advantage of the practical application methods of the iEPM approach as stated above.

Business Requirements

The business process "mortgage application" comprises the following tasks: If an application for a mortgage is available, the construction reference documents and the collaterals of the applicant must be checked. The construction reference documents are checked for completeness. The collaterals are checked whether they are sufficient for the applied mortgage. If the construction reference documents are incomplete, the missing documents are requested from the applicant and checked again when they are available. If the collaterals are insufficient, the mortgage will be rejected. If the documents are complete and the collaterals sufficient, the mortgage is granted. Table 9.13 shows the corresponding decision table comprising three rules.

Table 9.13.: Mortgage business process - decision table.

	Rule 1	Rule 2	Rule 3
Collaterals sufficient	Yes	Yes	No
Construction Reference Documents complete	Yes	No	-
Grant Mortgage	X		
Reject Mortgage			X
Request Missing Documents		X	

Based on these business requirements, three process designs are possible. In option A (see Fig. 9.13(a)), the activities "Check Construction Reference Documents" and "Check Collaterals" are modeled in parallel. In option B (see Fig. 9.13(b)) these checks are modeled in a sequence. The parallel design has the advantage that it can lead to a better cycle time than the sequential design. The disadvantage of the parallel design is that certain tasks may be executed unnecessarily. This is the case, when the mortgage is rejected due to insufficient collaterals, while the construction reference documents are checked or even while further documents are requested. If there are sufficient resources available, this sunk work or sunk processing time does not have any negative effect on the cycle time. But it has a negative effect on the costs. The third option is retrieved if the order of the checks in option B is switched. This design has the disadvantage that the NO-GO decision regarding the collaterals is made at the end and the construction reference documents are always completely checked. Therefore, the third option is not analyzed further.

Let us assume that the objective is the minimization of the costs by assuring a specific service level agreement regarding the cycle time. Equation 9.1 defines the objective as follows:

$$\text{minimize } meanC \qquad\qquad\qquad [9.1]$$
$$\text{subject to: } meanCT < 1200$$

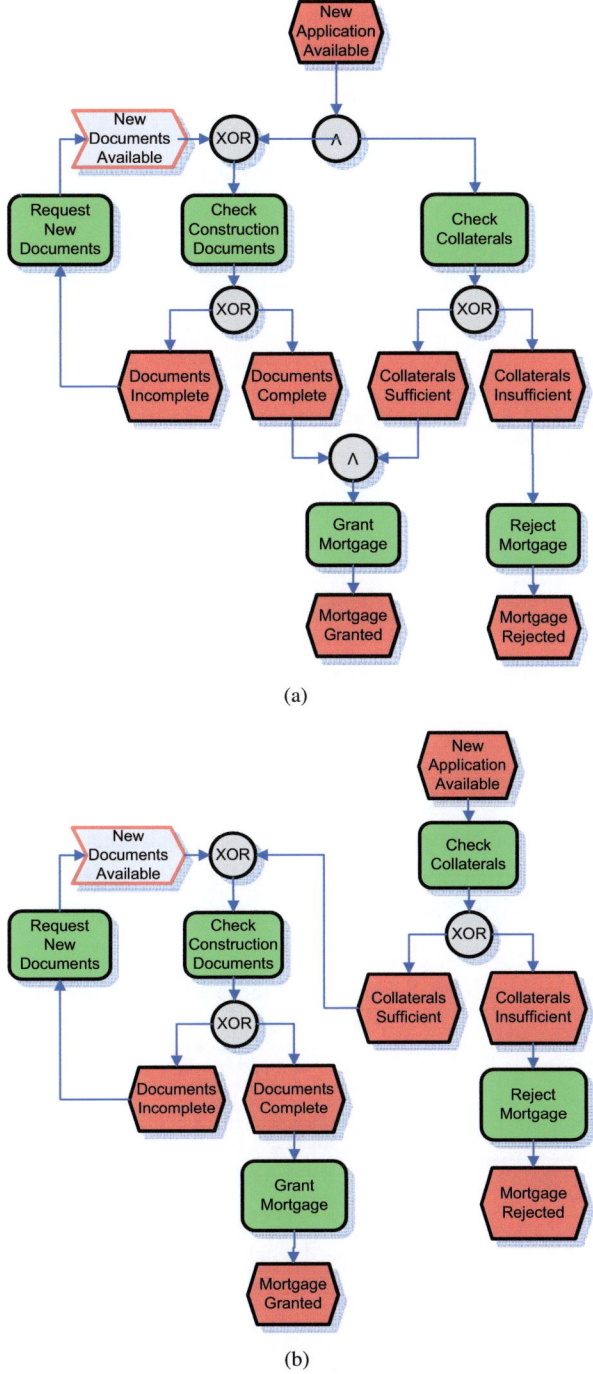

Figure 9.13.: Two design options of the mortgage process taken from [131]. (a) depicts option A in which the two checks are modeled in parallel. (b) depicts option B. Here, the two checks are modeled in a sequence.

where *meanC* are the average costs and *meanCT* the average cycle time which has to be less than a specific number of time units, here 1200.

This objective can be motivated by considering a cost reduction strategy with ensuring customer satisfaction at the same time. The customer should not wait too long for the decision about his application. The costs of executing a business process are determined on the basis of the processing times, one costs unit relates to one time unit. No fixed costs are considered. Thus, the costs are calculated by summing up the processing times of each finished and unfinished task.

The EPM

The creation of the EPM for the mortgage process implies the identification of the information elements and the dependencies between them. Table 9.14 contains the list of information elements.

Table 9.14.: Information elements of the mortgage application.

Information Element	Explanation
Collaterals	The collaterals of the applicant.
Construction Reference Documents	The construction reference documents of the applicant.
New Docs	New available documents due to a preceding request.
Final Decision	The final decision regarding the mortgage application. The application is either granted or rejected.

The identified information elements must be related to each other by defining the dependencies.[4] The resulting production rules of the mortgage application are listed in Table 9.15. The table contains a short description of each activity that is performed.

Table 9.15.: Production rules of the mortgage application.

ID	Activity	Dependency
0	Check collaterals	The values of the collaterals are checked whether they are sufficient for the applied mortgage.
1	Check construction reference documents	Completeness check of the construction reference documents.
2	Reject application	The application is rejected due to insufficient collaterals.
3	Request missing documents check	Missing documents must be requested if the preceding check determined that documents are incomplete.
4	Re-check construction reference documents	As production rule 1.
5	Grant application	The application is granted as documents are complete and collaterals sufficient.

---

[4]Remember that a dependency corresponds to a production rule.

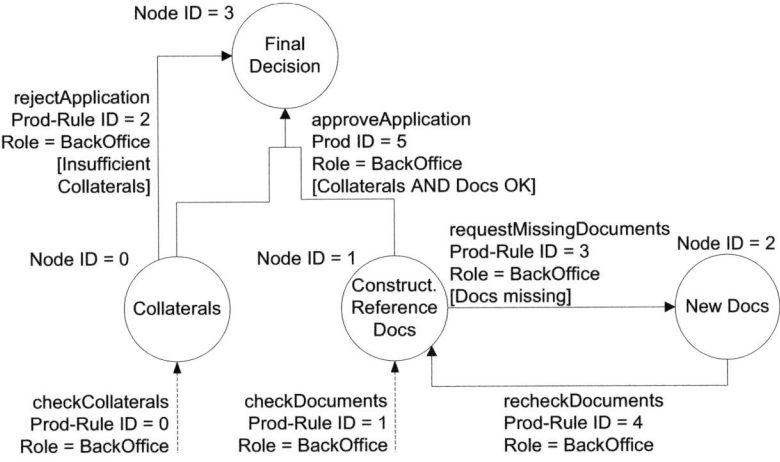

Figure 9.14.: Executable Product Model of the mortgage business process

The resulting EPM for the mortgage application business process is depicted in Fig. 9.14. The EPM comprises the execution paths of the three different aforementioned process designs (option A, B, and C). This is reason why an EPM may provide more flexibility as a regular process model. During runtime, the execution path can be switched if necessary. The following execution paths exist (for simplification the cycle is not considered here):

- Execution Path 1: $0 \rightarrow 2$

- Execution Path 2: $0 \rightarrow 1 \rightarrow 5$

- Execution Path 3: $1 \rightarrow 0 \rightarrow 5$

- Execution Path 4: $\{0 \text{ and } 1 \text{ in parallel}\} \rightarrow 5$

Experimental Setup

The mortgage process is analyzed based on two scenarios. The setting of scenario I is listed in Table 9.16 and Table 9.17. The former table contains the processing durations, the latter one contains the probabilities of the different events.

In scenario II, the situation is analyzed in which the completion of activity "Check Collaterals" is delayed. There can be various causes for such a delay: the occurrence of unexpected quality problems that lead to rework, a resource shortage due to illness or if new employees must be taught. Let us assume that quality problems lead to a longer processing time due to rework. The processing time of activity "Check Collaterals" is changed from 500 to 600 time units.

Table 9.16.: Mortgage business process - scenario I.

Activity	Duration
Check collaterals	500
Check construction reference docs	400
Reject application	200
Request missing documents	300
Re-check construction reference docs	400
Grant application	300

Table 9.17.: Mortgage business process - probabilities of the different events.

Event after XOR (see Fig. 9.13)	Probability
Construction Reference Documents complete	0.9
Construction Reference Documents incomplete	0.1
Collaterals sufficient	0.8
Collaterals insufficient	0.2

Based on these probabilities, the different cases (execution data instances) must be derived. In the aforementioned process simulation, probabilities are used for deciding which execution path is selected. In the EPM approach, this decision is made on the basis of the defined constraints and the execution data instances which provide consistent test data for the different cases as described in Sec. 5.3.2. The simplification was made, that if the construction reference documentation is incomplete, one request for missing documents is made at most. This results in four different cases. The probabilities of these cases are calculated on the basis of the probabilities of the decisions, e.g. for case 1: $0.8 * 0.9 = 0.72$. Table 9.18 contains the probabilities of the different cases.

Table 9.18.: Mortgage business process - probabilities of the different cases.

Case	1	2	3	4
Collaterals sufficient	Yes	Yes	No	No
Documents complete	Yes	No	Yes	No
Probability	0.72	0.08	0.18	0.02

The RRL-PSO-V approach is used for the experiments. As stop criteria 100 finished EPMs is selected with a maximum simulation duration that allows at most the complete execution of these 100 EPMs. As the objective is the minimization of the costs by assuring a specific service level agreement regarding the cycle time, these KPIs are included in the fitness function. Equation 9.2 defines the fitness function as follows:

$$f(\vec{x}) = meanC \qquad\qquad [9.2]$$
$$+ 1000 * max\{meanCT - 1200, 0\}$$
$$+ 1000 * max\{100 - meanFinishedEPMs, 0\}$$

where *meanC* are the average costs and *meanCT* the average cycle time which has to be less than 1200. If the average cycle time exceeds 1200 time units, a penalty will be added. The same pertains to *meanFinishedEPMs* which is the average total number of finished EPMs. If less than 100 EPM were executed, a penalty is enforced. The factor 1000 was determined for both penalties in preliminary experiments.

Business Process Optimization Methodology

Before the iEPM approach for intelligent business process optimization is discussed, the regular BPM optimization approach is explained. Both approaches are discussed on the basis of scenario I.

The regular optimization methodology requires the modeling of each design option. Here, this is done by modeling option A and B in the Business Process Modeling Notation (BPMN) using the commercial simulation tool iGrafx[5]. The process models are depicted in Fig. 9.15.

Table 9.19.: Mortgage business process - iGrafx simulation results for scenario I

Design	Mean Costs	Mean Cycle Time
A (parallel)	1165,88	835.48
B (sequential)	1165,88	1165.88

The simulation results are listed in Table 9.19. At first view, one could think that option A is better (in the sense of the objective - see Equ. 9.2) than option B as it has a smaller cycle time and the same costs. Unfortunately the iGrafx simulation does not include statistical data of canceled activities in the analysis. This means that the costs are not correctly calculated by iGrafx. Costs are only considered in the calculation if an activity is completely processed[6]. In the parallel model, the situation occurs that activities are canceled when the mortgage application is rejected. We refer to this kind of cost as sunk costs. Sunk costs can be considered as costs that were caused due to unnecessary work. Depending on the behaviour of the simulation engine, it can even happen that data of unfinished transactions is omitted. This can happen if a transaction reaches the end state and other running transactions (due to parallelism) are canceled.

---

[5]iGrafx website http://www.igrafx.de.
[6]The same pertains to the ARIS simulation as stated in [131].

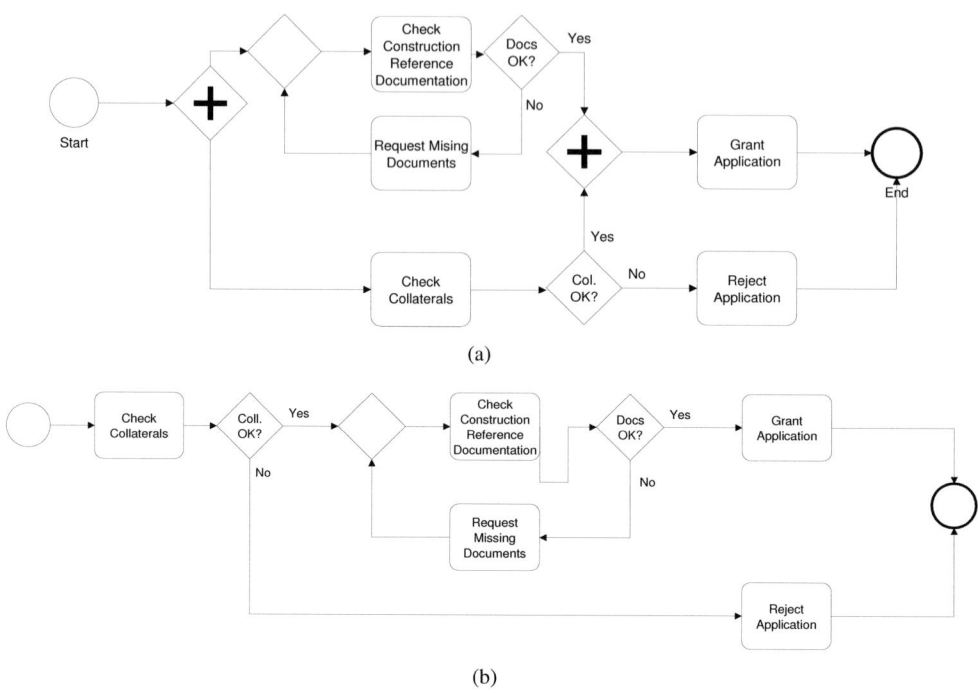

Figure 9.15.: The two design options of the mortgage process modeled in BPMN. (a) depicts option A and (b) depicts option B.

If sunk costs are considered, then option B is the design that leads to the smallest costs as there are no unnecessary tasks performed. As it fulfills also the Service Level Agreement (SLA) regarding the cycle time, it would be the preferred process design. In the following, the iEPM approach is discussed under consideration of sunk costs.

The iEPM optimization methodology does not require the modeling of different design options as already discussed. In the first step the heuristic is used to determine an optimal probability vector for scenario I. In the next step, the MAS simulates the execution of EPMs using Policy Iteration. The policy is configured with the probability vector determined in the previous step. During the execution, processing data is stored in a log file. This log file is analyzed with the open source process mining toolkit ProM. The analysis should show that the IBOs execute the EPM in a sequential order as this is the result of the regular optimization approach. In the following, the results of the logfile analysis are discussed.

Fig. 9.16 shows the pattern diagram that was created by using the performance sequence diagram analysis of the ProM tool.

This analysis compares the process instances against each other in order to determine whether they follow the same pattern. The found patterns are then displayed in the pattern diagram.

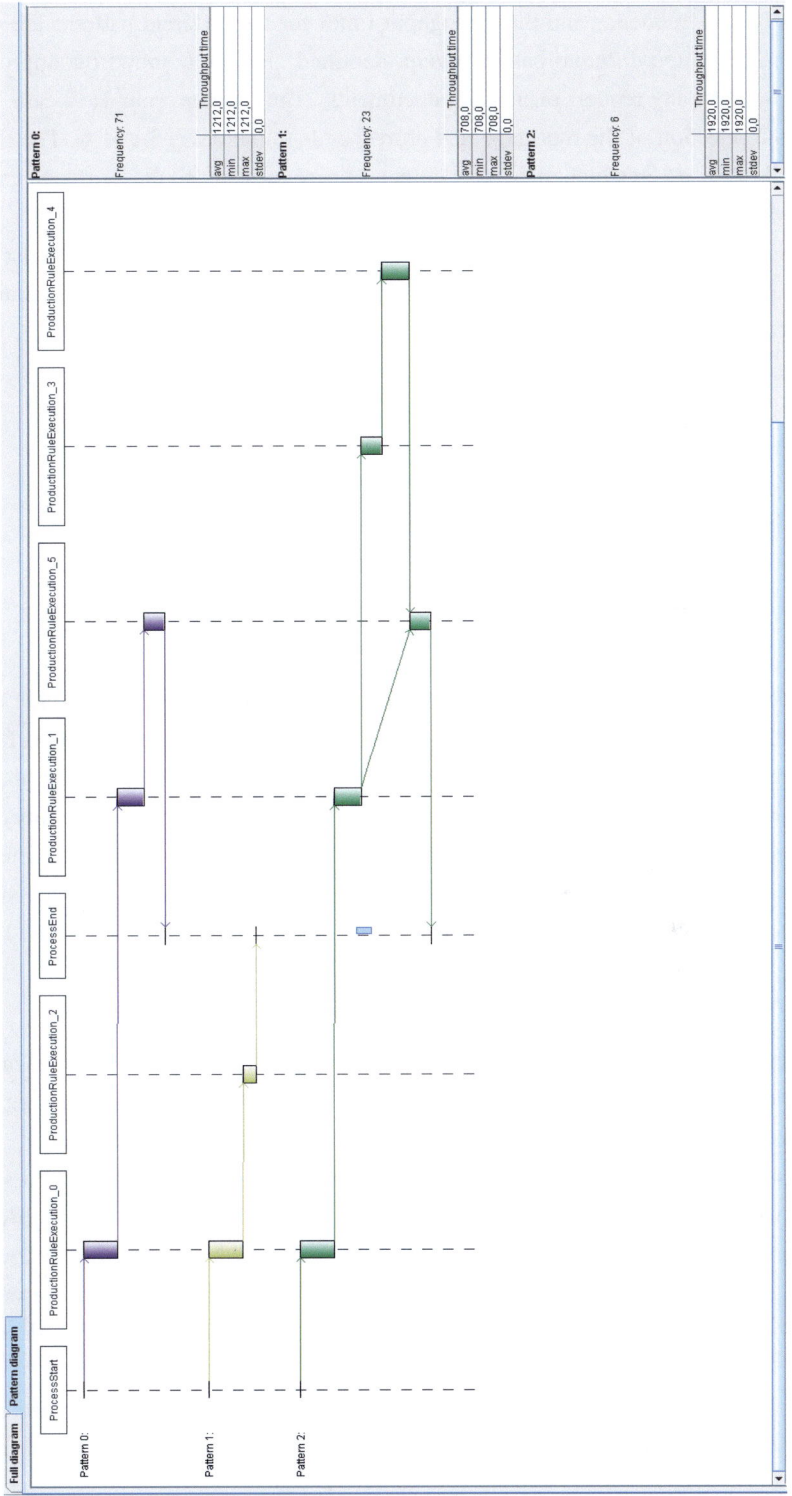

Figure 9.16.: ProM performance sequence diagram analysis - pattern diagram.

Furthermore, the frequency and the throughput times for the different patterns are displayed. As one can see, three different patterns were identified. Pattern 0 shows the approval of the mortgage without any request of missing documents. Thus, it corresponds to case 1. Pattern 1 shows the rejection of the mortgage and corresponds to the cases 3 and 4. The last pattern corresponds to case 2 in which missing documents are requested and the mortgage granted. All patterns show a sequential processing order of the activities.

The sequential processing order can also be seen if a Petri net is generated using the ProM tool. Fig. 9.17 shows the Petri net generated from the logfile using the Alpha++ mining plugin (for information about this algorithm see [319]).

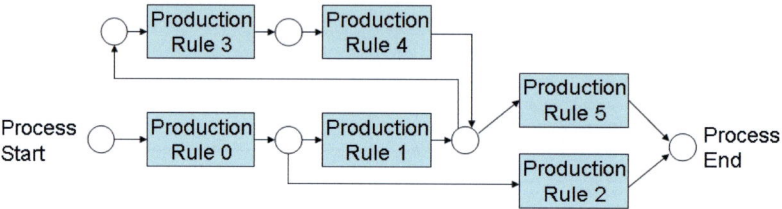

Figure 9.17.: ProM process mining result using Alpha++ algorithm (manually remodeled as original output was not readable).

Both diagrams show that the iEPM approach delivered the desirable result. The advantage of the iEPM approach as intelligent business process optimization methodology is that it does not require the manual creation of alternative process designs. As shown above, the standard approach requires the design of different models. If the iEPM approach is used, only one model is required. The analysis with ProM showed that the iEPM approach was able to determine the best process design in the given situation, here the option B (sequential design). In the next section, the application of the iEPM approach as intelligent BPM engine is evaluated.

Intelligent Business Process Engine

The first experiment analyzes the two design options for each scenario. The arrival rate and the resources are set so that no waiting times occur due to missing resources. Each experimental run is repeated 20 times.

The results of the simulation of scenario I and II are listed in Table 9.20. In scenario I, option B has lower costs than A. Thus, B is the preferable design. The situation in scenario II is different. As the cycle time of option B violates the constraint (see Equ. 9.2), option B is no longer the optimal process design. Therefore option A is preferable in scenario II as it satisfies the constraint regarding the cycle time. Thus far, it has been shown that depending on the scenario, different process designs can be optimal.

In the second experiment, the situation is analyzed, in which the processing time of activity "Check Collaterals" changes as described above in the middle of the simulation run. This

Table 9.20.: Mortgage business process - simulation results.

Scenario I		
Design	Mean Costs	Mean Cycle Time
Option A	1240.85 +/- 9.97	836.08 +/- 8.43
Option B	1159.0 +/- 14.76	1170.88 +/- 14.9
Scenario II		
Option A	1336.34 +/- 7.51	923.81 +/- 6.30
Option B	1257.51 +/- 14.04	1267.88 +/- 14.25

means, that in the first half of the simulation, the setting of scenario I is used and in the second half the setting of scenario II. Fig. 9.18 shows the results of this experiment.

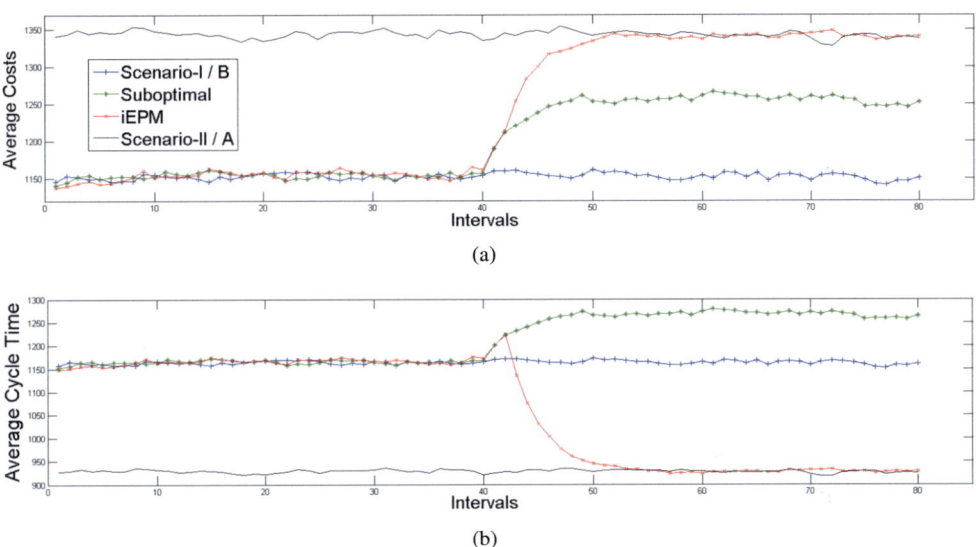

Figure 9.18.: Results of the different approaches. (a) depicts the average costs and (b) depicts the average cycle time.

The KPIs "average cycle time" and "average costs" are calculated after each interval. Run "Scenario-I / B" means that process design B is used in scenario I. Accordingly, run "Scenario-II / A" means that process design A is used in scenario II. These runs are included for comparison purposes. Run "Suboptimal" means that option B is used, but the situation changes from scenario I to scenario II in the middle of the simulation. As one can see, the cycle time increases and violates the constraint. Run "iEPM" shows the result of the iEPM approach. The first time that the offline learning takes place is before the simulation is started. The next time offline learning takes place is at interval 41 as the constraint regarding the mean cycle time was violated for the first time. The probabilities of the policy were updated at the beginning of the next interval. As one can see, the agents have autonomously adapted their behaviour in accordance to the changed scenario. First, they learned to execute the checks in a sequence and after the second learning phase to execute them in parallel.

The conducted experiments with the mortgage business process showed that the intelligent agents are capable of utilizing the flexibility of the EPM in order to optimize autonomously the business process execution in changing scenarios. By this, the advantages of the two practical application methods of the iEPM approach could be shown.

9.7.3. Credit Application Business Process

The advantage of the iEPM approach as intelligent BPM engine is once more demonstrated on the basis of a business process. This time, a credit application business process is evaluated in different scenarios.

Business Requirements

The simplified business process "credit application" comprises the following tasks: If an application for a credit is available, the financial situation and the customer history are checked. If one of the checks has a negative outcome, the application is rejected. If the results are positive, the contract conditions are calculated based on the application data (credit amount, collaterals, etc.) and the results of the checks. Afterwards, the calculated contract conditions must be approved (four-eyes principle). If the conditions are not approved, they must be recalculated until they are approved. Once they are approved, the application is granted.

Based on these business requirements, three process designs are possible. In option A, the activities "Financial Situation Check" and "Customer History Check" are modeled in parallel. In option B these checks are modeled in a sequence: "Financial Situation Check" followed by "Customer History Check". The parallel design has the advantage that it can lead to a better cycle time than the sequential design. The disadvantage of the parallel design is that certain tasks may be executed unnecessarily. This is the case, when the application is rejected due to a negative financial situation, while the customer history is still being checked. The third option is retrieved if the order of the checks in option B is switched. Fig. 9.19 depicts the parallel (option A) and sequential (option B) design options in BPMN.

Let us assume that the objective is the minimization of the average cycle time. Eqation 9.3

$$\text{minimize } meanCT \qquad\qquad [9.3]$$

where $meanCT$ is the average cycle time.

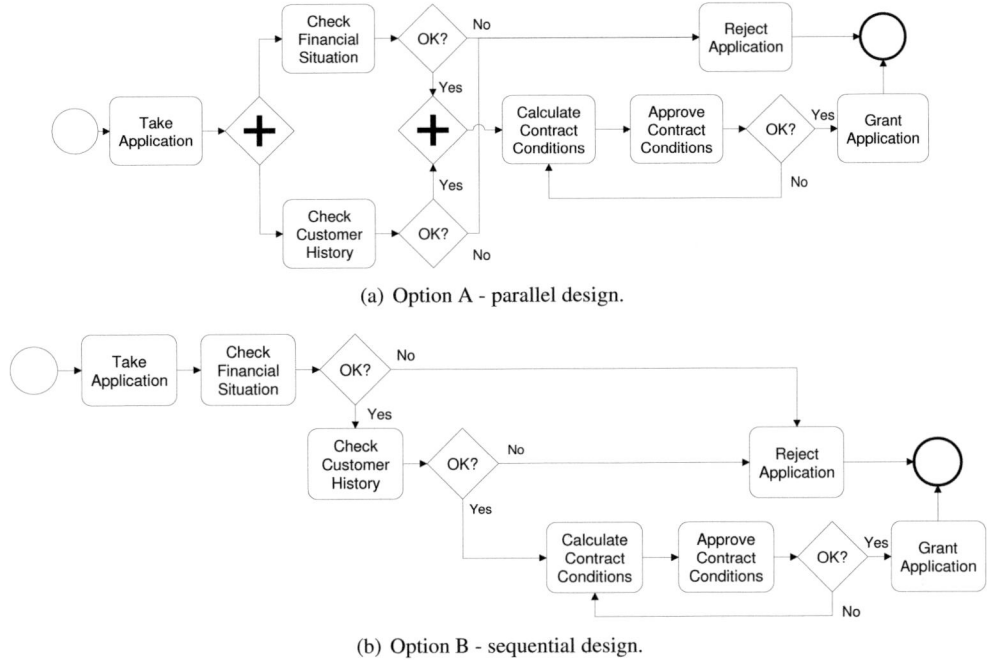

(a) Option A - parallel design.

(b) Option B - sequential design.

Figure 9.19.: Two design options for the credit application process as BPMN models.

The EPM

For creating the EPM, the information elements of the credit application process must be identified and the dependencies between them must be specified. For more information about this business process, in particular about the information elements and production rules see Sec. 3.4. The resulting EPM is depicted in Fig. 9.20.

The EPM "credit application" comprises the following execution paths[7]:

- Execution Path 1: $0 \rightarrow 1 \rightarrow 4$

- Execution Path 2: $0 \rightarrow 2 \rightarrow 8$

- Execution Path 3: $0 \rightarrow \{1 \text{ and } 2 \text{ in parallel}\} \rightarrow 3 \rightarrow 5 \rightarrow 7$

- Execution Path 4: $0 \rightarrow 1 \rightarrow 2 \rightarrow 3 \rightarrow 5 \rightarrow 7$

- Execution Path 5: $0 \rightarrow 2 \rightarrow 1 \rightarrow 3 \rightarrow 5 \rightarrow 7$

The execution paths 1 and 2 result in a rejection of the application. The execution paths 3, 4 and 5 (in combination with 1 and 2) correspond to the design options A, B and C, respectively.

---

[7]For simplification the cycle is not considered. If there are constraints specified, the feasibility of an execution path depends on whether the constraints of the production rules belonging to the execution path are fulfilled.

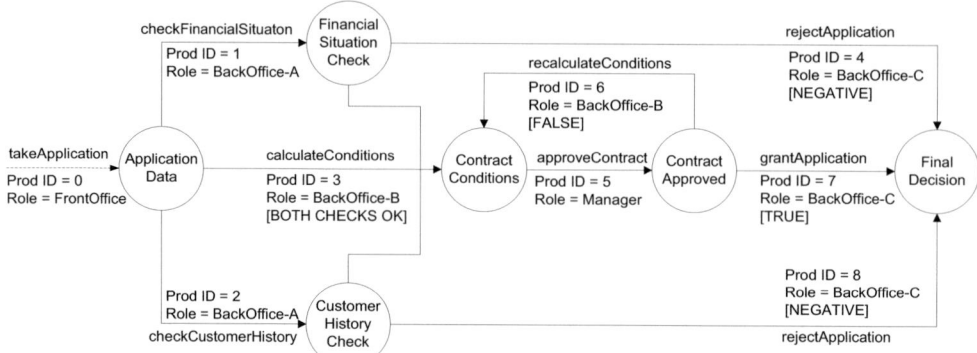

Figure 9.20.: Executable product model "credit application".

The EPM comprises the execution paths of the three different aforementioned process designs. This is the reason why an EPM may provide more flexibility as a regular process model as already argued for the mortgage process.

Experiments and Results

In the first experiment it is shown that a process model can become suboptimal if changes occur. In the second experiment it is shown how the iEPM approach is capable of handling such changes by adapting the behaviour of the intelligent agents.

The RRL-GA-V learning mechanism is used in this experiment. The GA is a real-vector GA using a Gaussian mutation and a population size of 20 individuals. The mutation operator is applied to 15 percent of the genes of every individual selected through a binary tournament selection. This setting was determined in preliminary experiments. As the objective is the minimization of the cycle time, this KPI is included in the fitness function. Equation 9.4 defines the fitness function as follows:

$$f(\vec{x}) = maxD - meanCT - 10 * meanN \qquad [9.4]$$

where $maxD$ is the duration of the simulation[8], $meanCT$ is the average cycle time, $meanN$ the average number of IBOs in execution which is used as penalty forcing the IBOs to execute all EPMs completely. Otherwise an IBO could also decide not to execute an EPM. The factor 10 is a weight that was determined in preliminary experiments.

---

[8]this constant ensures that the fitness values are nonnegative which is a requirement of the GA implementation

The credit application process is analyzed based on three scenarios. Scenario I is defined as follows:

- Table 9.21 contains the probability of the different cases. The probability reflects how often such a case occurs.

- Constant processing times as defined in Table 9.22.

- There are two resources for each role, except for role "BackOffice-A" to which three resources are assigned.

- Stop criteria: 2,000 executed EPMs.

- Constant arrival rate of 220 time units.

Table 9.21.: The different cases of the credit application.

Case	Description	Probability
1	Grant application without recalculation	0.4
2	Grant application with one recalculation	0.2
3	Reject application due to negative financial situation	0.3
4	Reject application due to negative customer history	0.1

Table 9.22.: Processing times of the production rules.

Prod-Rule ID	Activity	Duration
0	Take Application	300
1	Check Financial Situation	200
2	Check Customer History	300
3	Calculate Contract Conditions	200
4	Reject Application	100
5	Approve Contract Conditions	200
6	Recalculate Contract Conditions	200
7	Approve Application	200
8	Reject Application	100

Scenario II differs from I as only two resources of type "BackOffice-B" are available. This may happen e.g. due to illness. Scenario III differs from I as the arrival rate is decreased and set to 150 which results in a higher workload.

The first experiment analyzes the three design options for each scenario. Each experimental run is repeated 20 times. The results of the simulations are listed in Table 9.23 which contains the mean cycle time as well as the 0.95 confidence interval. In scenario I, option A has the minimum cycle time. Thus, A is the preferable design. The result for scenario II is different as option B is optimal. The same pertains to scenario III, in which also B is optimal. The results show that different process designs can be optimal in different scenarios. The parallel design has the disadvantage that resources are occupied by the customer history check which is unnecessary if the financial situation check is negative (sunk work).

Table 9.23.: Mean cylce time of the different process designs for each scenario.

Design	Scenario I	Scenario II	Scenario III
Option A	$1,073.3 \pm 4.5$	$10,486.1 \pm 635.9$	$6,275.3 \pm 260.3$
Option B	$1,215.5 \pm 4.9$	$1,399.0 \pm 17.4$	$3,285.9 \pm 8.0$
Option C	$1,286.6 \pm 3.7$	$33,853.5 \pm 606.2$	$19,294.9 \pm 398.5$

In the second experiment, the situation is analyzed, in which the scenario is changed in the middle of the situation. In the first half of the simulation, the setting of scenario I is used and in the second half the setting of scenario II. Fig. 9.21 shows the results of this experiment.

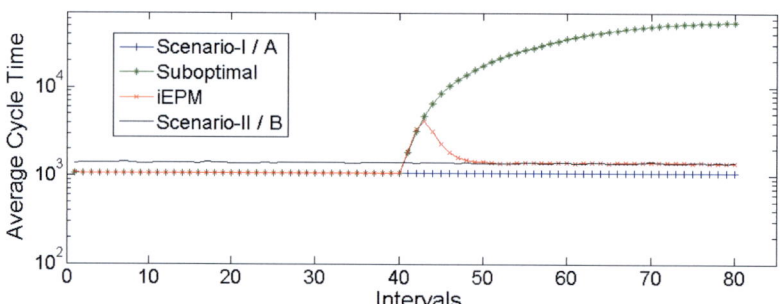

Figure 9.21.: The mean cycle time (logarithmic scale) of the different approaches in constant (Scenario-I/A and Scenario-II/B) and changing scenarios (Suboptimal and iEPM).

The KPI "average cycle time" is calculated after each interval. Run "Scenario-I / A" means that process design A is used in scenario I. Accordingly, run "Scenario-II / B" means that process design B is used in scenario II. These runs are included for comparison purposes. Run "Suboptimal" means that option A is used (which is optimal at the beginning), but the situation changes from scenario I to scenario II in the middle of the simulation. As one can see, the cycle time increases when the change occurs. Run "iEPM" shows the result of the iEPM approach. The first time that the offline learning takes place is before the simulation is started and after each interval. The probabilities of the policy are updated at the beginning of the next interval. As one can see, the IBOs have autonomously adapted their behaviour in accordance to the changed scenario. First, they learned to execute the checks in parallel (which corresponds to option A) and after the change to execute them in a sequence (which corresponds to option B). Thus, they utilized the flexibility of the EPM in order to optimize the KPI.

This evaluation showed the limitation of the standard BPM approach that uses a fixed business process model. If changes occur that have a significant negative impact on the KPIs, the process must be optimized manually, e.g. by finding an alternative process design. The iEPM approach has the advantage, that the optimization is done autonomously.

9.8. Summary

In this chapter, various simulation based experiments were conducted and statistically analyzed for evaluating the iEPM approach.

The first experiment showed successfully the proof-of-concept that EPMs can be executed with the MAS using the execute-all approach. The next experiments evaluated the different learning mechanisms. First, the RRL-GA approach was examined with different EPMs and policies. The results demonstrated that RRL-GA increases significantly the efficiency in comparison to the execute-all approach. Moreover, the results showed that the common goal of minimizing the average cycle time could be reached by the individual agent learning approach. In particular, the usage of a policy defined on a higher level of abstraction resulted in a significant performance gain, i.e. better results were obtained with the policy based on variants in comparison to the policy based on information elements and production rules.

Another aspect that was analyzed was the generalization which means to apply a policy learned for a specific scenario to a larger one. The results of the experiments showed that generalization is possible under specific circumstances only. Generalization is only successful if the larger scenario has the same characteristics as the smaller one. This aspect was evaluated in experiments by considering the relevance of workload information. If the usage of workload information is not necessary in the smaller scenario, the agents may not use workload information at all. But if the workload information is of importance in the larger scenario, the agents act suboptimal if the policy learned for the smaller scenario is used.

The critical aspect of the learning approach is the offline learning phase as each individual is evaluated on the basis of a simulation. Therefore, various optimization enhancements were implemented. One of these enhancements was the usage of PSO instead of GA. Moreover, an extension of PSO by Gap Search was introduced in the previous chapter. This extension was thoroughly evaluated and compared with standard PSO and GA. The results showed that PSO outperforms GA when applied in the offline learning phase of the iEPM approach. In particular, around one third of the generations can be saved if PSO is used in combination with Gap Search instead of standard PSO or GA. Alternatively, if the same number of iterations is carried out, a better solution is obtained with PSO and Gap Search.

The advantages of practical application methods of the iEPM approach were discussed in detail on the basis of three different business processes that were taken from literature and practice. The business process "new customer" was used to compare PSO and GA on the basis of a more complex business process. Additionally, preliminary experiments were conducted in order to demonstrate the capability of the IBOs to adapt their behaviour in dependence on the current scenario.

In order to get a deeper insight into the capability of the devised learning mechanism, further experiments were conducted with two business processes, a mortgage and a credit application business process. In experiments, the limitation of the standard BPM approach that uses a fixed business process model was discussed. It was shown that changes regarding the operating conditions can have a significant negative impact on the KPIs. If such changes occur, corrective actions have to be carried out such as the manual optimization of the process by finding an alternative process design. In experiments it was analyzed how the IBOs react to changes. The results showed that the IBOs adapted autonomously their behaviour in accordance to the changed scenario. Thus, the iEPM approach could be successfully applied for the autonomous optimization of the business process execution.

Summarizing the results obtained from the experiments evaluating the advantage of the iEPM approach, one has to observe the following: There is one common aspect in all three business processes derived from practical examples. In all three business processes there are tasks which are independent from each other, i.e. they can be processed either in a sequence or in parallel. Moreover, at least one of these tasks may lead to the end of the process. Thereby, the processing of the other tasks may be unnecessary. If the other tasks are processed anyways, this work is unnecessarily performed which is referred to as sunk work. The effect of sunk work depends on the operating conditions and the defined KPIs. For example, sunk work always has a negative impact on the costs as resources are occupied. The situation is different if the cycle time is considered as KPI. If the workload is high, this sunk work may have a significant negative effect on the KPIs as resources are occupied with unnecessary work. If workload is low (to be more precisely, no waiting times occur as the number of resources is sufficient for the volume of work) and the independent tasks are executed in parallel, sunk work may not have a negative impact one the average cycle time. It may only have a negative effect if the duration of the sunk work is longer than the other tasks that lead to the end of the process. Moreover, the execution of the independent tasks in parallel may result in a significant better cycle time. The significance of these effects depends on the distribution of the different cases. For example, considering the mortgage application process, the significance of the effect depends on the number of cases in which a customer applies for a mortgage with sufficient (no sunk work is possible) or insufficient (sunk work may be carried out) collaterals . The more cases exist in which an applicant has insufficient collaterals, the more sunk work may be carried out. The aforementioned limitation of regular process models is caused by the existence of sunk work in combination with changing operating conditions. In experiments it was shown that the iEPM approach manages the control-flow in such a way that leads to the optimization of the KPIs in changing operating conditions.

It has to be mentioned that there are simpler scenarios in which the iEPM approach provides advantages. Assume, that a business process consists of two independent variants that are processed by different resources. The iEPM approach is capable of using the different variants in terms of workload balancing. Variants can also be utilized if the execution of another one fails or if delays occur.

10. Conclusions and Future Work

> "The future influences the present just as much as the past."
>
> Friedrich Nietzsche

This chapter provides a summary and the conclusions regarding the presented intelligent Executable Product Model (iEPM) approach. Moreover, the directions of future work in the area of business process flexibility and autonomous optimization of business process execution are discussed.

10.1. Conclusions

This thesis presented a novel approach for enhancing the flexibility of service industry's business processes. The enhanced flexibility is utilized in order to autonomously optimize the execution of business processes. The developed approach is termed iEPM. It combines a special model for business processes with intelligent agents, that make use of sophisticated machine learning techniques.

Part of this work is a design methodology for business processes based on Executable Product Models (EPMs). An EPM provides a compact representation of the set of possible execution paths of a business process by defining information dependencies, instead of defining the order of activities as in regular process models. As EPMs are directly executed, different algorithms were developed for this execution. Due to the way of modeling, an EPM may provide more execution options, especially for complex business processes. In particular, OR dependencies provide flexibility as there are no precedence constraints between the production rules belonging to the OR dependency. Thus, they can be executed for example either in a sequence or in parallel. Modeling alternatives using one of the common process modeling languages may lead to a complicated and complex process model. A further advantage of the EPM is, that the variant in execution can be changed anytime during runtime. This is possible as an EPM comprises all possible variants in one model. As multiple EPMs can be defined, the simultaneous optimization of different business processes is supported, which allows an enterprise wide optimization.

The optimization of the execution of EPMs comprises the determination of a set of production rules, whose execution leads to the generation of the root information element, as well as the assignment of these production rules to resources in such a way, that leads to the optimization of the defined Key Performance Indicators (KPIs). It was shown, that the corresponding decision problem of a special case belongs to the class of NP-complete problems. This provided the argument as well as the motivation for applying approximation methods. Machine learning was selected to solve the multi-objective optimization problem, as it provides a flexible mechanism for the autonomous adaptation to changing conditions.

The flexibility provided by the Executable Product Model (EPM) is utilized by using a Multi-Agent System (MAS). A MAS based approach was selected, as MASs are capable of solving complex tasks in distributed environments and have been applied successfully in practice. The intelligent agents make use of machine learning techniques for managing and controlling the execution of EPMs. The devised hybrid learning mechanism was developed based on two machine learning approaches, Relational Reinforcement Learning (RRL) in combination with a heuristic. The actions of the Intelligent Business Objects (IBOs) are selected based on the RRL method Policy Iteration. The heuristic is used in an offline learning phase to adapt the behaviour of the agents. Initially a Genetic Algorithm (GA) was applied as heuristic, but later replaced by Particle Swarm Optimization (PSO) as part of the implemented performance enhancements.

Two practical application methods for the iEPM approach were identified:

- during runtime as intelligent Business Process Management (BPM) engine and

- during design time as intelligent business process optimization methodology.

To solve the time intensive optimization problem, a new search mechanism called Gap Search (GS) was introduced in [159], that aims at the acceleration of the PSO algorithm. The influence of using GS in combination with PSO in order to solve single, multi- and many-objective problems was studied on the basis of various standard test functions. GS was integrated into the three possible parts of a PSO and Multi-Objective Particle Swarm Optimization (MOPSO) namely as initialization, diversity and feasibility preservation mechanisms. The major result from the conducted experiments reveals, that GS improves the standard PSO and MOPSO methods even if it is deployed in solving many-objective problems. In particular, the results showed, that PSO outperforms GA when applied in the offline learning phase of the iEPM approach. Indeed, around one third of the generations can be saved if PSO in combination with Gap Search is used instead of standard PSO or GA. Alternatively, if the same number of generations is carried out, a better solution is obtained with PSO and Gap Search.

A prototype was implemented to be able to conduct experiments. The total number of classes sums up to *253* with around *39,750* total lines of codes. In order to perform a thorough evaluation of the iEPM approach, EPMs with different structures were used in the experiments. For that purpose, the EPMs were categorized into three different groups: pathological, large and practical EPMs (see Sec.9.1). Pathological EPMs have simple structures that represent some of the standard situations found in business processes, such as the processing of tasks in a sequence and in parallel. These EPMs were used to show the proof-of-concept of the developed approach and its implementation, as well as to analyze the capabilities of the learning mechanism. The scalability evaluation was mainly based on large EPMs, comprising up to 2000 production rules. Moreover, the advantages of the two mentioned application methods were analyzed and discussed in detail utilizing practical EPMs. This evaluation was performed on the basis of different business processes derived from examples found in the literature and in practice, e.g. the "new customer" example was derived from a business process implemented in a large German bank. The results of the conducted experiments showed the advantages as well as the applicability of the iEPM approach.

Applied as intelligent BPM engine, the results of the experiments showed, that the agents are capable of autonomously optimizing the execution. They utilized the flexibility of the EPM by choosing appropriate execution paths in dependence on the current operating conditions. The simulation on the basis of regular process models showed that process designs can become suboptimal, if changes occur, such as an increase of the volume of work. While the process design has to be changed manually in accordance to the new situation, the iEPM approach performs the optimization autonomously. The offline learning cannot only be used to adapt and optimize the behaviour of the agents, but also to perform what-if analyses, e.g. in order to make business forecasts.

During design time, the iEPM approach allows the analysis of the system behavior. In regular business process simulation approaches, alternative process models must be explicitly defined. The iEPM approach delivers the advantage, that the EPM already contains the possible variants. The advantage of this methodology over regular approaches is, that only one process model needs to be created.

Different prerequisites were identified under which the iEPM approach leads to advantages. Obviously, there is no room for improvement, if the business process and the EPM have a strictly linear structure. Therefore, the existence of different variants due to OR dependencies is the fundamental prerequisite. Which execution strategy[1] leads to the optimization of the KPIs is dependent on different influencing factors, such as KPIs, processing duration, distribution of cases, number of available resources. This was discussed in detail in Sec. 9.8. For example, the parallel execution of production rules can either have a positive or a negative impact on the KPIs. The iEPM approach is capable of deciding about the execution order in a way, that leads to the optimization of the KPIs. In general, variants that are processed by resources with different roles can be used to balance the workload. Moreover, different variants allow, for example, to choose alternative paths if one fails due to unavailability of resources or if quality problems lead to delays.

---

[1]In process model based approaches an execution strategy relates to a specific process design.

10.2. Future Work

Even though the current state of research presented in this work can provide substantial support in business process optimization, there are some aspects that have yet to be considered.

The following research directions were identified:

Tool Support The applicability of the iEPM approach in practice prerequisites tool support. Thus, a graphical editor could be implemented for designing EPMs. Moreover, if the iEPM approach is applied as optimization methodology, it has to support the definition of simulation configurations and the execution of simulations. Currently, this is done by manually writing an XML configuration file.

Enterprise-wide simulation As mentioned in the previous section, the simultaneous optimization of different business processes is supported. So far, the prototype does not allow to specify different KPIs for each EPM, e.g. it is not supported that in EPM A the cycle time is minimized and in EPM B the costs. Furthermore, the KPIs are not calculated separately for each EPM. The elimination of these restrictions requires that KPIs are defined and calculated EPM specific.

Scalability The scalability evaluation was discussed in Sec. 7.4. Three areas of improvement were identified:

    Parallelization For providing real scalability, the implementation of the developed prototype has to be optimized to support parallelism. There are two areas that can be parallelized, either the MAS or the heuristic. The MAS can be parallelized as follows: in one time slot, the IBOs and Resource Agents (RAs) can process their messages in parallel. The heuristic can be parallelized in such a way, that the evaluations of different solutions are performed in parallel. The former one should be implemented, if large scenarios are simulated, especially for enterprise-wide simulations. The heuristic needs to be parallelized, if the offline learning phase should be further optimized.

    Today, different kinds of distributed architectures exist, such as grid and cloud computing. Accordingly to [81, page 270] the main purpose of grid computing is the provision of resources, such as network, memory or processor capacities. Cloud computing can be considered as a logical extension of grid computing. It implies the provision of a specific service. Considering this differentiation, grid computing would be appropriate for the parallelization.

    The parallelization of an algorithm and its distribution on different processors or machines lead to a communication overhead. Especially if it is distributed on different machines, the communication overhead may be greater than the savings of parallel processing due to the network communication. As the computational time of the message processing is rather short, the distribution on different machines would probably not lead to a significant improvement. But the use of a multi-core processor could be advantageous. The situation for the heuristic is different, as the computational time of the evaluations is rather long, especially for very large scenarios. Here, the distribution on several machines could be beneficial. Note that parallel heuristics, such as parallel MOPSO, are already available [194]. Another method for potentially speeding up the offline learning phase is meta-modeling[2] which learns a cost landscape from a set of solution/cost pairs [155]. It was developed for applications with time-intensive function evaluations.

Executable Product Model In the current prototype all variants are evaluated. Heuristics could be applied as suggested in Sec. 7.4 in order to evaluate only a subset of promising variants. This could reduce the computational time if the EPM comprises a large number of variants (>1,000). As the number of variants must be quite large, this research direction pertains specifically to very complex EPMs.

Communication Topology The negotiation protocol makes use of multicast messages which have a negative affect on the computational time if there is a large number of IBOs and RAs. A more efficient communication topology (e.g. a central scheduling component which does not use multicast messages) or negotiation protocol (e.g. as in [77]) could be implemented in order to speed up the computational time.

Learning Mechanism There is a variety of possibilities to further extend the learning mechanism. One way is to learn not only probabilities, but the whole policy. A learning classifier system approach could be used for that purpose [40]. Learning the whole policy would be challenging due to the larger search space. Another possibility is to make use of process data, e.g. to classify process instances based on the process data in order to forecast the further course of the business process. Remember, that the routing in a business process and an EPM is dependent on the fulfillment of the constraints. A correct forecast could lead to a further optimization of the KPIs.

Integration in BPM tools In this thesis, only the idea was discussed how the learning mechanism can be integrated into commercial BPM tools. The future work in this direction would be the implementation of the required functionality.

Automatic Retrieval of Simulation Data In the conducted experiments, the simulation data was provided manually. Additionally, the simulation data could also be retrieved automatically from the operational database. Work in this area has already been started by other scientists (see e.g. [331]).

---

[2]In literature this is also referred to as surrogate or approximate modeling.

Multi-Objective Optimization Thus far, the iEPM approach uses scalarisation[3] to solve the multi-objective optimization problems. In this thesis, MOPSO was applied on standard multi- and many-objective test functions in order to evaluate the GS method. The future work in this area would be the replacement of PSO by MOPSO and its application for the optimization of the execution of EPMs.

Several future research directions were identified. In particular, the enterprise-wide simulation and optimization of business processes in combination with the implementation of the scalability enhancements would be a promising topic for future research.

---

[3]This means to combine the different objective functions to only one by using some weighting (see Sec. 2.4.2).

A. Business Process Management Standards

> "The wonderful thing about standards is that
> there are so many of them to choose from."
>
> Grace Hopper

This appendix contains information about the most relevant Business Process Management (BPM) standards. The major contributors for the development of Business Process Management (BPM) standards are the following organizations:

- Business Process Management Initiative (BPMI)

- Organization for the Advancement of Structured Information Standards (OASIS)

- Object Management Group (OMG)

- Workflow Management Coalition (WfMC)

A historical overview is depicted in Fig. A.1. It provides an insight in the development of the different standards that were released by standardization organizations and companies. In Fig. A.1 IDS pertains to IDS Scheer.

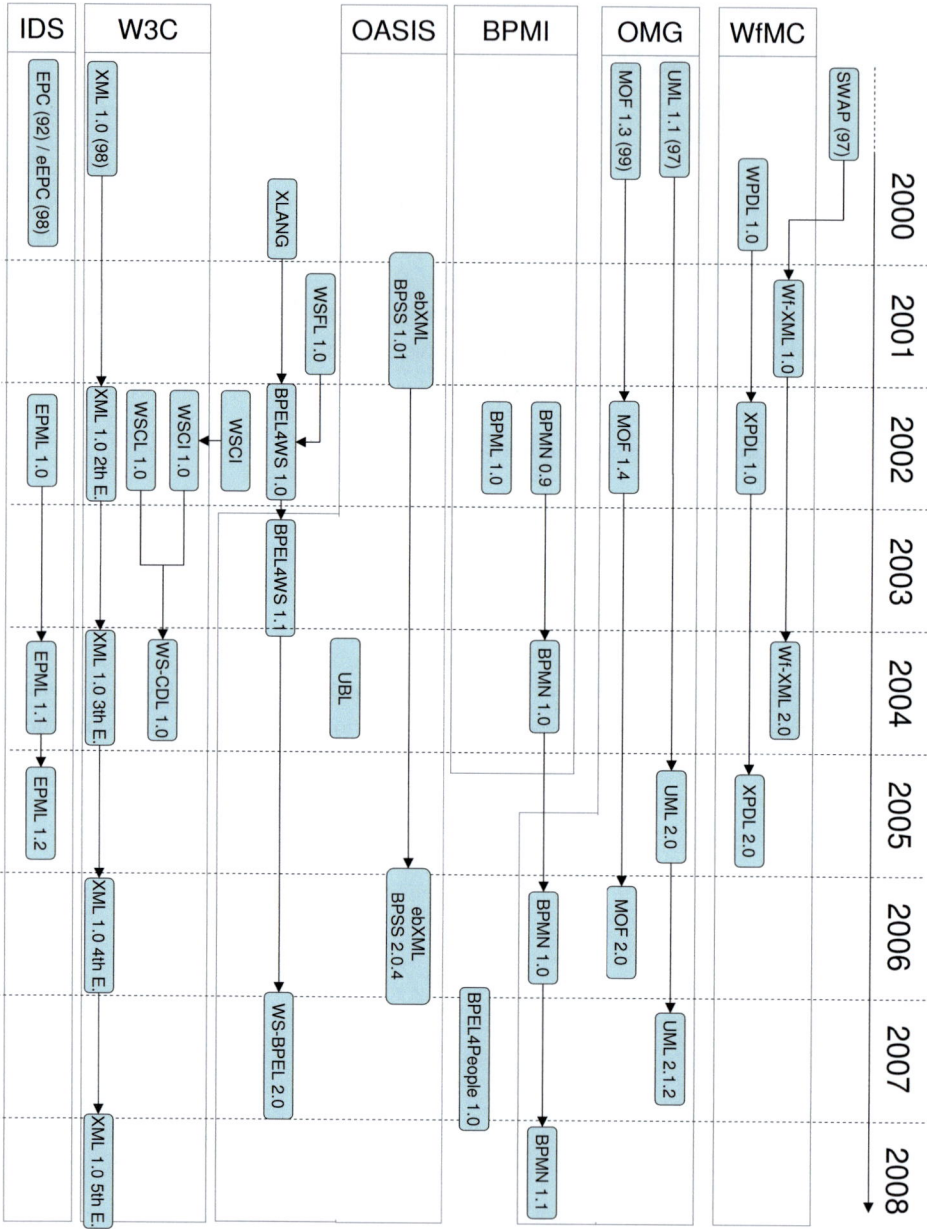

Figure A.1.: Historical overview about BPM relevant standards.

In Table A.1 an overview is given about the relevant standards in the area of BPM. It contains a short explanation of each standard.

Table A.1.: Business Process Management Standards

Standard	Description
BPDM	OMG's MOF[1] compliant Business Process Definition Metamodel. It is a subset of UML 2.0 metamodel and was developed for exchanging of process models between different modeling tools. The exchange format is defined by XML Schema (XSD) and XML for Metadata Interchange (XMI). BPDM is an alternative to the process interchange format XPDL.
BPEL4People	Business Process Execution Language for People (BPEL4People) is the WS-BPEL Extension for People. As interactions in WS-BPEL occur exclusively based on web services, BPEL4People was introduced to handle human interactions.
BPEL4WS	Business Process Execution Language for Web Services (BPEL4WS) has moved from a consortium of major software vendors to OASIS and has been incorporated into the WS–Specifications. In the course of this incorporation, BPEL4WS was renamed to WS-BPEL (often shortly termed BPEL). It is an XML based execution language for business processes, in which the activities are implemented on the basis of web services only.
BPML	The Business Process Modeling Language (BPML) proposed by Business Process Management Initiative (BPMI) is similar to BPEL. As the main difference BPML allows to specify multiple processes in one XML document and related communication between those processes. Furthermore, BPML is not tied to WSDL[2].
BPMN	The Business Process Modeling Notation (BPMN) specification developed by Business Process Management Initiative (BPMI) provides a graphical notation for specifying business processes. Its objective is to support both technical and business users by providing a notation that is intuitive to business users and yet able to represent complex processes. Additionally, the specification provides a mapping to BPEL4WS.
BPSS	Business Process Specification Schema (BPSS) is part of OASIS and UN/CEFACT's work on ebXML. It includes a metamodel and XML schema for web service choreography.
BPQL	Business Process Query Language (BPQL) is a query language which allows a GUI-based intuitive query formulation of business processes specifications. It also supports querying of execution business processes specifications in a distributed cross-organizational environment [24].
ebXML	Electronic Business using eXtensible Markup Language (ebXML) is a family of XML based standards sponsored by OASIS and UN/CEFACT. The objective is is to provide an open, XML-based infrastructure that enables the global use of electronic business information in an interoperable, secure, and consistent manner by all trading partners.
	Continued on next page

	Continued from previous page
Standard	**Description**
	ebXML has been approved as ISO standard (ISO 15000).
EPML	Event-Driven Process Chain Markup Language (EPML) aims to facilitate graphical model interchange for Event-Driven Process Chains (EPCs) [186].
PNML	Petri Net Markup Language (PNML) is a proposal for an XML interchange format for Petri net models[3] [28]
PSL	Process Specification Language (PSL) defines a neutral representation for manufacturing processes on the basis of an ontology. PSL is an ISO standard (ISO 18629 - industrial automation systems and integration).
UBL	Universal Business Language (UBL) is an OASIS specification for electronic XML business documents such as purchase orders and invoices.
WS-BPEL	See BPEL4WS.
WSCDL	Web Service Choreography Description Language (WSCDL) is an XML-based language that describes peer-to-peer collaborations of web services participants.
WSCI	W3C's Web Service Choreography Interface (WSCI) provides a set of extensions to WSDL in order to describe process behavior of message exchanges. It describes the flow of messages exchanged by a web service participating in choreographed interactions with other services.
WSCL	Web Services Conversation Language (WSCL) specifies abstract interfaces defining the business-level conversations. Business-level conversations define the order in which business payload (documents) is exchanged.
WSFL	Web Services Flow Language (WSFL) is an XML language for the description of web service compositions. It was originally proposed by IBM and is one of the predecessors of BPEL.
XLANG	XLANG is an XML-based extension of WSDL. The extensions describe process behavior of a web service similar to WSCI. XLANG is the second predecessor of BPEL.
XPDL	XML Process Definition Language (XPDL) is a format standardized by the Workflow Management Coalition (WfMC) to interchange business process models between different tools.
Wf-XML	This standard was developed by WfMC. It extends the Asynchronous Service Access Protocol (ASAP)[4] model to include BPM interchange capabilities. Wf-XML defines how process definitions can be retrieved from a BPM engine, as well as how to provide one.

---

[1]Meta Object Facility (MOF) is an OMG standard for model-driven engineering and defines a meta-modeling architecture. It is also an international standard: ISO/IEC 19502:2005 Information technology - Meta Object Facility. Additional information on OMG standards can be found in [210].

[2]Web Service Description Language (WSDL) is a W3C standard for describing web services as a set of end-points operating on messages containing either document-oriented or procedure-oriented information.

[3]Information about the PNML standard can be obtained from http://www.pnml.org/.

[4]ASAP was developed by OASIS and provides an extension of the Simple Object Access Protocol (SOAP). It enables generic asynchronous or long-running web services.

B. List Of Messages and Shared Knowledge

> "Knowledge is the conformity of the object and the intellect."
>
> Ibn Rushd (Averroes), Arab Andalusian Philosopher (520 - 595)

This appendix contains an overview about the knowledge that is shared between the agents by exchanging messages. In Table B.1 all messages are listed, that are exchanged within the Multi-Agent System (MAS). Additionally, Table B.2 contains a complete list of shared knowledge - the content of the messages.

Table B.1.: Complete list of agent messages

Message	Description
Adapted FIPA Contract Net Interaction Protocol specific messages	
Type	CALL_FOR_PROPOSAL
Sender	Intelligent Business Object (IBO)
Receiver	Resource Agent (RA)
Content	- Communication ID - Product Model ID - Production Rule ID - CfP-Deadline
Type	CALL_FOR_PROPOSAL_DEADLINE_DUE
Sender	IBO
Receiver	IBO
Content	- Communication ID
Type	PROPOSAL
Sender	Resource Agent
Receiver	IBO
Content	- Communication ID - Estimated Completion Time - Estimated Duration
Type	AWARD
Sender	IBO
Receiver	Resource Agent
Content	- Communication ID - Input Data - Execution Number

Continued on next page

Message	Description

Continued from previous page

Message	Description
Type	REJECT
Sender	IBO
Receiver	Resource Agent
Content	- Communication ID

Picking Protocol specific messages

Type	TASK_ANNOUNCEMENT
Sender	IBO
Receiver	Resource Agent
Content	- Communication ID - Product Model ID - Production Rule ID
Type	TASK_ANNOUNCEMENT_DEADLINE_DUE
Sender	IBO
Receiver	IBO
Content	- Communication ID
Type	PICKING_REQUEST
Sender	Resource Agent
Receiver	IBO
Content	- Communication ID
Type	PICKING_REQUEST_DEADLINE_DUE
Sender	Resource Agent
Receiver	Resource Agent
Content	- Task ID
Type	PICKING_GRANTED
Sender	IBO
Receiver	Resource Agent
Content	- Communication ID - Input Data - Execution Number
Type	PICKING_REJECTED
Sender	IBO
Receiver	Resource Agent
Content	- Communication ID
Type	WITHDRAW_TASK_ANNOUNCEMENT
Sender	IBO
Receiver	Resource Agent
Content	- Communication ID

Processing specific messages

Type	START_PROCESSING

Continued on next page

Message	Description
Sender	Simulation Control
Receiver	IBO
Content	- Product Model ID
Type	TASK_STARTED
Sender	Resource Agent
Receiver	Simulation Control
Content	- Production Rule ID - IBO ID - Task ID - Execution Number
Type	TASK_COMPLETED_RECHECK
Sender	Simulation Control
Receiver	Simulation Control
Content	- Resource Agent ID (RA that is processing the production rule) - IBO ID (ID of the IBO that processes the product model) - Processing Result - Sending Time
Type	TASK_COMPLETED
Sender	Simulation Control
Receiver	Resource Agent
Content	- Task ID - Processing Result
Type	TASK_COMPLETED
Sender	Resource Agent
Receiver	IBO
Content	- Task ID - Processing Result - Actual Start Time Slot - Waiting Time
Type	ESTIMATED_TASK_COMPLETION
Sender	IBO
Receiver	IBO
Content	- Task ID
Type	PROCESSING_COMPLETED
Sender	IBO
Receiver	Simulation Control
Content	- Final Result
Type	CANCEL_TASK
Sender	IBO
Receiver	Resource Agent

Continued on next page

Message	Description
	Continued from previous page
Message	**Description**
Content	- TASK ID
Type	SELF_ACTIVATION
Sender	IBO or Resource Agent
Receiver	same as sender
Content	-
Resource agent state specific messages	
Type	RESOURCE_AGENT_STATE_REQUEST
Sender	IBO
Receiver	Resource Agent
Content	-
Type	RESOURCE_AGENT_STATE_REQUEST_DEADLINE_DUE
Sender	IBO
Receiver	IBO
Content	- Resource Agent ID (ID of the resource agent to which the message RESOURCE_AGENT_STATE_REQUEST was sent
Type	RESOURCE_AGENT_STATE_INFO
Sender	Resource Agent
Receiver	IBO
Content	- Resource Agent State
Type	SET_RESOURCE_AGENT_STATE
Sender	Simulation Control
Receiver	Resource Agent
Content	- Resource Agent State
Background knowledge specific messages	
Type	RESOURCE_WORKLOAD_REQUEST
Sender	IBO
Receiver	Resource Agent
Content	-
Type	RESOURCE_WORKLOAD_REQUEST_DEADLINE_DUE
Sender	IBO
Receiver	Resource Agent
Content	- Role Name
Type	RESOURCE_WORKLOAD_INFO
Sender	Resource Agent
Receiver	IBO
Content	- Workload Information
	Continued on next page

Message	Description
	Continued from previous page
Message	**Description**
Type	RESOURCE_FAILURE_REQUEST
Sender	IBO
Receiver	Resource Agent
Content	-
Type	RESOURCE_FAILURE_REQUEST_DEADLINE_DUE
Sender	IBO
Receiver	Resource Agent
Content	- Role Name
Type	RESOURCE_FAILURE_INFO
Sender	Resource Agent
Receiver	IBO
Content	- Resource Failure Information

Table B.2.: List of shared knowledge

Knowledge	Explanation
Product Model ID	Unique identifier of the product model that has to be executed
Production Rule ID	Unique identifier of the production rule that has to be executed
Communication ID	Unique per IBO, identifier for the communication between IBO and resource agents
Task ID	Unique within simulation
CfP-Deadline	Deadline of the call for proposal
Estimated Completion Time	The estimated completion time of the production rule
Estimated Duration	The estimated duration for the processing of the production rule
Input Data	Origin information nodes of the production rule to be executed
Execution Number	A value of one indicates that the production rule is executed the first time, a value greater one means that a production rule is executed more than once which means it is part of a loop. The execution number is required as the process results depends on this information
Processing Result	Value of the information node that is created by the execution of the production rule
Actual Start Time Slot	Time slot in which processing was actually started by the resource agent
Waiting Time	Time between task assignment and the start of its execution
Resource Agent State	The state of the Resource Agent, either READY, PROCESSING, or ERROR
Sending Time	Time slot when the message was sent
Final Result	Denotes whether the execution of the product model was successful or not
Role Name	The role name of a resource agent
Workload Information	Information about the workload of a Resource Agent
Resource Failure Information	Information about the duration a Resource Agent was not able to work

C. Configuration

> "Everything should be made as simple as possible, but not one bit simpler."
>
> Albert Einstein

In this appendix information is provided how the Multi-Agent System (MAS) can be configured. There are different types of experiments that can be executed. These types require different configuration parameters. The types of experiments are:

- Regular run: The MAS executes the Executable Product Models (EPMs) based on the basic execute-all strategy or Policy Iteration approach. A regular run corresponds to the simulation of the real execution of EPMs.

- RRL-GA: This kind of experiment is executed in order to determine an optimal probability vector for the pre-defined policy making use of the Genetic Algorithm (GA) in the offline learning phase.

- RRL-PSO: This works as the RRL-GA, but with one difference: instead of the GA, the Particle Swarm Optimization (PSO) algorithm is used in the offline learning phase.

The MAS is configured by using an XML configuration file. The GA and PSO algorithm are configured by command line parameters in order to allow batch processing of experiments.

This appendix is structured as follows: First, the configuration parameters for the MAS are listed. Then, an example of an XML configuration file is given, followed by the DTD file for the validation of the XML configuration file. Afterwards, the command line parameters are listed for the configuration of GA and PSO.

C.1. Configuration Parameters

In this section, all configuration parameters are listed that are required for the MAS. Most parameters are defined in the XML configuration file. Table C.1 provides the list of parameters with the corresponding explanations. The parameter is either an XML tag or an attribute. In Table C.2, all hard-coded constants are specified.

Table C.1.: Configuration of the Multi-Agent System.

Parameter	Description
General Configuration	
MaxNumberOfTimeSlots	Stop criteria: maximum duration of simulation.
MaxNumberOfProduct-ModelExecutions	Stop criteria: maximum number of executed product models.
InterarrivalTimes-ProductModelInstances-ExponentialDistribution	The β value of the exponential distribution. It determines the inter-arrival time of product models.
ObservationWaitingTime	A percentage value greater than zero. Required for the task observation. The IBO expects the TASK_COMPLETED message within a specific time interval. This interval is calculated based on the estimated completion time and the ObservationWaitingTime: estimatedComplTime * (1+ObservationWaitingTime)
MaxNumberOf-ParallelEvents	This parameter denotes how many messages an agent can process per time slot. If the number of messages an agent has to process, exceeds the specified maximum, then the agent has to proceed the processing in the next time slot.
Adapted FIPA Contract Net Interaction Protocol Specification (ACNP)	
CallForProposalDeadline	Number of time slots, the call for proposal is valid.
MaxNumberOfCFP-_Retries	Number of call for proposals that are carried out for one production rule. If the IBO does not retrieve any proposals, the call for proposal has to be repeated.
WaitingTimeBetween-CFP_Retries	Number of time slots the IBO waits until it repeats the call for proposal.
Picking Protocol	
TaskAnnouncement-Deadline	Number of time slots, the task announcement is valid.
Role	
id	A unique ID of the role.
name	The name of the role, like manager or worker. Each name must exist only once.
errorInterarrivalTimeBeta	The beta value of the exponential distribution. It determines the inter-arrival time of resource failures.
errorDurationAlpha errorDurationBeta	Parameter α and β of the gamma distribution for the duration of a break down of a resource.
Resource Agent	
numberOfInstances	The number of Resource Agents of a specific role.

Continued on next page

Parameter	Description
	Continued from previous page
Parameter	**Description**
roleId	The ID of the role the Resource Agent belongs to.
willingnessToRiskFactor	Willingness to risk factor. The Resource Agent estimates the duration of a production rule based on this parameter and the gamma distribution for the estimated duration: $willingnessToRisk * estimatedDuration$

Executable Product Model - Information Node

Parameter	Description
id	Unique ID of the information node.
isArray	Possible values: yes or no. Determines whether an information node can store multiple values (array).
name	The name of the information node. Must not occur twice.
type	The data type of the information node. Possible values: Boolean, Date, Double, Integer, or String.

Executable Product Model - Production Rule

Parameter	Description
numberOfInstances	The number of Resource Agents of a specific role.
estimatedGammaAlpha estimatedGammaBeta	Parameter α and β of the gamma distribution for the estimation of the processing time of a production rule.
realGammaAlpha realGammaBeta	Parameter α and β of the gamma distribution for the calculation of the actual process time of a production rule.
costGammaAlpha costGammaBeta	Parameter α and β of the gamma distribution for the calculation of the costs.
roleId	ID of the role that is required for the processing of the production rule.
DestinationNode	The destination node that is created when the production rule has been executed successfully.
OriginNode	The origin nodes of the production rules. If no origin node has been defined, the production rule can be executed from the beginning. If multiple origin nodes have been defined, the production rule corresponds to an AND dependency. OR dependencies exist, if the same information node, has been defined as origin node in different production rules.
Constraint	A constraint can be defined that determines when a production rule becomes executable, e.g.: $StringNode(1) == "error"$. The constraint is fulfilled if the information node with $ID = 1$ of type String has the value *error*.

Executable Product Model - Execution Data Instance

Parameter	Description
probability	An execution data instance provides the data that is generated during the execution of an EPM. Multiple execution data instances may be defined. The probability determines how often a specific execution data instance is used during simulation.
	Continued on next page

	Continued from previous page
Parameter	**Description**
validFrom validTo	A time interval can be defined that determines when an execution data instance is valid. By this changing scenarios can be defined.
Result	An execution data instance must provide for each production rule a corresponding processing result (value of the destination node). In case of loops, multiple processing results must be provided for each rule that is executed multiple times.
Policy - Policy Rule	
condition	The condition of the policy rule. The condition must be fulfilled, before the action can be executed.
action	The action of the policy rule.
probability	The probability of the policy rule required for the policy iteration method. The probability determines whether the action is executed or the next policy rule is evaluated.

Table C.2.: Hard-coded configuration parameters.

Parameter	**Description**
PROLOG_ENGINE_TYPE	Type of the PROLOG engine. SWI-PROLOG or TU-PROLOG engine can be used.
USE_PROLOG_CACHE	Triggers the use of the PROLOG cache.
INFORMATION_VALIDITY _INTERVAL	Number of time slots after which information becomes outdated. Pertains to workload and resource failure information.
WORK_LOAD _REQUEST_PENALTY	Number of time slots that a work load request needs to be processed (penalty).
RESOURCE_FAILURE _REQUEST_PENALTY	Number of time slots that a resource failure request needs to be processed (penalty).
ABORT_CRITERIA_ENABLED	Triggers the abort criteria. The evaluation of an individual can be aborted before the simulation duration has ended.
TIMESLOTS_BETWEEN _PERIODIC_QUERY	Data is queried for the statistical analysis in time intervals.
USE_CONSTANT _PROCESSING_TIMES	If set to true, the α value of the gamma distribution is used as constant processing time.
USE_CONSTANT _ARRIVAL_TIME	If set to true, the β value of the exponential distribution is used as constant inter-arrival time.
	Continued on next page

	Continued from previous page
Parameter	**Description**
NUMBER_OF_PRODUCT _MODELS_TO_BE _GENERATED	Number of EPMs to be generated at one arrival event. The execution data instances are determined on the basis of the defined execution data instance probability.
PROBABILITY_PRECISION	Number of decimal places (positions after decimal point) of the probabilities. Pertains only to the GA.
USE_DATABASE	Triggers the use of a database for storing information about evaluated individuals. Pertains only to the GA.

C.2. Example of an XML Configuration File

In this section, an example of an XML configuration file is given. The following XML contains the configuration of the "Linear" EPM which was used in some of the conducted experiments (see e.g. Sec. 9.2.1):

```xml
<?xml version="1.0" encoding="UTF-8"?>

<!DOCTYPE Configuration SYSTEM "configuration.dtd">

<!-
Product Model:  Linear Structure
->

<Configuration>

    <RunningTime>
      <MaxNumberOfTimeSlots value="10000"/>
      <MaxNumberOfProductModelExecutions value="10000"/>
    </RunningTime>
    <InterarrivalTimesProductModelInstancesExponentialDistribution
    beta="55.0"/>
    <ObservationWaitingTime value="0.1"/>
    <MaxNumberOfParallelEvents value="1000000"/>

    <CallForProposalProtocol>
      <CallForProposalDeadline value="2"/>
      <MaxNumberOfCFP_Retries value="3"/>
      <WaitingTimeBetweenCFP_Retries value="10"/>
    </CallForProposalProtocol>

    <Roles>
      <Role id="0" name="Worker" errorInterarrivalTimeBeta="500000"
      errorDurationAlpha="3.0" errorDurationBeta="2.0"/>
      <Role id="1" name="Manager" errorInterarrivalTimeBeta="500000"
      errorDurationAlpha="2.5" errorDurationBeta="2.1"/>
    </Roles>

    <ResourceAgents>
      <ResourceAgent numberOfInstances="2" roleId="0"
      willingnessToRiskFactor="0.7"/>
      <ResourceAgent numberOfInstances="2" roleId="1"
      willingnessToRiskFactor="0.7"/>
    </ResourceAgents>
```

```
<ProductModels>
  <ProductModel>
    <InformationNodes>
      <InformationNode id="0" isArray="no" name="A" type="Integer"/>
      <InformationNode id="1" isArray="no" name="B" type="Integer"/>
    </InformationNodes>

    <ProductionRules>
      <ProductionRule estimatedGammaAlpha="100" estimatedGammaBeta="1"
      realGammaAlpha="100" realGammaBeta="1"
      costGammaAlpha="10" costGammaBeta="1" roleId="0">
        <DestinationNode id="0"/>
        <OriginNodes>
        </OriginNodes>
      </ProductionRule>

      <ProductionRule estimatedGammaAlpha="100" estimatedGammaBeta="1"
      realGammaAlpha="100" realGammaBeta="1"
      costGammaAlpha="10" costGammaBeta="1" roleId="1">
        <DestinationNode id="1"/>
        <OriginNodes>
          <OriginNode id="0"/>
        </OriginNodes>
      </ProductionRule>
    </ProductionRules>

    <ExecutionInstances>
      <ExecutionInstance>
        <Result productionRuleId="0" resultValue="1"/>
        <Result productionRuleId="1" resultValue="2"/>
      </ExecutionInstance>
    </ExecutionInstances>
  </ProductModel>
</ProductModels>

<Policy>
  <!- assure that work load information is requested->
  <PolicyRule condition="not workloads_available, not
  workloads_requested" action="request_workload" probability="0"/>
  <!- keep work load information updated, if it is outdated update it ->
  <PolicyRule condition="workloads_available, workloads_outdated, not
  workloads_requested" action="request_workload" probability="0"/>

  <!- analog work load information related rules ->
  <PolicyRule condition="not failure_rates_available, not
  failure_rates_requested" action="request_failure_rate"
  probability="0"/>
  <PolicyRule condition="failure_rates_available,
  failure_rates_outdated, not failure_rates_requested"
  action="request_failure_rate" probability="0"/>

  <!- assures that exactly one variant is executed - which is the
  variant with the minimum estimated weighted duration ->
  <PolicyRule condition="number_of_activated_variants(A),A=0,
  minimum_weighted_duration(V1, B)" action="activate(V1)"
  probability="1.0"/>
  <PolicyRule condition="activated_variant(V1),
  weighted_variant_duration(V1,A), minimum_weighted_duration(V2,B),
  A=&lt;B" action="proceed(V1)" probability="1.0"/>
  <PolicyRule condition="activated_variant(V1),
  weighted_variant_duration(V1,A), minimum_weighted_duration(V2,B),
  not V1=V2, A&gt;B" action="switch(V1,V2)" probability="0"/>
</Policy>
</Configuration>
```

C.3. DTD of the Configuration File

The XML configuration is validated on the basis of a DTD file which is presented here:

```
<?xml version="1.0" encoding="UTF-8"?>
<!ELEMENT Configuration (RunningTime,
InterarrivalTimesProductModelInstancesExponentialDistribution,
ObservationWaitingTime, MaxNumberOfParallelEvents,
(CallForProposalProtocol|PickingProtocol), Roles, ResourceAgents,
ProductModels, Policy?)>

<!ELEMENT RunningTime (MaxNumberOfTimeSlots,
MaxNumberOfProductModelExecutions)>
<!ELEMENT MaxNumberOfTimeSlots EMPTY>
<!ELEMENT MaxNumberOfProductModelExecutions EMPTY>
<!ELEMENT InterarrivalTimesProductModelInstancesExponentialDistribution
EMPTY>
<!ELEMENT ObservationWaitingTime EMPTY>
<!ELEMENT MaxNumberOfParallelEvents EMPTY>
<!ELEMENT CallForProposalProtocol (CallForProposalDeadline,
MaxNumberOfCFP_Retries,WaitingTimeBetweenCFP_Retries)>
<!ELEMENT PickingProtocol (TaskAnnouncementDeadline)>
<!ELEMENT CallForProposalDeadline EMPTY>
<!ELEMENT MaxNumberOfCFP_Retries EMPTY>
<!ELEMENT WaitingTimeBetweenCFP_Retries EMPTY>
<!ELEMENT TaskAnnouncementDeadline EMPTY>
<!ELEMENT Roles (Role+)>
<!ELEMENT Role EMPTY>
<!ELEMENT ResourceAgents (ResourceAgent+)>
<!ELEMENT ResourceAgent EMPTY>
<!ELEMENT ProductModels (ProductModel+)>
<!ELEMENT ProductModel (InformationNodes,ProductionRules,Cycles?,
ExecutionInstances?)>
<!ELEMENT InformationNodes (InformationNode+)>
<!ELEMENT InformationNode EMPTY>
<!ELEMENT ProductionRules (ProductionRule+)>
<!ELEMENT ProductionRule (DestinationNode,OriginNodes,Constraint?)>
<!ELEMENT DestinationNode EMPTY>
<!ELEMENT OriginNodes (OriginNode*)>
<!ELEMENT OriginNode EMPTY>
<!ELEMENT Constraint (#PCDATA)>
<!ELEMENT Cycles (Cycle+)>
<!ELEMENT Cycle (Node+)>
<!ELEMENT Node EMPTY>
<!ELEMENT ExecutionInstances (ExecutionInstance+)>
<!ELEMENT ExecutionInstance (Result+)>
<!ELEMENT Policy (PolicyRule+)>
<!ELEMENT PolicyRule EMPTY>
<!ELEMENT Result EMPTY>

<!ATTLIST MaxNumberOfTimeSlots value CDATA #REQUIRED>
<!ATTLIST MaxNumberOfProductModelExecutions value CDATA #REQUIRED>
<!ATTLIST
InterarrivalTimesProductModelInstancesExponentialDistribution
beta CDATA #REQUIRED>
<!ATTLIST ObservationWaitingTime value CDATA #REQUIRED>
<!ATTLIST MaxNumberOfParallelEvents value CDATA #REQUIRED>
<!ATTLIST CallForProposalDeadline value CDATA #REQUIRED>
<!ATTLIST MaxNumberOfCFP_Retries value CDATA #REQUIRED>
<!ATTLIST WaitingTimeBetweenCFP_Retries value CDATA #REQUIRED>
<!ATTLIST TaskAnnouncementDeadline value CDATA #REQUIRED>
<!ATTLIST Role
      id CDATA #REQUIRED
      name CDATA #REQUIRED
      errorInterarrivalTimeBeta CDATA #REQUIRED
      errorDurationAlpha CDATA #REQUIRED
      errorDurationBeta CDATA #REQUIRED
>
```

```
<!ATTLIST ResourceAgent
      numberOfInstances CDATA #REQUIRED
      roleId CDATA #REQUIRED
      willingnessToRiskFactor CDATA #REQUIRED
>
<!ATTLIST InformationNode
      id CDATA #REQUIRED
      isArray (yes|no) #REQUIRED
      name CDATA #REQUIRED
      type (Boolean|Date|Double|Integer|String) #REQUIRED
>
<!ATTLIST ProductionRule
      estimatedGammaAlpha CDATA #REQUIRED
      estimatedGammaBeta CDATA #REQUIRED
      realGammaAlpha CDATA #REQUIRED
      realGammaBeta CDATA #REQUIRED
      waitGammaBeta CDATA #IMPLIED
      waitGammaAlpha CDATA #IMPLIED
      costGammaBeta CDATA #REQUIRED
      costGammaAlpha CDATA #REQUIRED
      roleId CDATA #REQUIRED
>
<!ATTLIST DestinationNode id CDATA #REQUIRED>
<!ATTLIST OriginNode id CDATA #REQUIRED>
<!ATTLIST Node id CDATA #REQUIRED>
<!ATTLIST Result
      productionRuleId CDATA #REQUIRED
      resultValue CDATA #REQUIRED
>
<!ATTLIST ExecutionInstance
      validFrom CDATA #REQUIRED
      validUntil CDATA #REQUIRED
      probability CDATA #IMPLIED
>
<!ATTLIST PolicyRule
      condition CDATA #REQUIRED
      action CDATA #REQUIRED
      probability CDATA #IMPLIED
>
```

C.4. Genetic Algorithm Configuration

Table C.3 contains the list of existing command line parameters to configure the Genetic Algorithm (GA). The listing contains also an explanation of the possible values for each parameter.

In the following an example of a program call in order to start a GA experiment is given:

```
java -jar RRL-GA.jar xmlFile=config.xml popSize=30
noEvolutions=1000 noESRuns=20 initPop=random crossover=none
mutation=gaussian/0.15 selection=tournament noSimulationRuns=3
```

Table C.3.: Configuration of an RRL-GA experiment.

Command Line Parameter	Description and Values
xmlFile	Name of the XML configuration file.
noEvolutions	Number of evolution steps (generations). Minimum value is zero. If set to zero, only the initial population is generated.
popSize	Size of the population. Minimum value is 1
noSimulationRuns	Number of times a simulation is repeated for the fitness evaluation of an individual. Minimum value is one.
noESRuns	Number of times a GA experiment is repeated (different initial seeds). A higher number leads to an improved statistical significance of the results. Minimum value is one.
initPop	Method for the generation of the initial population. Possible values: GS (for Gap Search) or random.
selection	Selection operator. Possible values: best, roulette, or tournament.
crossover	Crossover operator. Possible values: none, average, onepoint.
mutation	Mutation operator. Possible values: none, random or gaussian/<Rate>, e.g. gaussian/0.1

C.5. Particle Swarm Optimization Configuration

Table C.4 contains the list of existing command line parameters to configure the Particle Swarm Optimization (PSO) algorithm. The listing contains also an explanation of the possible values for each parameter.

In the following an example of a program call in order to start a PSO experiment is given:

```
java -jar RRL-PSO.jar xmlFile=config.xml noEvolutions=30
noParticles=50 inertia=0.4 globalIncrement=1.0
particleIncrement=1.0 noSimulationRuns=3 noSWARMRuns=20
initPop=R-R outOfBoundary=Border-K craziness=none
topology=ring
```

Table C.4.: Configuration of an RRL-PSO experiment.

Command Line Parameter	Description and Values
xmlFile	Name of the XML configuration file.
noEvolutions	Number of evolution steps (generations). Minimum value is zero. If set to zero, only the initial swarm is generated.
noParticles	Number of particles of the swarm. Minimum value is 1
inertia	Inertia parameter (corresponds to w in Equ. 2.9). Possible values: nonnegative float, linDec (linear decreasing), or nonLinDec (non-linear descreasing).
particleIncrement	particle increment parameter (corresponds to c_1 in Equ. 2.9) Possible values: nonnegative float
globalIncrement	global increment parameter (corresponds to c_2 in Equ. 2.9) Possible values: nonnegative float
noSimulationRuns	Number of times a simulation is repeated for the fitness evaluation of a particle. Minimum value is one.
noSWARMRuns	Number of times a PSO experiment is repeated (different initial seeds). A higher number leads to an improved statistical significance of the results. Minimum value is one.
initPop	Method for the generation of the initial population. Format: <Position>-<Velocity>. Possible values: GS-0, GS-R, R-0, or R-R.[1]
outOfBoundary	Feasibility preservation method. Format: <Position>-<Velocity>. Possible values: GS-0, GS-R, GS-K Border-0, Border-R, or Border-K.[2]
craziness	Craziness method. Format: <Position>-<Velocity>. Possible values: none, GS-0, GS-R, GS-K, TF-0, TF-R, or TF-K.[3]
topology	Neighbourhood topology Possible values: star or ring

---

[1] GS is the abbreviation for Gap Search. -0, -R, and -K means either setting the velocity to zero, random, or keeping the current value.

[2] Border is the feasibility preservation strategy where the infeasible position is changed to the border of the feasible space.

[3] TF is the abbreviation for Turbulence Factor.

D. PROLOG

> "Language exerts hidden power, like a moon on the tides."
>
> Rita Mae Brown

This appendix contains a brief explanation about the use of PROLOG and the list of defined PROLOG predicates.

D.1. Use of PROLOG

PROLOG is a logic programming language which was created around 1972 by Alain Colmerauer together with Bob Pasero and Philippe Roussel. PROLOG stands for "Programming in Logic" (Programmation en Logique in French).

A PROLOG program (also termed PROLOG database) describes relations that are defined by means of clauses. A clause represents a statement about objects and relations between objects. Two types of clauses exist:

Rules A rule has the following structure: `Head :- Body.`
A rule represents conditional knowledge in the form of "head is true if body is true". Rules are used to derive further information from the information already stored in the database.

Facts A fact is a clause with an empty body that represents unconditional knowledge. An example of a fact is `executable(prodRule0)`.

All clauses (rules as well as facts) that have the same name (also termed functor) and the same number of arguments (also termed arity) comprise one predicate. Predicates are specified in the form Name/Arity, e.g. `executable/1`.

The PROLOG program (database) is the set of predicates available at the moment a query is executed. Queries can be used to evaluate whether a specific fact is true, e.g. "is production rule with ID 0 executable?" or which objects are part of a specific relation, e.g. "which production rules are executable?".

PROLOG is used within the intelligent Executable Product Model (iEPM) approach as follows: The system state perceived by the Intelligent Business Object (IBO) is stored by adding the related facts to the PROLOG database. Let us assume that production rule 0 has been executed, production rule 1 is executable and information node 0 has been created. Then, the following facts are added to the database:

- `executed(prodRule0).`

- `executable(prodRule1).`

- `created(infoNode0).`

As example, the policy consists of the following policy rule:

- `executable(X)` → `execute(X).`

The policy iteration approach requires the evaluation of the condition part of the policy. This is done by executing the query:

- `?- executable(X).`

which evaluates to true with the result `X = prodRule1`. If the IBO decides to execute the related action on the basis of the assigned probability, production rule 1 is executed.

D.2. List of Predicates

This section contains the list of PROLOG predicates used within the iEPM approach. The predicates are stored in the file predicates.pl and are loaded into the PROLOG database at startup of the program.

Predicates that are changed at runtime should be defined as dynamic as the SWI-Prolog engine throws an exception "operation undefined" if a query is executed before the predicate has been added to the database. Additionally, several PROLOG rules were defined.

In the following, the content of file predicates.pl is listed:

```
% Predicates related to the production rule status:

:- dynamic executable/1.
:- dynamic in_negotiation/1.
:- dynamic in_execution/1.
:- dynamic execution_failed/1.
:- dynamic execution_cancelled/1.
:- dynamic in_executed/1.

% Predicates related to the information node status:

:- dynamic not_yet_created/1.
:- dynamic created/1.
:- dynamic invalidated/1.
```

```
% Predicate that relates to the number of production rules in execution
% or in negotiation:

:- dynamic active_production_rules/1.

% Predicate that defines which production rule creates which information
% node:

:- dynamic creates_info_node/2.

% Predicate that defines the root information node:

:- dynamic root_info_node/1.

% Predicates related to the workload of production rules:

:- dynamic pr_workload_requested/1.
:- dynamic current_pr_workload/2.

% Variant specific predicates:

:- dynamic total_number_variants/1.
:- dynamic number_of_activated_variants/1.
:- dynamic weighted_variant_duration/2.
:- dynamic variant_execution_number/2.
:- dynamic estimated_variant_costs/2.
:- dynamic activated_variant/1.
:- dynamic execution_mode/1.

% Predicates related to the failure rates of variants:

:- dynamic failure_rates_requested/0.
:- dynamic failure_rates_available/0.
:- dynamic failure_rates_outdated/0.

% Predicates related to the workload of variants:

:- dynamic workloads_requested/0.
:- dynamic workloads_available/0.
:- dynamic workloads_outdated/0.

% Timestamp related predicates:

:- dynamic current_time/1.
:- dynamic processing_started/1.
:- dynamic last_failure_rate_update/1.
:- dynamic last_workload_update/1.

% Rule for determining the variant X with the minimum processing time
% left Y:

minimum_time_left(X,Y) :-
     findall(W, estimated_time_left(_,W), A),
     sort(A, [Y | _]), estimated_time_left(X,Y).

% Rule for determining the variant X with the minimum workload Y:

minimum_workload(X,Y) :-
     findall(W, current_workload(_,W), A),
     sort(A, [Y | _]), current_workload(X,Y).

% Rule for determining the variant X with the minimum weighted
% duration Y:

minimum_weighted_duration(X,Y) :-
     findall(W, weighted_variant_duration(_,W), A),
     sort(A, [Y | _]), weighted_variant_duration(X,Y).

% Rule for determining the variant X with the minimum costs Y:

minimum_estimated_costs(X,Y) :-
     findall(W, estimated_variant_costs(_,W), A),
     sort(A, [Y | _]), estimated_variant_costs(X,Y).
```

```
% Rule for determining the variant X with
% the maximum execution number Y
% (the variant that has been executed most frequently):

maximum_execution_number(X,Y) :-
      findall(W, variant_execution_number(_,W), A),
      msort(A, Z), last(Z,Y), variant_execution_number(X,Y).
```

E. Execution Semantics

Sir Edmund Blackadder: "I see, and the fact that this
secret has eluded the most intelligent people since
the dawn of time doesn't at all dampen your spirits?"
Percy: "Oh no; I like a challenge!"
Blackadder II:4

This appendix provides a formal definition of an EPM and its execution semantics. The definition which will be provided is similar to the definition of Petri nets. Petri nets allow a clear distinction between the structure of a business process and its dynamic states [233]. Moreover, Petri nets are based on a sound mathematical model. This appendix has the objective, to give a deeper insight into the execution semantics of EPMs. Note that the execution of an EPM has been explained on the basis of the developed execution algorithms in Sec. 3.3. Furthermore, a mathematical model for EPMs was provided in Sec. 4.3.2. As its purpose was to prove the NP-completeness, it was created for a special case only. Due to the different focus on the execution semantics, the mathematical model introduced in Sec. 4.3.2 will be adapted and extended.

This appendix is outlined as follows: First, a mathematical model for the EPM is introduced. As the execution semantics are rather complicated, they are introduced in multiple steps, starting with a basic mathematical model for the execution of an EPM. This model is explained in detail on the basis of various examples. Then, this basic model is extended and explained again. The appendix ends with a discussion about the different possibilities to further extent the mathematical model for the execution.

E.1. EPM Structure

As aforementioned, the EPM was mathematically defined in Sec. 4.3.2. For the NP-completeness proof, it was sufficient to define an EPM as a tuple (I, pre, P, f, R, g). This definition is used as a basis and extended in the following.

The execution of EPMs is based on the generated values of information elements and the defined constraints, i.e. production rules are executable only if the values of all input information elements of this production rule have been generated and the defined constraint evaluates to true. These constraints are defined on the basis of the input information elements of the corresponding production rule. In order to keep the definition simple, a generated value of an information element is considered to be an integer. Consequently, an integer variable is assigned to each information element.

The *indegree* of a production rule $p \in P$ equals the number of input information elements. Since $p = (d, os)^1$, the indegree of a production rule can be denoted by $|os|$. As production rules have always one output information element, their *outdegree* equals one. The *indegree* (*outdegree*) of an information element equals the number of incoming (outgoing) arcs.

Note that an EPM may also contain cycles. Thus, the set D_{pre} is defined not acyclic anymore as in the tuple (I, pre, P, f, R, g).

---

[1]d corresponds to the destination information element and os corresponds to the set of origin information elements of production rule p.

Definition: An Executable Product Model is a tuple
$(I, \hat{pre}, P, f, R, g, V, var, C, constr)$ with:

- I: Defined as in Sec. 4.3.2.

- $\hat{pre}$: Defined as pre in Sec. 4.3.2 with a different $D_{\hat{pre}}$:
  - $D_{\hat{pre}} = \{(d,o) \in I \times I | o \in \bigcup\limits_{es \in pre(p)} es\}$ is connected and each information node be-
    longs to at most one cycle.

- P: Defined as in Sec. 4.3.2.

- f: Defined as in Sec. 4.3.2.

- R: Defined as in Sec. 4.3.2.

- g: Defined as in Sec. 4.3.2.

- V: A finite set of integer variables with $|V| = |I|$.

- $var : I \rightarrow V$: This function assigns to each each information element $a \in I$ exactly one variable such that each variable is assigned to at most one information element.

- C: A finite set of constraints including a special nullary function which always yields to true denoted by $\underline{true}$. A constraint is defined as function:
  $f_c : V^{k_c} \rightarrow \mathbb{B}$, with $\mathbb{B} = \{0,1\}$, $c = 1, \cdots, |C|$; index k_c means that the arity of function f_c may be different for each constraint C.

- $constr : P \rightarrow C$: This function associates a constraint to each production rule, such that:
  - $\forall e \in I : pre(e) = \emptyset \Rightarrow constr(e, \emptyset) = \underline{true}$
    There are no constraining conditions on producing elements that do not require values of other information elements.

  - Let $p = (d, os) \in P$ and $o_i \in I, i = 1, \cdots, |os|$ be an arbitrary fixed enumeration of set os. Then $\forall p = (d, os) \in P$ with $os \not\subseteq \emptyset : constr(p) = f_c(var(o_1), \cdots, var(o_{|os|}))$
    Only variables assigned to the input information elements of the respective production rule appear in the constraint assigned to the production rule.

Thus far, the structure of the EPM was mathematically defined. Now, an example of this structure is provided. The EPM $(I, pre, P, f, R, g, V, var, C, constr)$ is defined as follows:

- $I = \{1, 2\}$

- $p\hat{r}e(2) = \{1\}$, $D_{p\hat{r}e} = \{(2, 1)\}$, $P = \{(1, \emptyset), (2, \{1\})\}$

- $f((1, \emptyset)) = 30, f((2, \{1\})) = 60$

- $R = \{worker, manager\}$

- $g((1, \emptyset)) = worker$, $g((2, \{1\})) = manager$

- $V = \{v_1, v_2\}$, $var(1) = v_1$, $var(2) = v_2$

- $C = \{f_1, f_2\}$ with $f_1 = \underline{true}$,

$$f_2(v_1) = \begin{cases} 1 & \text{, if } v_1 = 5 \\ 0 & \text{, otherwise} \end{cases}$$

- $constr((1, \emptyset)) = f_1$, $constr((2, \{1\})) = f_2$.

This EPM is depicted in Fig. E.1.

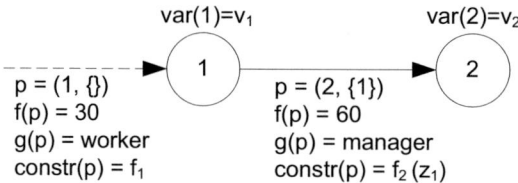

var(1)=v_1 var(2)=v_2

p = (1, {})
f(p) = 30
g(p) = worker
constr(p) = f_1

p = (2, {1})
f(p) = 60
g(p) = manager
constr(p) = f_2 (z_1)

Figure E.1.: Example of a linear EPM. Note that the constraint of production rule $(2, \{1\})$ was defined only for illustration purposes. If this constraint is not fulfilled, the EPM cannot be executed completely.

In the following, definitions are provided regarding the execution semantics of EPMs.

E.2. Basic Execution Semantic

This section introduces a basic mathematical model for the execution semantics of EPMs. First, some definitions are provided regarding the state of the execution. The definitions are partly derived from Petri nets. This basic definition considers the execution of exactly one EPM.

The execution of a production rule results in the generation of a value of its output information element. Thus, once a production rule has been executed, a value is assigned to its output information element based on the following function:

Definition: Value Assignment
A value assignment of a variable is defined by function $val : V \rightarrow \mathbb{N}$.

Note that the value assigned to a variable may change during the execution of the EPM. This may happen due to variants or cycles.

Definition: Marking
A marking of an EPM $(I, \hat{pre}, P, f, R, g, V, var, C, constr)$ is a mapping $M : I \rightarrow \mathbb{N}$. A marking is represented by the vector $(M(a_1), \cdots, M(a_n))$, where $a_1, \cdots, a_n$ is an arbitrary fixed enumeration of I. An information element $a \in I$ is marked if $M(a) > 0$.

The marking of an EPM, is the allocation of tokens over information elements. In graphical depictions of EPMs, a marking (token) is represented by black dots as in Petri nets.

A marking is equivalent to a bag. A bag is defined as a finite multi-set of elements of some alphabet A. The empty bag (denoted by $\mathbf{0}$) is the function yielding 0 for any element in A. An example of a non empty bag is$\| a^2, b, c^3 \|$ which denotes the bag containing two elements a, one b, and three elements c. An example of a marking of an EPM is e.g. $\| 1, 2, 3^2 \|$ which means that one token is in information element 1, one token is in information element 2, and two tokens are in information element 3.

Definition: Executable Production Rule
A production rule $p = (d, os) \in P$ is executable if:

(a) $\emptyset \in os$ or $\forall e \in os, \emptyset \notin os : M(e) > 0$ and

(b) $constr(p) = \underline{true}$ or $constr(p) = f_c(val(var(o_1)), \cdots, val(var(o_{|os|}))) = 1$

Condition (a) has the following meaning: Production rules creating leaf nodes ($\emptyset \in os$) are executable. If a production rule has input information elements, all input information elements have to be marked. Condition (b) means that the constraint assigned to the production rule is fulfilled. The notation $val(var(o_i)), i = 1, \cdots, |os|$ means that the generated (assigned) value is used for the evaluation of the constraint.

Definition: Production Rule Execution

Once a production rule $p = (d, os)$ is executable, it can be executed. This leads to a successor marking M' (written as $M \xrightarrow{p} M'$) which is defined for every $a \in I$ by:

$$
M'(a) = \begin{cases} 1 & \text{, if } a = d \text{ and } d = \underline{top} \\ \text{outdegree of } a & \text{, if } a = d \text{ and } d \neq \underline{top} \\ M(a) - 1 & \text{, if } a \in os \\ M(a) & \text{, otherwise} \end{cases}
$$

Remember, that production rules are executed by resources that must have the same role assigned as the production rule. Consequently, a production rule can only be executed if it can be assigned to an adequate resource. In Sec. 4.3.2 resources were already defined mathematically as a set of integers RS. Moreover, a specific role was assigned to each resource by function $h : RS \rightarrow R$ such that for each role $r \in R \exists rs \in RS$ with $h(rs) = r$.

Note that the dynamic aspects of the execution of an EPM are defined by the production rule execution as the marking changes if a production rule was executed. Thus, the execution of a production rule leads to a "movement" of tokens.

Definition: Execution Sequence

Let M be a marking of an EPM $(I, \hat{pre}, P, f, R, g, V, var, C, constr)$. If $M \xrightarrow{p_1} M_1, M_1 \xrightarrow{p_2} M_2, \cdots,$ $M_{n-1} \xrightarrow{p_n} M_n$ are production rule executions with $p_i \in P, i = 1, \cdots, n$ then $\theta = p_1 p_2 \cdots p_n$ is an execution sequence leading from M to M_n.

Definition: EPM Completion

An EPM is executed completely if $M(\underline{top}) = 1$.

Markings are also defined for the dynamic state of Petri nets. The main difference of the marking between EPMs and Petri nets is that the marking of a place in a Petri net is incremented at most by one. In an EPM, the outdegree (number of outgoing arcs of an information element) of an information element is used instead of the incrementation by one. This is required as all outgoing production rules of a created information element are potentially executable. In Fig. E.2 the situation is depicted in which at most one token is created at most.

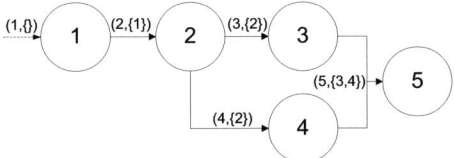

(a) Initially, there are no tokens. Thus, the marking equals $M_0(a) = 0 \forall a \in I$ or represented as a bag $\mathbf{0}$.

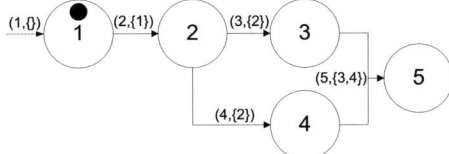

(b) After the execution of production rule $(1, \emptyset)$, information element 1 is marked: $M_1(1) = 1$ (bag $\|\ 1\ \|$).

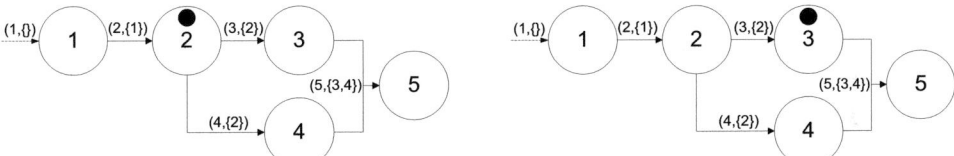

(c) After the execution of $(2, \{1\})$, the marking of 1 is decreased by one and the marking of 2 is incremented by one: $M_2(2) = 1$ (bag $\|\ 2\ \|$) Now, either $(3, \{2\})$ or $(4, \{2\})$ is executable.

(d) After the execution of $(3, \{2\})$, information element three is marked: $M_3(3) = 1$ (bag $\|\ 3\ \|$). At this point, the execution cannot proceed.

Figure E.2.: Marking of an EPM under the assumption that only one token is created at most. As one can see, the EPM cannot be executed completely as the production rule $(5, \{3, 4\})$ never gets executable due to one missing token. This is the reason for marking an information element based on its outdegree.

In Fig. E.3 an example of the execution of an EPM and its corresponding marking is illustrated. By marking information element 6 (see Fig.E.3(i)), the execution of the EPM is finished. Note that information element 1 is still being marked. This is due to the fact, that not all production rules have to be executed.

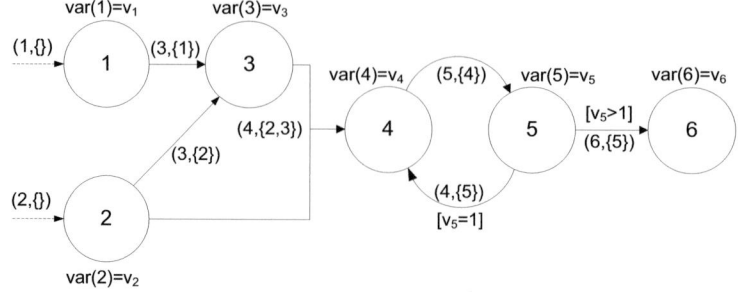

(a) Initially, there are no tokens. Thus, the marking equals $M_0(a) = 0 \forall a \in I$ or represented as a bag $\mathbf{0}$.

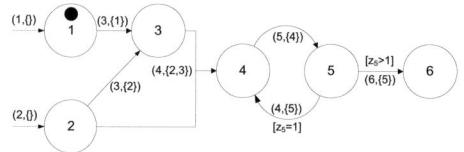

(b) After the execution of $(1, \emptyset)$, $M_1(1) = 1$.

(c) After the execution of $(2, \emptyset)$, $M_2(1) = 1$, $M_2(2) = 2$.

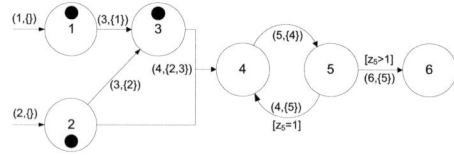

(d) After the execution of $(3, \{2\})$, $M_3(1) = 1$, $M_3(2) = 1$, $M_3(3) = 1$.

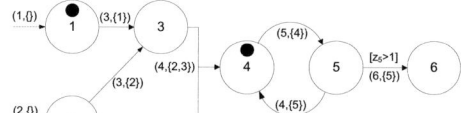

(e) After the execution of $(4, \{2, 3\})$, $M_4(1) = 1$, $M_4(4) = 1$.

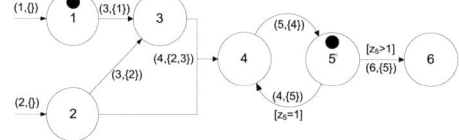

(f) After the execution of $(5, \{4\})$, $M_5(1) = 1$, $M_5(5) = 1$, assume that $v_5 = 1$.

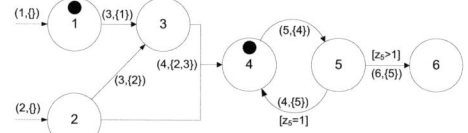

(g) After the execution of $(4, \{5\})$, $M_6(1) = 1$, $M_6(4) = 1$.

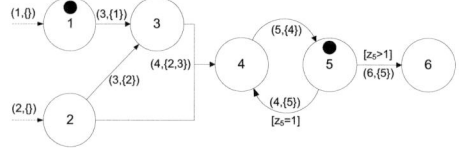

(h) After the execution of $(5, \{4\})$, $M_7(1) = 1$, $M_7(5) = 1$, assume that $v_5 = 2$.

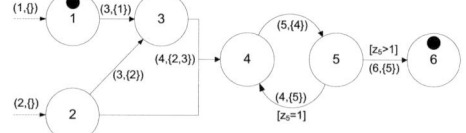

(i) After the execution of $(6, \{5\})$, $M_8(1) = 1$, $M_8(6) = 1$. Thus, the execution has finished.

Figure E.3.: Example of the execution of an EPM and its corresponding marking. Only markings which are unequal 0 are stated in the caption of the figures.

This basic execution semantic has one problem. As an information node may have multiple tokens due to its outdegree, it is not assured, that these tokens trigger the execution of the different outgoing production rules. It can happen for example, that these tokens trigger the execution of only one production rule multiple times. This situation is illustrated in Fig. E.4 in which production rule $(3, \{2\})$ is executed twice.

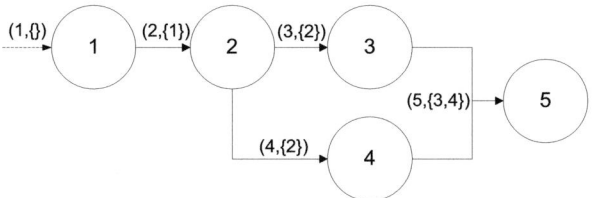

(a) Initially, there are no tokens $(M_0(a) = 0 \forall a \in I)$.

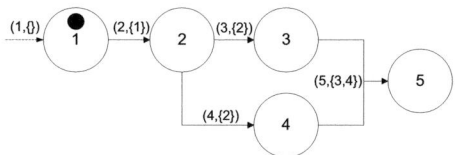

(b) After the execution of production rule $(1, \emptyset)$, information element 1 is marked: $M_1(1) = 1$

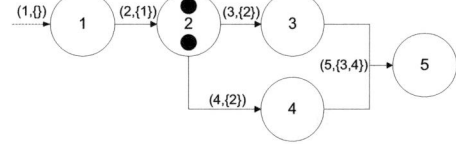

(c) After the execution of $(2, \{1\})$, information element 2 contains two tokens: $M_2(2) = 2$. Now, $(3, \{2\})$ and $(4, \{2\})$ are executable.

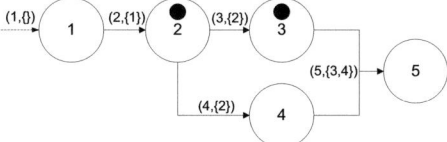

(d) After the execution of $(3, \{2\})$ information elements 2 and 3 are marked: $M_3(2) = M_3(3) = 1$.

(e) Production rule $(3, \{2\})$ is executed again. Consequently, information element 3 contains one token: $M_4(3) = 1$. At this point, the execution cannot proceed.

Figure E.4.: This example illustrates how the basic marking may result in a deadlock.

In order to handle this situation accordingly, an extended mathematical definition of the execution semantic is provided in the next section.

E.3. Extended Execution Semantic

The basic idea of handling situations as aforementioned is the usage of indexed tokens. First, each production rule gets a unique integer assigned by function $u : P \to \mathbb{N}$. The number of tokens still equals the outdegree of the created information node. But each of the tokens has an index corresponding to the unique integer of one of the outgoing production rules.

Let O_a be the set of outgoing production rules of information element $a \in I$.

Definition: Indexed Marking

An indexed marking of an EPM is a mapping $M(a) : I \to \mathbb{N}^{|O_a|}$. Thus, $M(a) = (m_1, \cdots, m_{|O_a|})$ is a vector and an element of this vector is denoted by $m_i, i = 1, \cdots, |O_a|$. An information element $a \in I$ is marked if $\exists i$ with $m_i > 0$.

Each m_i of a marking of an information element a relates exactly to one of the outgoing production rules of set O_a. This relationship is defined by function $s_a : \mathbb{N} \to \mathbb{N}$, e.g. $s_1(3) = 5$ means that in information element 1, the third position in vector $M(a)$ (which equals m_3) is related to the production rule with the unique integer 5.

Analog to the marking of the basic execution semantic, a marking can be represented by a bag. But it does not contain elements of $\mathbb{N}$ as defined in the basic execution semantics. Instead of that, a bag contains vectors.

A token is depicted as circle containing the unique integer of the related production rule, e.g. consider the marking $M(a) = (m_1, \cdots, m_{|O_a|})$ of an information element a. Then, for each $i = 1, \cdots, m_{|O_a|}$ with $m_i = 1$ and $s_a(i) = u(p)$, a token is depicted containing the value $u(p)$.

Definition: Executable Production Rule

A production rule $p = (d, os) \in P$ is executable if:

(a) $\emptyset \in os$ or $\forall e \in os, \emptyset \notin os : \exists m_i$ in $M(e) = (m_1, \cdots, m_{|O_a|})$ with $s_e(i) = u(p)$ and $m_i = 1$ and

(b) $constr(p) = \underline{true}$ or $constr(p) = f_c(var(o_1), \cdots, var(o_{|os|})) = 1$

Note that only the second part of condition (a) was adapted which has the following meaning: For each input information element e of production rule p, there must be one token whose index equals the production rule index $u(p)$.

Definition: Production Rule Execution

Once a production rule $p = (d, os)$ is executable, it can be executed. This leads to a successor marking M' (written as $M \xrightarrow{p} M'$) which is defined for every $a \in I$ by:

$$M'(a) = \begin{cases} \underline{top} & \text{, if } a = d \text{ and } d = \underline{top} \\ m'_i = 1 & \text{, if } a = d \text{ and } d \neq \underline{top} \text{ and } \forall i \text{ with } s_a(i) = u(p) \\ m'_i = 0 & \text{, if } a \in os \text{ and } \forall i \text{ with } s_a(i) = u(p) \\ M(a) & \text{, otherwise} \end{cases}$$

This indexed marking is illustrated in Fig. E.5. As aforementioned, a marking can be represented by a bag. As the EPM depicted Fig. E.5 comprises five information elements, a bag contains five vectors: $\| M(1), M(2), \cdots, M(5) \|$. Initially, the bag equals $\| (0), (0,0), (0), (0), (0) \|$ as there are no tokens. The relationships are defined as follows: $s_1(1) = 2$, $s_2(1) = 3$, $s_2(2) = 4$, $s_3(1) = 5$, $s_4(1) = 5$, $s_5(1) = 5$.

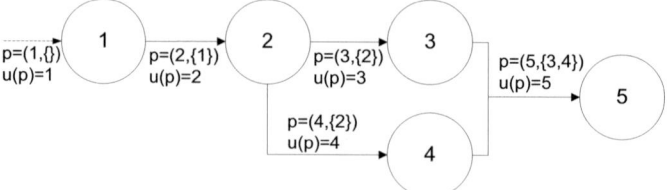

(a) Initially, there are no tokens: $\parallel (0),(0,0),(0),(0),(0) \parallel$.

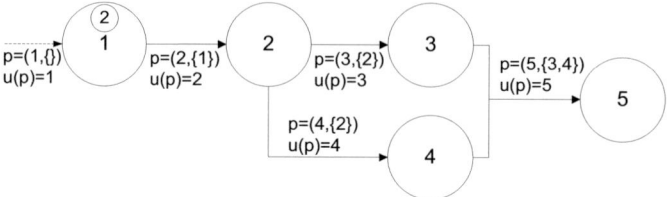

(b) After the execution of production rule $(1,\emptyset)$, information element 1 is marked: $\parallel (1),(0,0),(0),(0),(0) \parallel$.

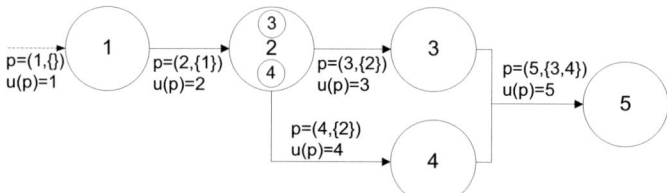

(c) After the execution of $(2,\{1\})$, information element 2 contains two tokens: $\parallel (0),(1,1),(0),(0),(0) \parallel$. Now, $(3,\{2\})$ and $(4,\{2\})$ are executable.

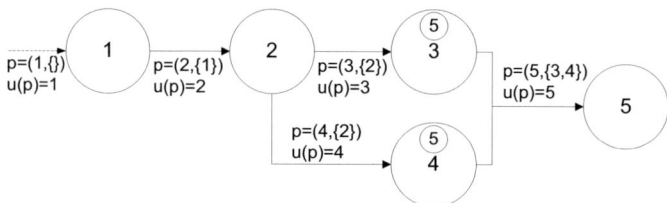

(d) After the execution of $(3,\{2\})$ and $(4,\{2\})$ the marking equals: $\parallel (0),(0,0),(1),(1),(0) \parallel$.

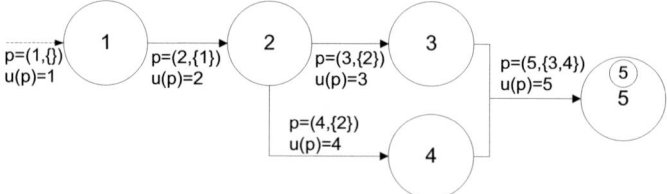

(e) After the execution of $(3,\{2\})$ the marking equals: $\parallel (0),(0,0),(0),(0),(1) \parallel$. The execution has completed.

Figure E.5.: Extended marking of an EPM using indexed tokens.

E.4. Further Extensions

There are some aspects that have yet to be considered to provide a complete mathematical model for the execution semantics of EPMs. As Petri nets provide a sound mathematical model for their execution, they will be used as a reference. In the following, the relevant aspects are shortly discussed.

Execution Semantics In order to avoid multiple executions of production rules due to the existence of variants in the EPM, the execution semantics have to be further extended. It has to be differentiated between multiple executions of production rules due to cycles and variants as the former one is allowed. The developed execution algorithms make use of a "history set" in order to identify the reason (cycle or variant) for the multiple execution of a production rule (see Sec. 3.3). The execution semantics could be extended accordingly to achieve the same behaviour regarding the execution.

Modeling Time In order to consider timing constraints, various aspects have to be considered. The location as well as the type of delay have to be modeled. The location of the delay of the execution of a production rule is the production rule. This means that once the execution of a production rule p has started, the output information element is marked after $f(p)$ time units. This pertains also to the assignment of a value to the variable assigned to the output information element. The type of delay can be distinguished between deterministic (the delay is fixed), non-deterministic (the delay is specified on the basis of constraints) and stochastic delays (the delay is sampled from a probability distribution). Note that in the EPM definition, the delay is defined deterministic by function f which could be changed if required.

Moreover, in stochastic Petri nets the dynamic behaviour is based on a timed state. This means that each token has its own time stamp. The marking of EPMs could be extended in a similar way that each token gets its own time stamp.

Race Conditions and Preselection The introduction of time may influence the execution semantics of EPMs. This pertains also to Petri nets. In Petri nets, conflicting transitions have to be resolved. Two transitions are said to be in conflict if a marking enables both transitions and firing either one of these transitions would disable the other. The firing/enabling semantic that is influenced by the introduction of time is called race semantics. Several ways exist to resolve conflicts in Petri nets, e.g. by using priorities or probabilities. If time is introduced in the mathematical model of the EPM execution, the affects on the execution semantics must be evaluated and resolved by an adequate method.

Modeling Resources In Petri nets, limited resources required for firing a transition can be explicitly modeled by using transitions and places. Resources are modeled as tokens whose number equals the number of available resources. The Petri net is modeled in such a way that a transition requiring a resource can only be fired if a token corresponding to the required resource is available. The EPM could be adapted in a similar way.

Multiple Executions In Petri nets, multiple executions of business processes are handled by introducing special Petri nets, termed coloured Petri nets. In a coloured Petri net, each token has a specific colour which corresponds to a specific process instance. The enabling of a transition considers the colour of the tokens. This can be adapted analogously for the execution of multiple EPMs.

F. List of Figures

G. List of Tables

H. Bibliography

[1] D. H. Ackley. *A connectionist machine for genetic hillclimbing*. Kluwer, Boston, 1987.

[2] Active Endpoints and Adobe and BEA and IBM and Oracle and SAP. WS-BPEL Extension for People (BPEL4People), Version 1.0. June 2007. http://download.boulder.ibm.com/ibmdl/pub /software/dw/specs/ws-bpel4people/BPEL4People_v1.pdf, last access: April 2009.

[3] E. R. Aguilar, F. Ruiz, F. García, and M. Piattini. Applying Software Metrics to evaluate Business Process Models. *CLEI Electronic Journal*, 9(1), 2006.

[4] D. M. Ahern, A. Clouse, and R. Turner. *CMMI Distilled: A Practical Introduction to Integrated Process Improvement*. Addison-Wesley, 3 edition, 2008.

[5] D. Ahlert. *Exzellenz in Dienstleistung und Vertrieb: Konzeptionelle Grundlagen und empirische Ergebnisse (in German)*. Gabler, 2002.

[6] G. I. Alkhatib. Web service standards road map. In *NWESP '05: Proceedings of the International Conference on Next Generation Web Services Practices*, page 445, Washington, DC, USA, 2005. IEEE Computer Society.

[7] T. Allweyer. Jenseits des Hype - die Wiederentdeckung der Geschäftsprozesse (in German). *Competence Site*, 2004. http://www.competence-site.de, last access: April 2009.

[8] J. E. Alvarez-Benitez, R. M. Everson, and J. E. Fieldsend. A MOPSO Algorithm Based Exclusively on Pareto Dominance Concepts. *Lecture Notes in Computer Science (LNCS), EMO 2005*, pages 459–473, 2005.

[9] S. W. Ambler. *The Object Primer : Agile Model-Driven Development with UML 2.0*. Cambridge University Press, 3 edition, March 2004.

[10] S. A. Amraii, M. Ajallooeian, and C. Lucas. A Dynamic Fuzzy-Based Crossover Method for Genetic Algorithms. In *ICTAI '07: Proceedings of the 19th IEEE International Conference on Tools with Artificial Intelligence - Vol.1 (ICTAI 2007)*, pages 465–471, Washington, DC, USA, 2007. IEEE Computer Society.

[11] T. Andres. From Business Process to Application: Model-Driven Development of Management Software. In *AGILITY by ARIS Business Process Management*, pages 221–231. Springer Berlin Heidelberg, 2006.

[12] P. J. Angeline. Evolutionary Optimization Versus Particle Swarm Optimization: Philosophy and Performance Differences. In *EP '98: Proceedings of the 7th International Conference on Evolutionary Programming VII*, pages 601–610, London, UK, 1998. Springer-Verlag.

[13] T. R. Ariyachandra and M. N. Frolick. Critical Success Factors in Business Performance Management-Striving for Success. *Inf. Sys. Manag.*, 25(2):113–120, 2008.

[14] T. Bäck. *Evolutionary algorithms in theory and practice*. Oxford University Press, 1996.

[15] J. D. Bagley. *The behavior of adaptive systems which employ genetic and correlation algorithms*. PhD thesis, University of Michigan, Ann Arbor, MI, USA, 1967.

[16] B. M. Baker and M. A. Ayechew. A genetic algorithm for the vehicle routing problem. *Computers and Operations Research*, 30(5):787–800, 2003.

[17] M. Baker and S. Hart. *The Marketing Book*. Butterworth-Heinemann, 6 edition, October 2007.

[18] M. Barret and E. Davidson. Exploring the Diversity of Service Worlds in the Service Economy. In *Information Technology in the Service Economy: Challenges and Possibilities for the 21st Century*, pages 1–10–, Boston, USA, 2008. Springer.

[19] J. Barry. Maiden Speak, House of Representatives. 108:164, 1978.

[20] J. Barry. *Sleepers Wake!: Technology & The Future Of Work*. Oxford University Press, New York, 1996.

[21] Basel Committee on Banking Supervision. Operational Risk - Supporting Document to the New Basel Capital Accord. 2001.

[22] J. Becker, C. v. Uthmann, and M. zur Mühlen. Identifying the Workflow Potential of Business Processes. In *HICSS '99: Proceedings of the Thirty-second Annual Hawaii International Conference on System Sciences-Volume 5*, page 5061, Washington, DC, USA, 1999. IEEE Computer Society.

[23] M. Beekman, G. A. Sword, and S. J. Simpson. Biological Foundations of Swarm Intelligence. In Blum and Merkle [31], pages 3–41.

[24] C. Beeri, A. Eyal, S. Kamenkovich, and T. Milo. Querying business processes with BP-QL. In *VLDB '05: Proceedings of the 31st international conference on Very large data bases*, pages 1255–1258. VLDB Endowment, 2005.

[25] G. N. Beligiannis, C. N. Moschopoulos, G. P. Kaperonis, and S. D. Likothanassis. Applying evolutionary computation to the school timetabling problem: The Greek case. *Computers and Operations Research*, 35(4):1265–1280, 2008.

[26] G. Beni and J. Wang. Swarm Intelligence in Cellular Robotic Systems. In *Proceedings NATO Advanced Workshop on Robots and Biological Systems*, Tuscany, Italy, 26-30 June 1989.

[27] K. Bennett, P. Layzell, D. Budgen, P. Brereton, L. Macaulay, and M. Munro. Service-based software: the future for flexible software. In *Software Engineering Conference, 2000. APSEC 2000. Proceedings. Seventh Asia-Pacific*, pages 214–221, 2000.

[28] J. Billington, S. Christensen, K. van Hee, E. Kindler, O. Kummer, L. Petrucci, R. Post, C. Stehno, and M. Weber. The Petri Net Markup Language: Concepts, Technology, and Tools. In *Applications and Theory of Petri Nets 2003: 24th International Conference*, pages 1023–1024, Eindhoven, The Netherlands, June 2003.

[29] J. Blazewicz, K. H. Ecker, E. Pesch, G. Schmidt, and J. Weglarz. *Handbook on Scheduling: From Theory to Applications (International Handbooks on Information Systems)*. Springer, July 2007.

[30] C. Blum and X. Li. Swarm Intelligence in Optimization. In Blum and Merkle [31], pages 43–85.

[31] C. Blum and D. Merkle, editors. *Swarm Intelligence: Introduction and Applications*. Natural Computing Series. Springer, 2008.

[32] D. W. Boeringer and D. H. Werner. Particle swarm optimization versus genetic algorithms for phased array synthesis. *Antennas and Propagation, IEEE Transactions on*, 52(3):771–779, 2004.

[33] R. Bordini, L. Braubach, M. Dastani, A. Seghrouchni, G. J. Sanz, and Others. A Survey of Programming Languages and Platforms for Multi-Agent Systems. In *Informatica*, volume 30, pages 33–44, 2006.

[34] E. Börger. A critical analysis of workflow patterns. Technical report, University of Pisa, Computer Science Department, 2007.

[35] O. Bousquet, U. von Luxburg, and G. Rätsch, editors. *Advanced Lectures on Machine Learning, ML Summer Schools 2003, Canberra, Australia, February 2-14, 2003, Tübingen, Germany, August 4-16, 2003, Revised Lectures*, volume 3176 of *Lecture Notes in Computer Science*. Springer, 2004.

[36] J. Branke and S. Mostaghim. About selecting the personal best in multi-objective particle swarm optimization. In T. P. R. et al., editor, *Parallel Problem Solving from Nature*, LNCS, pages 523–532. Springer, 2006.

[37] J. Branke, C. Schmidt, H. Schmeck, and V. Klohr. Evolutionäre Algorithmen zur Standortplanung (in German). *Industrie Management*, 18(6):37–40, 2002.

[38] D. Bratton and J. Kennedy. Defining a standard for Particle Swarm Optimization. In *Proceedings of the 2007 IEEE Swarm Intelligence Symposium*, 2007.

[39] M. Bruhn. *Internes Marketing: Integration der Kunden- und Mitarbeiterorientierung; Grundlagen - Implementierung - Praxisbeispiele*. Gabler, Wiesbaden, 1995.

[40] L. Bull and T. Kovacs. Foundations of learning classifier systems: An introduction. In L. Bull and T. Kovacs, editors, *Foundations of Learning Classifier Systems*, volume 183 of *The Studies in Fuzziness and Soft Computing series*. Springer, 2005.

[41] E. Burke, D. Elliman, and R. Weare. A genetic algorithm based university timetabling system. In *East-West Conference on Computer Technologies in Education, Crimea, Ukraine*, pages 35–40, 1994.

[42] R. Burke, S. Gustafson, and G. Kendall. A survey and analysis of diversity measures in genetic programming. In *GECCO '02: Proceedings of the Genetic and Evolutionary Computation Conference*, pages 716–723, San Francisco, CA, USA, 2002. Morgan Kaufmann Publishers Inc.

[43] S. Bussmann and K. Schild. Self-organizing manufacturing control: An industrial application of agent technology. In *Proceedings of the 4th International Conference on Multi-Agent Systems*, pages 87–94, Boston, MA, 10-12 July 2000.

[44] C. Caldwell and V. S. Johnston. Tracking a criminal suspect through face-space with a genetic algorithm. In *Proceedings of the Fourth International Conference on Genetic Algorithm*, pages 416–421. Morgan Kaufmann Publisher, July 1991.

[45] M. Calisti and D. Greenwood. Goal-oriented autonomic process modeling and execution for next generation networks. In *MACE '08: Proceedings of the 3rd IEEE international workshop on Modelling Autonomic Communications Environments*, pages 38–49, Berlin, Heidelberg, 2008. Springer-Verlag.

[46] J. Calladine. Giving legs to the legacy — web services integration within the enterprise. *BT Technology Journal*, 22(1):87–98, 2004.

[47] J. Cardoso. About the data-flow complexity of web processes. In *6th International Workshop on Business Process Modeling, Development, and Support: Business Processes and Support Systems: Design for Flexibility*, 2005.

[48] J. Cardoso. How to measure the control-flow complexity of web processes and workflows. In L. Fischer, editor, *Workflow Handbook 2005*, pages 199–212. Future Strategies Inc., 2005.

[49] J. Cardoso. Process control-flow complexity metric: An empirical validation. In *SCC'06: Proceedings of the IEEE International Conference on Services Computing*, pages 167–173, Washington, DC, USA, 2006. IEEE Computer Society.

[50] J. S. Carson, II. Introduction to modeling and simulation. In *WSC '05: Proceedings of the 37th conference on Winter simulation*, pages 16–23. Winter Simulation Conference, 2005.

[51] J. W. Chang and C. T. Scott. Agent-based workflow: TRP Support Environment (TSE). In *Proceedings of the 5th International World Wide Web Conference*, pages 1501–1511, Paris, France, 6-10 May 1996.

[52] J.-S. Chen, J.-L. Hou, and S.-M. Wu. Building investment strategy portfolios by combination genetic algorithms. In *ICNC '07: Proceedings of the Third International Conference on Natural Computation (ICNC 2007)*, pages 776–780, Washington, DC, USA, 2007. IEEE Computer Society.

[53] P. Chen. Entity-relationship modeling: historical events, future trends, and lessons learned. In *Software pioneers: contributions to software engineering*, pages 296–310, New York, NY, USA, 2002. Springer-Verlag New York, Inc.

[54] P. P.-S. Chen. The entity-relationship model - toward a unified view of data. *ACM Trans. Database Syst.*, 1(1):9–36, 1976.

[55] A. S. Chernobai, S. T. Rachev, and F. J. Fabozzi. *Operational Risk - A Guide to Basel II Capital Requirements, Models, and Analysis*. John Wiley & Sons, Inc., Hoboken, New Jersey, USA, 2007.

[56] C. Chiranjeevi and V. N. Sastry. Multi objective portfolio optimization models and its solution using genetic algorithms. In *ICCIMA '07: Proceedings of the International Conference on Computational Intelligence and Multimedia Applications (ICCIMA 2007)*, pages 453–457, Washington, DC, USA, 2007. IEEE Computer Society.

[57] H. Cho, F. Olivera, and S. D. Guikema. A derivation of the number of minima of the griewank function. *Applied Mathematics and Computation*, 204(2):694–.701, 2008.

[58] C.-H. Chou and J.-N. Chen. Genetic algorithms: initialization schemes and genes extraction. In *FUZZ IEEE 2000. The Ninth IEEE International Conference on Fuzzy Systems*, volume 2, pages 965–968, San Antonio, TX, USA, 2000. IEEE.

[59] M. B. Chrissis, M. Konrad, and S. Shrum. *CMMI(R): Guidelines for Process Integration and Product Improvement (2nd Edition) (SEI Series in Software Engineering)*. Addison-Wesley Professional, 2 edition, November 2006.

[60] A. D. Cioppa, C. D. Stefano, and A. Marcelli. On the role of population size and niche radius in fitness sharing. *IEEE Trans. Evolutionary Computation*, 8(6):580–592, 2004.

[61] P. Clark, B. Cestnik, C. Sammut, and J. Stender. Applications for machine learning: notes from the panel members. In *EWSL-91: Proceedings of the European working session on learning on Machine learning*, pages 457–462, New York, NY, USA, 1991. Springer-Verlag New York, Inc.

[62] P. D. Coddington and A. J. Newell. JAPARA: A Java Parallel Random Number Generator Library for High-Performance Computing. *Parallel and Distributed Processing Symposium, International*, 6, 2004.

[63] C. A. Coello, D. A. V. Veldhuizen, and G. B. Lamont. *Evolutionary Algorithms for Solving Multi-Objective Problems*. Kluwer Academic Publishers, 2002.

[64] S. B. Cooper. *Computability Theory*. Chapman Hall / Crc Mathematics Series, July 2003.

[65] T. H. Cormen, C. E. Leiserson, R. L. Rivest, and C. Stein. *Introduction to Algorithms*. The MIT Press, 2nd edition, 2001.

[66] T. Croonenborghs, K. Tuyls, J. Ramon, and M. Bruynooghe. Multi-agent relational reinforcement learning - explorations in multi-state coordination tasks. In *LAMAS*, volume 3898 of *Lecture Notes in Artificial Intelligence*, pages 198–212, 2006.

[67] F. A. Cummins. *Building the Agile Enterprise: With SOA, BPM and MBM*. Morgan Kaufmann Publishers Inc., San Francisco, CA, USA, 2008.

[68] T. Dahl, M. J. Mataric, and G. S. Sukhatme. A machine learning method for improving task allocation in distributed multi-robot transportation. *Complex Engineered Systems*, 2006.

[69] C. Darwin. *On the origin of species by means of natural selection*. John Murray, 1859.

[70] T. H. Davenport and J. E. Short. The new industrial engineering: Information technology and business process redesign. *Sloan Management Review*, 31(4):11–27, 1990.

[71] A. K. A. de Medeiros, A. J. M. M. Weijters, and W. M. P. van der Aalst. Genetic process mining: A basic approach and its challenges. In C. Bussler and A. Haller, editors, *Business Process Management Workshops*, volume 3812, pages 203–215, 2005.

[72] L. H. de Mello and A. C. Sanderson. And/Or graph representation of assembly plans. *Transactions on Robotics and Automation*, 6(2):1113–1121, 1990.

[73] K. Deb, S. Agrawal, A. Pratab, and T. Meyarivan. A fast elitist non-dominated sorting genetic algorithm for multi-objective optimization: NSGA-II. In *Parallel Problem Solving from Nature*, pages 849–858, 2000.

[74] K. Deb, L. Thiele, M. Laumanns, and E. Zitzler. Scalable test problems for evolutionary multi-objective optimization. Technical report, Computer Engineering and Networks Laboratory (TIK), Swiss Federal Institute of Technology (ETH), 2001.

[75] J. Debenham. A multi-agent architecture for process management accommodates unexpected performance. In *SAC '00: Proceedings of the 2000 ACM symposium on Applied computing*, pages 15–19, New York, NY, USA, 2000. ACM.

[76] J. Desel and T. Erwin. Modeling, simulation and analysis of business processes. *Lecture Notes in Computer Science: Business Process Managements - models, techniques and empirical studies*, 1806:129–141, 2000.

[77] U. Deshpande, A. Gupta, and A. Basu. Performance enhancement of a contract net protocol based system through instance-based learning. *IEEE Transactions on Systems, Man, and Cybernetics, Part B*, 35(2):345–358, 2005.

[78] R. D'Ippolito, K. Lee, C. Plinta, M. Rissman, and R. V. Scoy. Prototype real-time monitor: Requirements. Technical report, Software Engineering Institute, Carnegie Mellon University, 1987.

[79] K. Driessens. *Relational Reinforcement Learning*. PhD thesis, Katholieke Universiteit Leuven, Heverlee, Belgium, 2004.

[80] M. Dumas, W. M. van der Aalst, and Arthur. *Process Aware Information Systems: Bridging People and Software Through Process Technology*. Wiley-Interscience, September 2005.

[81] J. Dunkel, A. Eberhart, S. Fischer, A. Koschel, and C. Kleiner. *Systemarchitekturen für verteilte Anwendungen: Client-server, Multi-tier, SOA, Event-driven Architectures, P2P, Grid, Web 2.0 (in German)*. Hanser Verlag, 2008.

[82] S. Dzeroski, L. de Raedt, and K. Driessens. Relational reinforcement learning. *Machine Learning*, 43(1-2), April 2001.

[83] S. Dzeroski, L. D. Raedt, and H. Blockeel. Relational reinforcement learning. In *Machine Learning*, pages 7–52. Morgan Kaufmann, 1998.

[84] A. E. Eiben and J. E. Smith. *Introduction to Evolutionary Computing*. Springer, 2003.

[85] C. Ellis. Information control nets: a mathematical model of office information flow. *Proceedings of ACM Conference on Simulation, Measurement and Modeling of Computer Systems*, pages 225–39, 1979.

[86] M. R. Endsley. Design and evaluation for situation awareness enhancement. *Proceedings of the Human Factors Society 32nd Annual Meeting*, 1988.

[87] A. Engelbrecht. *Fundamentals of Computational Swarm Intelligence*. John Wiley, 2006.

[88] M. Faggini and T. Lux, editors. *Coping with the Complexity of Economics*. Springer, 2009.

[89] D. Fahland and W. Reisig. Asm-based semantics for bpel: The negative control flow. In *Proc. 12th International Workshop on Abstract State Machines*, pages 131–151, 2005.

[90] N. E. Fenton and S. L. Pfleeger. *Software Metrics: A Rigorous and Practical Approach*. PWS Publishing Co., Boston, MA, USA, 1998.

[91] J. E. Fieldsend and S. Singh. A multi-objective algorithm based upon particle swarm optimisation, an efficient data structure and turbulence. In *The 2002 U.K. Workshop on Computational Intelligence*, pages 34–44, 2002.

[92] H. Fischer, A. Fleischmann, and S. Obermeier. *Geschäftsprozesse realisieren: Ein praxisorientierter Leitfaden von der Strategie bis zur Implementierung (in German)*. Vieweg+Teubner, Wiesbaden, 2006.

[93] D. B. Fogel and H.-G. Beyer. A note on the empirical evaluation of intermediate recombination. *Evolutionary Computation*, 3(4):491–495, 1995.

[94] D. B. Fogel, G. B. Fogel, and K. Ohkura. Multiple-vector self-adaptation in evolutionary algorithms. *BioSystems*, 61:2001, 2001.

[95] Foundation for Intelligent Physical Agents. Fipa contract net interaction protocol spec-ification, std. 00029, rev. H, 2002. http://www.fipa.org/specs/fipa00029/SC00029H.pdf, last access: April 2009.

[96] M. Fowler. *Analysis Patterns: Reusable Object Models*. Addison-Wesley Professional, October 1996.

[97] A. A. Freitas. A survey of evolutionary algorithms for data mining and knowledge dis-covery. In *Advances in Evolutionary Computation*, pages 819–845. Springer-Verlag, 2002.

[98] A. A. Freitas. A review of evolutionary algorithms for data mining. In O. Maimon and L. Rokach, editors, *Soft Computing for Knowledge Discovery and Data Mining*, pages 61–93. Springer, November 2007.

[99] M. Gallaher, A. Link, and J. Petrusa. Measuring service-sector research and develop-ment. Technical report, RTI International - Health, Social, and Economics Research, 2005.

[100] E. Gamma, R. Helm, R. Johnson, and J. Vlissides. *Design patterns: elements of reusable object-oriented software*. Addison-Wesley Professional, 1995.

[101] M. R. Garey and D. S. Johnson. *Computers and Intractability : A Guide to the Theory of NP-Completeness (Series of Books in the Mathematical Sciences)*. W. H. Freeman & Co Ltd, January 1979.

[102] C. Gersung and W. Resengren. *The Service Society*. Schenkmann Publishing Company, Cambridge, MA, 1973.

[103] B. Godoall. *he Penguin Dictionary of Human Geography*. Penguin Books Ltd, 1987.

[104] E. M. Goldratt and J. Cox. *The Goal - A Process of Ongoing Improvement*. North River Press Publishing Corporation, Great Barrington, MA, second rev. edition, 1992.

[105] J. Gordijn, H. Akkermans, and H. van Vliet. Business modelling is not process mod-elling. In *ER Workshops*, pages 40–51, 2000.

[106] G. Görz, C.-R. Rollinger, and J. Schneeberger. *Handbuch der Künstlichen Intelligenz (in German)*, volume 3. Oldenbourg, 2000.

[107] J. Gottmann. *Megalopolis.: The Urbanized Northeastern Seaboard of the United States*. Twentieth Century Fund, New York, 1961.

[108] J. Gottmann. *Since Megalopolis: The Urban Writings of Jean Gottmann*. Johns Hopkins University Press, Baltimore, 1990.

[109] D. Greenwood and G. Rimassa. Autonomic goal-oriented business process management. In *ICAS '07: Proceedings of the Third International Conference on Autonomic and Autonomous Systems*, page 43, Washington, DC, USA, 2007. IEEE Computer Society.

[110] J. Grefenstette. Optimization of control parameters for genetic algorithms. *IEEE Trans. Syst. Man Cybern.*, 16(1):122–128, 1986.

[111] A. Gregoriades and A. Sutcliffe. A socio-technical approach to business process simulation. *Decision Support Systems*, 45(4):1017–1030, 2008.

[112] U. Greiner, S. Lippe, T. Kahl, J. Ziemann, and F.-W. Jaekel. A multi-level modeling framework for designing and implementing cross-organizational business processes. In S. W. Sadiq, M. Reichert, and K. Schulz, editors, *CEIS 2006, Workshop Technologies for Collaborative Business Process Management (TCoB)*, pages 13–23. INSTICC Press, 5 2006.

[113] A. Gustafsson and M. Johnson. *Competing in a Service Society: How to create A Competitive Advantage through Service Development and Innovation*. John Wiley and Sons, Inc., San Fransisco, 2003.

[114] M. Hammer and J. Champy. *Reengineering the Corporation: A Manifesto for Business Revolution*. HarperBusiness, April 1994.

[115] P. Harmon. Service oriented architectures and BPM. *BPTrends*, February 2005. http://www.bptrends.com, last access: April 2009.

[116] K. Harrison-Broninski. *Human Interactions: The Heart And Soul Of Business Process Management: How People Reallly Work And How They Can Be Helped To Work Better*. Meghan-Kiffer Press, February 2005.

[117] M. Havey. *Essential Business Process Modeling*. O'Reilly Media, Inc., 2005.

[118] M. J. Healey and B. W. Ilberry. *Location and Change: Perspectives on Economic Geography*. Oxford University Press, Oxford, 1990.

[119] S. Helwig and R. Wanka. Particle Swarm Optimization in High-Dimensional Bounded Search Spaces. In *Proceedings of the 2007 IEEE Swarm Intelligence Symposium*, pages 198–205, Honolulu, Hawaii, USA, April 2007. IEEE Press.

[120] J. C. Henderson and N. Venkatraman. Strategic alignment: leveraging information technology for transforming organizations. *IBM Syst. J.*, 38(2-3):472–484, 1999.

[121] M. Hepp, F. Leymann, J. Domingue, A. Wahler, and D. Fensel. Semantic business process management: a vision towards using semantic web services for business process management. In *e-Business Engineering, 2005. ICEBE 2005. IEEE International Conference on*, pages 535–540, 2005.

[122] A. E. E. R. Hinterding and Z. Michalewicz. Parameter control in evolutionary algorithms. *IEEE Transactions on Evolutionary Computation*, 3:124–141, 1999.

[123] S. Hinz, K. Schmidt, and C. Stahl. Transforming bpel to petri nets. In *Proceedings of the International Conference on Business Process Management (BPM2005), volume 3649 of Lecture Notes in Computer Science*, pages 220–235. Springer-Verlag, 2005.

[124] J. H. Holland. Outline for a logical theory of adaptive systems. *J. ACM*, 9(3):297–314, 1962.

[125] T. Holmes, H. Tran, U. Zdun, and S. Dustdar. Modeling human aspects of business processes - a view-based, model-driven approach. In I. Schieferdecker and A. Hartman, editors, *ECMDA-FA*, volume 5095 of *Lecture Notes in Computer Science*, pages 246–261. Springer, 2008.

[126] B. Hommes and J. Dietz. Business process modeling for the purpose of applying internet technology. In J. Krogstie, K. Siau, and T. Halpin, editors, *EMMSAD'01: proceedings. 6th CAiSE/IFIP8.1 International Workshop on Evaluation of Modeling Methods in Systems Analysis and Design*, pages 1–8, Interlaken, Switzerland, 2001.

[127] J. E. Hopcroft, R. Motwani, and J. D. Ullman. *Introduction to Automata Theory, Languages, and Computation*. Addison Wesley, 2nd edition, November 2000.

[128] R. Horst and H. Tuy. *Global Optimization: Deterministic Approaches*. Springer, April 2003.

[129] E. J. Hughes. Multi-objective Binary Search Optimisation. In *Evolutionary Multi-Criterion Optimization: Second International Conference (EMO)*, pages 72–87, 2003.

[130] D. Hvalica. Best first search algorithm in AND/OR graphs with cycles. *J. Algorithms*, 21(1):102–110, 1996.

[131] W. Ibert and M. Unterstein. Ansätze zur Bewertung alternativer Geschäftsprozessvarianten hinsichtlich der Durchlaufzeit (in German). *HMD - Praxis der Wirtschaftsinformatik*, 241, 2005.

[132] H. Itoh and K. Nakamurra. Learning to learn and plan by relational reinforcement learning. In *Proceedings Workshop on Relational Reinforcement Learning*, July 8 2004.

[133] A. Jaliniauskas. The analysis of unstructured processes in business administration. *Informatica, Lith. Acad. Sci.*, 11(2):125–136, 2000.

[134] W. Janke. Pseudo random numbers: Generation and quality checks. In J. Grotendorst, D. Marx, and A. Muramatsu, editors, *Quantum Simulations of Complex Many-Body Systems: From Theory to Algorithms*, volume 10 of *Lecture Notes*, pages 447–458, Jülich, 2002. John von Neumann Institute for Computing.

[135] N. Jennings and M. Wooldridge. Application of intelligent agents. In N. Jennings and M. Wooldridge, editors, *Agent Technology - Foundations, Applications, and Markets*, pages 3–28. Springer Verlag, 1998.

[136] N. R. Jennings. An agent-based approach for building complex software systems. *Commun. ACM*, 44(4):35–41, April 2001.

[137] N. R. Jennings, T. J. Norman, P. Faratin, and B. Odgers. Autonomous agents for business process management. *Journal of Applied Artificial Intelligence*, 14:145–189, 2000.

[138] P. V. Jenster and D. Hussey. *Company Analysis: Determining Strategic Capability*. John Wiley & Sons, 2001.

[139] J. Jeston and J. Nelis. *Business Process Management*. Elsevier/Butterworth-Heinemann, Amsterdam, 2006.

[140] K. A. D. Jong. *An analysis of the behavior of a class of genetic adaptive systems*. PhD thesis, University of Michigan, Ann Arbor, MI, USA, 1975.

[141] D. Judge, B. R. Odgers, J. W. Shepherdson, and Z. Cui. Agent enhanced workflow. *BT Technology Journal*, 16(3):79–85, 1998.

[142] L. P. Kaelbling, M. L. Littman, and A. W. Moore. Reinforcement learning: A survey. *Journal of Artificial Intelligence Research*, 4:237–285, May 1996.

[143] J. Kamleiter, M. Langer, and M. Kresse. *Business IT Alignment mit ITIL, COBIT, RUP: Gegenüberstellung und Integration der Referenzmodelle von IT Service Management, IT Governance und Anwendungsentwicklung (in German)*. Serview Gmbh, August 2006.

[144] S. H. Kan. *Metrics and Models in Software Quality Engineering*. Addison-Wesley, 2nd edition, 2002.

[145] R.-G. Kang and C.-Y. Jung. The improved initialization method of genetic algorithm for solving the optimization problem. In I. King, J. Wang, L. Chan, and D. L. Wang, editors, *ICONIP (3)*, volume 4234 of *Lecture Notes in Computer Science*, pages 789–796. Springer, 2006.

[146] R. S. Kaplan and W. Bruns. *Accounting and Management: A Field Study Perspective*. Harvard Business School Press, 1987.

[147] P. Karsten, J. Recker, and M. Rosemann. Towards a Classification and Lifecycle of Business Process Change. In N. Selmin, R. Schmidt, and P. Soffer, editors, *9th Workshop on Business Process Modeling, Development and Support*, 2008.

[148] G. Keller, M. Nüttgens, and A.-W. Scheer. Semantische Prozessmodellierung auf der Grundlage Ereignisgesteuerter Prozessketten (in German). Technical Report 89, Veröffentlichungen des Instituts für Wirtschaftsinformatik (IWi), University of Saarland, January 1992.

[149] J. Kennedy and R. Eberhart. Particle swarm optimization. In *Proceedings of IEEE International Conference on Neural Networks*, volume 4, pages 1942–1948, Perth, Australia, 1995.

[150] J. Kennedy and R. C. Eberhart. *Swarm Intelligence*. Morgan Kaufmann, 2001.

[151] B. Kiepuszewski. *Expressiveness and Suitability of Languages for Control Flow Modelling in Workflows*. PhD thesis, Queensland University of Technology, Brisbane, Australia, 2002.

[152] H. M. Kim and R. Ramkaran. Best practices in e-business process management: Extending a re-engineering framework. *Business Process Management Journal*, 10(1):27–43, 2004.

[153] J.-L. Kim. Permutation-based elitist genetic algorithm using serial scheme for large-sized resource-constrained project scheduling. In *WSC '07: Proceedings of the 39th conference on Winter simulation*, pages 2112–2118, Piscataway, NJ, USA, 2007. IEEE Press.

[154] G. Knolmayer, R. Endl, and M. Pfahrer. Modeling processes and workflows by business rules. In W. M. P. van der Aalst, J. Desel, and A. Oberweis, editors, *Business Process Management*, volume 1806 of *Lecture Notes in Computer Science*, pages 16–29. Springer, 2000.

[155] J. Knowles and E. J. Hughes. Multiobjective optimization on a budget of 250 evaluations. In C. Coello et al, editor, *Evolutionary Multi-Criterion Optimization (EMO-2005)*, volume 3410 of *LNCS*, pages 176–190. Springer-Verlag, 2005.

[156] A. Koschmider and A. Oberweis. How to detect semantic business process model variants? In *Proceedings of the 2007 ACM Symposium on Applied Computing*, volume 2,

pages 1263–1264, Seoul, Korea, March 11 - 15, 2007, 2007. Association for Computing Machinery.

[157] G. Kramler and W. Retschitzegger. Towards intelligent support of workflows. In *Proceedings of Americas Conference on Information Systems (AMCIS 2000)*, pages 581–585, Long Beach, USA, August 2000.

[158] M. Kress, J. Melcher, and D. Seese. Introducing Executable Product Models for the Service Industry. In Sprague and R. H., editors, *Proceedings of the 40th Annual Hawaii International Conference on System Sciences (HICSS 2007)*, page 46, 2007.

[159] M. Kress, S. Mostaghim, and D. Seese. Intelligent Business Process Execution using Particle Swarm Optimization. *Nature-Inspired Informatics for Intelligent Applications and Knowledge Discovery: Implications in Business, Science and Engineering*, 2009.

[160] M. Kress and D. Seese. Executable Product Models – The intelligent way. In *Proceedings of the International Conference on Systems, Man, and Cybernetics (SMC 2007)*, Montreal, Canada, 7-10 October 2007.

[161] M. Kress and D. Seese. Flexibility Enhancements in BPM by applying Executable Product Models and Intelligent Agents. In *Business Process and Services Computing (BPSC 2007)*, pages 93–104, Leipzig, Germany, 2007.

[162] M. Kress and D. Wölfing. Operational metrics and technical platform for measuring bank process performance. In *Handbook on Information Technology in Finance*. Springer, August 2008.

[163] J. Küster, K. Ryndina, and H. Gall. Generation of business process models for object life cycle compliance. In *Business Process Management (BPM 2007)*, pages 165–181, 2007.

[164] A. M. Latva-koivisto. Finding a complexity measure for business process models. Technical report, Helsinki University of Technology, Systems Analysis Laboratory, 2001.

[165] A. M. Law and W. D. Kelton. *Simulation Modeling and Analysis*. McGraw-Hill, Boston, MA, 3 edition, 2000.

[166] M. Lazarova, P. Borovska, and S. Mabgar. The impact of the mutation strategy on the quality of solution of parallel genetic algorithms. In *EC'08: Proceedings of the 9th WSEAS International Conference on Evolutionary Computing*, pages 63–68, Stevens Point, Wisconsin, USA, 2008. World Scientific and Engineering Academy and Society (WSEAS).

292

[167] G. S. Lee and J.-M. Yoon. An empirical study on the complexity metrics of petri nets. *Microelectronics and Reliability*, 32(3):323–329, 1992.

[168] J. Lee, D. Lee, and S. Kang. An Overview of the Business Process Maturity Model (BPMM). In K. C.-C. Chang, W. Wang, L. C. 0002, C. A. Ellis, C.-H. Hsu, A. C. Tsoi, and H. Wang, editors, *Advances in Web and Network Technologies, and Information Management, APWeb/WAIM 2007*, volume 4537 of *Lecture Notes in Computer Science*, pages 384–395. Springer, 2007.

[169] K. Lenz and A. Oberweis. Modeling Interorganizational Workflows with XML Nets. In *HICSS '01: Proceedings of the 34th Annual Hawaii International Conference on System Sciences (HICSS-34)-Volume 7*, page 7052, Washington, DC, USA, 2001. IEEE Computer Society.

[170] K. Lenz and A. Oberweis. Interorganizational Business Process Management with XML Nets. In H. Ehrig, W. Reisig, G. Rozenberg, and H. Weber, editors, *Petri Net Technology for Communication-Based Systems, Advances in Petri Nets*, volume 2472 of *LNCS*, pages 243–263. Springer-Verlag, 2003.

[171] F. Leymann and D. Roller. *Production workflow: concepts and techniques*. Prentice Hall PTR, Upper Saddle River, NJ, USA, 2000.

[172] Z. Liu and D. Towsley. Optimality of the round robin routing policy. Technical report, University of Massachusetts, Amherst, MA, USA, 1992.

[173] F. G. Lobo, C. F. Lima, and Z. Michalewicz, editors. *Parameter Setting in Evolutionary Algorithms*. Studies in Computational Intelligence. Springer, 1 edition, April 2007.

[174] M. Locatelli. A note on the griewank test function. *Journal of Global Optimization*, 25(2):169–174, 2003.

[175] M. Lovberg and T. Krink. Extending particle swarm optimization with self-organized criticality. In *Proceedings of IEEE Conference on Evolutionary Computation*, pages 1588–1593, 2002.

[176] R. F. Lusch, S. L. Vargo, and M. O'Brien. Competing through service: Insights from service-dominant logic. *Journal of Retailing*, 83:5–18, 2007.

[177] A. Mahanti and A. Bagchi. AND/OR graph heuristic search methods. *J. ACM*, 32(1):28–51, 1985.

[178] S. L. Mansar and H. A. Reijers. Best practices in business process redesign: validation of a redesign framework. *Comput. Ind.*, 56(5):457–471, 2005.

[179] V. Marík, O. Stepánková, H. Krautwurmova, and M. Luck, editors. *Multi-Agent-Systems and Applications II, 9th ECCAI-ACAI/EASSS 2001, AEMAS 2001, HoloMAS 2001, Selected Revised Papers*, volume 2322 of *Lecture Notes in Computer Science*. Springer, 2002.

[180] R. Marinescu and R. Dechter. AND/OR graph search for genetic linkage analysis. In *Workshop on Heuristic Search, Memory Based Heuristics and Their Applications, AAAI'06*. American Association for Artificial Intelligence, 2006.

[181] J. Melcher and D. Seese. Process measurement: Insights from software measurement on measuring process complexity, quality and performance. Technical report, Universität Karlsruhe (TH), Institut für Angewandte Informatik und Formale Beschreibungsverfahren, August 2008.

[182] J. Melcher and D. Seese. Towards validating prediction systems for process understandability: Measuring process understandability. In V. Negru, T. Jebelean, D. Petcu, and D. Zaharie, editors, *Proceedings of the 10th International Symposium on Symbolic and Numeric Algorithms for Scientific Computing (SYNASC 2008)*, pages 564–571, Timisoara, Romania, September 2008. IEEE Computer Society.

[183] J. Melcher and D. Seese. Visualization and clustering of business process collections based on process metric values. Technical report, Universität Karlsruhe (TH), Institut für Angewandte Informatik und Formale Beschreibungsverfahren, November 2008.

[184] J. Mendling, M. Moser, G. Neumann, H. M. W. Verbeek, B. F. van Dongen, and W. M. P. van der Aalst. Technical report, 2006. BPM Center Report BPM-06-08, 2006.

[185] J. Mendling and M. Nüttgens. A Comparison of XML Interchange Formats for Business Process Modelling, 2006.

[186] J. Mendling and M. Nüttgens. EPC markup language (EPML): an XML-based interchange format for event-driven process chains (EPC). *Information Systems and E-Business Management*, 4(3):245–263, July 2006.

[187] J. Mendling, H. Reijers, and J. Cardoso. What makes process models understandable. In *Business Process Management*, pages 48–63. Springer Berlin / Heidelberg, 2007.

[188] Z. Michalewicz. *Genetic Algorithms + Data Structures = Evolution Programs*. Springer-Verlag Berlin Heidelberg, 3rd edition, November 1998.

[189] D. Miers. BPM: Driving Business Performance. 2005. http://bptrends.com/publicationfiles/07-05%20WP%20BPM%20Driving%20Business%20Performance%20-%20Derek%20Miers1.pdf, last access: April 2009.

[190] R. Milner. *A Calculus of Communicating Systems*. Springer-Verlag New York, Inc., Secaucus, NJ, USA, 1982.

[191] T. M. Mitchell. *Machine Learning*. McGraw-Hill Science, March 1997.

[192] T. M. Mitchell. The discipline of machine learning, July 2006. http://www.cs.cmu.edu/ tom/pubs/MachineLearning.pdf, last access: May 2009.

[193] W. Y. Mok and D. P. Paper. Using Harel's Statecharts to Model Business Workflows. *Journal of Database Management*, 13(3):17–34, 2002.

[194] S. Mostaghim, J. Branke, A. Lewis, and H. Schmeck. Parallel multi-objective optimization using a master-slave model on heterogeneous resources. In *IEEE*, pages 1981–1987, Congress on Evolutionary Computation, 2008.

[195] S. Mostaghim, W. E. Halter, and A. Wille. Linear multi-objective particle swarm optimization. In Abraham, A., Grosan, C., Ramos, and V., editors, *Stigmergy optimization*, volume 31 of *Computational Science*, chapter 9, pages 209–237. Springer Verlag, 2006.

[196] S. Mostaghim and H. Schmeck. Distance based ranking in many-objective particle swarm optimization. In G. R. et al., editor, *Parallel Problem Solving from Nature (PPSN)*, pages 753–762, 2008.

[197] S. Mostaghim and J. Teich. Strategies for finding good local guides in multi-objective particle swarm optimization. In *IEEE Swarm Intelligence Symposium*, pages 26–33. IEEE, 2003.

[198] H. Mühlenbein, D. Schomisch, and J. Born. The Parallel Genetic Algorithm as Function Optimizer. *Parallel Computing*, 17(6-7):619–632, 1991.

[199] D. Müller, M. Reichert, and J. Herbst. Data-driven modeling and coordination of large process structures. In *On the Move to Meaningful Internet Systems (OTM 2007)*, pages 77–94, 2007.

[200] T. J. Muller and M. van Otterlo. Evolutionary reinforcement learning in relational domains. In *Proceedings Rich Representations for RL workshop ICML'05*, Bonn, Germany, August 2005.

[201] M. Netjes, H. Reijers, and W. P. v. d. Aalst. Supporting the BPM life-cycle with FileNet. In J. Krogstie, T. Halpin, and H. E. Proper, editors, *Proceedings of the Workshop on Exploring Modeling Methods for Systems Analysis and Design (EMMSAD'06), held in conjunctiun with the 18th Conference on Advanced Information Systems (CAiSE'06),*

Luxembourg, Luxembourg, EU, pages 497–508. Namur University Press, Namur, Belgium, EU, 2006.

[202] D. W. Nickels. It-business alignment: What we know that we still don't know. *Proceedings of the 7th Annual Conference of the Southern Association for Information Systems*, February 2004.

[203] N. J. Nilsson. *Principles of Artificial Intelligence*. Morgan Kaufmann Publishers, January 1993.

[204] R. Normann. *Service Management: Strategy and Leadership in Service Business*. John Wiley & Sons, Inc., 2002.

[205] R. Normann and R. Ramirez. From value chain to value constellation: Designing interactive strategy. *Harvard Business Review*, pages 65–77, July - August 1993.

[206] S. Nurcan. A survey on the flexibility requirements related to business processes and modeling artifacts. In *HICSS '08: Proceedings of the Proceedings of the 41st Annual Hawaii International Conference on System Sciences*, page 378, Washington, DC, USA, 2008. IEEE Computer Society.

[207] M. Nüttgens, A.-W. Scheer, and V. Zimmermann. Objektorientierte Ereignisgesteuerte Prozesskette (oEPK) - Methode und Anwendung (in German). Technical Report 141, Veröffentlichungen des Instituts für Wirtschaftsinformatik (IWi), University of Saarland, 1997.

[208] A. Oberweis. *Modellierung und Ausführung von Workflows mit Petri-Netzen (in German)*. Teubner Verlag, 1996.

[209] A. Oberweis, V. Pankratius, and W. Stucky. Product lines for digital information products. *Information Systems*, 32(6):909–939, 2007.

[210] Object Management Group. *Catalog of OMG Business Strategy, Business Rules and Business Process Management Specifications*. http://www.omg.org/technology/documents/ br_pm_spec_catalog.htm, last access: April 2009.

[211] J. O'connell. *Mastering Your Organization's Processes - A Plain Guide to Business Process Management*. Cambridge University Press, Cambridge, 2006.

[212] B. Oestereich, C. Weiss, Chr.and Schröder, T. Weilkiens, and A. Lenhard. *Objektorientierte Geschäftsprozessmodellierung mit der UML (in German)*. Dpunkt Verlag, July 2003.

[213] G. M. P. O'Hare and N. Jennings. *Foundations of Distributed Artificial Intelligence*. John Wiley & Sons, New York, New York State, United States of America (USA), 1996.

[214] D. Ortiz-Boyer, C. Hervás-Martínez, and N. García-Pedrajas. Improving crossover operator for real-coded genetic algorithms using virtual parents. *Journal of Heuristics*, 13(3):265–314, 2007.

[215] C. Ouyang, M. Dumas, A. H. M. ter Hofstede, and W. M. P. van der Aalst. From BPMN Process Models to BPEL Web Services. In *Web Services, 2006. ICWS'06. International Conference on*, pages 285–292, 2006.

[216] M. S. Pallos. Service-Oriented Architecture: A Primer. *EAI Journal*, (12), 2001. http://www.eaijournal.com/PDF/SOAPallos.pdf, last access: April 2009.

[217] V. Pankratius. *Product Lines for Digital Information Products*. PhD thesis, University of Karlsruhe, Karlsruhe, Germany, 2007. Printed by Karlsruhe University Press.

[218] C. H. Papadimitriou. *Computational complexity*. Addison-Wesley, 1994.

[219] M. P. Papazoglou and W.-J. van den Heuvel. Business process development life cycle methodology. *Communications of the ACM*, 50(10):79–85, 2007.

[220] U. Paquet and A. P. Engelbrecht. A new particle swarm optimiser for linearly constrained optimization. In *Proceedings CEC'03, the Congress on Evolutionary Computation*, pages 227–233, 2003.

[221] M. Pesic, M. H. Schonenberg, N. Sidorova, and W. M. P. van der Aalst. Constraint-based workflow models: Change made easy. In *On the Move to Meaningful Internet Systems (OTM 2007)*, pages 77–94, 2007.

[222] C. A. Petri. *Kommunikation mit Automaten (in German)*. PhD thesis, Institut für instrumentelle Mathematik, Bonn, 1962.

[223] F. Puhlmann and M. Weske. Using the pi-Calculus for Formalizing Workflow Patterns. In W. M. P. van der Aalst, B. Benatallah, F. Casati, and F. Curbera, editors, *Business Process Management*, volume 3649, pages 153–168, 2005.

[224] J. Pyke. Waking up the BPM paradigm. 2005.

[225] T. Pyzdek. *The Six Sigma Handbook: The Complete Guide for Greenbelts, Blackbelts, and Managers at All Levels*. McGraw-Hill, New York, 2 edition, 2003.

[226] J. B. Quinn, J. J. Baruch, and P. C. Paquette. Technology in services. *Sci. Am.*, 257(6):50–58, 1987.

[227] S. Rahnamayan, H. R. Tizhoosh, and M. M. A. Salama. A novel population initialization method for accelerating evolutionary algorithms. *Computers & Mathematics with Applications*, 53(10):1605–1614, 2007.

[228] S. F. Railsback, S. L. Lytinen, and S. K. Jackson. Agent-based simulation platforms: Review and development recommendations. *Simulation*, 82(9):609–623, 2006.

[229] K.-H. Rau. *Objektorientierte Systementwicklung: vom Geschäftsprozess zum Java-Programm (in German)*. Vieweg, Wiesbaden, 2007.

[230] M. Razavian and R. Khosravi. Modeling variability in business process models using uml. In *ITNG '08: Proceedings of the Fifth International Conference on Information Technology: New Generations*, pages 82–87, Washington, DC, USA, 2008. IEEE Computer Society.

[231] I. Rechenberg. *Evolutionsstrategie: Optimierung technischer Systeme nach Prinzipien der biologischen Evolution (in German)*. Frommann-Holzboog, 1973.

[232] G. Regev, P. Soffer, , and R. Schmidt. Taxonomy of flexibility in business processes. In *BPMDS'06: Proceedings of the 7th Workshop on Business Process Modelling*, 2006.

[233] H. A. Reijers. *Design and Control of Workflow Processes: Business Process Management for the Service Industry*. Springer, Berlin, 2003.

[234] H. A. Reijers, M. H. Jansen-Vullers, M. zur Muehlen, and W. Appl. Workflow management systems + swarm intelligence = dynamic task assignment for emergency management applications. In G. Alonso, P. Dadam, and M. Rosemann, editors, *BPM*, volume 4714 of *Lecture Notes in Computer Science*, pages 125–140. Springer, 2007.

[235] H. A. Reijers and I. T. Vanderfeesten. Cohesion and coupling metrics for workflow process design. In *Business Process Management: Second International Conference, BPM 2004. Proceedings*, volume 3080, pages 290–305, 2004.

[236] M. Reyes-Sierra and C. A. C. Coello. Multi-objective particle swarm optimizers: A survey of the state-of-the-art. *International Journal of Computational Intelligence Research*, 2(3):287–308, 2006.

[237] D. Riehle and H. Zllighoven. Understanding and using patterns in software development. theory and practice of object systems. In *VCK96 John Vlissides, James O. Coplien and Norm Kerth*, pages 3–13, 1996.

[238] S. Rinderle, M. Reichert, and P. Dadam. Correctness criteria for dynamic changes in workflow systems - a survey. *Data & Knowledge Engineering*, 50:9–34, 2004.

[239] P. Rittgen. Business processes in UML. In *UML and the unified process*, pages 315–331, Hershey, PA, USA, 2003. IGI Publishing.

[240] G. D. Robson. *Continuous Process Improvement*. Free Press, New York, NY, USA, September 1991.

[241] J. M. Robson. The complexity of go. In *IFIP Congress*, pages 413–417, 1983.

[242] M. Rosemann. Potential pitfalls of process modeling: part a. *Business Process Management Journal*, 12(2):249 – 254, 2006.

[243] M. Rosemann. Potential pitfalls of process modeling: part b. *Business Process Management Journal*, 12(3):377–384, 2006.

[244] M. Rosemann. Understanding and impacting the practice of business process management. In M. Dumas, M. Reichert, and M.-C. Shan, editors, *Business Process Management, 6th International Conference, BPM 2008, Milan, Italy, September 2-4, 2008. Proceedings*, volume 5240 of *Lecture Notes in Computer Science*, page 2. Springer, 2008.

[245] M. Rosemann and J. Recker. Context-aware process design: Exploring the extrinsic drivers for process flexibility. In T. Latour and M. Petit, editors, *18th International Conference on Advanced Information Systems Engineering. Proceedings of Workshops and Doctoral Consortium.*, pages 149–158, Luxembourg, 2006. Namur University Press.

[246] M. Rosen. BPM and SOA - Orchestration or Choreography? *BPTrends*, April 2008. http://www.bptrends.com, last access: April 2009.

[247] P. Ross, E. Hart, and D. Corne. Genetic algorithms and timetabling. In *Advances in evolutionary computing: theory and applications*, pages 755–771, New York, NY, USA, 2003. Springer-Verlag New York, Inc.

[248] R. G. Ross. *Principles of the Business Rule Approach (Addison-Wesley Information Technology Series)*. Addison-Wesley Professional, February 2003.

[249] T. Rozman, G. Polancic, and R. Vajde. Analysis of Most Common Process Modeling Mistakes in BPMN Process Models. In L. Fischer, editor, *2008 BPM & Workflow Handbook - Spotlight on Human-Centric BPM*. Future Strategies, Inc., May 2008.

[250] N. C. Russell. *Foundations of Process-Aware Information Systems*. PhD thesis, Queensland University of Technology, Brisbane, Australia, December 2007.

[251] SAP BPX Community. Process Management Lifecycle (PML). https://www.sdn.sap.com/irj/bpx/bpx-cycle, last access: April 2009.

[252] A. Schnieders and F. Puhlmann. Variability mechanisms in e-business process families. *9th International Conference on Business Information Systems (BIS 2006)*, pages 583–601, 2006.

[253] T. J. Schriber, J. Banks, A. F. Seila, I. Ståhl, A. M. Law, and R. G. Born. Simulation text books - old and new (panel). In *WSC '03: Proceedings of the 35th conference on Winter simulation*, pages 1952–1963. Winter Simulation Conference, 2003.

[254] H.-P. P. Schwefel. *Evolution and Optimum Seeking: The Sixth Generation.* John Wiley & Sons, Inc., New York, NY, USA, 1993.

[255] G. Seliger. Nachhaltige industrielle Wertschöpfungsnetze (in German). Technical report, Institut für Werkzeugmaschinen und Fabrikbetrieb, TU Berlin, Berlin, Germany, 2008.

[256] R. M. Selvi and R. Rajaram. Performance study of mutation operator in genetic algorithms on anticipatory scheduling. In *ICCIMA '07: Proceedings of the International Conference on Computational Intelligence and Multimedia Applications (ICCIMA 2007)*, pages 511–518, Washington, DC, USA, 2007. IEEE Computer Society.

[257] Y.-W. Shang and Y.-H. Qiu. A note on the extended rosenbrock function. *Evolutionary Computation*, 14(1):119–126, 2006.

[258] M. Singer and P. Berg. *Genes & Genomes: A changing perspective.* University Science Books, 1991.

[259] G. Sirilli and R. Evangelista. Technological innovation in services and manufacturing: results from italian surveys. *Research Policy*, 27(9):881–899, December 1998.

[260] S. N. Sivanandam and S. N. Deepa. *Introduction to Genetic Algorithms.* Springer, 2008.

[261] H. Smith. P-triz in the history of business process - part 3 in a series on p-triz. *BPTrends*, 2006. http://www.businessprocesstrends.com/publicationfiles/04-06-COL–P-TRIZ-3-Smith.pdf, last access: April 2009.

[262] R. F. Smith. *Business Process Management and the Balanced Scorecard: Focusing Processes as Strategic Drivers.* Wiley & Sons, New Jersey, USA, 2006.

[263] R. Snee. Why should statisticians pay attention to six sigma? *Quality Progress*, 32(9), 1999.

[264] Software & Information Industry's eBusiness Division. Strategic backgrounder: Software as a service (white paper). February 2001. http://www.siia.net/estore/ssb-01.pdf, last access: April 2009.

[265] J. W. Stepherdson, S. G. Thompson, and B. R. Odgers. Cross organisational workflow co-ordinated by software agents. In *Proceedings of the Workshop on Cross-Organisational Workflow Management and Co-ordination*, San Franciso, CA, 22 February 1999.

[266] H. Stormer. Task scheduling in agent-based workflow. In *International ICSC Symposium on Multi-Agents and Mobile Agents in Virtual Organizations and E-Commerce*, Wollongong, Australia, 11-13 December 2000.

[267] P. Strassmann. What is alignment? alignment is the delivery of the required results. *Cutter IT Journal*, 1:1–8, August 1998.

[268] M. W. Strickberger. *Evolution*. Jones and Bartlett Publishers, New Jersey, USA, 3nd edition, January 2000.

[269] R. S. Sutton and A. G. Barto. *Reinforcement Learning: An Introduction (Adaptive Computation and Machine Learning)*. The MIT Press, March 1998.

[270] P. Tadepalli, R. Givan, and K. Driessens. Relational Reinforcement Learning: An Overview. In *Proceedings of the ICML'04 workshop on Relational Reinfocement Learning*, Banff, Canada, 2004.

[271] R. M. Tagg. A new look at the dimensions of flexibility in workflow management. In *Proceedings of the 5th EURO/Informs Joint International Meeting*, Istanbul, Turkey, 2003.

[272] H. Takagi. Interactive evolutionary computation: Fusion of the capacities of ec optimization and human evaluation. In *Proceedings of the IEEE*, volume 89, pages 1275–1296, 2001.

[273] H. Tamura. A new multiobjective genetic algorithm with heterogeneous population for solving flowshop scheduling problems. *International Journal of Computer Integrated Manufacturing*, 20(5):465–477, 2007.

[274] F. W. Taylor. *The Principles of Scientific Management*. 1911.

[275] O. Thomas, O. Adam, and C. Seel. Business process management with vague data. In *Proceedings of the 16th International Workshop on Database and Expert Systems Applications (DEXA'05)*, 2005.

[276] J. Tien and D. Berg. Systems engineering in the growing service economy. *IEEE transactions on systems, man, and cybernetics*, 25(5):321–326, 1995.

[277] J. Tien and D. Berg. On services research and education. *Journal of Systems Science and Systems Engineering*, 15(3):257–283, 2006.

[278] A. Törn and A. Zilinskas. Global Optimization. *Lecture Notes in Computer Science*, 350, 1989.

[279] B. Tozawa, N. Bodek, and S. Rivoli. *The idea generator: quick and easy Kaizen*. PCs Press, Vancouver, WA, 2002.

[280] A. Tsalgatidou and T. Pilioura. An overview of standards and related technology in web services. *Distrib. Parallel Databases*, 12(2-3):135–162, 2002.

[281] O. Turetken and O. Demirors. Process modeling by process owners: A decentralized approach. *Software Process: Improvement and Practice*, 13(1):75–87, 2008.

[282] K. Tuyls, T. Croonenborghs, J. Ramon, R. Goetschalckx, and M. Bruynooghe. Multi-agent relational reinforcement learning. In *Proceedings of the Learning and Adaption in MAS Workshop 2005*, pages 123–132, 2005.

[283] P. Vajda, A. E. Eiben, and W. Hordijk. Parameter control methods for selection operators in genetic algorithms. In *Proceedings of the 10th international conference on Parallel Problem Solving from Nature*, pages 620–630, Berlin, Heidelberg, 2008. Springer-Verlag.

[284] W. van der Aalst, T. Weijters, and L. Maruster. Workflow mining: Discovering process models from event logs. *IEEE TKDE*, 16(9):1128–1142, 2004.

[285] W. M. P. van der Aalst. The application of Petri nets to workflow management. *The Journal of Circuits, Systems and Computers*, 8(1):21–66, 1998.

[286] W. M. P. van der Aalst. Business process simulation - lecture notes 2ii75, 2008. Deptartment of Mathematics and Computer Science, Technical University Eindhoven, http://wwwis.win.tue.nl/ mvoorhoe/sim/ln2II75.pdf, last access: April 2009.

[287] W. M. P. van der Aalst, Arthur, B. Kiepuszewski, and A. P. Barros. Workflow patterns. *Distributed and Parallel Databases*, 14(1):5–51, July 2003.

[288] W. M. P. van der Aalst, H. A. Reijers, and S. Limam. Product-driven workflow design. In W. Shen, Z. Lin, J.-P. A. Barthès, and M. Kamel, editors, *Proceedings of the 6th International Conference on Computer Supported Cooperative Work in Design*, pages 397–402, London, Ont., Canada, 12-14 July 2001. IEEE.

[289] W. M. P. van der Aalst, N. Russell, A. T. Hofstede, and D. Edmond. Workflow resource patterns. Technical report, Eindhoven University of Technology, Eindhoven, 2004.

302

[290] W. M. P. van der Aalst, N. Russell, A. T. Hofstede, and D. Edmond. Workflow data patterns: Identification, representation and tool support. In *Conceptual Modeling - ER 2005*, pages 353–368. Springer Berlin / Heidelberg, 2005.

[291] W. M. P. van der Aalst, N. Russell, and A. H. M. ter Hofstede. Workflow exception patterns. In E. Dubois and K. Pohl, editors, *CAiSE*, volume 4001 of *Lecture Notes in Computer Science*, pages 288–302. Springer, 2006.

[292] W. M. P. van der Aalst, M. Schonenberg, R. Mans, N. Russell, and N. Mulyar. Towards a taxonomy of process flexibility (extended version). Technical report, BPMcenter.org, 2007.

[293] W. M. P. van der Aalst and A. ter Hofstede. Yawl: yet another workflow language. *Information Systems*, 30(4):245–275, June 2005.

[294] W. M. P. van der Aalst and K. v. van Hee. *Workflow Management: Models, Methods, and Systems (Cooperative Information Systems)*. The MIT Press, January 2002.

[295] W. M. P. van der Aalst, M. Weske, and D. Grünbauer. Case handling: A new paradigm for business process support. *Data and Knowledge Engineering*, 53:2005, 2005.

[296] W. M. P. van der Aalst, P. Wohed, M. Dumas, A. T. Hofstede, and N. Russell. On the suitability of BPMN for business process modelling. In S. Dustdar, J. L. Fiadeiro, and A. Sheth, editors, *Proceedings of the 4th Int'l Conference on Business Process Management (BPM 2006)*, LNCS, pages 161–176, Wien, Austria, 2006.

[297] W. M. P. van der Aalst, P. Wohed, M. Dumas, A. H. M. ter Hofstede, and N. Russell. Pattern-based analysis of the control-flow perspective of uml activity diagrams. In L. M. L. Delcambre, C. Kop, H. C. Mayr, J. Mylopoulos, and O. Pastor, editors, *ER*, volume 3716 of *Lecture Notes in Computer Science*, pages 63–78. Springer, 2005.

[298] F. van Harmelen, V. Lifschitz, and B. Porter, editors. *Handbook of Knowledge Representation (Foundations of Artificial Intelligence)*. Elsevier Science, 2007.

[299] M. van Otterlo. Relational expressions in reinforcement learning: Review and open problems. In E. de Jong and T. Oates, editors, *Proceedings of the ICML'02 Workshop on Development of Representations*, 2002.

[300] M. van Otterlo. A survey of reinforcement learning in relational domains. Technical report, Centre for Telematics and Information Technology (CTIT) Technical Report Series, 2005. http://www.ub.utwente.nl/webdocs/ctit/1/00000137.pdf, last access: April 2009.

[301] I. Vanderfeesten. An evaluation of case handling systems for product based workflow design, June 2007. http://is.tm.tue.nl/staff/ivanderfeesten/ICEIS2007.pps, last access: April 2009.

[302] I. Vanderfeesten, H. A. Reijers, and W. M. van der Aalst. Product based workflow support: Dynamic workflow execution. In *CAiSE '08: Proceedings of the 20th international conference on Advanced Information Systems Engineering*, pages 571–574, Berlin, Heidelberg, 2008. Springer-Verlag.

[303] S. Vandermerwe and J. Rada. Servitization of business: Adding value by adding services. *European Management Journal*, 6, 1988.

[304] S. L. Vargo and R. F. Lusch. Evolving to a new dominant logic for marketing. *Journal of Marketing*, 68:1–17, January 2004.

[305] S. L. Vargo and R. F. Lusch. The four service marketing myths: Remnants of a goods-based, manufacturing model. *Journal of Service Research*, 6:324–335, 2004.

[306] S. L. Vargo and R. F. Lusch. Service-dominant logic: Continuing the evolution. *Journal of the Academy of Market Science*, 36:1–10, 2008.

[307] G. Venter and J. Sobieszczanski-Sobieski. Particle swarm optimization. *AIAA Journal*, 41(8):1583–1589, 2003.

[308] H. M. W. Verbeek. Analyzing bpel processes using petri nets. In *Florida International University*, pages 59–78, 2005.

[309] K. Vergidis, A. Tiwari, B. Majeed, and R. Roy. Optimisation of business process designs: An algorithmic approach with multiple objectives. *International Journal of Production Economics*, 109(1-2):105–121, 2007.

[310] J. Viega. Practical random number generation in software. In *ACSAC '03: Proceedings of the 19th Annual Computer Security Applications Conference*, page 129, Washington, DC, USA, 2003. IEEE Computer Society.

[311] C. R. von Hagen, D. Ratz, and W. Stucky. Simulation of business process improvement by a customized genetic algorithm. In *Proceedings of the European Simulation and Modelling Conference (ESMc2004)*, pages 252–256. EUROSIS, October 2004.

[312] B. Von Halle. *Business Rules Applied: Building Better Systems Using the Business Rules Approach*. Wiley, 1st edition, September 2001.

[313] G. Vreede. Modeling and simulating organizational coordination. *Simulation & Gaming*, 29:60–87, 1998.

[314] N. W. M. P. van der Aalst, Russell, A. T. Hofstede, and N. Mulyar. Workflow control-flow patterns: A revised view. Technical report, BPMcenter.org, 2006.

[315] C. Wagenknecht. *Algorithmen und Komplexität (in German)*. Informatik interaktiv. Fachbuchverl. Leipzig im Carl Hanser-Verl., January 2003.

[316] P. Walter and D. Werth. Collaborative business process lifecycles. In S. W. Sadiq, M. Reichert, and K. Schulz, editors, *Technologies for Collaborative Business Process Management*, pages 84–96. INSTICC Press, 2006.

[317] B. Weber, S. Rinderle, and M. Reichert. Change patterns and change support features in process-aware information systems. In *Advanced Information Systems Engineering*, pages 574–588, 2007.

[318] I. Wegener. *Complexity Theory. Exploring the Limits of Efficient Algorithms*. Springer, Berlin, Germany, 2004.

[319] L. Wen, J. Wang, and J.-G. Sun. Detecting implicit dependencies between tasks from event logs. In X. Zhou, J. Li, H. T. Shen, M. Kitsuregawa, and Y. Zhang, editors, *APWeb*, volume 3841 of *Lecture Notes in Computer Science*, pages 591–603. Springer, 2006.

[320] M. Weske. *Business Process Management: Concepts, Languages, Architectures*. Springer, Berlin, Heidelberg, 2007.

[321] B. Wetzstein, Z. Ma, A. Filipowska, M. Kaczmarek, S. Bhiri, S. Losada, J.-M. Lopez-Cobo, and L. Cicurel. Semantic business process management: A lifecycle based requirements analysis. In *Proceedings of the Workshop on Semantic Business Process and Product Lifecycle Management (SBPM 2007)*, volume 251, pages 1–11, 2007.

[322] D. Weyns and T. Hovoet. An architectural strategy for self-adapting systems. In *SEAMS '07: Proceedings of the 2007 International Workshop on Software Engineering for Adaptive and Self-Managing Systems*, page 3, Washington, DC, USA, 2007. IEEE Computer Society.

[323] J. White. Mobile agents. In J. Bradshaw, editor, *Software Agents*, pages 437–472. AAAI Press, 1997.

[324] D. Whitley. A genetic algorithm tutorial. *Statistics and Computing*, 4(2):65–85, June 1994.

[325] D. Whitley, K. Mathias, S. Rana, and J. Dzubera. Building better test functions. In *Proceedings of the Sixth International Conference on Genetic Algorithms*, pages 239–246. Morgan Kaufmann, 1995.

[326] D. Wodtke and G. Weikum. A formal foundation for distributed workflow execution based on state charts. In *ICDT '97: Proceedings of the 6th International Conference on Database Theory*, pages 230–246, London, UK, 1997. Springer-Verlag.

[327] D. H. Wolpert and W. G. Macready. No free lunch theorems for search. Technical Report 95-02-010, Santa Fe Institute, 1995.

[328] M. Wooldridge. *Introduction to MultiAgent Systems*. John Wiley & Sons, June 2002.

[329] M. Wooldridge and N. R. Jennings. Intelligent agents: Theory and practice, 1994.

[330] Workflow Management Coalition. Wfmc-tc-1011 ver 3 terminology and glossary english, 1999.

[331] M. Wynn, M. Dumas, C. Fidge, A. Ter Hofstede, and W. van der Aalst. Business Process Simulation for Operational Decision Support. In *Business Process Management Workshops*, pages 66–77. Springer Berlin / Heidelberg, 2008.

[332] X.-F. Xie, W.-J. Zhang, and Z.-L. Yang. Adaptive particle swarm optimization on individual level. In *Proceedings of the 6th International Conference on Signal Processing*, volume 2, pages 1215–1218. IEEE, 2002.

[333] G. Xue, J. Lu, and S. Yao. Investigating workflow patterns in term of pi-calculus. In *11th International Conference on Computer Supported Cooperative Work in Design*, pages 823–827. IEEE, Melbourne, Victoria, April 2007.

[334] T. Yamada and R. Nakano. Genetic algorithms for job-shop scheduling problems. In *In Proceedings of Modern Heuristic for Decision Support*, pages 67–81, 1997.

[335] S. Yang. Adaptive crossover in genetic algorithms using statistics mechanism. In *ICAL 2003: Proceedings of the eighth international conference on Artificial life*, pages 182–185, Cambridge, MA, USA, 2003. MIT Press.

[336] F. Zambonelli, H. Van, and D. Parunak. Towards a paradigm change in computer science and software engineering: a synthesis. *The Knowledge Engineering Review*, 18, 2004.

[337] L. Zhu, Y. Chen, Y. Lu, C. Lin, and A. Yuille. Max margin AND/OR graph learning for parsing the human body. In *Computer Vision and Pattern Recognition, CVPR 2008*. IEEE, 2008.

[338] M. D. Zisman. *Representation, Specification and Automation of Office Procedures*. PhD thesis, Wharton School, University of Pennsylvania, 1977.

[339] E. Zitzler. *Evolutionary Algorithms for Multiobjective Optimization: Methods and Applications*. Shaker, 1999.

[340] M. zur Mühlen. *Workflow-based Process Controlling*. Logos Verlag, Berlin, Germany, 2004.

I. Index